Dear Reader,

Welcome to the Galileo Press Discover SAP series. This new s  has been developed as part of our official SAP PRESS imprint to you discover what SAP is all about and to show you how to use wide array of applications and tools to make your organization more efficient and cost effective.

Each book in the series is written in a friendly, easy-to-follow style that guides you through the intricacies of the software and its core components. If you are completely new to SAP, you can begin with "Discover SAP," the first book in the series, where you'll find a detailed overview of the core components of SAP, what they are, how they can benefit your company, and the technology requirements and costs of implementation. Once you have a foundational knowledge of SAP, you can explore the other books in the series covering NetWeaver, Financials, CRM, HCM, BI, and more. In these books you'll delve into the fundamental business concepts and principles behind the tool, discover why it's important for your business, and evaluate the technology and implementation costs for each.

Whether you are a decision maker who needs to determine if SAP is the right enterprise solution for your company, you are just starting to work in a firm that uses SAP, or you're already familiar with SAP but need to learn about a specific component, you are sure to find what you need in the Discover SAP series. Then when you're ready to implement SAP, you'll find what you need in the SAP PRESS series at *www.sap-press.com*.

Thank you for your interest in the series. We look forward to hearing how the series helps you get started with SAP.

Jenifer Niles
Vice President

Galileo Press, Inc.
100 Grossman Drive
Suite 205
Braintree, MA 02184

 **PRESS**

SAP PRESS is a joint initiative of SAP and Galileo Press. The know-how offered by SAP specialists combined with the expertise of the publishing house Galileo Press offers the reader expert books in the field. SAP PRESS features first-hand information and expert advice, and provides useful skills for professional decision-making.

SAP PRESS offers a variety of books on technical and business related topics for the SAP user. For further information, please visit our website: *www.sap-press.com*.

Aylin Korkmaz
Financial Reporting with SAP
ISBN 978-1-59229-179-3
2008, 550 pages, $79.95

Manish Patel
SAP Account Determination
ISBN 978-1-59229-110-6
2007, 90 pages, $85.00

Michael Scott
US Tax and SAP
ISBN 978-1-59229-155-7
2007, 360 pages, $69.95

Naeem Arif
Financials: Configuration and Design
ISBN 978-1-59229-136-6
2008, 464 pages, $79.95

Manish Patel

Discover SAP® ERP Financials

Galileo Press

Bonn • Boston

ISBN 978-1-59229-184-7

1st Edition 2008

Editor Jenifer Niles
Copy Editor Julie McNamee
Cover Design Silke Braun
Layout Design Vera Brauner
Production Todd Brown
Typesetting Publishers' Design and Production Services, Inc.
Printed and bound in Canada

© 2008 by Galileo Press
SAP PRESS is an imprint of Galileo Press,
Boston (MA), USA
Bonn, Germany

German Edition first published 2008 by Galileo Press.

This book is dedicated with respect
and gratitude
to the memory of my father
the late Shri Bhailal C. Patel

Contents at a Glance

Contents

17 Treasury and Risk Management 495

A Glossary 523

Acknowledgment

I would like to thank SAP PRESS for giving me this opportunity to make this book possible. In particular, I would like to thank my editor Jenifer Niles for her support and patience during the process of writing this book. I would also like to thank SAP for the permission to use their reference materials in this book for the purpose of illustrations, examples, and case studies.

Preface

In writing this book, I tried to address what I felt was a gap in the available information about SAP ERP Financials by providing an easy to understand overview of SAP ERP Financials, its components, and its approach to enterprise computing, financial accounting and management (cost) accounting.

My objective is simple and straightforward. I have made every effort to explain features of SAP ERP Financials components, not in technical jargon or by using marketing brochure benefits, but by simply describing all of the benefits and by being specific about what these components can do for your business.

The following sections outline who will benefit from this book, how I have structured the book, and what topics are covered.

Who This Book is For

If you're a business decision maker considering implementing SAP ERP Financials components in your business, this book will help you to become familiar with the terminology, concepts, components, and technology you will be encountering.

If you're a manager who is dealing with new SAP ERP Financials components in your group, and you want to help your people succeed and become more productive, this book gives you the information you need to appreciate how all of the various features and tools in SAP components might make your people more efficient.

If you're an IT person who has never worked with SAP ERP Financials components, you'll get a quick, solid grounding in those components, and be able to make the connection between how those components can solve your business problems.

If you're a consultant considering entering the world of supporting SAP ERP Financials, this book can serve as a kind of tutorial to help you to better understand the SAP universe, including SAP's extended partner community and how it works to support customers.

What You'll Discover

My goal in writing this book is to introduce and explain in a simple and straightforward way SAP ERP Financials components, concepts and terms; how its different components approach solving real-world business problems; the technology behind SAP ERP Financials components; and what you can expect during an SAP implementation. Each chapter covers a different component of SAP ERP Financials in considerable details so that you can see the available functionality and relate it to how each component works in a real business.

I have been careful to define business and SAP relevant terms throughout the book so anybody from an SAP specialist unfamiliar with business terms or a business person unfamiliar with SAP terms can understand the information that has been provided. I have also made every attempt to give you examples and case studies to make SAP and its products relevant to you, your business, and your industry.

Navigational Tools for This Book

Throughout the book, I've tried to provide several elements that will help you access useful information. These include:

 > Tips call out useful information about related ideas or helpful suggestions.

 > Notes provide other resources to explore or special tools or services from SAP that will help with the topic being discussed.

 > Examples provide you with real-world illustrations of functions at work.

 > TechTalk examples provide a look into the technology behind the functions covered.

> Marginal texts provide a useful way to scan the book to locate topics of interest for you. Each appears to the side of a paragraph or section with related information.

This is a marginal note

> Warnings draw your attention to areas of concern or pieces of information that you should be aware of while evaluating specific functionality.

What's In This Book?

After a brief introduction to SAP ERP Financials in the first chapter, we'll move on to the different components of the core accounting, also referred to as the Financials component (FI). These components serve to improve your financial processes geared towards meeting external, statutory requirements. Next, we'll explore different components of management accounting, also referred to as the Controlling component (CO). These components help you with improving business processes for internal, management, cost accounting requirements. Finally, we'll look at the components of SAP ERP Financials in the area of Financial Supply Chain Management (FSCM). These components help you improve your business processes targeted at cash, liquidity, and capital management.

The following is an overview of what the book covers by chapter:

Chapter 1

This Introduction chapter provides you with an overview of SAP ERP Financials and highlights some of the numerous benefits that you can achieve by using such an integrated system. This chapter also provides you some examples of how SAP is increasingly becoming first choice across industries and different countries.

Read the book in sequence or go to specific chapters or sections as needed

As mentioned earlier, the components in core accounting (the Financial component (FI)) support business processes in finance that are typically originated based on external requirements, so the next chapters cover the SAP ERP Financials components that help you streamline business processes, improve operational efficiency, and increase automation in these areas.

Chapter 2

Read all of the chapter descriptions to get an idea of what's included in each

This chapter explains how you use *General Ledger (GL) accounting* to record accounting transactions and prepare financial statements to fulfill legal requirements. The GL is fully integrated with other SAP components and also helps you with the powerful integration of legal and management reports, segment reporting, and cost-of-sales reporting.

Chapter 3

Using *Accounts Receivable (AR) and Accounts Payable (AP)* components, you can record and administer invoices, payments, and other business activities with your customers and vendors. Seamless integration with sales and procurement, and a range of invoicing, payments, and electronic communication functions enable these components to alleviate costly and time-consuming manual operational processes in these areas.

Chapter 4

Even though you can't legally avoid or ignore taxes, you can certainly make recording, processing, and reporting of the various types of taxes easier by using the *Tax Accounting* component. The highly versatile tax calculation framework provided in this SAP component enables you to support tax calculation and accounting for almost any country in the world.

Chapter 5

The Bank Accounting component helps you make your banking activities such as applying cash, processing lockbox payments, carrying out bank reconciliation, and so on more efficient. Support for a large number of standard electronic formats helps you easily establish electronic communication with the banks worldwide.

Chapter 6

Using the *Investment Management* component, you can plan, manage, and monitor capital investment initiatives in your company. Comprehensive functionality enables you to plan and evaluate investment alternatives, whereas budget monitoring, distribution, and controlled release of funding help you keep investment costs in check.

When investments are ready to be capitalized, *Asset Accounting* provides end-to-end functionality to support fixed assets from acquisitions to retirements. Multiple depreciation books and complex depreciation rules help you manage not just fixed assets but also other types of assets such as intangible assets, financial assets, and so on.

Chapter 7
Recording, accounting, and reimbursing travel expenses in your company can be streamlined using the *Travel Management* component. Additionally, this component helps you request and plan for trips and even carry out trip booking by using interfaces with external reservation systems.

Chapter 8
The Payroll Accounting component helps you process employee payrolls and the inherent complexities involved in managing employee benefits, deductions, taxes, loans, and payments. In addition to the generic payroll processing functionality, this component provides specific functionalities to support payroll requirements of more than 35 countries.

Chapter 9
Consolidation helps you consolidate data across companies as well as across profit centers. It provides robust support for data collection, currency translation, eliminations, and investment consolidation processes. A single user interface helps you initiate, manage, and monitor the customized sequence of consolidation processes.

Management accounting (the Controlling component (CO)) on the other hand is more targeted toward the internal requirements of your company and provides necessary information to management for decision making. Apart from helping you analyze different types of manufacturing costs and overhead costs, it also helps you provide the planning and budgeting framework for your company. We'll discuss the following components of SAP ERP Financials that support management accounting:

Chapter 10

Use the index as a
navigational tool

Overhead Cost Accounting supports planning, measuring, allocating, controlling, and monitoring of overhead costs. You can use different mechanisms provided in this component to allocate overhead costs true to their origins.

Chapter 11

Project Accounting can be used for managing considerably more complicated overhead, investment, or production initiatives in your company. At your disposal are sophisticated techniques to help you evaluate revenues and costs of your initiatives.

Chapter 12

Product Costing can help you plan, manage, calculate, and analyze costs of your products and services. This component provides an extensive range of tools and functionalities that can support almost all types of manufacturing environments.

Chapter 13

Profitability Analysis helps you achieve one of the ultimate objectives of most companies when they invest in an ERP solution: the ability to easily plan, calculate, and analyze profitability by products, customers, regions, and any other criteria relevant for your business.

Chapter 14

Finally, *Planning and Budgeting* discusses how you can carry out integrated financial planning across different business areas and SAP components. By using the different tools and functions that are available, you can reflect your corporate planning process in SAP regardless of its complexity.

The third area of SAP ERP Financials that we'll discuss in this book is financial supply chain management (FSCM). This area provides you with a suite of application components that helps you optimize financial and information flows within a company and between business partners. This area includes several components:

Chapter 15

This chapter discusses three components from FSCM. To improve efficiency of managing incoming payment flows, *Collections Management* helps you proactively follow up on due and overdue receivables and record the history of customer contacts. *Dispute Management* helps you efficiently process receivables-related dispute cases and integrates dispute resolutions with AR. On the other hand, *Credit Management* helps you support and automate your credit decisions related to the creditworthiness of your customers and business partners.

Chapter 16
To help you better plan for required cash and working capital, the *Cash and Liquidity Management* component is provided. This highly integrated component helps you analyze incoming and outgoing payment flows for the purpose of liquidity planning.

Chapter 17
To manage surplus liquidity invested in the market and your exposure to different types of risks, SAP ERP Financials includes the *Treasury and Risk Management* component. This component provides highly advanced trading functionality to manage investments in stocks, bonds, derivatives, and other financial instruments; it also helps you keep an eye on risk exposures.

> At the end of the book, there is a glossary of SAP and enterprise computing terminology.

> In addition, the book also includes an index that you can use to go directly to certain points of interest.

I hope that this straightforward overview of SAP ERP Financials and its components will give you the information you need to assess your own business needs, determine which SAP components to explore further with your SAP support team, SAP implementation partner, or an SAP account representative, and help you take advantage of the many benefits that SAP ERP Financials has to offer for solving enterprise challenges.

Overview

In today's world, the responsibilities of the finance department go well beyond bookkeeping and financial accounting. While streamlining financial processes and managing working capital requirements, finance also has to provide analysis and reports to help management measure the costs and profitability of different business segments, activities, and initiatives. In addition, finance has to balance these internal expectations with the increasingly demanding compliance expectations from governmental and regulatory authorities.

Obviously, these challenges increase greatly as companies expand their operations and customer base globally, but the finance departments of local, small- and medium-sized companies are not immune to these expectations either. They have to contend with similar challenges and operate in an equally competitive market environment but with fewer resources.

What all of these companies have in common is a need for a system that is robust enough to meet their current business environment while providing a solid foundation for anticipated challenges as the company grows (Figure 1.1).

Figure 1.1 Business Challenges in Financials

The business environment was quite different in the early 1970s, however, when a small company called Systems Applications and Products in Data Processing (SAP) was launched in Germany. Even then though, the first financial accounting software introduced by the company reflected its vision to develop a standard application software for real-time business processing.

As early as the mid-1980s, the company's SAP software was able to handle multiple languages and multiple currencies for its customers. Throughout the years SAP anticipated and recognized the requirements, opportunities, and challenges of their customers and continued to incorporate them into its software. That small company has now evolved into a formidable, multinational juggernaut with a large portfolio of solutions catering to the diverse and unique needs of hundreds of thousands of customers in more than 25 industries and 100 countries. The leading enterprise-wide, financial application, now called SAP ERP, addresses the core business requirements for any company.

SAP ERP software consists of the following solutions:

> SAP ERP Human Capital Management (SAP ERP HCM)

> SAP ERP Operations

> SAP ERP Corporate Services

> SAP ERP Financials

The primary focus of this book is on SAP ERP Financials and how you can streamline and enhance your business processes with it. So if you're just starting with SAP, considering it for your business, or just want to know what SAP offers, you'll find what you're looking for here. You'll learn how it enables you to standardize and integrate your business processes, improve your operational efficiency and transparency, implement and analyze manufacturing and overhead costs, forecast and measure profitability, as well as prepare accurate, consolidated, timely and real-time reports. Additionally, it helps you address critical financial functions in the areas of core accounting, management reporting, working capital management, and so on. So let's take a look at what you'll learn.

What Does SAP ERP Financials Offer You?

As you'll see in this chapter, and throughout the book, one of the greatest strengths of SAP ERP Financials (and, of course, of the SAP ERP software itself) is the legendary integration of its components. SAP ERP Financials components aren't just limited to integration with each other but also with other SAP components. Because almost all business activities have a direct or indirect financial impact, a system with such strong integration provides you with unparalleled visibility into the business processes and business information in your company.

Legendary integration

Figure 1.2 provides an overview of how SAP helps you respond to today's business challenges. Here are just some of the benefits offered by SAP ERP Financials.

> **Standardized business processes**
> SAP ERP Financials enables you to establish standardized business processes across all of your subsidiaries, divisions, and departments, while factoring in individual requirements. And consistent business processes can help you improve productivity and interoperability of your employees. SAP ERP Financials also supports a powerful business workflow that can improve your efficiency by reflecting real-life decision-making processes in the system. Your

operational efficiency is further boosted by the elimination of data duplications, departmental handovers, and multiple, incompatible systems.

> **Single version of the truth**

Because everyone in the company can access the same data, the same transactional details, and the same reports, silos in your company can come down as quickly as the management chooses. Enhanced information sharing across departmental boundaries helps your employees make informed decisions by eliminating typical time delays involved in requesting and obtaining necessary information.

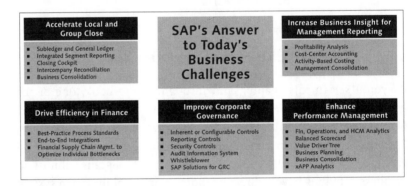

Figure 1.2 SAP's Answer to Today's Business Challenges

> **Improved transparency**

SAP ERP Financials provides you with the ability to drill-down from summarized, consolidated statements to the individual financial entries and associated information such as when (timestamp) and who (user). Such functionalities combined with detailed audit trails institute accountability and improve financial transparency in the company.

> **Accurate prediction of future costs and profits**

The software also provides you with the ability to integrate business processes in SAP across sales, manufacturing, procurement, and other systems, giving you access to detailed business information. You can use the insights gleaned from this information to predict future costs and profits as accurately and practically possible.

> **Tighter control of overhead**
> SAP ERP Financials supports planning, budgeting, analyzing, and controlling of direct and indirect costs at the departmental level. The support of activity-based costing provides you with even greater control over planning, budgeting, and analyzing the costs of business activities across your company. With the improved visibility of costs and cost origins, you can take actions to reduce your operating costs.

Managing overhead costs

> **Analyses of profitability based on criteria that is important to you**
> With the fully customizable framework for profitability analysis, you can calculate and analyze the contribution margin not only by departments, products, and customers; but also by any criteria relevant to your business. With this meaningful and actionable information, you can shift focus to more profitable areas while also concentrating on improving less profitable areas of your business.

> **Improved control of project initiatives**
> Using SAP ERP Financials, you can manage, control, and analyze costs and revenues on complex initiatives. You can analyze your complex projects for recording overhead costs, capitalizing investments, or manufacturing products per customer specifications. A much needed but seldom available attribute of these features is that they are completely integrated with other operational areas of your business.

> **Accurate and timely reporting**
> With the numerous standard reports and reporting tools you can quickly design custom reports that generate consistent, timely, and accurate reporting across all levels of your company. Access to the information can be limited based on user authorizations.

It's important to understand, however, that achieving these numerous benefits from an enterprise-wide integrated system such as SAP does not depend *only* on what the system has to offer. Atypical business processes, existing infrastructure, user training, user acceptance, management support, resources and constraints during project implementation, ongoing user support, people issues, and similar factors also impact directly or indirectly on the extent to which you can realize such benefits.

Reporting and analysis

Warning

Remember the widely known, often forgotten, and seldom acknowl-
edged truism: Automating a mess usually results in an automated mess!

Now let's see if SAP ERP Financials is right for your company.

Where Can You Use SAP ERP Financials?

The short and simple answer to this question is anywhere. The functionality and associated benefits of SAP, as we'll discuss throughout
the book, are relevant for companies of any size, in any country, and
in any industry. The standard SAP software supports all necessary aspects for global implementations such as multiple currencies, multiple languages, and so on. So what does this mean for you?

Multicurrency accounting

Such a design provides some obvious advantages for global companies
or the companies planning to expand their operations or customer
base into foreign countries. For example, you can record and process
business transactions in any currency and have your accounting ledgers updated in real time in the functional currency of the company
and reporting currency of the worldwide group. You can design your
core business processes independent of the operating currencies of
your subsidiaries, and at the same time, carry out currency-specific
processes such as currency valuations and inflation accounting. All
the functionalities and processes discussed in this book are capable of
handling multiple currencies.

Support for multiple languages

Support for multiple languages means that when your employees
worldwide are carrying out a business transaction in SAP, they'll view
the same screen but in their own language. This will help you considerably expedite user acceptance and user training of your SAP projects and initiatives. So, you and your coworkers at subsidiaries can
view the same document posted in SAP or the same report printed
from SAP but in different languages. This can be especially important
during month-end closing when frequent, and sometimes frantic, in-

formation exchanges occur between the head office and the world-wide branch offices. Your challenges may be even greater if you not only have customers in foreign countries but also have an actual presence (e.g., office) or operations (e.g., plant) there. Fortunately, as the leading provider of enterprise-wide solutions, SAP provides country-specific developments for more than 40 countries!

Country-Specific Features

As anyone who has worked in a large, global company knows, taking into account the nuances of the accounting, statutory, and business requirements of different countries can be challenging. However, regardless of whether you have a small sales office, large fulfillment plant, or a full-fledged manufacturing company operating in a different country, SAP ERP Financials can easily meet your country-specific requirements.

 Tip

All of the standard country versions provided by SAP are mutually compatible. For example, you can use the country versions for the United States, India, Brazil, Singapore, and France on the same system.

Obviously, payroll processing is considerably different in each country, but as you'll see in Chapter 8, the elegant design of the SAP Payroll component easily manages this requirement. Numerous other country quirks are included in SAP country versions to make your business operations as efficient as possible—no matter where you are. Here are some other examples:

Country-specific functionalities

> Country-specific sales and purchase tax calculations

> Country-specific asset depreciation rules and methods

> Formats for electronic data exchange with banks in different countries

> Country-specific rules for accounting of travel expenses

> Country-specific payment methods in addition to checks and bank transfers

> Numerous reports in various areas of financial accounting to meet country-specific requirements

SAP continues to work on the release of additional country versions. In addition to country-specific requirements, companies in different industries also require functionalities specific to their industries, and SAP provides industry-specific solutions for more than 25 industries.

Industry-Specific Features

Even though core financial processes mostly remain the same across different industries, understandable process differences exist among industries. For example, if, when, and how often you check customer creditworthiness depends on whether you're issuing a credit card, selling a car, building an aircraft for the government, selling a widget on an Internet store, or providing legal services to your clients. What's important to you is whether SAP ERP Financials supports the business requirements of *your* industry.

 Warning

Not all SAP industry solutions were developed with concurrent usage in mind. You should consider this aspect if your company intends to use multiple industry solutions in the same SAP system.

Industry-specific functionalities

The following are some examples of industry-specific functionalities in SAP:

> Grouping multiple customer services on a single bill (e.g., utilities, telecommunications companies)

> Real-time distributing of premiums, claims, and costs from accounting documents to multiple coinsurers (e.g., insurance companies)

> Determining operating profit of a hospital based on services provided to the patients (e.g., healthcare providers)

> Distributing production cost to the original project item requesting it, even if requirements from multiple project items were grouped together at the time of production (e.g., aerospace manufacturers)

> Synchronizing changes to software licenses reflected in sales orders to corresponding customer billing (e.g., high-tech companies)

> Revenue distributing/allocating of product volume and product values based on ownership (e.g., companies in the oil and gas industry)

Of course, these are just some of the finance-specific functionalities available to you in the industry solutions provided by SAP. It's also interesting that across different industry-specific solutions, SAP supports requirements ranging from those that are shared across multiple industries (e.g., incentives and commissions calculation) to those that have their own country-specific versions (e.g., patient accounting for healthcare). New industry solutions and new functionalities are regularly introduced by SAP. Table 1.1 provides a list of industry-specific solutions available from SAP as of the writing of this book.

Financial and Public Services	
SAP for Banking	SAP for Higher Education and Research (SAP for HE&R)
SAP for Defense and Security	SAP for Insurance
SAP for Healthcare	SAP for Public Sector
Manufacturing	
SAP for Aerospace and Defense (SAP for A&D)	SAP for Industrial Machinery and Components (SAP for IM&C)
SAP for Automotive	SAP for Life Sciences
SAP for Chemicals	SAP for Mill Products
SAP for Consumer Products	SAP for Mining
SAP for Engineering, Construction, and Operations (SAP for EC&O)	SAP for Oil & Gas (SAP for O&G)
SAP for High Tech	

Table 1.1 Industry Solutions Available from SAP

Service	
SAP for Media	SAP for Travel and Logistics Services
SAP for Professional Services	SAP for Utilities
SAP for Retail	SAP for Wholesale Distribution
SAP for Telecommunications	

Table 1.1 Industry Solutions Available from SAP (cont.)

Challenges of distributed systems

Having considered country-specific and industry-specific requirements, another aspect to your "where can you use SAP ERP Financials" question may be with reference to the organizational structure of your company. Different companies are structured differently in terms of divisional, functional, and geographical distribution of different business activities. For example, you would want your ERP system to support any combination of centralized and decentralized business activities (e.g., among head office and branch offices), shared services (e.g., customer support, travel management), and outsourced activities (e.g., payroll, accounts payable), etc. SAP supports all such organizational structures and many more, even if different divisions or subsidiaries of your company are using different versions of SAP. However, as a business user, you may want to consider the following:

> How will you get data from your subsidiaries at the global head office for financial consolidation?

> How will your regional treasury get their information from regional companies for their daily cash management and liquidity reports?

> If you have "loaned" employees to your subsidiary to work on a project, how and when will the accompanying costs be posted to your ledger?

Of course, SAP ERP Financials supports all such business scenarios, but keeping these types of questions in mind will be beneficial when you embark on any new SAP initiative in a distributed environment.

Throughout this book, we'll focus on the different components in the areas of core accounting (FI), management accounting (CO), and financial supply chain management (FSCM). As you can see in Figure 1.3, the components of SAP ERP Financials provide you with one consistent platform for all people involved in your financial processes. Of course, the figure also shows that this book will give you a flavor of only some of the components of SAP ERP Financials. It would be impossible to cover all of the components in one book, so they are not all covered in this book.

Figure 1.3 SAP ERP Financials

Please keep in mind that there is no single, right way to read or use this book, but you may find it most useful to read the book sequentially because the concepts explained in earlier chapters are referenced in subsequent chapters. However, if you're already familiar with some functionality, or if you're interested only in specific functionalities, by all means go straight to the chapter of your interest. Also, you may encounter scenarios where different parts of a topic are distributed across different chapters. For example, internal orders (a type of cost collector used in SAP software) are discussed in chapter 10; but planning on internal orders is discussed in chapter 14, and their usage for investment capitalization is discussed in Chapter 6. More than anything else, this distribution of information across different chapters represents how closely different components of SAP are integrated with each other!

In the next chapter, we'll begin our discovery of SAP ERP Financials starting with the core Financials component of General Ledger (GL) accounting.

General Ledger

The general ledger forms the backbone of any accounting system. It records the financial impact of all the business transactions in your company, provides necessary information to prepare your financial statements and helps you track and preserve the information you need for internal or external audits of your company. The General Ledger (GL) is also one of the core Financial Accounting components in SAP ERP Financials. It provides you with functions for entering, recording, and evaluating accounting entries to make daily accounting operations fast and efficient.

This component is fully integrated with other SAP application components, such as accounts receivable, accounts payable, asset accounting, sales, materials management, and others. This integrated design allows other application components to automatically post accounting entries for relevant business transactions. These automatic entries ensure accurate, efficient, and real-time recording of financial transactions, which in turn, enables you to carry out real-time analysis and reporting of financial information.

Overview

The GL in SAP ERP Financials records all business transactions for statutory and management reporting purposes. Full integration of the

GL with all of the other operational areas of a company helps ensure that the accounting data is always complete and accurate. In addition, by integrating all operational areas, entries in subledger accounts are automatically and simultaneously posted to appropriate control reconciliation accounts in the new GL.

GL accounting also supports many other functions, including parallel accounting which allows for multiple accounting principles, Profit Center Accounting (PCA), segment reporting, and cost of sales accounting. You can maintain multiple charts of accounts to meet recording and reporting requirements, and by splitting maintenance of GL account data at the chart of accounts and company level, you can manage a number of GL accounts in your primary chart of accounts while taking care of local nuances. In addition, GL accounting allows you to create groups and hierarchies of profit centers to generate profit center reports at multiple levels of responsibility areas.

Another advantage of the new GL is the online document splitting functionality, which lets you prepare financial statements based on profit centers, functional areas, business areas, or other user-specified segments. As we'll discuss in more detail later in this chapter, you can use the Accrual Engine to automate accruals processing by using complex calculation rules, and you can use the Closing Cockpit to obtain a single view of the status of the closing activities across your companies.

GL reporting

One of the really important features of SAP ERP Financials is the standard reports it provides for financial statements and other reports required to meet country-specific reporting requirements. This large number of standard reports provides visibility to ledger account balances and GL entries posted from other application areas. And you can use report development tools provided in the system to develop additional reports to meet your own requirements.

Functions in Detail

We'll start this section by talking about how to set up the GL in SAP ERP Financials to deal with the most fundamental aspects of any accounting system, such as your corporate structure, fiscal years, chart of accounts, currencies, and so on. Then we'll discuss some of the key features of the new GL, followed by posting of accounting transactions and integration of the new GL with other SAP application areas. We'll wrap up with coverage of two really important and useful features: financial closing and financial reporting.

Corporate Structure

One of the key things to consider if you choose to implement SAP ERP Financials is how you'll represent your corporate structure, consisting of different companies and operating units within the SAP system. The decisions you make at this stage are extremely important and can have a considerable, far-reaching impact. SAP ERP Financials provides several different organizational units to map your corporate structure into financial accounting, company code, company, business area, profit center, functional area, and segments.

Company Code

The most important organizational unit in SAP ERP Financials is the *company code*. Business transactions relevant for financial accounting are entered, saved, and evaluated at the company code level. As a rule of thumb, for every legal entity for which you want to generate statutory reporting financial statements (balance sheet and income statements), you'll need to create a separate company code. Figure 2.1 shows some of the control parameters for a company code.

 Tip

Even if you only have one unit in your company, you'll need to set up at least one company code.

You can use the *company* organizational unit to group one or more company codes together so that you can prepare consolidated financial statements. However, unlike company codes, companies should be defined only after careful consideration of your financial consolidation requirements. (We'll cover consolidation more in Chapter 9.) For the sake of simplicity, company code and company will be referred to interchangeably throughout the rest of the chapters.

Figure 2.1 Company Code Control Parameters

Business Area *The organizational unit business area* was introduced so that in addition to company codes, you can generate financial statements based on key operational areas, such as product lines, branch locations, strategic business units, and so on. Because business area functionality isn't being developed or enhanced any further, however, SAP recommends that if you have a new installation, you should consider using other organizational units such as profit centers or segments to meet your business requirements.

Profit centers represent management-oriented structures of the corporation (e.g., departments) for the purpose of internal controls. You can analyze operating results of profit centers based on costs and revenues posted to it. You can also prepare financial statements by profit centers. Another relatively new organizational unit in SAP ERP Financials is the segment. Segments can be freely defined, are generally derived from profit centers, and are used across all companies for reporting. This allows companies to insert their own organizational units into transactional data. For example, an insurance company may decide to use its Line of Business (LoB) as a Segment so that transactions can be allocated to appropriate LoBs, and the company can prepare financial statements by LoB. Even though profit centers and segments appear to cater to similar requirements, nuances between them will become clear later in this chapter.

If you need to prepare reports per Cost of Sales Accounting, you have to use an organizational unit called the *functional area*. Functional areas are used in the system according to functions, for example, production, testing, sales, support, admin, and so on. Functional areas can be linked to P&L accounts so that you can group operating expenses for preparing financial statements. There are several other organizational units to be discussed, but we'll get to those in later chapters when we discuss the relevant functionality. For now, let's discuss the key settings that impact SAP ERP Financials.

Functional Area

Basic Settings

After you set up organizational units to represent your corporate structure, you need to set up other fundamental areas of any financial system, including fiscal year, ledger, currencies, and chart of accounts.

Fiscal Year

You first need to define your fiscal year. A *fiscal year* in SAP ERP Financials can follow the calendar year (Jan.–Dec.), or it can be different from the calendar year (e.g., Apr.–Mar., Sep.–Aug., etc.). The fiscal year can consist of posting periods that correspond to calendar months, or you can define posting periods that have different start and end dates than calendar months. Not only that, a fiscal year can consist of 12 posting periods or any number of posting periods.

 Tip

> All accounting transactions in SAP ERP Financials are posted to GL accounts as of the posting date, and so they impact account balances in the posting period corresponding to the posting date. The system determines the posting date and posting period based on how you have defined the fiscal year associated with the company code.

This design makes several variations of fiscal year definitions possible (see Figure 2.2) to meet different business requirements. For example, you can set up the following:

> A fiscal year corresponding to a calendar year, with 12 posting periods corresponding to a calendar month.

4/4/5 Fiscal Year

> A fiscal year corresponding to a calendar year, with 12 posting periods, but the posting periods don't correspond to calendar months (e.g., 4/4/5). You define the start and end dates of each posting period.

> A fiscal year corresponding to the calendar year with more or less than 12 posting periods. You also define the start and end dates of each posting period.

> A fiscal year that is any variation of the preceding, but the fiscal year doesn't correspond to the calendar year.

FV	Description	Year-depend	Calendar yr	No. of posting	No.of spe
24	Half periods	☐	☐	24	
C1	1st period (calendar year)	☐	☐	1	
K0	Calendar year, 0 spec. period	☐	☑	12	
K1	Cal. Year, 1 Special Period	☐	☑	12	1
K2	Cal. Year, 2 Special Periods	☐	☑	12	2
K3	Cal. Year, 3 Special Periods	☐	☑	12	3
K4	Calendar year, 4 spec. periods	☐	☑	12	4
R1	Shortened fisc.year Jan-Sep'94	☑	☐	12	4
V3	Apr.- March, 4 special periods	☐	☐	12	4
V6	July - June, 4 special periods	☐	☐	12	4
V9	Oct.- Sept., 4 special periods	☐	☐	12	4
WK	Calendar weeks	☑	☐	53	

Figure 2.2 Setting Up Your Fiscal Year

In addition, you can define up to four "special posting periods" for a fiscal year. All special periods post on the last date of the last posting period, but they let you separate year-end accounting entries. For example, any adjustment entries for a "soft" year-end closing can be posted to period 13, adjustment entries after internal audit review can be posted to period 14, adjustment entries after external audit review can be posted to period 15, and so on.

If at a later date, you need to change your fiscal year (e.g., changing from an Apr. - Mar. to a Jan. - Dec. fiscal year), SAP ERP Financials provides you with functionality to make this transition as easy and transparent as possible in other areas of the business. Now let's take a look at the accounting ledger.

Accounting Ledger

At least one accounting ledger must be designated as the leading ledger for the company. The *leading ledger* records and reports on financial transactions with the accounting principles, currencies, fiscal year, and other parameters that are exactly the same as the company.

Accounting ledgers

Additionally, if required, you can create a number of parallel ledgers called non-leading ledgers. Non-leading ledgers can be different from leading ledgers in terms of different accounting principles (IAS versus US GAAP), different currencies, or even a different fiscal year.

Keep in mind, however, that by default, all accounting entries are posted to all ledgers. You can selectively post to only specific ledgers, however, thus giving you flexibility to carry out adjustment entries per IAS in one ledger and per US GAAP in another ledger. Automatic accounting entries originating in other SAP application areas can be grouped based on accounting principles, which in turn can be used to determine the ledger to which those entries are posted.

Parallel accounting

 Tip

If you're using older versions of SAP ERP (prior to SAP ECC 5.0) for which the new GL is unavailable, you can carry out parallel accounting (e.g., valuation using different accounting principles) by using additional GL accounts, using additional company codes, or by creating additional ledgers in the Special Ledger component.

It's important to note that these leading and non-leading accounting ledgers are GLs consisting of GL accounts that only carry GL transactions. Customers, vendors, and asset transactions are represented in the GL only as a summary/control/reconciliation account and are posted to respective subledgers. After your ledgers are set, another setting to address is your choice of currencies.

Currencies

Standard SAP ERP Financials comes ready with close to 200 currencies along with their relevant information (e.g., Japanese Yen with zero decimal places, Dinar with three decimal places, etc.). You can maintain exchange rates between currency pairs manually, or you can use an interface program to obtain and automatically update exchange rates from an external service. For each currency pair, you can maintain multiple types of exchange rates, including month-end rates, monthly average rates, and so on.

As long as you have proper conversion rates and exchange rates in the system, you can post an accounting entry in pretty much any currency. SAP calls this currency transaction currency, or the currency in which a transaction is posted to the ledger. Apart from transaction currency, you can define three currencies for each accounting ledger you use. One of the currencies in the leading ledger must be *company code currency*, which is the functional currency in which a company's statutory financial statements are prepared.

Currency types and exchange rates

You can choose additional ledger currencies from group currency (for the purpose of consolidation), hard currency (if the company is based in a country with a highly volatile currency), index-based currency (if the currency is indexed), and so on. Now let's look at the functionality available in SAP ERP Financials to represent the cornerstone of any financial system: the chart of accounts.

Chart of Accounts

In the GL in SAP ERP Financials, one or more charts of accounts are used to group GL accounts. A chart of accounts that is associated with a company is referred to as its primary chart of accounts, and you can share one chart of accounts across multiple companies. Details of GL accounts are maintained at two levels:

> Information that is unique to the chart of accounts and can't be different in different companies, for example, the GL account number, account name, whether the account is a balance sheet or an income statement account, corresponding account in group chart of accounts, and so on.

> Information that isn't unique to the chart of accounts and that can be different in different companies, for example, currency in which the account balances are maintained, controls for sales and purchase taxes, whether accounting entries to the account can be posted through manual journal entries, and so on.

 Tip

SAP provides chart of accounts templates for more than 25 North American, European, and Asian countries. These templates provide you with typical setups for revenue and expense accounts, bank accounts, inventory and consumption accounts, payroll accounts, tax accounts, and various other types of accounts.

Depending on your consolidation process and how your group companies are structured, you have an option to set up two additional charts of accounts: group chart of accounts and country chart of accounts.

One approach is to set up every company with its own chart of accounts, and then use group chart of accounts for consolidation purposes. Another approach is to share the primary chart of accounts across all companies, and handle country-specific accounting by using country charts of accounts. Every GL account in your primary chart of accounts is linked to a corresponding account in the group chart of accounts or the country chart of accounts. This makes preparing financial statements for consolidation (if you're using group chart of accounts) or for local statutory reporting (if you're using country chart of accounts) extremely efficient because every accounting entry is automatically recorded to the appropriate account.

Multiple charts of accounts

This design helps you contain proliferation of GL accounts in your primary chart of accounts and also meets the unique or one-off accounting requirements of your companies. So let's learn how to set up your GL.

The New GL

Before we discuss more typical accounting transactions such as journal entries, let's discuss some of the unique functionality offered, supported, and integrated in the new GL. Whether you choose to use this functionality and how, depends entirely on your business requirements. Except for setting up retained earnings accounts, whether you use the other functionalities discussed in this section is optional.

Document Splitting

One of the decisions you need to make while setting up the new GL is whether you want to activate the document splitting functionality. *Document splitting* can be used to produce balanced financial statements at lower levels than company code, for example profit center. For the GL, this functionality can be enabled for profit centers, business areas, and segments. Because segments represent user-defined criteria, you have a lot of room to enrich your GL postings by carefully selecting segments for document splitting.

 Example

> Consider a simple scenario where a customer invoice for $5,000 is posted with revenue entries posting to two profit centers: $3,000 and $2,000, respectively. Without document splitting, revenue numbers—$3000 and $2,000—are posted to individual profit centers. However, the customer receivable entry isn't assigned to any profit center, which means that if you want to prepare accurate balance sheets by profit center, you have to do additional processing.

As shown in the preceding example, with document splitting activated, customer receivables are split by profit center. The splitting process is automatic in real time and performed in the background, so it's transparent to the user. You can view an invoice document as it was entered or with all automatically generated entries.

Document splitting in subsequent postings

The power of document splitting is evident when you consider its impact on subsequent entries. When a customer makes a payment against the invoice discussed previously, but there is a difference due to a cash discount (or it could be a short-payment or exchange-rate loss), those entries are split as per the original profit centers as well. Figure 2.3 shows an example of the document-splitting process for a customer invoice.

```
┌─────────────────────────────────────────────────────┐
│  Example of Document Splitting                        │
│                                                       │
│  Customer invoice (as entered)                        │
│  Receivable Account              $  5,000             │
│  Revenue Account      PrCtr 001  $ (3,000)            │
│  Revenue Account      PrCtr 002  $ (2,000)            │
│                                                       │
│  Customer invoice (after document splitting)          │
│  Receivable Account   PrCtr 001  $  3,000             │
│  Receivable Account   PrCtr 002  $  2,000             │
│  Revenue Account      PrCtr 001  $ (3,000)            │
│  Revenue Account      PrCtr 002  $ (2,000)            │
│                                                       │
│  Customer invoice with discount (as entered)          │
│  Bank Account                    $  4,700             │
│  Receivable Account              $ (5,000)            │
│  Cash Discount Given             $    300             │
│                                                       │
│  Customer payment (after document splitting)          │
│  Bank Account         PrCtr 001  $  2,820             │
│  Bank Account         PrCtr 002  $  1,880             │
│  Receivable Account   PrCtr 001  $ (3,000)            │
│  Receivable Account   PrCtr 002  $ (2,000)            │
│  Cash Discount Given  PrCtr 001  $    180             │
│  Cash Discount Given  PrCtr 002  $    120             │
└─────────────────────────────────────────────────────┘
```

Figure 2.3 Document Splitting Example

Zero-balancing by Segments

For any object or combination of objects that you've selected for document splitting, you can set the system to ensure zero-balancing. In the example in Figure 2.3, after document splitting, if the net balance for a profit center is not zero, SAP automatically carries out balancing entries so that the net balance by profit center becomes zero.

In SAP ERP Financials, different business transactions, such as invoices, payments, and so on, are grouped into document-splitting rules that determine document-splitting triggers. These rules are grouped into a document-splitting method. All companies that belong to the same client (consider "client" as a "slice" of your SAP ERP database as set up by people managing your software installation) must use the same technical method for document splitting. You can choose to exclude a company from using the same document splitting method, but you should consider how that will impact your inter-company accounting entries. You also need to decide whether to activate functionality of negative postings in the new GL.

Negative Postings

Typically, when you reverse an accounting entry, debits and credits are posted to accounts that are opposite of those in the original accounting entry, which increases debit and credit transaction totals in each account. However, if you activate *negative posting*, debits and credits are posted as negative entries to the original accounts of the accounting entry, thereby reducing debit and credit transaction totals.

Reconciliation of negative postings

You can use this functionality to reverse incorrectly posted entries without having to increase debit and credit transaction numbers in the GL accounts. At the same time, this functionality can create confusion for an unknowledgeable person who is carrying out reconciliation between account balances and transaction figures. Therefore, SAP ERP Financials provides you with two levels of control: document types that are specifically identified to allow negative postings, and a control setting at the company code level to allow negative postings.

In addition, if a reversal is posted using a posting date other than the one for the original accounting entry, a setting for negative posting isn't taken into account. This built-in control avoids negative transaction figures in individual periods. And it's compatible with reversal entries originating in other SAP areas such as materials management, sales, purchasing, and so on, although each of those applications must specifically indicate that the reversal entry is to be posted as negative posting.

When making decisions about document splitting and negative postings, you should also consider how SAP handles the posting of retained earnings at the end of the fiscal year.

Retained Earnings

At year end, balances of all P&L accounts are transferred to a retained earnings account. In many lower-end accounting systems, this is done by actually posting a document that zeros out the P&L accounts and by transferring balances as opening balances of the balance sheet in the new fiscal year. However, this method makes it impossible to prepare an income statement for the last period in the fiscal year after the fiscal year closing has been carried out. In SAP ERP Financials, only the net balance is transferred as an opening balance of the retained earnings account, so that you can go back in history and create financial statements of any period.

In addition, you can set up more than one retained earnings account. Of course, one P&L account can be mapped to only one retained earnings account, but you can carry forward balances of different sets of P&L accounts to different retained earning accounts. This feature lets you create different financial statements at different levels by using different retained earnings accounts, which is yet another feature to assist you in carrying out parallel accounting.

Parallel accounting

Earlier, we already talked about using the profit center organizational unit for reporting purposes, so let's look at that functionality in a little more detail now.

Profit Center Accounting

Profit Center Accounting (PCA) lets you determine profits and losses by areas of responsibility within your company for management controlling and reporting purposes (Chapter 13 goes into more details of PCA from a profitability analysis viewpoint). In SAP ERP Financials, it's also possible to prepare complete balance sheets for each profit center by assigning asset portfolios, payables, receivables, material stocks, WIP (Work In Process) and other balance sheet items to profit centers; or you can choose to only selectively analyze balance sheet items (e.g., receivables and payables) by profit centers.

You can link default profit centers to cost centers, assets, GL accounts, products, and so on. For example, when an accounting entry is posted to a cost center, SAP ERP Financials automatically posts that accounting entry in parallel to the corresponding profit center. You can create as many multilevel profit center groups as required for reporting. You have to create at least one profit center group to which all profit centers are linked; this profit center group is called *standard hierarchy*. The profit center standard hierarchy acts as a catchall profit center group and ensures that at least one profit center group represents your whole enterprise. In addition, you can group profit centers into additional groups for reporting purposes.

Standard hierarchy

New GL versus classic PCA

PCA setup is decidedly different depending on whether it's integrated with the new GL or whether you're using it as delivered in prior versions (called classic PCA). Although most of these differences concern "how to do it" and not "what functionality is available," PCA using the new GL provides similar functionality more efficiently and with reduced effort. You can approach it in two ways:

> To integrate PCA with the new GL, you define the profit center as one of the criteria on which document splitting is carried out. This setting ensures that accounting entries (e.g., receivables and payables entries) are split by profit centers and enables you to report on receivables and payables by profit center. If you want to prepare complete balance sheets by profit centers, you have to set the system so that the profit center is always required, and *zero-balance check* for profit centers is always performed in all accounting entries.

> If you intend to use or continue to use classic PCA with the new GL, then automatic splitting by profit centers won't occur, and you need to run additional programs at month end, so that all accounting entries are analyzed and balance sheet entries are updated with appropriate profit centers.

Each of these approaches has its unique reporting capabilities and constraints, and it's possible—although not suggested—to continue using classic PCA independent of using the new GL. It's also possible—although not recommended due to large data volume—to run classic PCA and the new PCA in parallel. You should make your final decision after carefully evaluating both approaches.

What we've discussed so far mostly refers to the commonly used accounting approach of *period accounting*. Under this approach all of the costs incurred in a period are reported in that period, regardless of whether the corresponding revenue was earned then. In the next section let's see how SAP can be used to implement a different type of accounting approach called cost of sales accounting.

Cost of Sales Accounting

In the *cost of sales accounting* approach, only the costs for which corresponding revenues were earned are reported. We've already discussed the fact that if you're planning to use cost of sales accounting, you have to set up functional areas. To do this, you need to assign these functional areas to GL accounts, cost centers, and other organizational objects.

Compared to period accounting, relatively few standard reports are available for the cost of sales accounting method, although SAP does provide you with templates for preparing financial statements. But you'll need to modify these templates or create additional reports to meet your requirements.

At this point, you should have a good idea of the unique features offered by the new GL. In the next section, we'll take a look at how typical accounting transactions (e.g., journal entries) are processed in SAP ERP Financials.

Accounting Transactions

All accounting transactions are posted to the GL as financial documents, which, in SAP ERP Financials, consist of a document header and two or more document line items. Irrespective of the SAP application area, all business transactions that have financial impact create a financial document in SAP ERP Financials. Thus, a goods receipt in purchasing, which increases the value of an inventory account, creates a financial document; similarly, posting travel expenses in travel management increases the value of employee payables and creates another financial document. You'll come across different types of these documents throughout this book, so this section only focuses on some very basic features of them.

Accounting Documents

In a financial document, the attributes associated with the document header and two or more line items make the document in the GL very important for recording and reporting financial activity. Some of these attributes capture standard information, such as the document date (typically the date when the document is entered in the system), posting date (the date the GL account balance is updated), company code, tax details, and so on. So, let's discuss two extremely important attributes of a financial document: document types and posting keys.

Document Types   *Document types* help to distinguish between business transactions. SAP provides more than 40 document types for different business transactions in receivables, payables, asset accounting, inventory accounting, and payroll (see Figure 2.4). Even though it's recommended to use these document types as-is for their intended purpose, you can choose to create your own document types, modify existing ones, or use them for a different purpose than recommended. How you use document types to distinguish different transactions is largely a business decision.

Type	Description
AA	Asset posting
AB	Accounting document
AF	Dep. postings
DG	Customer credit memo
DR	Customer invoice
DZ	Customer payment
KG	Vendor credit memo
KR	Vendor invoice
KZ	Vendor payment
RB	Reserve for Bad Debt
RE	Invoice - gross
RN	Invoice - net
RV	Billing doc.transfer

Figure 2.4 Financial Document Types in SAP ERP Financials

Financial document types influence several important factors while posting accounting documents. For example, document types control which types of accounts can be posted to. So, if document type KR (which represents a vendor invoice) is set up to allow posting to vendor accounts and GL accounts, and you try to use that document type to post an invoice from a customer, SAP ERP Financials displays an error. Document types also control the document numbering of accounting documents. If you're using secondary/non-leading ledgers, you can specify the number range by ledger for the same document type. This ensures that different ledgers can have continuous document numbers. Document numbers can continue across fiscal year boundaries or can reset to the initial document number every fiscal year.

Posting keys are two-digit codes that determine two main attributes of every line item in an accounting document: 1) whether the line item is debit or credit, and 2) whether the line item posts to a GL account, customer account, vendor account, asset account, or inventory account. Many GL reports include posting keys, and a few of the posting transactions also require them, so it helps to be familiar with some of the most commonly used posting keys; for example, you use 01 to debit the customer account and 50 to credit the GL account, and so on. Figure 2.5 shows some examples of available posting keys.

Posting keys

01	Invoice	Debit	Customer
04	Other receivables	Debit	Customer
11	Credit memo	Credit	Customer
15	Incoming payment	Credit	Customer
21	Credit memo	Debit	Vendor
25	Outgoing payment	Debit	Vendor
31	Invoice	Credit	Vendor
39	Special G/L credit	Credit	Vendor
40	Debit entry	Debit	G/L account
50	Credit entry	Credit	G/L account
70	Debit asset	Debit	Asset
75	Credit asset	Credit	Asset
89	Stock inwrd movement	Debit	Material
99	Stock outwd movement	Credit	Material

Figure 2.5 Posting Keys Used in SAP ERP Financials Documents

Posting Aids

After a document has been posted, you cannot change the account number, amount, debit or credit, or other key information. Standard system behavior is to allow changes to very few fields after a document has been posted, although this behavior can be changed through configuration for certain fields such as document text. All changes are automatically recorded with user name and timestamp, thus providing you with a detailed audit trail.

If all of the information required to post an accounting document isn't available, complete, or confirmed, you can *park* the accounting document. Parked documents *don't* have any impact on account balances, but they can be reviewed later and then approved or rejected. Parked documents also support SAP workflow, which enables you to automatically forward a parked document for review, and then post it to the new GL, if approved.

Document parking

If, while posting accounting entries, the standard SAP applications display too many fields that aren't always relevant (an accounting entry screen can have upwards of 30 fields for every line), you can create *fast entry screens* for different transactions. These are user-defined data entry screens in which you can choose to display only the fields you need. You can create one or more fast entry screen templates that display only those fields for which an entry is expected (e.g., GL account, Amount, Debit or Credit, Cost Center, Description, and so on), so that document entry screens look simpler. In addition, users can set their own editing controls to make posting accounting documents easier. Figure 2.6 shows some of the parameters that an SAP ERP Financials user can set while posting accounting entries.

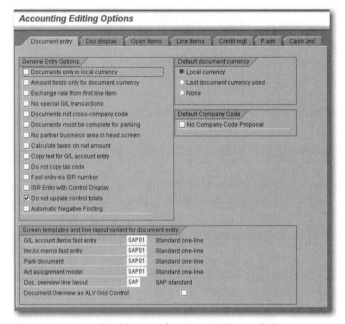

Figure 2.6 Personalized Settings for SAP ERP Financials Documents

Recurring entries   SAP ERP Financials supports recurring entries by enabling you to create a recurring entry master document. Recurring entries can be posted using periodic intervals (e.g., every month, every other month, every quarter, etc.) or by using a *run schedule*. You can define a run schedule so that instead of a fixed date each month or each quarter, recurring entries are posted on specific dates, for example, on the 10th of April, 17th of May, 21st of June, and so on. So, a run schedule can be useful for recurring entries that do not conform to monthly periodicity. By using posting keys that post to customer or vendor accounts, you can easily create recurring entries for accrual postings such as rent. Using a standard program, you can select and post all recurring entries that are due for posting. If recurring entries are in different currencies, you can use the original exchange rate or current exchange rate for each recurring posting run.

Recurring entries are useful if the posting information such as accounts and cost centers remain the same each period. However, if the posting details change each period, you can use the Act Assignment Model entry. Account assignment models act as templates in which GL accounts, cost centers, comments, and so on already exist, and you can change whatever information you like.

Account Assignment Model

You can also use any existing document as a reference while posting new documents; or you can specifically create *sample documents* to be used as a reference. Sample documents don't impact the ledger account balances. When using reference documents, you have the options to generate reverse posting, transfer entries with or without line item texts entered in the original document, recalculate amounts using current exchange rate, and so on. The following section describes how cross-company documents can be posted.

Cross-Company Documents

SAP ERP Financials easily handles cross-company scenarios that involve more than one company. All you have to do is set up which GL accounts should be posted for debits and credits for each pair of companies. Consider a scenario where Company 1001 is making a payment to a vendor on behalf of Company 2001.

When you post this payment in Company 1001, you can specify that the payment is on behalf of Company 2001. SAP automatically creates a cross-company accounting document that posts receivables from Company 2001 into Company 1001 and payables to Company 1001 into Company 2001. All of these documents are linked with each other by a cross-company document number.

You can also use this functionality to post to more than two companies in the same document. While entering individual document lines, specify which company that line belongs to, and in the background, SAP creates all of the necessary cross-company postings. Of course, just like any other accounting documents, these cross-company documents can be displayed, changed, or reversed. Now that we've looked at how typical accounting transactions are posted in GL, let's consider how financial documents posted in GL are integrated with business transactions posted in other SAP application areas.

Integration of the New GL

One of the most powerful features of the new GL is its full integration with other SAP application areas. For example, you can display a goods receipt against a purchase order, and from there, you can navigate to corresponding accounting entries posted to inventory accounts.

On the other hand, you can display any accounting document. If the document wasn't directly posted to the new GL, you can navigate back to the original business transactions that caused this accounting entry by using the Document Relationship Browser.

Document Relationship Browser

Figure 2.7 shows a sample Document Relationship Browser screen for a relatively simple business scenario. The scenario corresponds to revenue posted by GL document 90001735, for which you want to review where those postings originated.

Figure 2.7 Document Relationship Browser

Even though we haven't yet discussed the SAP application areas from which other documents shown in Figure 2.7 have originated, most of these are intuitive. You can see the following from this document relationship tree:

> The new GL document under consideration was created with reference to customer billing document 0090001735.

> The billing document was created with reference to delivery document 0080000928 in shipping.

> The delivery document was created with reference to customer order 1402 in sales.

> Goods issue for that order was posted with document 4900002697 in materials management.

> Inventory account entries corresponding to that goods issue were posted with document 4900001801 in GL.

> Profit centers were posted with documents 15111 (goods issue) and 15121 (customer billing).

> Cost centers were posted with documents 12391 (goods issue) and 12401 (customer billing).

If you have enough authorization, you can even display any of these documents from the Document Relationship Browser. If you've spent time reconciling accounting entries in other systems, you can appreciate the tremendous power that this type of integrated view can give you.

Financial Closing

Depending on how many application areas you're using, the month-end and year-end closing process in SAP ERP Financials can be as simple as running a few simple balance carry-forward programs, or as complex as running a large number of programs across different application areas in a carefully planned sequence across multiple companies.

This section discusses some of the major month-end activities from the point of view of the new GL, such as allocations, currency valuation, and accruals. In addition, it discusses the Closing Cockpit, which can act as a single interface for your closing activities. You'll find details of other closing activities in the relevant chapters of this book. For example, bank statement reconciliation is discussed in Chapter 5 on banking, and asset depreciation run is discussed in Chapter 6 on investment capitalization.

Allocations

Allocations enable you to periodically allocate amounts from senders to receivers. This section only refers to the allocation process in profit centers, but the new GL supports the allocation process for business areas, functional areas, and user-defined segments.

Assessment versus distribution

SAP ERP Financials supports two types of allocations: *assessment* and *distribution*. The assessment process posts amounts from the sending profit centers to the assessment account, from which amounts are debited to the receiving profit centers. Sending profit centers retain their original amounts. The distribution process credits sending profit centers and debits the receiving profit centers, thereby actually reducing balances of the sending profit centers by allocation amounts.

Allocation rules determine whether amounts should be allocated from the sending profit centers to the receiving profit centers using posted amounts (everything posted to the sending profit centers), fixed amounts, or fixed percentages. By associating ledger groups in definition of allocation cycles, you can use amounts posted in one ledger to carry out allocation postings in all ledgers belonging to the ledger group.

 Tip

> It's highly recommended that these allocations be used for profit centers or user-defined segments. For allocation of costs, the corresponding allocation functions in Overhead Cost Accounting should be used.

Currency Valuation

SAP supports currency valuation of accounting entries to the functional currency of the company. Depending on which other currencies are set up, you can also carry out foreign currency valuations in group currencies, hard currencies, or index currencies. SAP also supports currency translation as per FASB 52 under US GAAP to any of these currencies.

Currency valuation of ledger accounts that are maintained based on ending balance (e.g., bank accounts in foreign currency) is handled differently from valuation of accounts maintained on a clearing basis (e.g., receivables accounts to which invoices and payments in foreign currency are posted). This difference ensures, for example, that any exchange gain or loss calculated on an open invoice at month end can be accurately adjusted based on the actual gain or loss realized when the payment against that invoice is received in subsequent months.

Revaluation of open items

In addition to the standard valuation procedure where the exchange gain or loss is always recorded, SAP also supports other currency valuation procedures such as the lowest value principle, where only the exchange loss is booked; and the strict lowest value principle, in which the exchange gain or loss is booked only if the newly calculated gain or loss is more than the gain or loss calculated during the previous revaluation. Another important month-end activity is posting accruals.

Accrual Engine

If your month-end accrual requirements are relatively few and easy, then you can use the simple accrual programs provided in SAP ERP Financials. Using these programs, you specify the reversal date while posting accrual entries. Subsequently, you run another program that reverses all relevant accrual entries en mass. You can also use recurring entries described in the previous section to carry out accruals.

However, if your accrual requirements are pretty complex, such as a large number of active customer contracts involving different types of revenue and cost components that you have to accrue over different timeframes, then you can use the Accrual Engine to efficiently process accruals.

The Accrual Engine can be set up to suit your requirements for accrual types, accrual components, accounting principles under which you carry out accruals, and other relevant parameters. Figure 2.8 shows how you can set up a simple one-year customer contract involving a revenue component and an expense component.

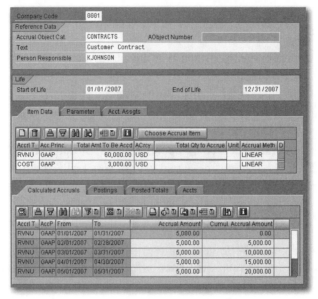

Figure 2.8 Setting Up a Customer Contract in the Accrual Engine

After such a contract has been set up, the Accrual Engine can accurately calculate and post summarized accrual entries each month. Not only that, if the original contract undergoes changes (e.g., early termination, addition of new services), the Accrual Engine can account for those changes.

 Tip

> SAP provides template programs that can be used to transfer accrual information from other application areas. Examples of contracts that originate in different application areas but can be set up in the Accrual Engine are lease contracts, financial contracts, customer service contracts, real estate contracts, and so on.

Closing Cockpit

The Closing Cockpit provides a single interface to all closing activities. You first set up a master list of all activities that you have to carry out during period end. These activities can include SAP programs, SAP reports, and manual activities done outside of the SAP application, along with detailed comments. With each activity, you assign its ownership to a user and assign the expected day relative to the close date; for example, depreciation run is carried out by Mr. Bob on "closing day–3."

Every month, when this list is released, planned start and end dates are calculated for every closing activity and working list. You can start SAP programs or reports directly from the Closing Cockpit. Results of that activity (e.g., carry-forward ledger account balances) are updated back to the Closing Cockpit, indicating whether the process was successful or whether there were any errors.

For activities that are outside of SAP, you have to update the start and end status manually. Actual starting and ending dates and times are then updated for every activity, so that you can compare them with the planned dates and times.

You can duplicate this activity list for other group companies in your organization and then customize the activity lists of individual companies. For example, manufacturing companies will have more closing activities compared to service companies. This ability to maintain closing activities and track status in real time across all companies (even worldwide) gives you a very effective tool to improve your closing process. Figure 2.9 shows you a sample Closing Cockpit screen.

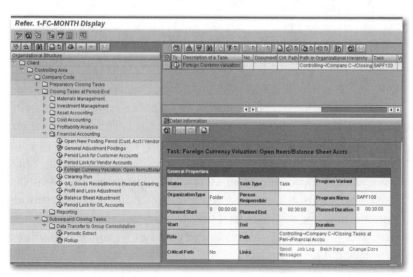

Figure 2.9 Closing Cockpit

Financial Reporting

SAP provides a large number of standard reports to prepare financial statements, cash flow statements, and additional reports to meet country-specific requirements for a large number of countries. Other reports provide different views to GL account balances and accounting entries. You'll find most of these reports neatly organized under the Information System heading in the new GL area.

Financial statements Using financial statement definitions, you can prepare one or more additional variations of financial statements (balance sheets and income statements) in multiple languages, different currencies, and at different levels—by individual companies, by business areas, or for a corporate group across multiple companies—to suit your requirements.

 Tip

> These financial statements provide income statement information only by GL accounts. If you want to have expense details by cost centers and revenue details by profit centers, you need to prepare those statements from Cost Center Accounting (CCA) or Profit Center Accounting (PCA).

Normally, one of the goals of an SAP implementation project is to make information more visible, so as business users get comfortable with new processes, you'll inevitably end up developing more reports to slice and dice the vast amount of integrated information available.

Report Painter SAP ERP Financials also provides a *Report Painter* tool so that you can create additional reports. Report Painter is an extremely powerful tool for designing reports that easily fit into a row and column design. For example, if you want to carry out a comparative analysis of your expenses, you can create groups of accounts (sales, marketing, R&D, finance, etc.) and define them as rows of the report. Then you can create columns of that report to correspond to different time periods (current month, quarter-to-date, year-to-date, last year - same month, etc.), and your report is ready! The Report Painter tool can be a little technical, but it's formidable.

You can also use the SAP Query tool to get data out of SAP ERP Financials. After your technical team sets up the source of information that you can query on, this tool lets you pick and choose what information you want to display. This tool is really powerful if you want to report a large volume of data without the need for complex formatting but with the ability to slice and dice information.

SAP Query

Internal correspondence enables you to print accounting documents or accounting statements from GLs or subledgers. You can design and link forms to individual companies, so that you can use a single program to gather required data, but you can use different forms for different companies while printing account statements. You should keep in mind that the SAP software differentiates between a customer invoice printed from finance (that includes GL accounts and dollar amounts) and a customer billing document printed from sales, which typically includes stock and quantity details.

Summary

In this chapter, we covered key information about the diverse functionality of the new GL as summarized here:

> The ability to set up SAP ERP Financials to accommodate your organizational structure for external and statutory requirements, as well as for internal, management purposes

> The ability to create user-defined segments, and associate or allocate accounting entries to segments for preparing LoB or segment reporting

> The ability to use multiple charts of accounts that are seamlessly linked with each other to meet group requirements as well as local statutory requirements

> The availability of multiple ledgers to accommodate parallel valuation requirements per multiple accounting principles or for differing management reporting requirements

> Document splitting with zero balancing functionality to produce balanced financial statements at lower levels than company code

> Full integration of the GL with other SAP application areas providing you with visibility and traceability of accounting entries

> System-delivered multi-currency, multi-language reports that also meet country-specific requirements for many countries in the world

> The availability of tools to create your own reports for financial reporting and analytics

> The ability to use the Closing Cockpit to improve visibility and control of closing activities across different functional areas across multiple companies in the organization

> The Accrual Engine to handle posting of accruals irrespective of volume and the complexity involved

Next, in Chapter 3, we'll explore receivables and payables.

3

Receivables and Payables

In today's business environment, managing accounts payables and receivables is a critical function. This mechanism essentially keeps companies running because without cash flow, it's difficult to operate. SAP ERP Financials offers powerful tools for managing these processes, and throughout this chapter, we'll discuss the basic functionality and business requirements for them. And, because accounts receivables and accounts payables are also closely linked with the banking functionality for receiving and making payments, you'll benefit from reading this chapter in conjunction with Chapter 5 on Banking Transactions. More specific functions, such as liquidity management, credit management, risk management, and dispute management, are discussed in separate chapters.

Overview

As you would expect, the accounts payable (AP) component records and administers accounting data for vendors. It's also an integral part of the purchasing process, because vendor invoices for purchase orders are posted and paid in AP. But unlike many other available systems, SAP ERP Financials provides vendor invoice verification that is rich in functionality and can be used for two-way or three-way matching, identifying and analyzing variances, and carrying out follow-up or corrective actions.

In addition to the typical processing of vendor invoices, several other automatic invoicing functions, such as self-invoicing based on goods receipts, Evaluated Receipt Settlement, consignment settlement, and pipeline settlement, are also supported. (We'll discuss all of these functions shortly.) Invoicing plans and revaluation of invoices add to the functionality available to you for enhancing the vendor invoicing process. Payables to vendors, and if necessary, customers, are paid with the Payment Program. Payments can be made in printed and electronic form, and SAP supports a wide range of payment methods required or applicable in countries around the world.

Similarly, the accounts receivable (AR) component records and administers accounting data for customers and is an integral part of the sales system. SAP ERP Financials provides functionality to carry out billing for services and products based on orders, contracts, or deliveries. Using a generic interface, you can also load data from external systems to be used as the basis for customer billing. Other available options include retroactive billing, periodic billing, summary billing, billing based on milestone achievements, and after-the-fact billing based on actual resources consumed. Incoming payments can be matched with open invoices using the powerful cash application program discussed in Chapter 1. AR also records and provides data required for other SAP software components such as credit management, liquidity planning, collection and dispute management, and other integrated applications.

Integration with the new GL

Postings made in AP and AR are automatically and simultaneously recorded in the new General Ledger (GL) using the reconciliation (control) accounts associated with vendors or customers. Using special GL indicators, you can support business transactions such as bank guarantees, down payment requests, and others not typically recorded in GL. And, automatic or manual document-clearing processes can be used to match debits and credits in a customer or vendor account to reduce open items in receivables and payables.

When creating customer and vendor accounts in your SAP system, you can mirror complex customer and vendor organizations and their interrelationship. You do this by linking customer accounts or vendor accounts among each other based on partner functions to indicate the account to be used for selling, shipping, billing, paying, and performing other functions. In addition, you can maintain customers in the system who are also your vendors and vice versa. This can be especially useful because it enables you to link the customer and vendor accounts to carry out netting for payment settlement purposes. You can also maintain accounts that represent head-office and branch-office relationships with each other for the purposes of invoicing, paying, dunning, or creating other correspondence.

When you need to communicate with your customers or vendors, you can use the business correspondence functionality to design balance confirmations, account statements, and other forms of reports to suit your requirements. The system contains due date forecasts, balance lists, journals, balance audit trails, and other internal evaluations in AR and AP.

Functions in Detail

In this section, we'll discuss different AR and AP functionalities in detail. We'll start with how customer and vendor master data is maintained, followed by the four most commonly used and important business processes: sending invoices, receiving payments, receiving invoices, and making payments. We'll end by reviewing the other supporting processes.

Master Data

Before discussing customer and vendor master data, it's important to understand the organizational units involved in data maintenance. From an accounting point of view, the only organizational unit relevant for AR and AP is a company code in which debits and credits to customer and vendor accounts are recorded. However, in an integrated system such as SAP ERP Financials, it also helps to understand how sales and purchasing functions of your organization are mapped.

Organizational units in the sales and purchasing application

Sales organizations in SAP ERP Financials represent sales responsibility by geography (regions or countries), *distribution channels* represent responsibility by method of fulfillment (wholesale, retail, or online), and *divisions* represent responsibility by product groups. Similarly, on the purchasing side, *purchasing organizations* represent purchasing responsibility by geography, and *plants* correspond to the plants of your organization where goods receipts and goods issues take place. These are the typical uses of these organizational units, but you can use them differently to match your sales and purchasing requirements.

Sales organizations, purchase organizations, and plants are linked to a company code, in which accounting entries for sales and purchase transactions with customers and vendors are posted. This type of design flexibility enables you to set up SAP to meet your sales and purchasing business requirements largely independent of whether your receivables and payables operations are centralized, distributed, or outsourced.

Customers and Vendors

Customer master data is created at three levels in SAP ERP Financials: General level, company code level, and sales organization level. General-level customer data includes information such as name, address, phone, fax, emails, and information relevant for marketing (e.g., industry, sales, Nielsen ID), customer tax numbers, and similar other information that remains the same for all companies and all sales organizations.

The company code level customer data includes the reconciliation account (control account in GL where the customer balance is posted), customer bank information for electronic payments, lockbox information, information relevant for cash and liquidity planning, dunning information, and other details relevant for AR. On the other hand, customer data at the sales organization level includes information that is relevant for sales, such as order probability, rebates and pricing information, billing information, and so on.

Similarly, vendor master data is also maintained at three levels. Information at the general level is similar to that maintained for customers, including name, address, communication details, and such. Company code level information such as reconciliation account, withholding tax (e.g., 1099) information, eligible payment methods for vendors is maintained as relevant for AP. The purchasing organization level includes information relevant for purchasing such as Incoterms, control parameters relevant to goods receipt, and invoice settlement, purchasing group, etc.

Multilevel master data

This design of maintaining master data enables you to maintain single customers or vendor numbers, while taking care of disparate, local requirements of individual companies and sales or purchasing departments. So, you can maintain single customer or vendor master records that can be extended to the relevant company codes.

 Example

> If your U.S. and Canadian companies have relationships with the same customers, you can maintain different pricing and rebate information and different bank accounts for receiving electronic payments under a single customer number, but in separate U.S. and Canadian sales organizations or company codes.

Partner Functions

For larger customers and vendors, their addresses for order receiving, goods delivery, billing, and payment receipts are likely all different. SAP ERP Financials handles this type of requirement by allowing you to create multiple customer and vendor accounts that can be linked with each other by specifying the partner relationship between them. So you can create four different customer accounts—each representing selling, shipping, billing, and payment addresses for the customer—and link all of them together using partner functions. Of course, if all of these addresses are the same, you can use the same account number for all four partner functions. SAP ERP Financials provides more than 90 partner functions that can be used to signify business partner relationships. Figure 3.1 shows a sample list of partner functions.

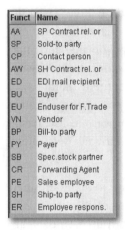

Funct	Name
AA	SP Contract rel. or
SP	Sold-to party
CP	Contact person
AW	SH Contract rel. or
ED	EDI mail recipient
BU	Buyer
EU	Enduser for F.Trade
VN	Vendor
BP	Bill-to party
PY	Payer
SB	Spec.stock partner
CR	Forwarding Agent
PE	Sales employee
SH	Ship-to party
ER	Employee respons.

Figure 3.1 Partner Functions

 Warning

Without clear logic or decisions, assigning appropriate partner functions for customer and vendor master data can be complicated and confusing during data conversion from other systems.

When master data is maintained in the system, you can start processing business transactions with customers and vendors. Let's begin with the customer billing process.

Customer Billing

Billing document versus accounting document

In a typical sales cycle, after the customer order is received, the next step is manufacturing or procuring the goods and delivering the goods to the customer, or performing services as requested by the customer. After goods are delivered or services are performed, customer billing is the final processing stage of the sales cycle. Unlike many other systems, in SAP ERP Financials, a billing document only refers to the document sent to a customer from the sales application with details of products and quantities billed. This is a different document from the accounting document posted to AR, which contains amounts and GL accounts. Typically, you configure the software so that both of these document numbers are the same. The billing document sent from the sales application is linked to a Sales Organization, Distribution Channel, and Division; whereas accounting documents in AR are linked to a Company Code. Let's now see how to generate these billing documents.

Billing Process

You can create billing documents in different ways. You can have a daily background process to create all billing documents that are due; you can selectively create billing documents online from a billing due list proposed by the software, or you can explicitly create billing documents for an order or a delivery. Figure 3.2 shows the program screen to select and process billing documents.

Billing documents can refer to customer invoices, credit memos, debit memos, pro-forma invoices, and cancellations. These billing documents can be created based on orders, deliveries, or services.

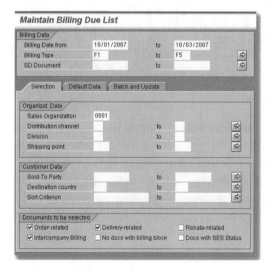

Figure 3.2 Billing Due List

Billing Process
Options

If more than one order or delivery for a customer is due for billing, you can choose to create a separate billing document for each delivery (individual billing documents) or one combined billing document across all orders and deliveries (collective billing documents). You also have an option to split one billing document into multiple billing documents based on user-defined criteria. SAP automatically creates separate billing documents if some of the important criteria (e.g., sales organization, payment terms) are different.

The process for determining GL accounts that billing documents post to can be as simple or as complex as required by your business. This decision largely depends on the level of visibility you require in the revenue accounts section of your chart of accounts. Geography, customer base (wholesale, retail, online, etc.), and revenue streams (sales, service, consulting, etc.) are some typical criteria for segregating revenue numbers while posting accounting entries from customer billing.

 Tip

Even though it's tempting to create separate revenue accounts in your chart of accounts for every conceivable combination of revenue criteria, doing so will make reporting more difficult. Creation of revenue GL accounts should be primarily driven by the requirements of preparing income statements. For reporting and analysis by other criteria, such as a distribution channel or smaller, regional offices, you may want to use the Sales Information System in SAP ERP Financials.

Sales accruals

By properly identifying business requirements and setting up revenue account determination, you can also automate accrual entries (e.g., for shipping costs, marketing promotions, etc.) or accounting entries in accordance with rebate agreements. So far, we've discussed a straightforward billing process where customers are invoiced based on orders received. SAP ERP Financials also supports special types of billing processes.

Special Scenarios

SAP ERP Financials supports the process of *self-billing*, so that instead of you sending out billing documents to your customers, your customers can send you self-billing documents that contain information about deliveries they have received and the amount that they are settling.

Typically, self-billing data is received and updated electronically. Afterwards, the self-billing program attempts to locate corresponding data in SAP ERP Financials using a delivery number. If the program finds a match, it attempts to compare material, quantity, and price information. Any discrepancies within the tolerance limits are written off, whereas any discrepancy greater than the tolerance limit automatically creates an open entry for the difference in customer receivables.

You can use the *retroactive-billing* functionality to process and re-price billing documents that have already been processed. This can be necessary if, for example, your customer pricing agreements change frequently and retroactively (fairly common in the consumer electronics industry). Using retroactive billing, you can revalue affected documents and automatically create debit memos or credit memos for the differences. You can even carry out retroactive billing in simulation mode to analyze potential changes.

Retroactive billing

Another scenario may involve the requirement to bill your customer periodically at a specific frequency (monthly, quarterly, etc.) or based on the completion of specific tasks or events. SAP provides two types of *billing plans* for this purpose: the *periodic billing plan* and the *milestone billing plan*. Using the periodic billing plan, you can specify the frequency of billing, and SAP automatically proposes billing dates and billing amounts—both of which can be modified to meet a specific requirement.

The milestone billing plan is used to trigger customer billing when a mutually agreed upon "milestone" has been completed. For example, for an SAP rollout project, different milestones include signing the contract, finalizing requirements, signing off on deliverables, and so on. In the SAP project system (discussed in Chapter 11), you specify project tasks as milestones and assign milestones to billing dates in billing plans. Subsequently, when a milestone is reached and confirmed in the project system, the corresponding customer billing is released for further processing. In complex projects, the schedule of

Billing plans

actual deliverables may differ from the originally planned schedule, so you have an option to choose whether milestone billing should be based on planned dates or actual dates.

Resource-related billing provides yet another method of billing your customers. This type of billing is required in situations where customers are to be billed for work done, materials used, and other expenses, but actual details are not known until completion of services (e.g., consulting or maintenance contracts) or completion of production (e.g., in make-to-order production). You can handle these situations by creating billing requests.

Billing requests

A billing request document contains expenditure items to be billed and presents relevant details in expenditure view and sales pricing view. The expenditure view enables you to change proposed amounts and quantities to be billed, choose whether an item is to be billed partially or not at all, and determine whether items should be locked against any future changes. In the sales pricing view, you control how these items are billed to the customer by entering or changing the pricing of the items in the billing request.

So far all of the discussion in this section has assumed that billing documents are generated based on the order and delivery data in SAP ERP Financials. But, using the general billing interface, you can also generate billing documents based on data loaded from external systems. This data has to be prepared as a sequential file in a specific format and can include document data (e.g., deliveries or orders generated externally) or master data (e.g., customer addresses or taxability). Typically, you will use general billing interface to interface with your legacy systems.

Regardless of how a customer is billed, from an accounting point of view, the timing and process for recognizing sales revenues can be totally different.

Revenue Recognition

Depending on statutory or business-specific requirements, the timing when revenue is recognized can be different from the timing when the customer is billed. SAP revenue recognition supports different methods of revenue recognition: at the time of billing, time-related, or service-related.

Recognizing revenue at the time of billing is the standard system response. Time-related revenue recognition enables you to recognize revenue periodically over a specific time frame, for example, billing a customer in advance for one year of maintenance contract and recognizing 1/12th of the billed amount as revenue each month. Service-related revenue recognition enables you to recognize revenue after a specific event, such as delivery completed or services performed.

Types of revenue recognition

If you're using time-related or service-related revenue recognition, SAP ERP Financials posts to accrued revenue accounts at the time of customer billing. Subsequently, using the revenue recognition program, you can recognize revenue from accrued revenue accounts to regular revenue accounts. You can also start recognizing revenue before the customer is billed. The revenue recognition program tracks this portion of revenue into an unbilled receivables account.

Independent of the revenue recognition process (which is internal to your company) is the cash application process during which payments received from the customer are applied against customer invoices in AR.

Incoming Payments and Cash Application

Figure 3.3 shows a sample screenshot of the program for entering incoming payments. The program displays all open debit and credit documents based on parameters such as customer account, company, date, and so on. You can choose to display documents from more than one account or even from more than one company.

After a list of documents is displayed, you can sort and search for items, select items based on amounts, select or unselect multiple items, and organize the display so that you can easily find invoices to apply payment against. You also can choose whether documents on the screen are automatically selected for payment based on amount or based on oldest first. If you choose one of those options, the program

Automatic matching of payments and invoices

makes an attempt to suggest documents that can be settled by the payment.

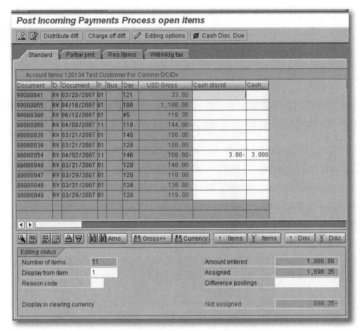

Figure 3.3 Cash Application to Customer Invoices

Partial payments and Residual payments

If a customer underpays, you can post the payment in two different ways. You can apply the incoming payment as a *partial payment* against the invoice. With this approach, payment is posted with reference to the customer invoice, and both the invoice and payment remain as open items on the customer account. All documents are cleared when the remaining payment is received. Another option is to post the incoming payment as a residual payment. In this case, the original invoice is cleared with the incoming payment, and a new document equal to the balance amount is posted to the customer account. Whether you post an incoming payment as a partial payment or as a residual payment is largely a business decision. Figure 3.3 shows an example in which a $1,000 payment is to be allocated to net receivables of $1,698.35.

Notice the Reason Code field in Figure 3.3. You can assign one or more reason codes to the payment difference and post these differences back on the customer account. In addition to reason codes, you can also enter two freely definable reference keys for every difference line so that it's easier to analyze these differences. This functionality can be useful when processing an incoming payment with many chargeback amounts.

You can also choose to write off the difference that is within tolerance limits. This is an appropriate place to introduce how SAP ERP Financials handles tolerances. You can associate tolerance limits (as percentages and absolute amounts) with customers, vendors, and employees. A difference is considered within tolerance limits only if it's within the lowest of the limit determined by the percentage and the amount associated with the customer or vendor and the employee processing the payment.

Based on your system configuration, SAP ERP Financials automatically posts any discount adjustments, tax adjustments, or exchange loss or gain entries while processing an incoming payment.

The last two sections discussed the AR business processes of sending invoices to customers and receiving payments from customers. The next section discusses the AP process of validating and posting invoices received from vendors.

Vendor Invoice Verification

In invoice verification, incoming invoices from vendors are verified, matched against purchase orders or service orders if they exist, and released for payment after all information is verified. SAP ERP Financials provides Logistics Invoice Verification (LIV) to handle a multitude of business requirements that revolve around vendor invoice verification.

LIV supports posting vendor invoices, vendor credit memos, and subsequent debits and subsequent credits for any adjustments. Unlike vendor invoices and vendor credit memos, subsequent debits and subsequent credits only change payable amounts without changing quantities. Figure 3.4 shows the LIV screen with some of the available options highlighted in inset windows. For goods procured using purchase orders, invoices received from vendors are matched with purchase orders and goods receipts. Additionally, SAP ERP Financials also provides you with many other options to meet different types of requirements.

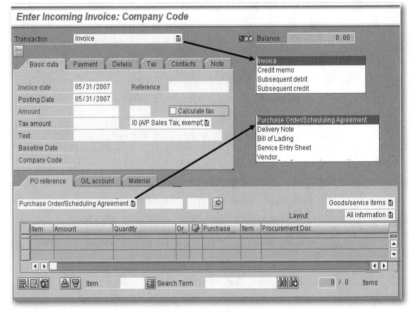

Figure 3.4 Vendor Invoice Verification in Logistics

Allocation and Assignment of Invoices

Different vendors at different times can send you invoices based on different criteria, and SAP ERP Financials provides functionality to enter and associate vendor invoices for any such scenarios. Following are some of the scenarios for which you can enter vendor invoices:

Different types of vendor invoices

> Invoices with reference to purchase orders for goods delivery, services performed, and delivery costs.

> Invoices with reference to scheduling agreements (an agreement between your company and the vendor to procure goods at specific points in time over a certain time period).

> Invoices against goods deliveries from vendor. While processing goods receipts, you can associate them with delivery note numbers from vendors so that these deliveries can be referenced at the time of processing vendor invoices.

> Invoices for planned and delivery costs for goods deliveries from vendors. These invoices can be referenced by bill of lading numbers associated with each goods delivery from vendors.

> Invoices for services performed as requested in service orders.

Unless the vendor invoice exactly matches in all respects with corresponding purchase order(s) and goods receipt(s), there will be some variances.

Variances and Invoice Blocking

Based on allocations you have specified for invoices, the LIV program checks whether any variances exist in invoiced quantities and/or amounts. SAP ERP Financials can check for any quantity variance (quantity delivered versus quantity invoiced), price variance (unit price in invoice versus unit price in purchase order), variances in both quantity and price, and what SAP calls *order price quantity variance*. Order price quantity variance is the variance calculated if a vendor invoices you in different units from the units in which you had placed an order.

For each of these variances, you can specify tolerance limits in the system. Tolerance limits allow you to focus on major differences while ignoring relatively smaller, acceptable differences. These tolerance limits can be set as specific percentages, that is, absolute amounts for positive as well as negative variances. Not only that, but you can also specify different tolerance limits depending on whether an invoice is received before receiving goods or after receiving goods. These combinations allow you to fine-tune system behavior to meet your unique requirements.

Tolerance limits for variances

While entering vendor invoices, the LIV process identifies one or more variances and checks whether these variances are within tolerance limits for every invoice item. Even if one type of variance for one invoice item isn't within tolerance limits, the complete invoice is blocked for payment.

In addition to the system automatically blocking invoices because of variances, you can choose to block invoices above a certain threshold amount, block any invoice manually for any reason, or use *stochastic blocking to block random invoices*. Stochastic blocking is relevant only if an invoice isn't blocked due to any other reason. You can activate stochastic blocking in the system by specifying the threshold amount and probability percentage. For example, if you've set a threshold amount as $1,000 with a probability of 30 %, vendor invoices over $1,000 have a 30 % chance of being blocked for payments.

Releasing blocked invoices

All blocked invoices must be released before they can be processed for payment. You can release these invoices manually or automatically. If you attempt to release invoices automatically, SAP ERP Financials checks to see if any additional activities have occurred based on which the invoice block can be removed. For example, you may have worked with the vendor to resolve any price variances and posted subsequent debit or credit adjustments. Another example might be an invoice that was blocked because the invoiced quantity was higher than the received quantity, but then subsequently an additional quantity was received. None of these subsequent activities in themselves remove the payment block from the original invoice, but invoice blocks are no longer valid, so invoices can be automatically released for payments.

The vendor invoice process discussed so far is fairly typical, in which the vendor sends an invoice after delivering goods or performing services per the purchase order. However, you have several other options at your disposal to make this process more efficient.

Automatic Settlement of Invoices

Apart from typical vendor invoice processing, SAP ERP Financials supports a few other variations to handle vendor invoicing based on your relationship and contractual agreements with a vendor:

> **Evaluated Receipt Settlement (ERS)**
> The vendor does not send you any invoices. Instead, you create

invoices based on information contained in purchase orders and goods receipts.

> **Consignment and Pipeline Settlement**
This scenario is applicable when your production uses consignment materials (vendor supplies you with stock but does not invoice until you actually withdraw it for usage) or pipeline materials (e.g., water, oil, etc.). Based on your usage and goods withdrawal, you carry out settlement to the vendor account.

> **Invoicing plan**
You negotiate the invoicing plan when you place the purchase order and then create invoices automatically on scheduled dates per the plan, independent of goods delivered or services performed.

> **Revaluation**
If prices and conditions have retroactively changed, you can use this process to revaluate goods receipts from the vendor that have already been settled. Control parameters in vendor master data and material master data control whether and how these processes can be used for settling vendor invoices. After vendor invoices are received, verified, and posted in AP, the next step is to make payment against the invoices.

Retroactive changes

Payment Program

Every company has to make payments, and all financial systems support making payments. What makes the payment program in SAP ERP Financials unique is its ability to combine highly complex and different payment processes and present them in a simple to use, consistent user interface.

The focus of this section is to discuss features of the payment program. For details on how to set up different payment methods and bank accounts, refer to Chapter 5 on banking transactions. Parameters and rules for controlling the payment program are set up in the vendor master, in individual document lines, via system configuration, and in individual payment runs.

The payment program is used to process payment runs for outgoing payments to vendors and employees (the latter are also created as

Payments to
customers

vendors). However, you can also use this payment program to make payments to customers if they have credit balances. In addition, you can set up the system so that depending on the amount threshold, payments have to go through one or more levels of approvals before they are released. Figure 3.5 shows a completed payment run.

Figure 3.5 Automatic Payment Run

To start a payment run, you first have to specify parameters indicating who, when, what, and how. This is when you specify vendor accounts that should be considered for payment; payment methods (check, wire transfer, etc.) for which payment is to be made; companies—yes, you can specify more than one company—for which payment runs should be carried out; as well as a number of other user-defined selection criteria.

Payment proposal

The second step in the payment process is to create the proposal run. The payment proposal lists all items that meet the selection criteria entered in the payment run parameters while taking into account other control parameters configured in the system. The proposal also proposes items that are not due yet, but you can access the payment discount if they are paid in the current payment run. The payment program uses the "next payment run date" entered in the parameters to make this determination.

Exception list

The proposal run also creates an exception list, if applicable, of items that are selected based on selection parameters but can't be paid because, for example, the item has been blocked for payment or the item does not indicate the payment method by which it should be paid. At the end of the proposal run, you can display or print the proposal list and exception list for review. You can also prepare a detailed log that shows how each item in the proposal was selected. At this point, you also can edit the proposal list so that you can correct any items on the exception list so that they're included in the payment run, or you can manually block items from the proposal list so that they aren't paid in the current payment run.

The next step in the payment process is the payment run during which accounting entries are posted to vendor accounts and general ledger accounts such as bank accounts, clearing accounts, discount accounts, etc. These accounting entries post payments to vendor accounts and update cleared document items with payment information. Control parameters in the vendor master data control whether payments are made to an alternate payee, whether every open item is paid by separate check, or whether payments are grouped based on any other criteria. By default, the payment program attempts to make a single payment to each vendor in every payment run. Payments are posted to each vendor account.

 Note

If payments are made by check, check numbers are assigned to each payment document during the payment run before checks are physically printed. This is different from some other systems where checks are assigned to payments only after they have been printed.

The final step in this process is to carry out physical payments. At this point, you can print checks, print payment authorization forms, and create data files to be sent to the bank for electronic payments. Technically, you can include different types of payments (checks, wire transfers, etc.) in a single payment run, so it's a business process decision on whether to create separate payment runs for different types of payments.

You also have an option to choose vendor items manually for payments and print a one-off check. This process of manually selecting items is similar to the one used for posting incoming payments discussed before.

Check management   SAP ERP Financials provides a large number of check management programs. These programs can be used to display check information (by check number, by payment document, or as a check register), void checks (whether checks have been issued or are still unused), reset information from checks that are incorrectly voided or marked as cashed, and so on.

So far, we've discussed the four most commonly used AR and AP processes that either post debits or credits to customer and vendor accounts. So now, we'll discuss the other functionality available for analyzing and processing AR and AP.

Document Clearing Process

For customer and vendor accounts with a high transaction volume (e.g., in the automotive business), by clearing (or matching) open debit and credit entries posted to a customer or vendor account, you can reduce the time it takes to analyze open receivables and payables. If you're used to matching debits and credits manually in other systems, you'll love the clearing program in SAP ERP Financials that you can use to clear entries in a customer or vendor account.

 Tip

Even though account clearing is more typically associated with customer and vendor accounts, the program in SAP ERP Financials can be used to carry out clearing in GL accounts as well. For example, account clearing is often used for GL bank accounts and other open item managed balance sheet accounts.

Automatic Document Matching   By default, this program carries out the clearing of debits and credits if they match exactly or are within tolerance limits. In addition, entries that are cleared should also have the same business area (if applicable), same trading partner (if used), same reconciliation account, and same currency in which the GL is updated. In addition, you can specify two additional criteria by which you would like this clearing to occur. These additional fields can be almost any field from customer or vendor master data or from document data. You can fine-tune the clearing process by making sure fields are used consistently in document data entry, for example, entering the contract number in document reference for every customer transaction.

The clearing process can be carried out in a currency that is different from the currency in which the original documents have been posted. Depending on documents being cleared, SAP ERP Financials can automatically post additional entries for cash discounts, gains, or losses due to overpayment or underpayment, bank charges, exchange gain or loss, and so on.

SAP ERP Financials also provides a manual clearing program that you can use to manually clear debits and credits posted to an account. Even though the automatic clearing program is useful, the manual clearing program is most commonly and most frequently used for the clearing process because it provides more control and flexibility for matching debits and credits. The process of matching debits and credits is almost exactly like the one for posting incoming or outgoing payments manually as discussed earlier.

Program for manual clearing

The clearing process for most of the GL accounts, even though beneficial, is optional—except for the goods receipt/invoice receipt (GR/IR) clearing account.

GR/IR Clearing Account
The GR/IR account is a special type of clearing account used to match goods receipts and invoice receipts from vendors. A goods receipt from a vendor posts a credit to the GR/IR account, and an invoice receipt from a vendor posts a debit to the GR/IR account, regardless of whether the invoice is received before or after the goods receipt. Postings to this account are matched with each other based on the purchase order. Figure 3.6 shows an illustration of postings made to the GR/IR account at the time of goods receipt and invoice receipt.

This account is typically reviewed as part of the month-end processing. The GR/IR clearing process analyzes quantity and amount differences between the goods receipt and invoice receipt and clears corresponding entries if there are no differences or differences are within tolerance limits. At the end of this process, entries in the GR/IR account only refer to those goods receipts that haven't been completely invoiced and those invoices for which all goods are not yet received.

Check for quantity differences and amount differences

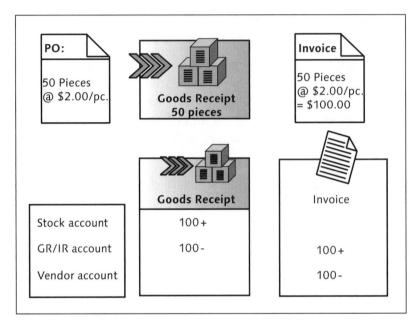

Figure 3.6 Posting to a GR/IR Account

Another frequently used AR process (especially in the utilities industry) is the dunning process.

Dunning Process

In SAP ERP Financials, as with most accounting systems, you can send dunning notices to customers who are behind on payments. Unlike many other financial systems, in SAP ERP Financials, the same program can be used to dun vendors if they have long overdue debit balances. The dunning process in SAP ERP Financials is very flexible because it can be controlled through parameters in the customer master data, in individual documents, and via system configuration settings.

Settings

You may have a single dunning group in your company, or you may have multiple dunning groups responsible for dunning customers based on geographical areas or types of customers. Dunning areas allow you to divide your organization in terms of dunning responsibilities. Every customer transaction carries dunning areas in which it may be dunned, so it's possible that the same customer can be dunned by more than one dunning area.

Based on the number of days for which an item has been overdue, the item is assigned a dunning level. The higher the dunning level, the longer the item has been overdue and thus potentially warrants higher attention. Dunning levels also control whether interest should be calculated on arrears and whether/how much information is included on dunning notices that are sent out. After the maximum dunning level is reached, the overdue item is typically transferred to the legal department for further processing.

For each dunning level, you can specify the minimum amount and minimum percentage. If the total (or percentage) of overdue items at a dunning level is less than the minimum amount (or percentage) specified for that level, a dunning notice for that level isn't triggered. Instead, those items are assigned to the next lowest dunning level . This design prevents any long overdue item of a relatively small amount from being assigned a very high dunning level. Of course, you can always manually override the dunning level associated with an item to take care of special business circumstances.

Dunning Levels

Dunning procedures in SAP ERP Financials determine additional controls as well:

Dunning Procedure

> The maximum number of dunning levels that an overdue item can be dunned for

> The grace period before an overdue item is considered for dunning

> How interest on arrears is calculated

> If or how much dunning charges are added to dunned amount

Obviously, these parameters can be different depending on the customer base that is being dunned, so you can create multiple dunning procedures (e.g., one procedure for your large, high-volume customers, and a different procedure for your smaller, low-volume customers) and then assign the appropriate dunning procedure in the customer master.

After the required settings are made in the documents, in the customer master, or in the system configuration, you're ready to carry out the dunning run.

Dunning Run

Figure 3.7 shows an overview of the dunning process in SAP ERP Financials.

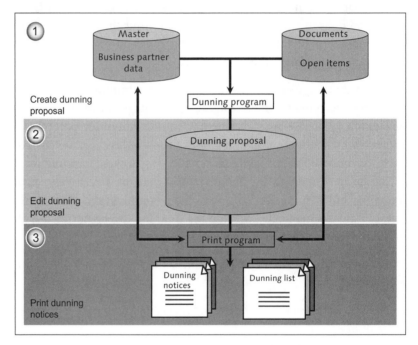

Figure 3.7 Dunning Process

The first step in the dunning run is to enter the selection parameters. These parameters determine which customers (and vendors) from which companies are analyzed for overdue items. You can fine-tune this selection further by specifying an additional selection. While considering whether an item should be included in the dunning proposal, the dunning program checks the last time when the account was dunned and whether any dunning blocks exist. After the system has carried out the dunning selection, you can check the log for errors.

After the dunning proposal has been created, you can review and edit the dunning proposal as well as items and accounts that are dunned. Some of the edits you can do at this time include the following:

Dunning proposal

> Raise or lower the dunning level of an overdue item

> Block an item or an account from being dunned in the current dunning run

> Change the dunning block in account master data

The final step in the dunning run is, of course, to issue dunning notices. The dunning procedure determines whether separate dunning notices are issued for each dunning area or whether a single dunning notice is issued for a company. You also can print all items from a specific dunning level separately from all other items. You can create different dunning forms for each company, and you can decide the wording to be printed based on the dunning level.

Following are some of the special scenarios and their handling by the SAP ERP Financials dunning process:

> You can exclude specific items from dunning by assigning dunning blocks, or you can assign a dunning block to the customer master to stop it from being dunned at all.

Dunning flexibility

> You can use grouping keys to dun groups of customer items together based on specific criteria, for example, all items with same contract number are to be dunned together.

> All open credit memos (barring few exceptions) on account are assigned the highest dunning level so that for dunning purposes, they offset the oldest invoices.

> If you've maintained a head office-to-branch office relationship in the customer master, you can choose to do decentralized dunning to branch offices. Standard program behavior is to dun the head office for all overdue items.

> If customer and vendor accounts are linked with each other in SAP ERP Financials, the dunning program carries out dunning based on the joint balance after considering all open items in both accounts.

> You can specify an alternative recipient for dunning notices in customer master.

SAP ERP Financials also supports many other AR and AP transactions, as you'll see next.

Other Processes

In this section, we'll discuss other supported AR and AP business processes. Even though you may not use some of these processes frequently, their availability and seamless integration with the rest of the AR and AP processes makes it easier to use them if you need to.

Nontrade Customers and Vendors

Invoicing from finance

To process nontrade transactions, you can set up customers and vendors that are valid in company codes but not in any sales or purchase organizations. Examples of these transactions are making payments for utilities, receiving payments for sublease, and so on that do not typically involve the creation of sales and purchase orders. You can debit or credit any such customer or vendor account using document entry in AR or AP directly, without having to go through the complete invoicing process in sales or purchasing.

These document entry transactions in AR and AP can also be used to post corrections and adjustments to trade accounts. So, you can offset or correct a sales or purchase invoice by posting an entry directly in AR or AP.

Special Transactions

SAP uses special GL indicators to represent transactions such as down payments, bank guarantees, and so on. These special transactions are reported in different reconciliation accounts, separately from other receivables and payables, for statutory or management reasons.

A few additional controls influence the behavior of special GL transactions. For example, one control flag indicates that the transaction is only for statistical purpose (e.g., down payment request), another control indicates that the transaction impacts credit limit evaluation (e.g., actual down payment posting), and another control is available to issue a warning message if a nonzero balance occurs (e.g., if you're posting an invoice for a vendor where the down payment already exists).

SAP ERP Financials provides special GL transactions to handle down payments, down payment requests, payment requests, bank guarantees, security deposits, bad debt reserves, and bill of exchanges. You can also create your own special GL transactions to meet any additional business requirements, such as to differentiate between down payments received against sales and down payments received against maintenance contracts.

Bank guarantees and down payments

Payment Card Processing

SAP ERP Financials supports the end-to-end process of accepting credit card payments from customers. At the very minimum, you require an interface to send details from SAP ERP Financials to the merchant bank clearing system that handles credit card transactions. In addition, you may also obtain services to verify and authorize credit card information as soon as it's available. SAP provides template programs to carry out these functions.

 Tip

> You can modify and use template programs delivered with SAP ERP Financials to interface with systems that validate, authorize, and clear credit card transactions. However, many credit card verification companies and merchant banks also provide ready-to-use interfaces that integrate with SAP ERP Financials.

Customer credit card information is accepted at the time of creating the sales order. At this time, the credit card information is validated and authorized, and authorization information is stored in the sales order. Credit card authorization is checked again before goods delivery is processed in SAP ERP Financials, so that you can take corrective action if the credit card authorization fails. When invoices are created, the credit card information is transferred to accounting documents.

Credit card
settlement

When customer invoices paid by credit card are posted to accounting, the customer receivable is automatically cleared to indicate that invoices are no longer due. Instead, receivables are transferred to credit card clearing GL accounts. Periodically, you carry out settlement runs to settle or send credit card transactions from SAP to the clearing bank. Payments received from the clearing bank against credit card receipts are posted similar to any other incoming payments, and that bank account is reconciled similar to other bank accounts.

SAP ERP Financials supports the necessary encryption methods and routines to keep credit card information as secure as possible.

Balance Confirmation

The balance confirmation process involves verifying your AR and AP balances with corresponding customers and vendors. SAP ERP Financials supports different variations of this process so that you can use whichever best meets yours requirements.

> If you're using the balance confirmation process, you notify customers or vendors with balance information per your accounts and ask for a reply regardless of whether they agree or disagree with the information.

> If you choose to use the balance notification process, you notify customers or vendors with balance information per your accounts and ask them to respond only if they disagree with the balance stated.

> You can also choose to use the balance request process, in which you ask customers or vendors to notify you of balance amounts per their records.

All responses to these notices are stored in SAP ERP Financials so that you can compare them with your balances and take appropriate action for any discrepancies. If necessary, you can also send out reminder notices to those who haven't responded.

Sample balance
confirmations

On the other hand, if your balance confirmation process doesn't require being this comprehensive, you can randomly select accounts for a balance confirmation process instead of carrying it out for all customers and vendors.

Reporting and Communication

In AR and AP, *correspondence* refers to account statements, open item lists, balance confirmations, and other such communications sent to customers and vendors. SAP ERP Financials provides programs and forms for various types of correspondence that you can modify (e.g., adding your company's logo on customer account statements) and use. You can also combine details from several companies and send those details in a single letter, as long as it pertains to the same account.

Internal evaluations for customers and vendors provide fairly simple ways to analyze your receivables and payables. Standard SAP ERP Financials supports evaluations for customers and vendors for due date analysis, payment history analysis, currency analysis, overdue items analysis, and days sales outstanding (DSO) analysis. Many of these analyses report information that can be grouped by company code, country, industry, and other such criteria. Figure 3.8 shows different evaluations available for analyzing AR.

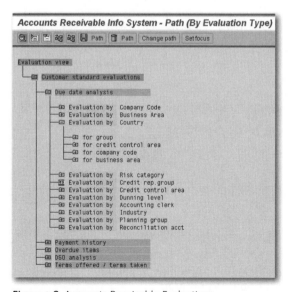

Figure 3.8 Accounts Receivable Evaluations

SAP reporting   SAP ERP Financials provides many standard reports that are neatly grouped under the Information System node in the Accounts Receivable and Accounts Payable menu. For example, standard AR reports are available to generate a list of customer balances; comparison of sales and receivables; aging analysis; due date analysis by document date, posting date, and net payment due date; payment history analysis; customer account line item details for printing or for online analysis; list of down payments; and more. Almost the exact same types of reports are available in AP for vendor account analysis.

Summary

This chapter discussed some of the functionality of the AR and AP components of SAP ERP Financials. In addition, because of the integrated nature of this system, we also discussed the invoicing process in sales and purchasing. Following is a summary of what you can do with AR and AP:

> Maintain customer and vendor master data at three levels: General data, company code data, and sales or purchasing organization data.

> Represent complex relationships between various customer or vendor addresses using partner functions to identify different types of accounts.

> Bill customers based on orders, contracts, or deliveries, and use the most appropriate billing method: self-billing, retroactive billing, billing plans, or resource-related billing.

> Apply incoming payments to open invoices, post any residual entries for follow-up; partial pay against open invoices; automatically post entries for cash discounts, tax adjustments, and exchange gain or loss—all in one single program.

> Verify vendor invoices by comparing them against orders, deliveries, or contracts; post direct adjustments to GL accounts and to materials; and analyze and post variances through the powerful Logistics Invoice Verification (LIV) program.

> Carry out payment runs that can automatically select payables for vendors (and if required, customers) across multiple companies, make payment using a wide variety of payment methods, and generate printed checks or create data files for electronic payments.

> Carry out manual or automatic document clearing in the customer and vendor account to match debit and credit entries based on user-defined criteria.

> Use a large number of standard reports for analyzing, monitoring, and reporting of business transactions in AP and AR.

AR and AP transactions are commonly subject to sales or purchase taxes, which are discussed in the next chapter.

4

Taxation

Every company involved in the manufacturing or trading of goods or services must pay, collect, or at least report taxes on their business transactions. Although most people aren't excited by the hairsplitting nuances, taxes are part of every business. In some industries, calculating taxes may be as simple as applying a flat rate to all customer invoices. But in large, manufacturing companies with multiple product lines, the taxes can be so complex that these companies need separate corporate sales tax planning departments who analyze the sales and procurement activities to find ways to legally reduce the tax liability.

SAP ERP Financials provides you with the necessary end-to-end functionality to make these processes as automatic, efficient, and manageable as possible. This chapter discusses how to manage your business processes for sales, purchase, and withholding taxes. We'll discuss the calculation of payroll taxes in Chapter 8.

Overview

SAP ERP Financials provides you with comprehensive tax function-ality for calculating, posting, and reporting different types of taxes according to the legal requirements of a country or region. Your tax calculations can be highly customized to handle your businesses tax calculation requirements, while taking into consideration relevant statutory requirements. After the software has been properly config-ured, tax postings to the GL occur automatically and are mostly trans-parent to the business users processing the transactions. You can also adjust tax entries manually or automatically based on cash discounts, deductions, and other differences.

In addition, you can use this comprehensive tax reporting solution to prepare transaction-level tax reports for analysis, reporting, and reconciliation, or even to prepare final tax returns. And you can in-terface with external programs for tax calculation and reporting. Tax processing is carried out in application areas such as sales and pur-chasing and when taxes are incurred. These tax calculations are later used to post tax-relevant entries in accounting.

 Note

> In SAP terminology, all taxes charged by the vendor are called input taxes, and all taxes levied on customers are called output taxes. This chapter refers to sales (output) taxes and purchase (input) taxes unless noted otherwise.

Sales and purchase taxes

The software supports calculating taxes on sales and purchases, and provides detailed reports to list taxable and nontaxable sales and pur-chase transactions. These reports not only provide verifiable audit trails, but if applicable, they allow you to calculate tax remittance (or credit) by calculating the difference between taxes collected (output tax) and taxes paid (input tax). Template calculation procedures are also provided for calculating other types of taxes, such as acquisition tax, investment tax, and so on. Additionally, the tax procedures can be easily modified to include any country-specific or industry-specific taxes.

Depending on the tax structure of a country, these tax calculations can be performed at one or more levels, such as federal, state, county, and so on. For the countries that require granular tax calculations, you can use the tax jurisdictions functionality. You'll also find support for the comprehensive calculation of withholding taxes. These are the taxes withheld from payments, and most countries have detailed regulations controlling the types of transactions for these withholdings.

In this chapter, we'll review the different types of sales and purchase taxes, VAT, and withholding taxes and explain how SAP ERP Financials helps you manage these. Please note that we'll cover property taxes and other fixed asset taxes in Chapter 6, "Capitalization of Investments," and payroll taxes will be covered in Chapter 8, "Payroll Accounting."

Functions in Detail

In this section we'll show how you can effectively use the software for sales and purchase taxes, and explain how you can use the tax calculation functionality to meet your statutory, organizational, and business requirements. Then we'll discuss the tax calculation and tax exemption processes, and show how you can generate tax reports. We'll also cover two other major tax topics: calculation of VAT, and calculation of withholding taxes. We'll wrap up with a look at some other types of tax calculations supported by SAP ERP Financials and show how you can use these calculations as templates to meet any other requirements.

Setting Up Taxes

Sales and purchase tax calculation is influenced by statutory requirements, organizational requirements, and business requirements:

> Statutory requirements are specified by relevant tax authorities of a country.

> Organizational requirements are based on how the company is structured from a tax point of view.

> Business requirements determine industry-specific taxes as well as taxability of customers and products that the company is dealing with.

So let's look at each of these requirements in more detail.

Statutory Requirements

Tax calculation procedure

Statutory guidelines for tax calculations cover the taxes for domestic business transactions and for import and export business transactions. In particular, these guidelines specify the tax authorities that are responsible for levying taxes and the applicable tax rates in the country.

In SAP ERP Financials, tax calculation procedures provide the framework to calculate sales and purchase taxes. You can assign only one tax calculation procedure to a country, which means that the procedure needs to provide the calculation framework for all types of taxes that are relevant for sales and purchase transactions in that country. For example, sales tax, purchase tax, and use tax for the United States; input tax, output tax, consumption tax, and service tax for China; and so on. The software provides templates for tax procedures to meet the requirements of almost 50 countries, but if required, you can easily create new procedures or modify existing ones to meet your requirements.

Tax codes

Tax codes are used to specify tax percentage rates, tax calculation, and whether the tax code is relevant for sales or for purchases. You simply specify the tax codes while processing business transactions, and the tax calculation procedure calculates the actual tax based on the tax rates associated with the tax code and a number of other control parameters. Figure 4.1 shows a sample list of tax codes delivered for a European country.

In many countries, sales and purchase taxes are calculated at a national level, and at a state or province level. You'll find a list of codes for the states and provinces of more than 50 countries. But if you need to carry out tax calculations for countries for which such codes aren't provided, you can create additional tax region codes or fiscal region codes.

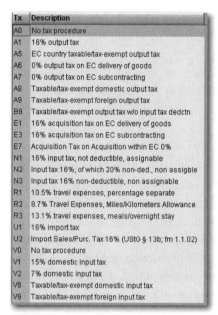

Tx	Description
A0	No tax procedure
A1	16% output tax
A5	EC country taxable/tax-exempt output tax
A6	0% output tax on EC delivery of goods
A7	0% output tax on EC subcontracting
A8	Taxable/tax-exempt domestic output tax
A9	Taxable/tax-exempt foreign output tax
B9	Taxable/tax-exempt output tax w/o input tax dedctn
E1	16% acquisition tax on EC delivery of goods
E3	16% acquisition tax on EC subcontracting
E7	Acquisition Tax on Acquisition within EC 0%
N1	16% input tax, not deductible, assignable
N2	Input tax 16%; of which 20% non-ded., non assigble
N3	Input tax 16% non-deductible, non assignable
R1	10.5% travel expenses, percentage separate
R2	8.7% Travel Expenses, Miles/Kilometers Allowance
R3	13.1% travel expenses, meals/overnight stay
U1	16% import tax
U2	Import Sales/Purc. Tax 16% (UStG § 13b; fm 1.1.02)
V0	No tax procedure
V1	15% domestic input tax
V2	7% domestic input tax
V8	Taxable/tax-exempt domestic input tax
V9	Taxable/tax-exempt foreign input tax

Figure 4.1 Tax Codes for a European Country

You'll also find support of tax jurisdictions to meet requirements in countries with a very large number of tax authorities. Each tax jurisdiction uniquely identifies a tax authority; for example, in the United States, tax jurisdiction codes uniquely identify a combination of the state, county, and city. The jurisdiction code always describes the location where goods were delivered or where services were provided. In some countries, sales tax is paid at a local and national level. To handle these types of calculations, tax rates are maintained for a combination of tax codes and tax jurisdiction codes.

Tax jurisdiction codes

Depending on the number of jurisdictions, products, customers, and business transaction volumes in each jurisdiction, manually maintaining tax rates for all required combinations can quickly become resource intensive. In these situations, you may choose to use commercially available bolt-on tax calculation systems such as Vertex, Taxware, and Sabrix that seamlessly integrate with SAP tax calculations.

More than any other application area in SAP ERP Financials, this is an area where SAP partner products play an important role. In some countries, it's due to the large number of tax regions (the United States has more than 67,000 tax jurisdictions) for which taxes have to be calculated, administered, and reported; whereas in other countries, it's due to the volume and frequency of changes to tax rules. Let's consider the organizational requirements that impact the calculation of sales and purchase taxes.

Organizational Requirements

Sales and purchase tax calculations are also influenced by how the organization is structured in terms of the main registered company address and locations of its plants, warehouses, and other offices, As discussed, the tax calculation procedure is assigned to a country, so a company set up in the software inherits tax calculations for the country in which it operates. This may imply that you need to set up at least one company for each country where you have business operations. However, if no other statutory requirements exist, and the reason for setting up companies in other countries is because there are company warehouses, distribution centers, or plants; you can use the Plants Abroad functionality.

Plants Abroad functionality

Using the plants abroad functionality, you can process tax returns for warehouses, distribution centers, and plants in foreign countries without having to set them up as additional companies. Even though plants abroad may seem like a decision that has more technical benefits in terms of system setup and configuration, it has a very distinct and beneficial impact on business operations in terms of transaction processing and reporting.

 Warning

The software currently does not have functionality that supports companies that are set up to use jurisdiction code functionality for tax calculations but that also want to set up plants abroad functionality.

Business places

Another possible variation in structuring a company from a tax point of view is the requirement of different tax identification numbers for its locations. Typically, the tax identification number of the main company (the legal entity) is valid and applicable to all of its locations. However, in some countries, tax authorities assign a separate tax identification number to different locations of a company and require separate tax calculations and remittance for every location. You can use an organization unit called a business place to support this requirement. Business places are created at a level below a company code and are associated with other organizational units such as plants, sales offices, or other units. For all tax-relevant transactions, a business place is determined based on this assignment to ensure the accuracy and integrity of tax reporting.

The software currently supports functionality of business places for specific countries, including Brazil, Philippines, Taiwan, and a few others. So carefully consider any new requirements and their possible impact across the system before activating business place functionality for any other country. The third area influencing sales and purchase tax calculation refers to the business requirements of your company.

Business Requirements

Each company is different. Some manufacture or trade different types of products, provide different types of services, interact with different types of customers, but not all products, services, and customers are always taxable. For example, business deals with nonprofit organizations or governmental agencies aren't taxable in many countries. With SAP ERP Financials, though, you can specify the tax classification for your products, services, and customers as required by the tax requirements of the countries in which you do business. You use this classification to group products, services, and customers into tax classifications such as taxable, nontaxable, partially taxable, or any such classification for every country in which you do business.

Taxability of customers and products

The tax classification of products depends on whether they are being sold or purchased. On the sales side, product taxability is maintained for every combination of sales organization and the countries in which products are sold. On the procurement side, only local regulations are relevant for product taxability, so you specify the tax classification only once for each plant that receives or manages the product.

Ex **Example**

> A chemical company, with plants in California and Texas, sells to its customers in the United States and Canada from its North American Sales Organization, and to its customers in the United Kingdom, Germany, and France from its Europe Sales Organization.
>
> For the raw materials, the company needs to maintain tax classifications only for the California and Texas locations. For the finished goods, product tax classification is required for every country in which the product is sold by the company: United States, Canada, United Kingdom, Germany, and France. And, for trading goods, the tax classification needs to be maintained for procurement as well as sales.

Similarly, customers are allocated their tax classification in their master data to indicate whether they should be taxed, never taxed, or any other classification as dictated by the statutory requirements. For example, in many countries, nonprofit organizations aren't subject to tax. For every combination of customer tax classification and product tax classification, you need to indicate the applicable tax code and applicable tax rates.

Let's consider a business model where the American and European sales groups of a company sell the same product to customers located in different countries. By maintaining a tax classification for every combination of sales organization and destination country, you can accurately calculate the sales tax for any possible business transaction.

Tax Calculation and Posting

Tax processing and GL accounts

When posting a sales or purchasing document to accounting, tax items are created and posted automatically. Without getting into too much technical detail, the tax code entered in a business transaction indirectly determines the GL accounts the taxes are posted to. The setup of tax GL accounts can be as simple or as complex as needed to meet your requirements. For example, you can choose to post all types of taxes to a single account, separate input taxes and output taxes to different accounts (more typical setup), or have separate accounts for each tax code or for each tax jurisdiction level.

Another aspect to consider is control parameters in the GL account master data, which determines how sales and purchase taxes are calculated, validated, and posted to each account. The tax category specified in the GL master record determines whether the GL account is a tax account itself, a tax-relevant account, or a nontax-relevant account. For tax relevant accounts, you can further specify which types of tax codes are allowed for transactions posted to that account. Figure 4.2 shows some of the available tax categories for setting up a GL account.

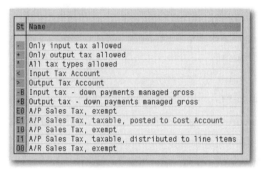

St	Name
-	Only input tax allowed
+	Only output tax allowed
*	All tax types allowed
<	Input Tax Account
>	Output Tax Account
-B	Input tax - down payments managed gross
+B	Output tax - down payments managed gross
E0	A/P Sales Tax, exempt
E1	A/P Sales Tax, taxable, posted to Cost Account
I0	A/P Sales Tax, exempt
I1	A/P Sales Tax, taxable, distributed to line items
O0	A/R Sales Tax, exempt

Figure 4.2 Tax Categories for a GL Account

As you can see, the first three tax categories in Figure 4.2 control the types of taxes allowed in business transactions posted to tax-relevant accounts. The next two tax categories are used in GL tax accounts, and tax categories -B and +B are relevant only for down payments (discussed in more detail in the "Taxes on Down Payments" section). These tax categories are available for all GL accounts.

Tax categories

Following these seven tax categories are the categories representing tax codes. These tax categories are used with tax-relevant GL accounts to restrict posting to the account of only those business transactions that carry that specific tax code; however, this level of control is typically not used or required.

Another important tax calculation setting in the GL account master is posting without taxes allowed. By selecting this field, you can indicate that an account is tax relevant, but you can post nontax-relevant transactions to it as well.

Tax Postings

Taxes and cash discounts

When you post a tax-relevant document, the tax base amount is calculated first and may include a cash discount. But whether or not a cash discount is included in the tax base amount is determined independently for each company code based on the configurable setting in your system. Similarly, you can set a control indicator for each company that determines whether the discount is calculated on an after-tax or before-tax amount.

The following combinations of how discounts and taxes are calculated are available:

> Calculation of a cash discount on an after-tax amount and of taxes on a before-discount amount.

> Calculation of a cash discount on a before-tax amount and of taxes on a before-discount amount.

> Calculation of a cash discount on a before-tax amount and of taxes on an after-discount amount.

> Calculation of a cash discount on an after-tax amount and of taxes on an after-discount amount. This method is supported only if a tax calculation is carried out at the jurisdiction code level.

Default tax codes

As discussed earlier, the tax code entered into the document determines how the tax calculation is carried out. Tax codes in business transactions are defaulted from the customer or vendor account, or they can be automatically derived based on your system configuration (e.g., for intercompany or cross-country business transactions). While entering invoices manually, you can change these default tax codes.

You can also enter or change tax amounts manually while posting a document. SAP checks whether the tax amount entered manually matches the automatically calculated tax amount. If these amounts are different, the system issues a warning message. You can change this warning message to an error message to prevent users from entering any different tax amounts; however, this may create problems in AP because you have to enter whatever tax amount is on the invoice when entering vendor invoices.

Tip

SAP always issues a warning message if the difference in a manually entered tax amount and the automatically calculated tax amount is more than the maximum possible rounding difference. SAP calculates the maximum possible rounding difference as the number of lines in the document multiplied by the smallest rounding difference possible. So in a document consisting of five lines posted in USD, SAP issues a warning message if the difference is more than $0.05.

After the tax is calculated, SAP determines the GL accounts to be posted based on the tax codes and creates additional line items in the document, so that taxes are automatically posted to the GL.

Tax Exemption

One approach we discussed for posting tax-exempt transactions is to select the "posting without tax allowed" indicator in the tax-relevant ledger accounts. These types of transactions don't require you to enter tax codes, and postings without tax codes don't generate any tax information. But because no tax information is generated, these transactions aren't displayed in any standard tax reports.

There is a different approach for posting tax-exempt transactions, however, where you use the tax codes for which the tax rate is 0 %. When these tax codes are used in relevant transactions with a tax rate of 0 %, taxes aren't calculated, and no tax entries are posted. However, these transactions store tax codes, so they are displayed in standard tax reports. This can be especially useful for reconciliation and tax audits because most standard SAP reports list information and transactions separated by tax code. Thus, by careful use of the posting without tax allowed indicator on GL accounts and tax codes with 0 %, you can separate business transactions that aren't tax relevant from the business transactions that are tax-exempt.

Tax-exempt and not relevant for taxes

Additionally, for a tax-exempt customer, you can maintain exemption certificate details in the customer master. Each certificate is stored with validity dates, so that customer is considered exempt only if the certificate entered in the master data is valid. Figure 4.3 shows a screen where you can enter the customer tax-exemption certificates into the customer master data.

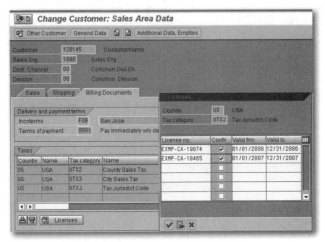

Figure 4.3 Customer Tax-Exemption Certificates

However, if you choose to use third-party software for calculating taxes, you'll need to decide whether tax exemptions will be handled by the third-party software or by SAP. This decision will have an impact on how you set up your tax codes and customer master data.

Tax Reporting

As shown in Figure 4.4, SAP provides many standard tax reports to meet specific requirements of several countries. These reports provide transactional details as well as summarized analysis for reconciling, auditing, and tax filing. If you've integrated third-party software with SAP for tax calculation, then typically, you can generate tax reports from that software as well. You'll also find functionality to verify the accuracy and completeness of such reports and to reconcile these reports with the transactional data you posted.

Preparing tax returns

Standard SAP functionality can be used to prepare sales/purchase tax returns. These returns can be prepared in the local currency of the company or in a different, alternate currency such as the Euro. Typically, these returns are prepared separately for individual companies. However, SAP also supports preparing these returns at a combined, higher level across multiple companies. This can be useful, for example, if multiple companies are set up for operational convenience but from a tax point of view represent the same entity.

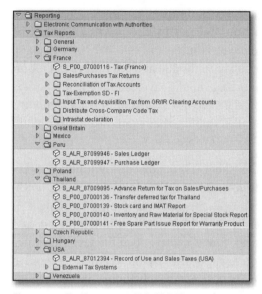

Figure 4.4 Tax Reports in SAP ERP Financials

The program used to prepare advanced tax returns can also be used to automatically post accounting entries for tax payables. Of course, if you don't use this feature, entry for tax payables is made manually.

In addition, tax-relevant transactions can be grouped based on specific criteria to arrive at individual line item amounts that can be filled in for tax returns. Alternatively, if tax authorities accept tax returns electronically, you can prepare data files for sales/purchase returns and submit the returns and supporting details electronically using SAP XI (Exchange Infrastructure).

In addition to these generic reports, you can also generate country-specific reports for several countries to meet local statutory tax reporting requirements. For intercompany business activities, usually only the total due tax is posted in the company in which the transactions originated. To handle special requirements for countries that require tax amounts to be reported in both companies, a report is available to list intercompany transactions, base amounts, and tax amounts involved.

Withholding Tax

1099 processing

The withholding tax functionality is used to withhold specific amounts from payments based on the required tax regulations. Typically, tax payments to the appropriate tax authorities are made by the party that carries out this deduction and not by the party subject to the deduction. However, if the payee is subject to self-withholding taxes, it's also possible to pay the full amount due and only provide a report to tax authorities on amounts that should have been withheld. For example, in the United States, the 1099 form is used to report amounts paid to individuals to show the amount that should have been withheld (e.g., work-for-hire, freelance work, etc.).

You should be sure to use the newer extended withholding tax functionality even though you can use the simplified classic withholding tax functionality as well because, as shown in Table 4.1, there are many differences between the classic withholding tax and the extended withholding tax functionality. (X in the table indicates that the individual function is supported by the classic or extended withholding tax). If you're an existing SAP customer, and you're using the classic withholding tax functionality, SAP provides tools and programs to convert from the classic to the extended withholding tax functionality.

Table 4.1 also shows that with extended withholding tax functionality, you can process withholding taxes in AP and in AR. In AP, vendors (or employees set up as vendors) are subject to withholding tax, and your company can choose to deduct or report those taxes. Whereas in AR, your company is the one subject to the withholding tax, and customers may deduct withholding taxes from their payments.

 Tip

> This section only discusses tax withholding from payments to vendors and customers. For tax withholdings from employee payroll, see Chapter 8 "Payroll Accounting."

Individual Functions		Classic Withholding Tax	Extended Withholding Tax
Withholding tax on outgoing payment		X	X
Withholding tax on incoming payment			X
Withholding tax posting at the time of payment		X	X
Withholding tax posting at the time of invoice			X
Withholding tax posting on partial payment			X
Number of withholding taxes for each document item		Maximum 1	Several
Withholding tax base	Net amount	X	X
	Modified net amount		X
	Gross amount	X	X
	Tax amount		X
	Modified tax amount		X
Rounding rule for calculation			X
Cash discount considered in calculation			X
Accumulation of period of time (e.g., quarterly, annually, etc.)			X
Min/Max amounts and exemption limits			X
Certificate numbering			X
Calculation formulas		X	X

Table 4.1 Classic and Extended Withholding Tax Comparison

For several countries, SAP provides ready-to-use setup for types of recipients (pensioner, agent, partnership, corporation, etc.), types of income (interest income, insurance commission, rent, professional services, etc.), and country pairs (for withholding on foreign payments) that are subject to withholding tax. The withholding tax can be posted at the time of invoicing or at the time of payment because SAP sup-

Ready to use withholding taxes

ports both of these options and also supports the third option of only calculating withholding tax. Under the third option, withholding tax isn't deducted from the payment, but instead it's calculated and later reported to the tax authorities.

SAP uses withholding tax types to differentiate between types of withholding taxes that may be applicable on business transactions. Withholding tax types provide a number of control parameters that impact how the withholding tax is calculated. Figure 4.5 shows an example of the withholding tax type setup for the United States. The example shows a withholding tax type that is posted at the time of payment. Setup for a withholding tax type that is posted at the time of invoice is similar but with fewer control parameters.

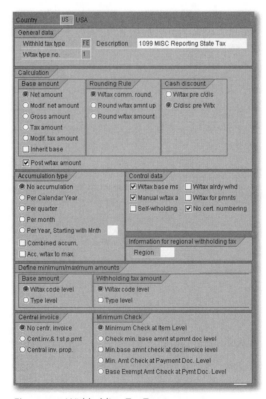

Figure 4.5 Withholding Tax Type

So as you can see, SAP provides all of the options you need for setting up your withholding taxes, and you can control many parameters for the withholding tax calculation:

> What amount is used as the base amount for tax calculation (Base amount)

> Whether the base amount should be accumulated over month, quarter, or year for tax calculation (Accumulation type)

> Whether the tax is calculated before or after calculating cash discounts (Cash discount)

> Whether the tax is posted in accounting entries or only calculated for reporting purposes (Post w/tax amount)

> Whether tax amounts and tax base amounts can be manually changed at the time of posting (W/tax base manual and Manual w/tax amount)

Withholding tax type definitions are valid for a country; for example, the one in Figure 4.5 can be used for any company configured for the United States. Ultimately, however, the control parameters for individual companies determine which withholding tax types can be used for posting. This design enables you to maintain multiple SAP companies in parallel and control the available withholding tax types.

Sliding-scale calculation

The withholding tax codes determine tax rates and the percentage of the withholding tax base (calculated per withholding tax type) to which those rates are applicable. You can also specify tax rates based on a sliding-scale calculation of the base amount. For every withholding tax type, you can set up as many withholding tax codes as you need. These codes are then specified in the vendor master to indicate whether a vendor is subject to withholding tax or not. If the vendor is subject to multiple withholdings, you can assign multiple codes in the master data. In many countries, the tax authorities control the numbering of withholding tax certificates, so SAP provides you with the flexibility to number tax certificates by company, by types of withholding tax, by branch offices, or at the lowest level by type of payee (customers, vendors, etc.), which allows you to meet the diverse requirements of different tax authorities.

1099 reporting You also can prepare withholding tax reports electronically or in printed form for tax authorities. By associating states or provinces with withholding tax codes, you can easily prepare reports at the federal and regional levels. The software also provides additional reports to meet specific withholding tax functionality for several countries. For example, you get an updated 1099 form template every year that meets the latest IRS regulations.

Additional correspondence options are available for requesting exemption information from business partners or reporting account activity subject to tax withholding or for similar requirements.

 Example

Many companies in the northwestern United States have significant investment and operations in the United States and Canada. Per the tax treaty between the two countries, payments made by these U.S. companies to Canadian citizens are subject to up to 30 % withholding tax. Scholarship or fellowship payments made by universities to non-U.S. residents are also subject to up to 14 % withholding tax.

The European Union and VAT Processing

SAP also supports calculation and processing of VAT (Value Added Tax). This is a type of consumption tax levied, for example, in member states of the European Union. As a consumption tax, the VAT is designed to be paid by the end consumer. But because it's not feasible to collect VAT from individual consumers, the VAT system is structured so that each business collects the VAT on its sales and passes it down the economic chain to its customers. If these customers are businesses and not end consumers, they also collect VAT on their sales and pass the cost on to their customers by collecting the VAT from them, and so on.

However, businesses only have to remit to the tax authorities the difference between their input tax (tax paid to their vendors) and output tax (tax collected from their customers). This ensures that the VAT does not accumulate through the economic chain, and so that, in the end, consumers only pay the VAT once. Countries assign VAT registration numbers to companies.

Every transaction subject to the VAT carries the VAT registration number of the vendor and of the customer, as applicable. Deliveries made to companies in other EU countries are tax-exempt, but the supplier (vendor) reports those business transactions to its local tax authority, and the receiver (customer) calculates the applicable input tax.

VAT Processing

SAP provides complete support for managing, calculating, and reporting VAT and relevant business transactions. SAP also provides check rules for EU member states so that you can identify any incorrect VAT numbers and reduce the errors when the tax is remitted. Using SAP, you can maintain VAT registration numbers for your customers in their master data, and you can choose to maintain VAT registration numbers for your vendors. SAP ERP Financials does not currently use that information, however.

Validation of VAT numbers

For Austria, Belgium, Czech Republic, France, Germany, Italy, and many other countries that are members of the European Union, SAP provides tax calculation procedure templates that can be used "as is" with very little modification. For most of these countries, SAP also provides tax codes and tax percentages that can be used "as is" in business transactions.

To accurately calculate and display VAT on transactions with customers, SAP checks VAT registration numbers from the customer master, information on the reporting country where goods are delivered, and information on the delivery country from which delivery was made. If the goods delivery is part of a triangular deal, it must be marked as such when entering the transaction to ensure that the transaction is identified as a triangular deal in the EC sales list (European Community Sales List).

Another scenario to be considered in VAT transactions is when the customer who places an order (sold-to party), the customer who receives the goods (ship-to party), and the customer who pays the bill (payer) are different. If any or all of the accounts have VAT registra-

Derivation of VAT number

tion numbers, per priority rules, the first VAT registration number of the payer is used, as long as the payer isn't the same as the sold-to party. If the payer does not have a VAT number, or if the payer is the same as the sold-to party, the VAT number of the ship-to party is used. Finally, if the VAT number of the ship-to party isn't available, then the VAT number of the sold-to party is used.

In addition, SAP provides programs to carry out a pro-rata method of VAT calculation. This type of VAT calculation is necessary if company operations result in a combination of outputs, and only some of these outputs are exempt from VAT. For example, a manufacturer may pay input tax on procuring materials that are used to produce three products, two are subject to VAT, and one is exempt from VAT. For these companies, not all of the input tax paid by them can be offset against the output tax they collect. Instead, the deductible portion of the input tax is calculated based on the calculation of a pro-rata ratio of taxable turnover to total turnover of the business.

Because this pro-rata ratio can't be calculated accurately until after the period (month, quarter, or year) is over, at the end of the period, the correction documents are posted with adjustments calculated based on the difference between the two pro-rata ratios. Programs provided can be used to:

> Register the VAT pro-rata coefficient (ratio).
> Apply the pro-rata coefficient while posting incoming invoices.
> Calculate the difference based on periodic or annual recalculation of pro-rata coefficients.
> Post necessary adjustments.

VAT Reports

EC sales list   Another important feature of SAP VAT processing is the reporting functionality. Every organization subject to VAT processing is required to prepare an EC sales list for the relevant tax authorities. This EC sales list provides information on tax-exempt deliveries of goods within the European Union and goods movement to other companies. SAP provides generic programs to prepare EC sales lists in printed and electronic form. To meet country-specific requirements, SAP also provides specific EC sales list programs for Belgium, Spain, and other EU countries. As mentioned earlier, deals marked as triangular deals are listed separately on the EC sales list. Figure 4.6 shows the selection screen for a generic **EC Sales List** report.

Every organization subject to VAT processing is also required to file quarterly and annual returns to tax authorities listing tax-exempt export deliveries, tax-exempt EU-internal deliveries, base value of the goods on which acquisition tax was calculated, and other details. The software provides programs to prepare the return for sales and purchase taxes by using information taken from the tax codes.

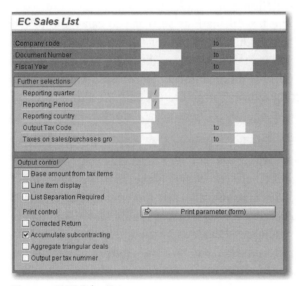

Figure 4.6 EC Sales List

Other Tax Scenarios

The taxes covered so far are typical of taxes levied on sales and purchases of goods and services in most countries, although they may be called different names (e.g., GST in Australia or GST, PST, and HST in Canada). In addition to these taxes, you can also use SAP to calculate other types of country-specific taxes. Let's review some of those taxes.

Taxes, taxes, and more taxes

119

Use Tax

Use tax is the tax assessed in the United States on goods transactions that may have been tax-free otherwise. For example, if companies sell goods to out-of-state customers, typically they do not collect sales tax unless they are registered or have a physical presence (such as plant, office, etc.) in that state. However, the purchaser of the goods is still required to calculate the tax equivalent to the sales tax they would have paid and remit payment to its own state as use tax. If the supplier of the goods does charge tax, then the purchaser can claim tax credit for such taxes from subsequent tax remittances.

SAP supports the calculation of use tax by allowing you to set the control parameters for the tax calculations so that you can indicate the tax codes that will trigger the calculation of the use tax. If a vendor invoice is subject to a use tax calculation, the tax calculation procedure automatically posts additional entries to record the use tax and increases the offsetting entries by the use tax amount. But posting of the use tax does not change the amount payable to the vendor.

In other scenarios, the purchaser may trigger payment of such taxes. Let's say a telecommunications supplier company purchases tax-free inventory using a resale certificate. If the company uses some of this inventory for its own offices, then the company is required to pay taxes proportional to the goods consumed versus the goods purchased. Another example is if goods purchased by an auto manufacturer for consumption in one state are later moved to a different state for consumption. In all such situations, companies are required to self-assess and pay applicable taxes.

Self-assessment permits Obviously, large manufacturing companies with their plants and locations in multiple states make many purchases that may be used for taxable or tax-exempt purposes. To facilitate easy calculation and remittance of applicable taxes, the companies can obtain licenses called self-assessment permits, which allow them to procure all goods on a tax-exempt basis. These companies then self-assess their tax liabilities based on their goods procurement and goods consumption and make remittance to the appropriate tax authorities.

Acquisition Tax

Another tax scenario handled is the acquisition tax, which is levied by some of the member states of the European Union, and is applicable for goods exported within the European Union. For cross-border movement of goods and services within the European Union, there is no input (purchase) tax, but the receiving company is required to post (recognize) an acquisition tax at the prevailing local rate. The acquisition tax is booked as a payable at the time the invoice is posted. Typically, acquisition taxes are recorded only for reporting to tax authorities, so the liability of the acquisition tax is offset automatically and simultaneously by posting the offsetting entry as a receivable/recoverable acquisition tax.

Acquisition tax

Using the tax calculation procedure template that calculates the acquisition tax, you can set up additional tax codes for the acquisition tax calculation. These tax codes post both sides of the tax entry—acquisition tax credit at the prevalent rate and offsetting debit entry as 100 % of the acquisition tax—having a zero net effect on the invoice posting.

 Tip

Even though the discussion of the acquisition tax, investment tax, and other taxes in this section is applicable to specific countries in the system setup, their tax calculation procedures can be used as templates to understand how to set up similar calculations for other countries.

Investment Tax

In countries such as Norway, in addition to VAT, *investment tax* is levied on capital investment goods such as machinery, vehicles, office equipment, and several consumables. Unlike VAT, however, the investment tax isn't refundable (although it can be deductible from your income), and it must be paid to the tax authorities by the receiving party.

Investment tax

You also have access to a tax calculation procedure template for Norway that shows the calculation of the investment tax in addition to VAT. When an invoice is posted, a payable line—separate from payable to vendor—is posted for the investment tax. The offsetting entry for the investment tax can then be charged either to a separate account or distributed proportionally to other GL items.

Sales Equalization Tax

Unlike the acquisition and investment taxes, the *sales equalization tax* is charged by the vendor or supplier of goods and services, for the sales made to tax-exempt customers. This requirement is more common in Belgium and Spain, and under this scenario, the vendor charges a sales equalization tax to customers in addition to an output tax. Then the vendor pays the tax to the tax authorities.

Depending on the statutory requirements, the sales equalization tax is calculated either as a percentage of the invoice amount or as a percentage of the output tax amount. SAP provides a tax calculation procedure template that can handle either of these requirements.

Non-deductible Input Tax

Deductibility of input tax

We said earlier that under the VAT system, businesses can deduct taxes paid to their vendors from the taxes collected from their customers and pay the difference to tax authorities. However, similar to other scenarios discussed before, input taxes paid on goods that are internally used by the company (e.g., upholstery outfitter using cloth or leather pieces for samples) aren't deductible. So, it's possible that part or all of the input tax on a business transaction may be nondeductible.

With SAP, you can specify percentage rates for the input tax and for the nondeductible portion of the taxes. When a vendor invoice is posted, the nondeductible portion of the input tax can be either posted to a separate account, or it can be distributed to other items in an invoice. Of course, if all of the input tax is nondeductible, the invoice doesn't post any entry for input tax; instead, the total tax amount is posted to a nondeductible account.

Other Transactional Taxes

You can also calculate additional types of transactional taxes without using tax codes. For example, in some regions or countries, there is an environmental tax, or white goods fees, charged on large, expensive electronic items. These taxes are collected from end consumers using a sliding scale based on the final sales price.

This requirement can be easily met by setting up calculations sales so that when products that meet the specified criteria are sold, the environmental taxes are automatically added to the invoice based on a final sales price. When these invoices are posted to the GL, accounting entries for the environmental taxes can be pointed to one or more ledger accounts.

Tax calculations in the sales component

However, transactions recorded in this manner might not be displayed in any standard sales and purchase tax reports. For the environmental tax, you can display the transaction activity from ledger accounts for reporting, but in other cases, you might have to develop additional reports.

Deferred Tax

The default system behavior is to recognize sales and purchase taxes at the time of invoice processing. However, in some countries, tax authorities require that taxes are recognized when invoice payments are made or received, not when the invoice is processed. For this purpose, the software provides deferred taxes.

The process of setting up, calculating, and processing deferred taxes has a few key differences from the standard process for setting up taxes. To begin with, you have to set up two sets of tax codes: deferred tax codes and target tax codes. Deferred tax codes are used in business transactions where taxes are to be deferred (e.g., while issuing an invoice). These codes are mapped to the corresponding target tax codes in the system setup. You also have to set up two sets of tax accounts: one to post deferred taxes and one to post recognized taxes.

Deferred tax codes and target tax codes

Using the deferred tax transfer program, you can periodically transfer taxes to recognized tax accounts. During this transfer, postings with deferred tax codes are converted to postings with target tax codes. Transfer is only proportional to the payments, so if an invoice is only 75 % paid, only 75 % of the taxes are recognized. The deferred tax transfer takes into account all other nuances, such as posting exchange gain/loss entries if tax clearing occurred in a foreign currency, and creating separate accounting entries to transfer tax amounts to provide a proper audit trail. You can even set up the program to recognize taxes only after payments are cleared in the bank.

Taxes on Down Payments

Net posting versus gross posting

One final tax scenario to consider is taxes on down payments. In the software, down payments from customers and down payments made to vendors are tracked in a separate reconciliation account, that is, the control account in GL for receivables or payables. Whether these down payments are subject to tax or not depends on local, statutory requirements. But you'll get support for two methods of posting tax on down payments: *net display* and *gross display*. The difference between the two methods is how the tax amount gets posted in customer or vendor accounts, then by extension to the corresponding reconciliation accounts in GL.

In the net display method, the customer account only shows the amount paid as a down payment, and the tax is posted to a separate tax account. In the gross display method, the amount total of the down payment and tax are posted to the customer account, and the tax entries are posted to tax accounts and tax clearing accounts. Settings that control the taxability of down payment accounts are set at the level of the chart of accounts, so they are applicable for all companies associated with that chart of accounts.

Now that you've learned about the various sales and purchase taxes, let's take a look at a case study of a company using SAP.

Case Study

Company Overview

A mid-sized U.S.-based manufacturer of consumer electronics has a retail presence in two states. The company is in a fast-growing business and expects to increase its retail presence to four additional states within the next year. The company is also in the process of aggressively expanding its customer base in Europe. Currently, the company is at a competitive disadvantage because although the company sells to its customers through product catalogs, it doesn't offer an option for customers to place product orders online.

The decision to use SAP as the main backend system was made in July 2005. This case study discusses the challenges and benefits of that decision and the subsequent SAP rollout from a tax accounting point of view. Keep in mind that the ability to handle sales tax calculation and compliance requirements was only one of the factors influencing this change.

Business Challenges

Before centralizing the business operations into SAP, this company used a combination of home-grown and third-party systems. Tax data from operations was scattered in multiple systems, so expansion of business into Europe would have required modification or development of additional home-grown systems to handle the unique VAT requirements.

Although competitive pressures demanded that products be made available for sale online, no backend systems were in place to support this initiative. In addition, enabling consumers to order products online presented issues of tax calculation and compliance with a large number of additional tax jurisdictions because products can be shipped to pretty much anywhere. Systems used by the company before the transition to SAP were woefully inadequate to handle this complexity.

On the purchasing side, no process was in place to validate tax information on invoices received from vendors, and random selection and checking of invoices had revealed the possibility that the company was overpaying taxes.

This hodgepodge of systems and rules created many problems for the tax department, such as information not being available in a timely fashion, which in turn caused delays in filing taxes, sometimes even resulting in tax penalties. Preparation for tax audits was also a time-consuming process, and because tax information went through multiple manual interventions before being used for reporting, there was always a risk of data not being accurate due to human errors.

The business process for identifying and managing 1099 payments was manual, and although the business process was good enough to handle the current workload, it was doubtful whether the process would be able to support much increase in volume.

As far as the tax department was concerned, an "as-is" situation would not meet the increasing requirements of their growing business.

Solution Deployment

When the decision was made by the company to implement SAP as the main operational backend system, it was decided, as part of that implementation, to review and fulfill as many tax requirements as possible.

A comprehensive requirements document was prepared to list existing requirements of the tax department for handling sales and purchase taxes in the United States as well as in Europe. The document also captured the anticipated future requirements in transactional taxes, based on the company's vision and business plan.

The company decided that the initial implementation of SAP should, at the very minimum, support tax calculation, posting and reporting on standard sales and purchasing processes, and catalog sales. In addition, custom interfaces were developed to integrate with POS systems supporting retail locations. These interfaces ensured two-way data exchange and thus ensured that any changes to the tax rates were reflected in POS systems in a timely fashion.

They also decided to use the tax calculation procedures provided for tax calculation in the United States and for VAT calculations in the European business unit. Anticipating future requirements, tax calculation by jurisdiction codes was enabled for U.S. operations. Considering the limited number of tax authorities the company was reporting to, they decided to maintain jurisdiction codes and tax rates, instead of using additional bolt-on software for tax calculation.

And although the classic withholding tax functionality was sufficient to meet their business requirements for 1099 reporting, they decided to implement enhanced withholding tax functionality because SAP recommended this for new implementations.

Value Achieved

Because multiple tax systems were combined into a single system, it eliminated the need to manually enter taxes in the GL. Instead, with SAP, all sales and purchase activity automatically and accurately posted tax-relevant entries to the GL.

There was also an immediate and noticeable effect of SAP in the area of catalog sales. Before SAP, there were numerous customer complaints and adjustments due to incorrect tax calculations. Now, with the new system in place, customer tax information was stored, including tax exemptions, if any. The accuracy of tax information on invoices increased dramatically, resulting in a reduced DSO (Days Sales Outstanding, a standard measure to see the number of days the customer took to clear an invoice) for the catalog customers.

AP started noticing warning messages on many of the vendor invoices indicating discrepancies in tax calculation, which allowed them to debit vendors for any tax differences and reduce overpayments. They were also able to use this information to follow up with vendors to ensure that future invoices would be received with accurate tax information.

By using the withholding tax functionality for 1099 processing, AP was able to focus on managing the whole process by exceptions, such as requesting information from new vendors, and keeping the withholding tax process current and valid for existing vendors. Additionally, with the new system in place, the department is confident it can meet increased transaction volume as well as any other complexity (such as the same account subject to multiple types of withholding) that may come in the future.

Although the European business operations are limited to only one country, and the business volume is smaller compared to the same in America, the experience gained in setting up the VAT calculation for one country and the availability of a large number of tax calculation procedure templates for other European countries makes future roll-outs to other European countries fairly easy.

One of the major, noticeable improvements was in the tax department's ability to prepare data for reporting, filing, auditing, or just analysis. A single source of information has improved confidence in tax numbers in the system and is helpful in preparing for audits. Details behind a number reported in any tax report are always just a few clicks away.

The availability of all transactions—whether taxable or nontaxable—by individual tax authorities has been of tremendous help, while preparing tax returns and determining taxes payable to each tax authority. In the older process, this involved multiple systems, and accuracy of tax data was always in question, especially when making sure that all product returns were accounted for in appropriate jurisdictions.

Looking Ahead
Calculating and reporting sales and purchase taxes with SAP ERP Financials is a huge improvement over the older process. Two areas are still under consideration for further improvement.

One of these is to focus on filing tax returns electronically. Using the SAP Data Medium Exchange Engine (DME Engine), the company can prepare data files to include the required data in the varied formats specified by the different tax authorities. After these files are ready, they can be electronically submitted to the respective tax authorities. This is a huge improvement over the current manual process of preparing and filing tax returns.

Another area under consideration is support for Internet sales, specifically for U.S. operations. The tax department has started evaluating SAP-certified, bolt-on software available for tax calculation. Management has yet to make a decision on whether to use Internet sales as a convenience for existing customers or promote it as a separate revenue stream. In the first case, the website may be coupled with some custom-developed logic for tax calculation. However, if the Internet store is intended to be a major revenue stream, then third-party bolt-on software may be necessary to allow them to calculate taxes for pretty much any jurisdiction.

Summary

In this chapter, we covered a lot of detail about the different functionalities offered for managing sales and purchase taxes. As you learned, this is a truly global tool that addresses numerous taxes from a wide variety of countries.

Following is a summary of the functionalities available for managing sales and purchase taxes:

> Comprehensive and customization functionality to support calculation, posting, and reporting of sales and purchase taxes with or without tax jurisdiction codes

> Templates of tax calculation procedures for more than 50 countries with ready-to-use setup of corresponding tax codes, tax rates, and other parameters

> Availability of SAP-certified, bolt-on solutions to handle extremely complex or voluminous tax calculation requirements

> Support for tax calculation at federal, regional, or for combination taxes at both federal and regional levels

> Plants Abroad functionality to accurately and easily prepare tax reports for warehouses, distribution centers, and plants located in foreign countries

> Support for business places to prepare tax returns at a lower level than a company

> Ability to classify and support products and customers based on their taxable or nontaxable status, and support for any combination of transactions

> Automatic calculation and accurate posting of taxes to GL accounts, while taking into consideration any adjustments needed for cash discounts or other deductions

> Comprehensive tax reporting to support reports for analysis, reconciliation, and preparation of tax returns and tax filing, most of which can be in printed form or in electronic form

> Support for withholding tax calculation, posting, and reporting in AP and AR

> Support for country-specific additional sales and purchase taxes such as acquisition tax, sales-equalization tax, investment tax, and many others

In the next chapter, we'll discuss bank accounting and banking transactions, and whether to manage your own bank accounts or to process payment transactions with customers and vendors.

Bank Accounting

In today's economy it's impossible to think of any type of business that doesn't use banking services. The requirements, complexity, and transaction volume may be different, but all businesses need to make payments to vendors, receive payments from customers, and transfer money between bank accounts. Obviously, these banking activities are coordinated with and influenced by a company's requirements for working capital and cash management.

So let's take a look at SAP's bank accounting features. Before we do though, keep in mind that there is a difference between the SAP Bank Accounting component and the SAP Industry Solution for Banking. The Bank Accounting component supports common banking activities and is useful for any company that transacts "with" banks as part of their regular operations. The SAP Industry Solution for banking, however, is more useful for companies that are "in" the banking industry and can use functionality such as deposits management, collateral management, leasing, and so on. This chapter focuses on the Bank Accounting component, but keep in mind that we'll discusses the cash management functionality in more detail in Chapter 16.

Overview

The bank accounting component allows you to manage house banks and bank accounts, to create and process different types of payments, and to process follow-up and month-end activities such as bank statement reconciliations. (We'll define house banks shortly). A central bank directory ensures common and consistent use of bank data throughout banking transactions for house banks and partner banks. Support for a large number of payment methods such as checks, electronic bank transfers, bill of exchange, direct debit, etc allows you to use the same banking processes worldwide, regardless of the country or the bank involved.

SAP also supports a complete range of transactions for manual and electronic processing of data files, which can perform many common business processes, such as bank statement reconciliation, processing of deposited checks and issued checks, processing of cash journals, and more. The large number of international and country-specific file formats supported for exchanging data with banks and business partners also helps you make your bank process more efficient.

Many parts of this chapter discuss how you would set up an SAP system. because as a business user, it's important to understand the bank accounting components and become familiar with the technical processes, such as selecting a bank account for making payments and matching incoming payments to invoices. Let's take a look at these functions in detail.

Bank Accounting Functions

We'll first consider how you can use SAP ERP Financials to support your global banking relationships and different payment methods. Then we'll talk about additional controls you can use to fine-tune your payment processing, followed by the payment aids you can use to make your banking activities more efficient. We'll finish this section with a look at reconciling bank statements, processing issued and deposited checks, and handling other bank accounting activities.

Banks and Bank Accounts

Bank directories can be extremely useful for large, global companies doing business in multiple countries, and they can also be used while setting up house banks and bank accounts. The bank directory can be updated using bank directories electronically available in the United States, Canada, Germany, and other countries; or the bank directory can be imported from BIC Database Plus©, which is supported by the SWIFT Network.

Bank directories

House Banks

House banks are the banks where your company operates its accounts for making and receiving payments. These banks represent the banking relationship of a company with different banks or different locations of a bank, and they can represent multiple bank accounts. For example, a small retailer may only have one account at one house bank; whereas a large multinational retailer may have several bank accounts at multiple house banks.

For every house bank, you specify relevant details such as a unique bank key (bank routing number); a bank number, if different from the bank key; address; SWIFT code or BIC code, and so on. If you upload the bank directory, these details are automatically copied while setting up house banks. In addition, you also get some unique functionality:

SWIFT code

> You can specify country-specific checks to validate whether bank key and bank account numbers conform to specific standards. This can be useful if you maintain bank information manually because the system can reject erroneous entries. Additionally, complete validation of IBAN numbers for many countries is supported.

> You can maintain a reference to another bank location that is responsible for receiving electronic data files. This can be useful, for example, if you have banking relationships with multiple branches, but your bank has a centralized location for processing electronic payments.

> You can specify a separate bank account from which bank charges are debited. This can be useful if bank charges on foreign payments, such as wire transfers, are to be paid from a different bank account than the one actual payment is made from.

Tip

For every house bank, you can set up multiple bank accounts corresponding to your actual bank accounts.

Bank Accounts

Integration with the new GL

To continue with the example discussed earlier, a multinational retailer may require multiple bank accounts at different house banks (e.g., Citibank, Bank of America, HSBC, etc) for different purposes, such as savings, bank deposits, payroll, trade receivables, trade payables, expense reimbursement, and so on. These different types of accounts and what they will be used for can be configured. So, for example, you can ensure that a vendor isn't paid from the employee expense reimbursement account. Figure 5.1 shows a bank account that is set up with information such as Bank Account Number, IBAN, Currency (e.g., a U.S. company may maintain a bank account in Euro), and primary G/L account number. This GL account number represents the bank account in the chart of accounts, and it integrates accounting transactions posted to the bank account with the new GL. In addition to this primary GL account, for cash management, you can use subaccounts for incoming and outgoing payments. Subaccounts in this context represent other GL accounts that you use as clearing accounts for different types of incoming and outgoing payments.

Subaccounts for cash management

We'll discuss cash management in more detail in Chapter 15, but for now, an example of cash management is when you deposit a check or make a check payment, the bank account balance is increased or decreased only when the check is cleared. Depending on your business volume, this can amount to a significant difference between the actual bank balance and the bank balance reported in your financial system. But you have an option to manage these cash flows by using GL accounts that act as subaccounts. When incoming or outgoing payments are processed, instead of the primary GL account, the balance of these subaccounts is debited or credited. And the balance of the primary GL account is changed only when the actual clearing of checks is processed, which is typically at the time of processing bank statements.

Depending on your cash-management requirements, you can set up as many subaccounts as required.

Figure 5.1 Bank Account in SAP ERP Financials

 Tip

If your bank manages different accounts (different types or in different currencies) under the same account number, you can maintain an alternative account number to differentiate between these bank accounts.

In addition to your own bank information, you can also maintain bank account information for your business partners.

Customer and Vendor Bank Accounts

For making and receiving electronic payments, it's important to maintain accurate and current information about customer and vendor bank accounts. Of course, if you've uploaded the bank directory, maintenance of this bank information is relatively easy. And, as we'll discuss later, lockbox processing can also extract bank information from customer payments received electronically and update that information in the customer master data.

Alternative payee or payer

For all of your customer and vendor bank accounts, you have to maintain similar details to those you maintain for your house banks, such as bank name, branch information, address, bank key, SWIFT code, account number, account type, IBAN number, and so on. Additionally, for each customer and vendor, you can maintain alternative payee or payer information that can be valid globally or only for a specific location.

 Ex Example

> While making a payment to a global supplier with whom you have purchasing relationships in multiple countries, you can use alternative payee information to make payments for one or all subsidiaries to their global headquarters.

To support today's global business environment, regardless of where the customer or vendor is located, the software supports making and receiving payments from its bank accounts in any country, which brings us to the concept of bank chains.

Bank Chains

Electronic payments between companies seldom occur directly between their banks, especially if the companies are in different countries. For example, when a retail company in Chicago receives payments from its subsidiary based in Vechta, Germany, the payment may be routed through a bank in San Francisco or New York, with possibly different bank charges. Typically, the House bank of the sender company decides how such payments are routed, which may or may not be cost effective. Many operational systems don't even provide the ability to specify bank accounts of business partners, let alone the ability to specify routes of such payment flows. But the *bank chain* functionality allows you to specify the route of these payment flows yourself, which helps you make decisions and reduces the associated time and costs.

Warning

The bank chain functionality is available only for automatic payment processing.

Bank chains are used to specify up to three banks in a payment flow. You can set up multiple strategies to determine a bank chain based on the sending bank, receiving bank, country of the receiving bank, or currency. For example, you can prioritize selection strategies so that if the program can't determine the bank chain based on the sending bank and receiving bank, it will attempt to determine the bank chain based on the sending bank and receiving country, or sending bank and currency, and so on. Figure 5.2 shows an example of bank chain determination for payments made in Euros between banks in Germany and the United States.

Crcy	Ctry	Bank Key	Ctry	Bank Key	PmtMthSu	BankChn ID
JPY						0002
EUR	DE					0002
EUR	IT		US			0001
EUR	DE	10020030	US			0003
EUR	DE	10020030	US	8897134132		0004
EUR						0005

Figure 5.2 Bank Chain Determination

If your business requirements are more complicated, you may appreciate the functionality that gives you even more flexibility to fine-tune how you use bank chains. The strategies discussed previously for determining the bank chain can be separately maintained for making payments and interbank transfers. If there is a better and more cost effective bank chain for making or receiving payments, you can maintain separate bank chains for individual customers or vendors as well. Now let's discuss how to make or receive these payments.

Bank chains for business partners

Payment Methods

A large number of payment methods for incoming payments (from customers) and outgoing payments (to vendors) are supported by the system. These include almost universally used payment methods such as checks, as well as unique payment methods, such as BACS in the United Kingdom, POR in Switzerland, and so on. A payment method has to satisfy not only the banking standards and guidelines of each country but also your operational requirements. This requirement can be satisfied by specifying the payment method parameters that are valid for a country and a company.

Country-Specific Parameters

These payment method parameters are valid for a country and are shared by all companies in that country. These parameters are mostly based on banking standards of the relevant country:

> Whether the payment method is used for incoming payments or outgoing payments.

> Whether the payment method represents a payment by check, bank transfer, or bill of exchange.

> Details and payee information required for the payee. For example, you may require bank details (IBAN, SWIFT code) for electronic payments.

> Whether payment method can be used for making personnel payments.

Foreign currency payments

> The currencies for which the payment method can be used. Without any restrictions, a payment method can be used for making payments in any currency.

> Posting specifications such as document types and the special GL indicator used in accounting entries posted to the new GL.

Even though more than 200 ready-to-use payment methods across almost 50 countries are provided, you may need to create additional payment methods. For example, a utility company may use different payment methods with different document types for making government payments and vendor payments. Apart from these country-specific parameters, you can also specify the number of company-specific parameters.

Company-Specific Parameters

Figure 5.3 shows an example of company-specific parameters. Because these parameters are company-specific, they can be different for different companies in the same country. These parameters are more relevant for operational reasons. For example, by using amount limits, you can control minimum and maximum amounts for which you want to use a payment method. So, you may choose not to pay by check for amounts over $100,000 or pay by bank transfer for payments less than $25.

Other parameters can be used to control if and how the payment method can be used for foreign payments. Consider a U.S. dollar bank account for a U.S. company. Using these parameters, you can control whether the payment method can be used for payments in a foreign currency, such as:

> Making EUR payments to pay foreign vendors

> Making payments to a vendor in Germany with a bank account in Germany

> Making payments to a foreign bank account, regardless of where the vendor is located

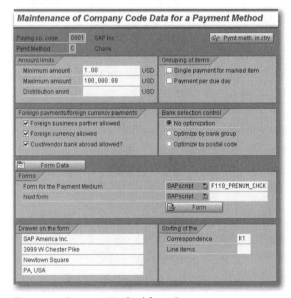

Figure 5.3 Payment Method for a Company

Payment printouts   Another very important company-specific parameter is the *payment form* or *printout*, which is printed for every payment made using this payment method. This printout can be an actual form of payment such as a check, or any other printout such as approval instructions for a bank wire transfer. Of course, you can also create additional payment methods for companies.

Because SAP's design is so flexible, a financial services company can create multiple payment methods for check payments made to vendors, employees, and government authorities. Or an investment group of three companies (assuming they're all in the same country) can share the same payment method for check payments but use different payment limits and different check layouts. Regardless of why and how the payment is made, it always requires some form of *payment media*.

Payment Media

A payment method typically requires printed or electronic payment media to process, instruct, or record the action of making the actual payment. *Payment media* can vary depending on the payment guidelines for a bank or country, and on the use, purpose, and business processes of your company. For example, check payments almost always require physical printouts, whereas electronic payments can be processed in several ways. You can prepare a data file and electronically send it to the bank, print fund transfer approval letters and fax them, or enter transfer requests directly using the bank's website. You can also customize the software to generate physical printouts and electronic data files for any payment method. Because the check is one of the most universally used payment mediums, let's discuss check management functionality in a little more detail.

Check Management

We already discussed how the software supports multiple house banks and bank accounts. You can set up multiple check lots for any bank account for which you have check writing privileges. Here are some unique features how management of check lots are handled:

140

> Check lots can be restricted for use with specific payment methods. So it's possible, for example, to use different check lots for vendor payments and employee payments.

> If you issue checks using a manual system or some other system, you can issue checks that aren't in sequence. For example, if a rebate-processing department distributes checks from one lot to several individuals, checks may not be issued in sequential order.

Out of sequence check issuing

There are several programs for handling check-processing activities, problems, or mistakes.

 Example

Using the check register, you can display check details based on a large number of selection criteria, such as amounts, currencies, payment methods, issue dates, cashing dates, etc., and to respond to payment status requests, you can easily display check information from a paid invoice or a list of paid invoices from check details.

As we'll discuss later, other programs can be used to manually update check cashing information for individual checks, to upload a file received from a bank, to update cashing information for multiple checks, or to void checks that are unused or have already been issued. The check voiding process in some systems can be unforgiving, so if you void a check by mistake, you have to maintain details of that check offline. But, if a check is marked as void by mistake; you can simply reset the voiding information. At this point, we should introduce different tools available for creating forms or printed layouts such as checks.

Voided checks

 Tip

These form development tools can be used for preparing forms and printouts across almost all Financials, Logistics, and Human Resources components and applications of SAP ERP 6.0.

Form Printouts

In previous versions of SAP ERP Financials, the only form development tool available for creating forms and layouts was SAPscript. Subsequently, another tool called SmartForms was introduced, and the current version also supports creating interactive PDF-based forms. Without getting into too many details of the technical capabilities and constraints of each tool, the following are some of the ways you can use them apart from creating check layouts and other printouts:

> You can create address labels for mailing check payments or payment notices.

> You can create forms that exactly match the formatting and details of the official bank transfer forms of your bank.

Payment forms on
an intranet

> You can create interactive forms in PDF format that can be displayed in a browser for users to fill in. For example, you can create a PDF-based payment request form and make it available on the company intranet.

> You can mass print or email forms. For example, you can send payment information to major suppliers via email when their invoices are processed.

Of course, many payment methods require electronic data files instead of, or along with, physical printouts. For this purpose, the *Payment Medium Workbench* is provided.

Payment Medium Workbench

In the older versions of SAP ERP Financials, different programs were used to prepare payment data for different payment methods in different countries. Considering that the format, structure, content, and level of details can vary by country, bank, and payment method, more than 150 programs for different payment methods have to be supported. This is not just a purely technical issue, because during a payment run, users had to make sure that the correct payment program and selection criteria were selected for every payment method to print checks or create payment data files. This can become problematic depending on the number of payment methods processed by AP, especially for centralized or outsourced AP operations. So, an extremely flexible tool called the Payment Medium Workbench (PMW) was introduced for creating payment data files.

*Criteria for separate
data files*

Using PMW has several advantages, but the primary one is that business users can see the process of selecting the appropriate program, format, or selection criteria. There are also more than 50 well documented, ready-to-use PMW formats provided for several countries, and these formats can be easily modified to meet any unique requirements of your bank. One of the important factors while designing a new format in PMW is to check with your bank to find out what its criteria are for receiving separate files. PMW is flexible enough to support creating separate payment files based on companies, banks, bank accounts, and payment methods. So, depending on your banking relationships and AP operations, you can create a consolidated data file for all payments across all companies or create separate data files for each payment method from individual bank accounts.

 Tip

PMW uses another tool called the Data Medium Exchange Engine (DMEE) to create electronic data file formats. The DMEE is also used in other SAP application areas that exchange data files in specific formats.

Another advantage of the PMW is that it's also possible to include non-SAP information in the payment file, if required by your bank. For example, you can combine, in the same payment file, bank-specific information (e.g., transmission codes) and the payment data generated. The next step is to decide on additional payment controls and to see how the payment program selects these payment methods and bank accounts during payment runs.

Payment Program

We've already discussed how multiple house banks, bank accounts, and payment methods are supported, but additional payment controls for the payment process are also supported.

Payment Controls for a Company

For every company, you can specify several parameters that control the payment process. So let's take a look at the parameters that control the cash discount calculation. Consider an invoice with a final due date of June 15th and a 2 % discount for payments received before June 1. The default behavior of the payment program is first to attempt to pay this invoice on or before June 1 and then automatically reduce the payable by 2 %; if that isn't possible, delay the payment until the due date and pay the invoice in full. You can influence this behavior in three different ways independently for each company:

> You can specify tolerance days to cash discount dates and final due date. So if the number of tolerance days for a company is five, the payment program will extend the automatic reduction of the payable by 2 % until June 6th.

> You can instruct the payment program to deduct the maximum possible cash discount (i.e., 2 %) regardless of the payment date, even if it's after June 15th.

> You can delay the payment of invoices until the final due date if the cash discount offered is below a certain percentage.

Each company typically decides these parameters based on their vendor relationships and working capital requirements.

Now consider an example of a small entertainment business that consists of three companies from a statutory point of view, but only one company handles payments for all three companies. You can easily support this requirement by setting up a relationship between the sending company codes and the paying company codes. In this example, all three companies are set up as sending company codes, with the company making payments set up as the paying company code for all three. During the payment run, the software automatically evaluates and pays outstanding invoices for all three companies while automatically creating intercompany accounting entries. For the paying company codes, you can specify additional control parameters, such as a minimum amount for processing incoming or outgoing payments, whether any exchange rate differences should be posted during payment processing, and so on. One of the most important setups for paying company codes is selecting the bank account.

Selecting the Bank Account

If a company has multiple accounts with multiple banks, how does the payment program know which bank account to use for making which payment? The software uses a bank selection control for making that decision. This setup is only required for the companies that make the payments. So if your main company makes payment on behalf of one of your subsidiaries, this setup is not required to be done for that subsidiary. As shown in Figure 5.4, the bank account determination in the payment program can be best described as a three-step process, each step influenced by a different set of parameters.

❶ The first set of parameters control the selection of a bank based on payment method and currency. In the entertainment example, for check payments (payment method C), BANK1 is evaluated before BANK2; whereas for electronic payments (payment method D), BANK2 is evaluated before BANK1.

The process explained

❷ The second set of parameters influences the selection of the bank account based on payment method and currency. So for BANK1, check payments in U.S. dollars are made from account CHEK1, and in any other currency are made from CHEK2; whereas for BANK2, electronic payments in U.S. dollars are made from account CHEK1.

❸ The third set of parameters specifies the maximum amount for a bank account in different currencies up to 1 million U.S. dollars but only up to 50,000 in Japanese Yen and Euro.

Paying co. code   0001

❶ Ranking Order

PM	Crcy	Rank.order	House Bk
C	USD	1	BANK1
C	USD	2	BANK2
D	USD	1	BANK2
D	USD	2	BANK1

❷ Bank Accounts

House b	P	Curr	Account ID	Bank subaccount
BANK1	C		CHEK2	113001
BANK1	C	USD	CHEK1	113001
BANK2	D	USD	CHEK1	113002

❸ Available Amounts

House ba	Account ID	Curr	Available for outgoing
BANK1	CHEK1	USD	999,999.00
BANK2	CHEK2	EUR	50,000.00
BANK2	CHEK2	JPY	50,000

Figure 5.4 Bank Account Determination

145

Payment proposal and exception list

The automatic payment program selects the bank account for a payment after taking into consideration the payment method, payment currency, and payment amount parameters. These parameters are evaluated in the sequence depicted in Figure 5.4. If the payment program doesn't find the required information at any level, it evaluates the next value from the previous level. If the payment program finds the required parameters, the corresponding open items are included in the payment proposal; otherwise, those open items are placed in an exception list.

 Tip

During a payment run, if you activate an additional log for payment method selection in all cases, the payment proposal log will contain the entire process of the bank account selection for all payments.

During the payment run, the program checks for items due for payments in customer and vendor accounts. These items typically reflect accounting entries corresponding to invoices and debit or credit adjustments. Additionally, several payment aids are provided to process payments for items that aren't already posted to customer and vendor accounts.

Payment Aids

This section discusses several payment aids available, such as payment requests, payment advice, payment orders, and repetitive codes.

Repetitive Codes

Recurring payments

Repetitive codes represent payment data that remains unchanged for frequently recurring payments, such as money transfers to foreign subsidiaries, payments to your favorite SAP consultant for project support, etc. Typically, for these transactions, only the payment amount is different in each payment transaction; whereas the sending bank and bank account, receiving bank and bank account, payment method, currency, and more remain the same. For these types of payments, you can use repetitive codes that correspond to the payment data that remains unchanged. For example, Figure 5.5 shows a repetitive code used to make a payment for office rent and utilities.

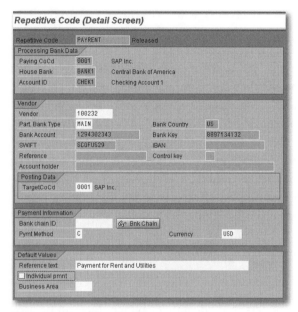

Figure 5.5 Repetitive Codes

In the United States, you can even agree upon mutually acceptable repetitive codes with your house bank, so that the bank only needs the repetitive code and the amount to process a payment. Regardless of whether repetitive codes are used to communicate with house banks or to improve operational efficiency, they provide quicker and faster ways to create payment requests.

Payment Requests

As the name implies, payment request documents can be used to make payment requests for vendor or customer payments, bank transfers, and so on. Payment requests capture all data relevant for making a payment, such as bank account, payment method, and amount. Similar to a payment program that processes open items posted to a vendor account, another program provides you with the ability to process payment requests and post payments against payment requests. Payment requests can be used to request advance payments to vendors, fund transfers between bank accounts, payments of customer refunds or rebates, sales commission, bonus payments, and more.

Payment approval process
You can use the approval process with SAP Business Workflow to make sure that the payment requests are reviewed, approved, and released before corresponding payment can be processed. Because there are diverse requirements and uses for payment requests, the software supports several options for processing payment requests after they are created. For example, a payment request to make a large customer payment for a refund can be sent for approval, automatically released for payment, processed to the point of posting the payment while waiting for the check to be printed, or processed all the way up to check printing. Of course, by routing a payment request through the approval process, you can reject or reverse it based on the recipient, purpose, and fund availability. Similar to payment requests used for outgoing payments, you also have *payment advice* notes for processing incoming payments.

Payment Advice

A payment advice note details an incoming payment that can be used to assign and clear open items. A payment advice note contains information on paid items, amount, reason for any payment differences, reference document numbers that can help identify items being paid, etc. Using a payment advice number, the program for processing incoming payments can automatically propose items that may have been paid along with proposals for any difference items.

 Tip

Payment advice notes are also created by the programs that automatically match incoming payments, such as programs to process bank statements, check deposits, lockboxes, and more.

Typically, payment advice notes are created automatically through electronic payment processing programs; these programs use interpretation algorithms to determine how to search for matching documents in customer accounts. For manually created payment advice notes, you can use completely customizable selection rules to interpret available information to search for corresponding documents. Also, even if payment advice notes are automatically created, they may have to be manually modified, for example, if the program can't find all of the invoices referenced in the payment. Creating payment advice notes manually can also be useful where for operational reasons the process of entering incoming payments is separate from the process of applying the payment to the customer account.

Another payment aid supported is the use of payment orders.

Payment Orders

Normally, when the payment process is carried out, the payment program posts payments and marks items as paid or cleared in a vendor account. However, payment methods that create payment orders to delay posting payments to the vendor account are also supported. Under this scenario, the payment program does not create payment documents and does not mark items as paid or cleared. Instead, the system creates a separate document called Payment Order that contains relevant information to be used later for processing payments.

Selection rules

When these payments are cleared in the bank account, the payment order numbers are referenced on bank statements; which triggers the payments to be posted and the items to be marked as paid. The program for electronic bank statement processing supports a search algorithm so that you can search for items based on payment order numbers. The paid items remain blocked for other clearing transactions and further payment runs until the payment has been posted. For example, by delaying posting of foreign currency payments until they are cleared in the bank account, you can post accounting entries using actual exchange rates. Otherwise, you have to separately record exchange gains or losses based on exchange rate fluctuations between the time the payment was posted and the time the payment cleared in the bank. This can be especially useful for companies that have a considerable supplier base in countries with volatile currencies with highly fluctuating exchange rates.

Delayed posting of payments

At regular intervals, typically weekly or monthly, a bank reconciliation process is carried out for every bank account. During this process, entries posted are reconciled with the entries reported by the bank.

Bank Statement Reconciliation

A complete range of functions are supported to convert, import, enter, process, match, reconcile, and post bank transactions reported in a bank statement. You can import bank statement data, or you can enter the information manually. Let's look at importing a statement.

Importing a Bank Statement

Banks in almost all major countries provide access to bank transaction data in electronic format. The structure and format of this information varies by country or even by banks, and many banks provide transaction data in multiple formats. Thus, the process of converting bank account information can quickly become daunting depending on the number and dissimilarities of your banking relationships.

Fortunately, a single and consistent method of converting bank information from a variety of formats and sources is provided. You may remember the DMEE tool from our discussion in Section 1.2.3. You can use the same DMEE tool to convert and load data files from any bank. You can also directly import bank data from many standard international formats such as BAI (U.S.), MultiCash (Germany), CSB43 (Spain), internationally recognized SWIFT MT940, and so on.

Posting to new GL and subledgers
During a typical bank statement import process, information from a file is loaded in the temporary bank data area; the program analyzes the postings (more on this later) and creates program sessions with the proposed accounting entries. A bank statement entry (e.g., incoming payment from a customer or outgoing payment to a vendor) may also require posting additional entries in subledgers (e.g., clearing invoices in receivables or payables). The bank statement program creates two separate sessions, one for accounting entries in the new GL and one for accounting entries in subledgers. While uploading the bank statement, several options are provided to influence how these sessions are created.

Tip

To improve operational efficiency, the program can group bank statement items into bundles and create separate posting sessions for each. A bundle can be based on the number of items (e.g., 100 items per bundle) or be based on the clerks responsible for managing customer or vendor accounts.

While testing an interface for a new bank account, you can choose to load the bank statement without creating any posting sessions so that you can analyze data loaded in temporary bank data area. On the other hand, for a fairly stable interface with long established bank accounts, you can choose to directly post accounting entries from a bank statement file. A third option lets you post to the new GL immediately while postponing subledger postings. This option can be useful if the complete processing of statements takes too long, and you want bank balances as soon as possible. So let's see how to enter bank statements manually.

Manual Bank Statement

Depending on the volume of bank transactions and the cost of the electronic bank interface, you may choose to manually enter bank statement. Figure 5.6 shows an example of a manual bank statement entry.

Process Manual Bank Statement

Bank a/c: 98124186127012399   GL Account   113000   CoCode 0001 Crcy USD

Bank statement items

Tran	Value date	Amount	Doc. no.	Bank ref	Allocation	Custom	Vendor
0003	03/10/2007	9,876.54	129121009			12111	
0003	03/10/2007	12,298.31	612191911	REF #45			
0004	03/11/2007	9,876.54-	691218788	REF #23	21039022		98312
0004	03/11/2007	21,210.09	691217979		90001239		97654
0005	03/15/2007	1,210.09-	208000199	REF #12	39009012	12111	
0005	03/17/2007	7,654.57	612191911	REF #87			94553

Amount entered   39,952.88   Bank statmnt   102,860.65   Line   1 / 6

Figure 5.6 Manual Bank Statement

The software is flexible enough to allow you to customize the screen layout so that you can process bank statements efficiently and effec-

Customized entry layout

tively while still capturing all of the necessary information. Fields displayed in the figure, such as Value date, Amount, Customer, Vendor, Bank ref (Bank Reference), etc., are self-explanatory. The first column Tran (Transaction Type) requires more explanation, so let's discuss.

Transaction Types

Transaction types are used in both manual as well as electronic bank statement processing. Even though transaction types have to be specified explicitly in manual processing, transaction types are easier to understand if discussed from the electronic statement viewpoint.

External and internal transaction types

In an electronic bank statement from any bank, different business transactions are classified using different transaction types. These transaction types classify different incoming payments, outgoing payments, bank charges, interest income, and other transactions. Different banks most certainly use different transaction types to refer to the same bank transaction (e.g., incoming check), but this complexity is easily handled by mapping these external transaction types to internal transaction types and specifying all processing parameters only to internal transaction types.

This unique design ensures that you can accommodate unavoidable variations in external bank data while still maintaining a consistent approach for processing bank statements. Thus, transactions for incoming wire transfers or checks reported by different banks using different transaction types are processed in the same way, as long as those external transaction types are mapped to the same internal transaction type.

Obviously, when a manual bank statement is processed, there are no external transaction types to map to, so the transaction type entered in Figure 5.6 refers to an internal transaction type. In manual bank statement processing, you can choose the customer, vendor, or bank account; debit or credit posting; and other details. For electronic bank statements, effectively and accurately determining these details requires additional processing.

Processing Electronic Bank Statements

SAP provides you with a large number of control parameters that influence the processing and posting of transactions reported in a bank
account statement. These control parameters determine and influence
several factors in bank statement processing:

Control parameters

> Whether the transactions are debits or credits, and whether the
  reported amount represents the opening balance, closing balance,
  total balance, adjustment balance, or any other type of balance

> Whether the transaction posts accounting entries only to the new
  GL (e.g., bank charges) or to the subledger as well (e.g., clearing a
  customer invoice)

> The determination of bank accounts, GL accounts, and correspond-
  ing debit and credit amounts for accounting entries

> How the reference information from the transaction is interpreted,
  and how the information is used to find a corresponding match

The last point mentioned in the previous list is crucial for automatic
bank statement processing because the more successful the automatic
search and matching, the less manual work is required to process the
statement. As discussed next, the software provides the highly customizable interpretation algorithm and search string techniques for
automating this process to the maximum extent possible.

Interpretation Algorithm
The interpretation algorithm concept is fairly simple. It represents the
strategy used by the bank statement processing program to search
for matching information for every item in the bank statement. This
information is usually contained in one or more fields of a bank statement item, and it's used during bank statement processing to match
and clear subledger items. For example, different algorithms can interpret this information as a document number (incoming payment)
or a check number (outgoing payment) to search for corresponding
customer or vendor documents; if a document match is found, the
program can create accounting entries for matching and clearing invoices against payments. More than 20 different algorithms are pro-

vided (see Table 5.1), and you can also create up to 9 additional algorithms.

No.	Algorithm Description
001	Standard algorithm: Document number or reference document number
011	Outgoing check: check number different from payment document number
020	Document number search
021	Reference document number search
025	Invoice list
033	Search for payment advice notes
060	Document number search for clearing documents
901–909	Customer-specific interpretation algorithms

Table 5.1 Sample List of Interpretation Algorithms

Processing cross-company cash receipts

Most of the interpretation algorithms search for a document referenced in a bank statement item in the company processing the bank statement, which satisfies most common requirements. However, consider again the example of the small entertainment business discussed previously. If one company carries out cash receipts and bank reconciliations for the other two companies, you need to process the bank statement in one company but search for reference documents that may have been posted in other companies. This requirement is supported with two special algorithms that don't check for the existence of reference documents in the company processing the bank statement. Try to find equivalent functionality in other financial systems!

When reference information in bank statement items does not exactly match with corresponding information, you can use the search string functionality.

Search strings

Business partners commonly truncate or modify document numbers and reference numbers on payment transactions. For example, a bank statement item referring to an invoice 1800000234, may reference it as 18–234, 180000234 (by mistake), 180 000 0234, 18000 00234, or any other variation. Obviously, if an interpretation algorithm attempts to find an exact match with any of these values, it will never find the corresponding SAP invoice.

Search strings

To improve the matching probability, you can use *search strings* to supplement the standard interpretation algorithms; which allows numbers to be automatically identified, even if they are incomplete or modified. The search string consists of special characters (see Figure 5.7) that let you override or interpret the value from bank statement items.

Character	Meaning	Example
|	Or	a|b finds a or b
()	Group	c(ac|b)d finds cacd or cbd
+	Repetition (as often as you like, must occur at least once)	(ab)+ finds ab or abababab
*	Repetition (as often as you like, must occur at least once)	ab* finds a or b or abbbbbbb
?	Wildcard	a?b finds a Qb or a1b
#	Digits 0-9	
\	Slash (searches for special characters)	\#\#\# finds ### and not 123, for example
^	Start of line	
$	End of line	

Figure 5.7 Special Characters in Search Strings

The search string functionality is so powerful that its use is also supported for other fields in electronic bank statement processing. Although unlike the search string for the Note to Payee field used to only search for document numbers, search strings for other fields

Search string for cost centers

(e.g., Cost Center) can actually replace the value of that field. For example, you can create a search string so that if a bank statement item contains the word maintenance, the Cost Center value is replaced with 5260. You can use a similar technique for other fields, such as Profit Center, Business Area, Account Type, Account Number, and so on.

You can also test and simulate search strings in the system by importing bank account statements. The simulation functionality enables you to review results of applying search strings and modify them as necessary until you obtain satisfactory results. This can be especially useful if you notice that the software isn't able to automatically match large number of invoices, and you would like to fine tune the matching capability of the program. You may not be able to find 100 % matches for all items in all bank statements, but you can modify search strings to maximize a number of transactions posted automatically during bank statement processing. For the accounting entries that can't be posted automatically, you need to carry out postprocessing of electronic statements.

Postprocessing

Postprocessing enables you to review and post bank statement items that could not be matched and posted automatically during electronic bank statement processing. The postprocessing program selectively displays bank statement items based on a number of parameters, such as company, bank, bank account, statement number, statement date, and so on, so that you can distribute the workload of investigating, processing, and posting these items as appropriate. When a user is editing a bank statement item during postprocessing, no other users can make changes to that item. For a bank statement item that couldn't be posted automatically, you can modify the value of the Note to Payee field, Customer field, and several other pieces of information so that the bank statement item is posted to the correct GL account and customer or vendor account.

Debits returns processing

When you carry out postprocessing of your bank statements, you may encounter returned checks or similar rejected payments that the program is unable to process automatically. But you can easily handle such bank statement items using the comprehensive returns

156

processing functionality Typically, such items also carry a reason for the return (e.g., insufficient funds), which can be used to classify and post such returns to the appropriate GL accounts. As a testament to the powerful integration capability, you can automatically reopen invoices in the corresponding customer account, based on the reason for the check return or rejection of payment. Not only that, but you can also change the payment method in the invoice items or block them from dunning or payment. For example, if a customer removes collection authorization from the bank account, an attempt by the utility company to auto debit the utility payment will be rejected. When this rejection of payment gets reported in their bank statement, the utility company may want to block invoiced items on payment block until the problem is resolved.

Now that we've looked at the bank statement reconciliation process, let's look at some other bank transactions.

Other Bank Transactions

In this section, we'll discuss some other commonly used bank transactions, such as lockbox processing, incoming check processing, and so on. You may notice that SAP's modular and completely customizable design of electronic bank statement processing is also used to process other bank account transactions. Let's start with lockbox processing.

Lockbox Processing

Lockbox is a banking service offered by U.S. banks. As part of this service, companies that receive a large number of payments (e.g., utility companies) request their customers to send payments to a central bank, typically a P.O. box. The bank processes these payments and periodically sends a data file to the company. The file contains the payment amount and other reference information so that the company can allocate payments to customer accounts. This lockbox service not only reduces workload for the company but also provides better liquidity because incoming payments are deposited and processed quicker.

BAI and BAI2
formats

The lockbox program supports the processing of lockbox files received in BAI format as well as the newer, BAI2 format. These file formats are commonly used by banks in US to electronically transmit lockbox information. The reference information in incoming payments usually refers to a document number that can be a customer billing document number or a corresponding accounting document number (refer to Chapter 2 for the difference between these two documents). During the import of a lockbox data file, you get the flexibility to search for a customer account based on either or both document numbers.

If a customer account is identified (e.g., based on bank information), the lockbox program uses powerful algorithms to match incoming payments with open items in the customer account. Depending on the results of the matching process, the incoming payment is posted to the customer account as a clearing payment (all documents provided in the file could be matched), partial payment (some of the documents couldn't be matched), or on-account payment (none of the documents could be matched). If the customer can't be identified, the incoming payment is posted to an unapplied payment clearing account such as an AR suspense account.

You can use the lockbox post-processing program for matching and posting any payments that couldn't be automatically processed. Of course, you also get other programs to process deposited checks, which can be used if the lockbox service isn't available.

Processing Deposited Checks

Even if your company doesn't use lockbox services, or your bank doesn't provide lockbox services, many banks do offer the service of sending daily data files of received checks. But if this information isn't received in the format required by the program, you may have to convert the file received from the bank so that the program can process the data.

Electronic
processing of check
file

Similar to the program for electronically processing bank statements, the program for electronically processing deposited checks transfers data from the bank file to a temporary bank data area. If you choose to interpret data in the file, the program searches for a customer match based on the bank key and bank account number from the data file. If a match is found, the corresponding customer number is transferred to the check deposit list. As discussed before in "Processing Electronic Bank Statements," this program also creates two program sessions to post accounting entries in the new GL and in the AR subledger.

Entries that can't be automatically processed by the electronic check deposit program can be processed using a manual check deposit program. The manual check deposit program can also be used if your bank doesn't offer electronic data file of deposited checks. The program attempts to search for customer accounts based on the document number entered from the check. Obviously, if the program can't find the customer account, you have to manually modify the details so that the check deposit can be posted in the system.

Similar to processing deposited checks, you also have the ability to process checks issued by you.

 Tip

If most of the entries in your bank account are for your deposited checks and issued checks, you can use programs discussed in this section along with a few manual entries (for bank charges, interest, etc.) in lieu of the bank statement processing functionality.

Processing Issued Checks

One of the most common requirements for processing checks after they have been issued is to record the date on which they were cleared in the bank account. This serves as proof that the payee received and deposited the check. Many banks offer services to send a list of cleared checks daily. For added verification, the files can also include the amount for which the check was cleared (positive pay service). This added information helps you catch any fraud or tampering with the check amount.

Positive pay

If you don't use the subaccount functionality discussed earlier and simply want to mark checks as cashed, you can update the check cashing date manually. However, if you use subaccounts, a program to read and process checks from a data file is provided. If a valid check is found, the program marks the check as cleared and automatically changes the account balance in the subaccount and primary GL account. Now let's see how cash-based payment transactions are supported.

Cash Journals

Typically, major payment transactions among business partners aren't conducted in cash. However, for companies doing business with individuals (e.g., utility companies), it's possible to receive cash payments from customers. Similarly, almost all companies maintain a petty cash account for carrying out nominal, daily cash expenses. You can also use one or more cash journals to track different types of cash receipts and cash payments.

Cash journals (see Figure 5.8) support different types of transactions, such as receipts from bank accounts, transfers to bank accounts, cash expenses, cash revenues, customer postings, and vendor postings. The cash journal allows you to post reversals and track such reversal postings, print the cash journal as well as individual cash receipts, and display corresponding entries in the new GL directly from the cash journal.

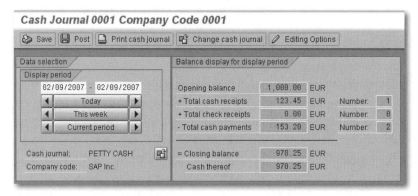

Figure 5.8 Cash Journal Summary

Before we end the chapter, let's take a quick look at other payment methods supported.

Other Payment Methods

Now let's talk about other supported payment methods that we haven't been able to discuss yet.

Bills of exchange are primarily used in international trade, mostly in Europe, as an unconditional mode of payment in which the payer agrees to make a payment to the payee on a specific future date. Bills of exchange are transferable and can be redeemed by the payee before the due date at a discount. Bills of exchange and reverse bills of exchange in AR as well as in AP are also supported. Bills of exchange are treated as special GL transactions, which we discussed in Chapter 2. Special GL transactions are also used to support other types of payment transactions, such as bank guarantees and letters of credit.

The need for companies to share financial data over the Internet, and the increasing popularity of personal financial software has given rise to the Open Financial Exchange (OFX) format. SAP provides ready-to-use OFX format files for payment data that can be used to transfer payments and account statements over the Internet to OFX partners. OFX partners specify the URL address and login information and typically represent house banks for which you have OFX access.

Payments over the Internet

Orbian Payments are special types of payments that are fully integrated with SAP ERP Financials (SAP is one of the original founders of the Orbian system) and are used by business partners who are members of the Orbian system. Orbian is the supply chain finance solution that provides a way for buyers to defer the cash payment of invoices while allowing their supplier(s) immediate access to the value of those invoices in the form of Orbian credits. Suppliers can use Orbian credits for making their own payments, for offsetting against their Orbian debits, or for converting Orbian credits to actual payments. Users can use the same interface to make Orbian Payments that they use for printing checks or making bank transfers.

Orbian payments

Now let's see how a city government was able to use lockbox to improve collections of its receivables.

Case Study

This beautiful border city in the Northeastern United States is becoming increasingly important for retail businesses, professional services, arts and education. The city's fire, police and other municipal and civic services departments strive to provide excellent services to its population of over 96300. To further improve quality of the services it provides, the city government is in the process of a major overhaul of its aging computer software and systems across all of its departments.

Business Challenges

Property taxes contributed to almost 45 % of the revenue, with charges for other services coming distant second. Thus, one of the main areas of focus for the administrative and finance department was making their collection of property taxes as automated as possible. Each year, the department received close to 100,000 property tax returns and payments by mail. The largely manual processing of these returns and payments led to many challenges for the limited city staff.

For example, since there were internal delays even in processing the payments that were actually received, city staff had little time to ensure the timeliness of the receipts. This resulted in many returns and payments filed way past their deadlines. This delay in processing caused cash flow problems considering that property taxes were the largest source of revenue for the city. Cash planning was considerably difficult due to the delays in receiving payments from property owners, which were further exacerbated by internal delays in processing these payments. After factoring in lost interest income and possibility of surplus liquidity, it was obvious that the processes, systems and the software had to change.

Council members were familiar with the extraordinary benefits reaped by other cities in the region by their usage of SAP. So once the budget was approved for implementing new ERP system across all departments, choice of SAP was non-contested.

Solution Deployment

With the primary focus of improving collection of property taxes, the city government evaluated several banks in terms of their lock-box services. Council members were aware that in such an initiative, support, efficiency and details provided by lockbox services were as important as the powerful processing functionality. After due deliberation and unavoidable government paperwork, a regional bank was selected to provide lockbox services for collection of property taxes.

Apart from electronically sending daily files for the receipts, the bank also offered electronic imaging services. The imaging services electronically converted all paperwork including tax return and any supporting documents, and made that information available for reference. The SLA (Service Level Agreement) called for this information to be available within 24 hours of processing a payment. Not only that, the bank also made all this information available over the Internet so that with secure login, any staff member can refer to the required information for further processing of taxes.

Realizing the importance of the success of this initiative, the city council also invested in several mailing campaigns introducing this new method of payment to its constituents. The campaigns also attempted to quantify savings from this initiative and how the city planned to use those savings for further improvements.

Value Achieved

Even though some of the savings and improvements were obvious and immediate, it took approximately three months before the operational staff was properly trained and comfortable acknowledging the benefits. Some of the major improvements included improved processing time, reduced labor and overhead costs, and increased and timely availability of funds.

For example, the average processing time for property tax returns was reduced from seven working days to only one day. This enabled the city to process 79 % of the property tax returns by the stipulated deadlines—a huge year-over-year improvement. Internally, there were equally noticeable reductions in labor and overhead costs. These reductions were due to the fact that there was no longer a need for personnel to handle the paperwork as most of the information was now only a mouse click away. In the past, the city had to sometimes hire temporary workers to cope with the deluge of paperwork. This considerable reduction in paperwork also helped the city in its "going green initiative" and helped improve its social image.

And obviously there was the undeniable benefit of reduced cash flow pressures. The city was able to immediately start earning interest on the deposits, and the finance department was now able to plan their expected property tax inflow with a reasonable level of certainty. Since most of the receivables were now processed electronically, the staff was able to concentrate on delayed and deliquent property tax payments.

Summary

In this chapter, we saw how you can improve the efficiency, automation, and standardization of your banking activities with SAP ERP Financials. After reading this chapter, you should have a good idea of the wide array of functionality provided, which allows you to:

> Use domestic and international payment methods, house banks, and bank chains to facilitate bulk payments and reduce the cost of moving funds

> Carry out electronic data exchange with banks worldwide using standard, international file formats or bank-specific, unique formats

> Use interpretation algorithms that use available information to match incoming payments with open items and to automatically carry out bank statement reconciliation

> Process partial payments, on-account payments, while taking into consideration payment differences and tolerances

> Use payment requests, payment advice notes, payment orders, and repetitive codes to streamline your bank accounting activities

In the next chapter, we'll discuss how the software can be used to support Capitalization of Investments and Asset Accounting.

6

Capitalization of Investments

In today's thriving investment environment, publicly traded companies have access to capital investments that can be used for business initiatives to meet their internal and external requirements. Capital investments fuel future growth and operational expansion, improve efficiency, and maintain existing infrastructure. They also help organizations meet governmental, environmental, and industry regulations.

In a large company, you could have hundreds of ongoing business initiatives at different levels, so it's important to get an overview of the planning and budgeting processes while maintaining strict budgetary control. And, after investment projects are capitalized to fixed assets, it's equally important that you maintain up-to-date information on the asset base for management, audit, tax, and insurance purposes. This is where the Investment component comes in. It helps you plan and execute investment initiatives. With the help of SAP Asset Accounting, you can also support the management of capitalized assets' lifecycles. Keep in mind that it's possible to use the Asset Accounting component independent of the Investment Management component.

Overview

In this chapter, we'll discuss the functionalities of investment management and asset accounting. We'll begin with an overview of investment management and then look at its specific functions. The term *investment* in this context refers to more than just capital investment. In fact, you can use the investment component for any initiative that is a cost but has the potential for long-term financial and non-financial returns. For example, the maintenance of a vehicle fleet, a research project, expansion of a warehouse, or an employee training initiative, all can be managed as investment projects. Figure 6.1 shows how investment management integrates with other SAP components.

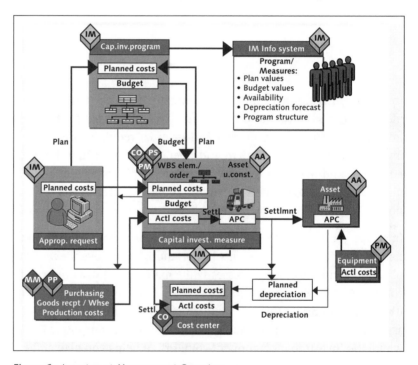

Figure 6.1 Investment Management Overview

Investment management overview

SAP provides investment programs for cyclical (typically annual) planning and management of investment budgets. The hierarchical structure of these investment programs enables you to create a structure that reflects your capital planning process. Requests for funding can be created using appropriation requests, which describe alternatives for what is to be done, who is requesting it, who is responsible for it, how much it will cost, and how much money it will make. Multiple planning versions support several iterations of the capital planning process. So after the requested funding is reviewed and approved, the approved budget can be distributed through the organizational hierarchy to investment measures to record and monitor transactional activities related to the investment initiative. Throughout the life of investment projects, real-time information can be obtained through standard reports, and real-time budget controls can be implemented using budget availability checks.

After investments are capitalized to fixed assets, asset accounting supports business transactions, such as acquisitions, retirements, transfers, adjustment of capitalized values, and depreciation values. Several ancillary functions support analysis and valuation of fixed asset data for management, audit, insurance, and tax purposes. In addition, a variety of reports are available, including country-specific reports, to meet asset reporting requirements for management, accounting, and tax purposes. Now, let's look closely at the specific functions of investment management and asset accounting.

Functions in Detail

You can use the comprehensive functionality available investment management for planning, financing, and capitalizing investment projects. After investments have been capitalized to assets, you can use asset accounting to support end-to-end business processes required for managing assets. So let's look at the functionality available to support each stage of this process, starting with investment programs.

Investment Programs

You use investment programs to plan and monitor capital investments and other projects in your corporate group. Investment programs represent business initiatives for capital investments in a corporation, but because capital-planning processes can vary widely, SAP provides

Capital planning process

a highly flexible way to organize investment projects in a hierarchical structure.

Hierarchical Structure

Investment programs are organized in a multilevel hierarchical tree structure, allowing you to create a hierarchy that matches the capital planning process of your business. For example, a multinational electronics manufacturer can create a hierarchy to correspond to its country headquarters, various company locations, and plants; or a software development company can create its hierarchy based on industry verticals and the size of project investments.

 Warning

You can create an investment program hierarchy that is 99 levels deep. However, before you get carried away, you may want to consider its impact on system performance.

Approval year An investment program is always assigned an approval year, which is the year the investment budget was approved. This budget may be used in the approval year, in subsequent years, or not at all. However, the approval year forms an integral part of the investment program definition. If the program continues to the next fiscal year, you can keep the program definition as is and copy it to the new approval year. This unique design allows you to compare the capital spending of a certain year with that of the budget approval year.

During the life of an investment program, it may undergo many changes, such as being transferred from one cost center/company to another. Likewise, investment programs may correspond to capital investments in multiple companies. SAP handles this type of complexity by providing you with the program position of an investment program.

Program Position

The *program position* represents a node in the investment program hierarchy, and it links an investment program to organizational units, such as company, plant, and so on. The topmost node in an investment program hierarchy is called *top position*, under which you can create as many lower-level positions as required. Different program positions in a hierarchy can correspond to different companies, profit centers, plants, or other organizational units. For example, a manufacturing company represented by a top-level investment program can have lower-level positions representing investment programs in its plants. These organizational assignments are time-dependent, so that you can easily handle changes such as an investment program being transferred from one plant to another.

The positions of investment programs play an important role in the hierarchy because company, plant, controlling area, and other organizational units from investment projects at one position in the hierarchy (e.g., for company code) are defaulted to its lower-level positions (e.g., plants). In addition, you can associate investment priority, investment reason, and any other classification criteria with program positions for reporting purposes. This combination of investment program definition and investment program position enables you to make the investment program hierarchy as simple or as complex as necessary.

Default organizational units

You can create investment programs that correspond to capital investments in multiple companies, as long as the companies share the same fiscal year, functional currency, and controlling area. The controlling area is discussed in Chapter 10, but basically, it represents an organizational unit from a cost-controlling viewpoint.

Now that we've discussed how the capital planning process is supported from an organizational viewpoint, let's move on to another important business process: request for capital funding.

Appropriation Requests

During the capital planning process, individual units in the companies (cost centers, profit centers, plants, etc.) submit their capital funding requests, which are used as input for capital spending decisions. These capital funding requests are created as appropriation requests.

Appropriation requests are created for investments when the costs involved are high, and capital planning and approval is required. Corporate policy determines the threshold over which appropriation requests should be created (e.g., for expenditures over $5,000). SAP provides a complete range of functions for creating, processing, approving, monitoring, and analyzing appropriation requests. Let's start at the beginning, the creation of an appropriation request, by looking at the data captured in one.

Appropriation Request Data

SAP supports several methods of creating and maintaining appropriation requests. You can choose any method depending on operational convenience, available information and your corporate policy. For example, for smaller projects, project managers can use a single program to create detailed appropriation requests that contain all required information; whereas for larger projects, project planners may use one program to create appropriation requests with only general information, and later on project managers may use another program to update those requests with relevant financial information.

A detailed and complete appropriation request can contain the following information:

> Reference to the investment program, if applicable

> Organizational units (company, cost center, etc.) requesting the investment and responsible for carrying out the investment activity

> Parameters such as investment reasons, investment priority, investment scale, and other classification parameters that can be used for reporting and analysis

> People involved with the request, such as the applicant, approver, and so on

> Expected costs and revenues and any pre-investment analysis information

Appropriation request approval process

Corporate policy determines the number of approvals required after appropriation requests are created. Using the status management functionality, any type of sophisticated approval process can be implemented. Status management allows you to control different stages of appropriation requests, such as creation, ready for approval, approved or rejected, released for processing, and so on. Using this design, you can gain visibility into appropriation requests at different stages of the approval process and also ensure that only approved appropriation requests are turned into actual projects.

We need to discuss two important features of appropriation requests: the appropriation request variants used to analyze investment alternatives and the information available in appropriation requests for pre-investment analysis.

Investment Alternatives

You have already seen that it's necessary to specify the expected costs and revenues while creating an appropriation request. But what if there is more than one alternative for fulfilling the same requirement? You have two options to handle such scenarios.

The first option is to create a different appropriation request for each alternative. One of the requests is designated as the original appropriation request, and the other requests maintain references to that number. For reporting purposes, these requests can be evaluated together based on the original request number. This option is relevant if different organizational units are involved, for example, a pharmaceutical corporation evaluating investment requirements of a drug research project by its two different research companies.

The second option is to evaluate alternatives using appropriation request variants (see Figure 6.2). An appropriation request variant contains expected costs, revenues, and other information for one alternative. Every appropriation request has at least one variant. To represent more than one alternative, you create multiple appropriation request variants. An example of this is a pharmaceutical company evaluating investment requirements of a drug research project based on two different methodologies. In this option, organizational units such as company, cost center, and so on remain the same, but different descriptive details, project deadlines, assessment information, and pre-investment analysis can be entered for different variants.

Appropriation request variants

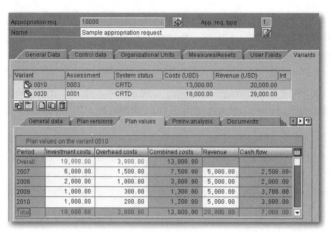

Figure 6.2 Appropriation Request Variants

Pre-investment Analysis

Pre-investment analysis refers to different information provided in an appropriation request about the viability of an investment approach. For example, you can enter a text comment to describe the subjective assessment of an investment alternative, or you can use a subjective score such as good, satisfactory, etc., to indicate your opinion of the investment alternative. You can also maintain other objective, empirical information such as payback period and internal rate of return (yield on invested capital) for an investment alternative.

Net present value and discounted cash flow

SAP also supports automatic calculation of net present value (NPV) and the discounted cash flow (DCF) rate based on expected costs and revenues provided in an appropriation variant. NPV calculation is a standard method for financial appraisal of long-term capital projects. It's a calculation of the difference between the present value of cash inflows and the present value of cash outflows over an investment time frame. Similarly, DCF is also a widely used method for evaluating an investment option. Under the DCF method, the present value of all future cash flows is calculated after discounting it for opportunity costs and risk adjustments.

A detailed discussion of these calculations is beyond the scope of this chapter, but you should be aware that these calculations use reference interest rates to calculate the possible return on capital that will be deployed for an investment option. And you can maintain annual interest rates in the form of a yield curve, which in turn is used to calculate NPV and DCF. If information about expected revenues isn't available, or if you choose not to use system calculations, you can also maintain NPV and DCF values directly in appropriation requests. After appropriation requests have been evaluated, approved, and released, they're converted into investment measures.

Investment Measures

Investment measures are used to manage capital investment projects and provide the ability to plan and monitor capital investments that aren't fully capitalized yet. Investment measures can be really complex (e.g., multi-year construction of a new manufacturing plant) or relatively simple (e.g., buying 30 computers over 6 months). In this chapter, we'll use the phrases investment measure (SAP terminology) and investment projects (common business terminology) interchangeably. Unlike appropriation requests and investment programs, there's no separate master data for investment measures. Rather, an investment measure is either an internal order or a WBS element of a project.

 Tip

See Chapter 10 and Chapter 11, respectively, for more details on SAP functionality of internal orders and projects.

Internal Orders and Projects

Internal orders (also called overhead cost orders) provide functionality to plan for, collect, and settle costs of relatively simple activities, such as the earlier example of buying 30 computers. On the other hand, projects are used to manage very large and complex initiatives that have precisely defined goals and specific time-bound deadlines, and consume considerably more resources, such as the earlier example of constructing a plant. A project is represented by a multilevel task structure with different tasks broken down into Work Breakdown Structure Elements (WBS elements). Both internal orders and

WBS elements of projects can be used as investment measures for investment programs. Which one is used depends on business requirements, operational convenience, and existing infrastructure. You may want to get familiar with both SAP components before deciding whether your investment initiatives can be best represented by internal orders, projects, or a combination of both.

Shared investment projects

These investment measures capture transactional activities occurring in investment projects, and investment measures corresponding to one investment program can be in different currencies or even different companies. For more complex requirements, you can assign a percentage allocation of one investment measure to multiple companies or even multiple investment program positions. This can be useful if, for example, multiple companies are sharing the costs of a project, such as a statutory compliance project. Standard reports automatically break down budget, plan, and actual values according to these percentages.

Investment measures allow you to collect inflows of costs to investment projects, from purchase orders, production orders, overhead costs, and so on, and to settle these costs so that they are capitalized, expensed, or reported on a balance sheet in a Construction In Progress (CIP) account. All costs collected on an investment project that are neither capitalized nor expensed are reported as CIP on a balance sheet statement. The object used to capture these cost inflows and settlement outflows of an investment measure is called an Asset under Construction (AuC).

Asset Under Construction (AuC)

Creation of an AuC

An AuC acts as a link between your investment projects and fixed assets. AuCs are special types of assets even though the standard fixed asset transactions available can be used to manage AuCs. Although AuC assets contain depreciation parameters, these assets are not actually depreciated. Instead, the parameters are used for depreciation simulation and reporting purposes. As discussed, AuC costs are shown as CIP in a separate balance sheet item. An AuC is automatically created when an investment measure (internal order or WBS element) is released so that there is one AuC for each investment measure.

However, if required, you can choose to link multiple investment measures to one AuC or split one investment measure into multiple AuCs. You'll want to choose one of these approaches based on your depreciation simulation requirements.

Typically, an investment measure and an AuC are created in the same company; however, there are exceptions to this. Let's consider a business scenario where capital investment projects are managed by one company, but the resulting final assets are owned by a different company. If you specify different companies as the requesting company and the responsible company in an appropriation request, the investment measures are created in the one identified as the responsible company, whereas AuCs (and final assets) are created in the one identified as the requesting company. SAP provides this design flexibility so that you can create final fixed assets independent of capital investment projects. Let's now discuss transaction flows from investment measures to assets.

Postings and Settlement

Investment measures, such as internal orders or WBS elements, record actual costs from several sources. These costs can result from postings in Financial Accounting, allocation of overhead and other charges, or goods movements due to procurement or production. These costs are collected on investment measures in real time as the different transactions occur.

Every month, you analyze costs collected on active investment measures and capitalize them to AuCs. As you may remember, WBS elements in a project are structured in a hierarchy of tasks. So if there are costs accumulated on lower-level tasks in a project, you may have to first settle them (or accumulate them) to higher level tasks so that they can be settled to AuCs. So, AuCs serve as a cost collector to hold your costs until you're ready to finally set up fixed assets. From an accounting point of view, these costs are reported on balance sheets in a CIP account. When fixed assets are ready to be put in service, you can carry out the settlement process.

Capitalization to AuCs

Settlement options

The settlement process involves taking costs collected on AuCs and either capitalizing them to fixed assets or expensing them to cost centers. You may have to expense some costs if you determined that it was being incorrectly capitalized in the CIP account. Fortunately, you don't have to wait until the investment project is complete to settle costs from AuCs to final assets. For example, if you receive 5 out of 30 computers, you can start capitalizing and depreciating them immediately. The software supports several different ways for settling costs collected in AuCs to fixed assets. So, in our example, you can choose to capitalize costs by distributing the costs equally on 5 computer assets, or capitalize a specific percentage of costs on each asset, or even capitalize specific dollar amounts to each asset. The settlement process is extremely powerful and can be customized to meet the business requirements of any type of fixed assets capitalization.

Before we discuss fixed asset functionality, let's see how investment programs, appropriation requests, and investment measures all fit together into the capital planning and budgeting process.

Planning and Budgeting

Capital planning process

A typical capital planning process in a company starts with individual business units planning and requesting funding for their investment projects. These planned values are consolidated in a bottom-up planning process in higher-level business units within a company. For example, requested funding by plants is consolidated at the regional level, requested funding by regions is consolidated at the company level, and so on. Approval decisions are made so that requested funding is approved, rejected, or partially funded in the form of an approved budget. Finally, approved budget dollars are allocated in a top-down distribution process to business units at lower levels. For example, an approved budget for a company is allocated to regions, and an approved budget for a region is allocated to plants.

> **Tip**
>
> This section only discusses planning and budgeting of capital invest-
> ments. Planning and budgeting for revenues and expenses are discussed
> in Chapter 14.

As shown in Figure 6.3, you'll have support for both your bottom-up planning processes and your top-down budgeting processes for capital investments. So, let's look at these processes in more detail.

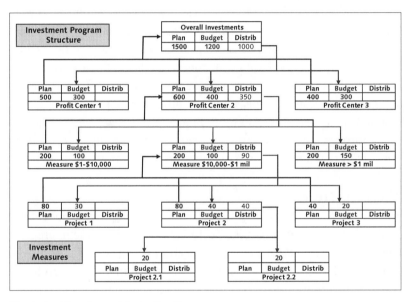

Figure 6.3 Planning and Budgeting Process

Planning Process

As discussed, when you create an appropriation request, you must enter expected or planned costs. If there are multiple alternatives, you'll have to create appropriation request variants for each alternative and then enter planned values separately for each variant. When investment measures are created from appropriation requests, these planned values are automatically copied from specified appropriation request variants. You can also enter plan values directly for individual investment measures, which can be especially useful if an investment project is already active, and you have to plan for more funding.

Because appropriation requests and investment measures are already assigned to organizational units, plan values can be easily consolidated and reported by plant, company, or any other level in your corporate hierarchy. During the planning process, you can roll up planned values to higher-level investment program positions to obtain an overview of funding requested by lower-level business units.

Plan versions
Occasionally, capital planning processes go through multiple cycles where plan values are revised and investment alternatives are reevaluated. To deal with this, you can repeat the roll up of planned values to replace old planned values in the hierarchy with new values, or you can create multiple plan versions to evaluate different alternatives. Both investment measures and investment programs support multiple plan versions. After funding requests have been reviewed and approved, and the planning process has been completed, the next step is to carry out top-down distribution of the approved budget.

Budgeting Process

Top-down budget distribution
During the budgeting process, you enter the approved budget for different investment program positions in the investment program hierarchy, starting with the top node and ending with the approved budget for investment measures (i.e., the actual investment projects). SAP ensures that approved budgets for lower-level positions in the investment hierarchy don't exceed approved budgets for higher-level positions. For example, the combined approved budget for all plants cannot be greater than the approved budget for the company they belong to. You can extend this budget control further and enforce in the system that individual projects can receive their approved budgets only from corresponding investment program positions in the hierarchy. For example, you can require that the combined approved budget for all of the plant's projects does not exceed the budget approved for that plant as a whole.

However, it's not always possible or practical to control budget approvals for investment projects using this method. For example, a budgeting process may approve budget dollars before any actual investment projects have been identified. For such cases, SAP enables you to budget individual investment projects separately and independent of the approved budget for the corresponding plant or company. If you choose this approach, you should periodically compare budgeted values on investment projects with the approved budget of the corresponding plant or a company.

 Tip

Investment programs differentiate between three different plan and budget values: values for the current approval year, values carried forward from previous approval years, and forecasted values for future approval years.

Another unique feature of the budgeting process is the support for managing different types of budgets identified by budget categories. By using different budget categories, you can manage separate budgets for costs that can be capitalized and incidental costs that are not capitalized. Note that even though budget management by budget categories is supported for investment programs, it isn't supported for investment measures. You can only approximate the division of approved budget by assigning percentages to budget categories. To divide actual costs by budget categories, you can get fairly accurate results by determining whether costs were settled (via AuCs) to fixed assets or to cost centers.

Budget categories

Now that you understand how budget distributions from investment program positions to investment measures are controlled, let's discuss how to control the available budget for individual investment projects.

Availability Control

Availability control is how you compare, in real time, actual costs posted to an investment project with a corresponding approved budget. Imagine an IT project approved for $12,000 for the purchase of 10 computers. Without any real-time checks in the system, the actual purchase order could be placed for more expensive computers and the project could end up costing $18,000.

By using availability control, you can determine what, if any, action to take for budget control. You can choose to display a warning message, send an email (e.g., to the project manager), or prevent the posting when total actual costs on an investment project reach a certain percentage of the approved budget. The extremely comprehensive budget availability check monitors the available budget in real time as costs are posted to an investment project by journal entries, goods issues from the warehouse, payroll postings, overhead costs, and through purchase requisitions and purchase orders. However, the availability check in the purchasing process is slightly different from other entries.

Commitment
management

First, when purchase requisitions or purchase orders are created for an investment project, actual costs haven't yet been incurred. Secondly, the actual cost of the purchase is known only when the vendor invoice is received, and it may be different from the cost mentioned in the purchase order. However, there is a potential that costs mentioned in a purchase order will be incurred in the future for that investment project. The software checks these costs by using commitment management. When commitment management is activated, potential costs indicated in purchase requisitions and purchase orders reduce the available budget for the investment projects. When a vendor invoice for a purchase order is received, commitments for corresponding investment projects are reduced, and actual costs are increased. While checking for the available budget, SAP keeps track of actual costs that have incurred on an investment project, even if some of those costs have been already capitalized to fixed assets.

So far, we've discussed how to plan, manage, and capitalize investment projects. In the remainder of the chapter, we'll take a look at managing fixed assets and other asset accounting processes.

Structuring Fixed Assets

In today's complex and global corporate environment, an asset management system needs to meet several requirements in parallel. From an organizational viewpoint, you need to manage assets by companies, plants, locations, and so on. For accounting purposes, you must be able to depreciate those same assets in multiple ways. And for reporting, you need to group similar types of assets (e.g., vehicles, equipment, and computers) and report their current values regardless of where they are located and how they are depreciated. The software not only provides comprehensive asset management functionality to meet such requirements, but it also seamlessly integrates this information with other SAP applications.

Even though most of our discussion focuses on fixed assets, the asset accounting component can also be used for many other types of assets. For example, it can be used to manage goodwill (intangible assets), treasury instruments (financial assets), assets rented on capital or operating lease (leased assets), plant machinery (technical assets), investment subsidies (negative assets), assets that are not depreciated in accounting but require tracking for physical inventory (low-value assets), and even real estate that uses the same, consistent user interface. Let's first consider structuring assets from an organizational perspective.

Types of assets

Organizational Viewpoint

The asset class represents the classification of assets by type, such as vehicles, machines, buildings, and so on. You can create as many types of asset classes as necessary. For example, a transportation company may create a large number of asset classes for different types of vehicles; an investment company may use different asset classes for fine arts, bullion, and so on, whereas other companies may not create any asset classes of these types. The asset class is extremely important because it controls many factors, such as asset numbering, calculating different types of depreciation, determining depreciation and asset capitalization, GL accounts, and so on.

GL account determination

In the software, assets are always assigned to a company code for calculating and posting depreciation. In addition, you can improve tracking and reporting by linking assets to plant, cost center, location, and even employee number. All these assignments are time-dependent, so any change in cost center, location, or employee ownership of an asset over a period of time can be easily managed. True to its design, the asset accounting component is completely integrated with plant maintenance, real estate, and other SAP applications. This means, for example, that you can link individual machines in a plant to corresponding assets in Asset accounting so that information between assets and machines can be automatically synchronized; or you can capitalize costs incurred for maintenance of a machine directly to a corresponding fixed asset.

Complex assets   A *complex asset* with numerous components can be created by using subassets (components of main assets). This is helpful because you can depreciate and post asset transactions directly to these subassets. For example, if an asset represents a building, subsequent major building improvements can be created as its subassets. On the other hand, if required for business or statutory reasons, you can use group assets to depreciate a number of assets together as a group. The following section tells you more about the depreciation calculation from an accounting point of view. Figure 6.4 shows how all these different elements are used in setting up assets.

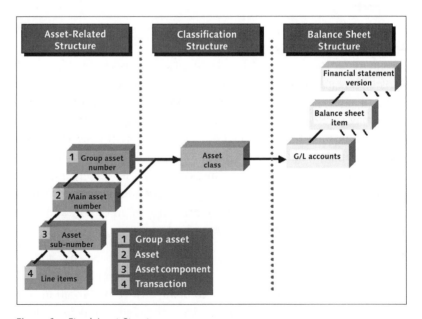

Figure 6.4 Fixed Asset Structure

Accounting Viewpoint

Typically, assets are subject to multiple types of depreciation calculations:

> For accounting books, assets are depreciated per local accounting rules or GAAP.

> For tax returns, they are depreciated differently for federal, local, and property taxes.

> For insurance purposes, they are depreciated based on their replacement values.

> For management, they may be depreciated so that the calculation also includes interest on tied up capital.

> For assets held by subsidiaries in different countries, assets are required to be depreciated differently for consolidation and possibly in different currencies.

The software enables you to easily meet these diverse requirements by using depreciation areas. A depreciation area represents depreciation calculation for specific purposes, such as GAAP, taxes, insurance, etc. You can create as many depreciation areas as required, group them into a chart of depreciation (ChoD), and link that ChoD to a company to ensure that all assets in that company are depreciated as required. So, for example, a global retailer can use multiple ChoDs for its companies located in different countries, where each ChoD consists of depreciation areas that meet local requirements as well as consolidation requirements. A depreciation calculation for accounting purpose is always calculated in and posted from Depreciation Area 01.

Depreciation areas and chart of depreciation

 Tip

Typically, you can use the same ChoD for all companies located in a country. ChoD templates are provided for more than 25 countries.

For every combination of asset class and depreciation area, you have to specify two important parameters: depreciation key and useful life. The depreciation key specifies how depreciation is calculated, such as a straight-line method, a declining balance method, and so on. On the

Depreciation key

other hand, the useful life of an asset represents the time frame over which the asset is depreciated. This unique way of specifying depreciation rules enables you to depreciate an asset using different methods simultaneously, over different useful lives for different purposes. For example, a construction company can depreciate construction equipment for accounting purposes over three years using a straight-line method and simultaneously depreciate it for tax purposes over five years using a declining balance method.

Types of depreciation

For every depreciation area, you can control which of the three types of depreciation can be calculated:

> **Ordinary depreciation**
> This type represents regular wear and tear of an asset.

> **Unplanned depreciation**
> This is used to post unplanned depreciation to an asset (e.g., damage to a plant due to a heavy flood).

> **Special depreciation**
> This can be used to depreciate assets due to special events or regulations (e.g., economic stimulus act passed in the United States).

Typically, assets are depreciated using the same fiscal year that the company uses. If you need to, however, you can depreciate assets over different fiscal years. This may be necessary if the fiscal year of a company is from April to March, but for tax purposes, assets should be depreciated from January to December. This may also be necessary if assets are required to be depreciated using the mid-quarter rule as is the case in the United States.

After you have set up a ChoD, depreciation areas, asset classes, and the required structure, you're ready to process asset transactions.

Asset Transactions

All asset-related business processes, ranging from asset acquisitions to asset retirements are supported with the software. But before we get into the details of asset transactions, you need to know two terms: transaction type and asset value date.

The *transaction type* in asset accounting is used to identify different business transactions. Over 100 different transaction types are supported, such as asset acquisition from a vendor or another group company, asset retirement with revenue or without revenue, asset transfer to a group company, and so on. By classifying asset transactions at such a detailed level, the asset accounting software is able to provide highly integrated functions (e.g., you can easily identify an asset transfer between group companies for consolidation) and some of the most comprehensive reports. In most of the asset accounting transactions, the appropriate transaction type is determined or defaulted to.

Transaction type

The *asset value date* is another unique and important concept in asset accounting. It identifies the date on which asset values are changed, which can be different from the date on which GL account balances are updated. Consider this example:

Asset value date

 Example

> A garment manufacturer realizes during the quarter-end audit in October, that, in July, the costs of repairing a machine should have been capitalized, but they were incorrectly expensed. Obviously, accounting books for July can't be reopened to make this adjustment, but for accurate depreciation calculation, this correction should be effective from July.

In the software, you can meet both of these requirements by creating an entry with a posting date in October and an asset value date in July.

Each asset transaction contains a transaction type and an asset value date regardless of whether they were posted automatically or manually. Now, let's take a look at some common asset transactions.

Common Asset Transactions

The flexible design of the asset accounting component gives you many ways to carry out common asset transactions such as acquisitions and retirements. For example, as you saw earlier, you can collect costs on purchase orders and investment measures and then capitalize those costs to fixed assets. A variation of this process involves creating a purchase order. Instead of associating it with an investment measure, you can directly associate it with an asset in asset accounting. In this case, asset acquisition is typically recorded when the goods receipt against the purchase order is posted. Similarly, you can post asset capitalization based on a goods issue from your warehouse inventory. This can be useful, for example, if you use inventory parts to replace or repair assets, and if inventory costs need to be capitalized.

Direct acquisitions and retirements

You can also post asset acquisition accounting entries directly in asset accounting. To post asset acquisitions, you can directly debit an asset using a specific posting key (discussed in Chapter 2), and a post offsetting credit to the vendor account or the clearing account depending on integration between your AP and asset accounting processes. If these processes are closely integrated, you can post vendor payables and asset acquisition in a single entry, or you can use a clearing account for offsetting entries from asset acquisitions and vendor payables. Similarly, when assets are sold to customers, you can post asset retirements by directly crediting an asset and debiting a customer account or a clearing account. The software automatically calculates and posts any gain or loss based on the remaining book value of the asset (the difference between acquisition cost and accumulated depreciation).

SAP ERP Financials also easily handles asset transfers between cost centers, plants, or even across companies. For example, you can transfer assets between companies at net book value or with details of original cost and accumulated depreciation. Before we continue talking about another important process of depreciation calculation, it's important to note that asset retirements and asset transfers can be carried out for a complete asset or for a partial value of an asset.

Depreciation Calculation

The depreciation calculation in SAP is different from other systems in that the process is completely customizable—you can even choose how frequently it's done: monthly, quarterly, annually, or any frequency you prefer. Figure 6.5 shows some control parameters for depreciation calculation.

Calculation process

During the depreciation calculation, the system first calculates year-to-date depreciation for an asset based on its current book value and current depreciation method; it then compares the calculation with the year-to-date depreciation that was actually posted and calculates the difference between the two as depreciation that needs to be posted. One benefit of this method of depreciation calculation is that it automatically takes into account any value corrections or changes made during the year.

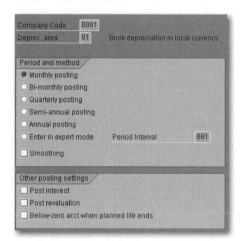

Figure 6.5 Depreciation Control Parameters

So, for example, if the depreciation method was changed in July, during a subsequent depreciation run, the process will use the new depreciation method as if it was changed in January (assuming the fiscal year begins in January). If an asset is determined to be under-depreciated or over-depreciated, the process automatically calculates and posts the depreciation correction to ensure that during a fiscal year, an asset is depreciated using the same method.

If an asset is deemed under-depreciated or over-depreciated during the depreciation calculation process, there are two possible options for posting a depreciation correction. You can distribute the depreciation correction over the remaining open periods of the fiscal year (the smoothing method), or you can post the entire depreciation correction in one month (the catch-up method). You should choose which method to use based on the applicable accounting rules and corporate policies. SAP ERP Financials ensures that the depreciation process can be carried out only per the schedule specified, which means that if the depreciation frequency is configured as monthly, you can't skip a month between depreciation runs unless you specifically designate it

Catch-up method versus smoothing method

as an unplanned depreciation run. However, if asset values change after a scheduled depreciation run, you can repeat a depreciation run.

Posting depreciation

The posting of depreciation expenses is handled in a rather unique way. By default, the depreciation expense is posted to the cost centers associated with the assets. However, you also have the option to collect depreciation costs on an internal order (discussed in Chapter 10) and settle it as required. For example, by using internal orders to collect depreciation costs, you can post depreciation to other projects or orders, or distribute it across multiple cost centers. By default, depreciation is posted to the new GL from Depreciation Area 01. You have to use a different program if you need to post depreciation from other depreciation areas. In the next section, we'll focus on other types of business transactions and assets.

Additional Functionality

So far we've only discussed functionality for processing typical business transactions for capitalized fixed assets. However, as we've already discussed in this section, the asset accounting functionality supports many other types of business transactions and assets.

Other Transactions

Postcapitalization process

Apart from acquisitions, retirements, transfers, and depreciations, many other business transactions can take place in asset accounting. For example, consider a multiyear construction project of an automotive manufacturing plant. Because such an endeavor is so complex, it's possible that after plant construction is complete, you'll realize that some costs or some assets should have been capitalized in previous years that are now already closed for accounting. You can use the post-capitalization process to capitalize an amount from any date from previous, closed fiscal years. And, asset accounting calculates the total depreciation amount and the useful life from the capitalization date and distributes the depreciation over the remaining open periods of the current fiscal year and future years.

Another common business process is receiving credit memos from vendors due to price adjustments, revisions, or corrections. These credit memos effectively reduce the acquisition cost of an asset and thus impact the depreciation calculation. Similar to the process discussed before, you can use direct accounting entries to post a credit to an asset and a debit to a vendor account or a clearing account. If the credit memo is posted in the same fiscal year as the asset was acquired, the depreciation calculation automatically adjusts to take into account the effect of this credit. However, if an asset was acquired in prior fiscal years, the system can't automatically correct the depreciation calculated in prior years. For such cases, you have to use the *write-up process*.

Typically, the write-up process is used to increase the book value of an asset. The best part about the write-up process is that it's completely flexible. Using the same program, you can post a write-up (increase in book value) or a write-down (decrease in book value) of an asset. You can post different write-up (or write-down) amounts in different depreciation areas and for different types of depreciation, such as ordinary, special, or unplanned depreciation. Additionally, numerous control parameters that can influence the depreciation calculation are provided. For example, you can specify:

Depreciation calculation control parameters

> Scrap value or scrap percentage so that an asset isn't depreciated below a certain amount

> Maximum amount limit on annual/accumulated depreciation

> Whether date specifications and controls are based on fiscal year or calendar year

> Whether the depreciation calculation should start from the beginning, middle, or end of a period (i.e., beginning of the next period), where a period can be a month, a quarter, or a year

> Whether the calculation should change to a different method when certain conditions are met, such as if the net book value of an asset is less than a specified amount or more than a specified percentage, if a specified number of years has passed, if the end of useful life has been reached, and so on.

In fact, there are too many parameters to list them all here, but note that you can access numerous parameters to customize and control the depreciation calculation. Let's discuss more complex business processes in asset accounting.

Additional Scenarios

Leased assets   A fairly common business requirement is managing leased assets, a special form of rented assets. During the lease period, the company owning the asset receives lease payments from the company using the asset. Most of the lease-relevant information, such as the number of lease payments, payment cycle, lease factor/interest rate, lease installment, and lease agreement details are maintained in the asset master. And, both the capitalization of lease payments (capital lease) and the expensing of lease payments (operating lease) are supported. For a capital lease, liabilities for lease payments are automatically created; whereas for an operating lease, you have to manually create documents in the new GL to represent lease payments.

Companies also commonly insure their assets to protect their investment. There is comprehensive functionality for reporting and valuating assets for insurance purposes. And using the asset master, for reporting and analysis purposes, you can maintain information such as insurance company, type of insurance (e.g., replacement value, market value), insurance premium, and so on. There is also support for revaluation of the asset base for insurance purposes by index series for annual revaluation.

Investment subsidies   In addition, all business activities for requesting, receiving, monitoring, and repaying investment subsidies are supported. Investment subsidies are received for capital-intensive, long-term investment projects typically in government, from government, and for government work. An investment subsidy is represented by an investment support measure. Figure 6.6 shows an example of an investment support for $100,000 for calendar year 2006. SAP also supports distributing the subsidy amount over multiple years, so that, for example, a city contractor can receive a five-year subsidy ($20,000 per year) for maintaining roads and bridges, and the limit can be checked annually or cumulatively, depending on whether the unused subsidy can be carried over to the next year.

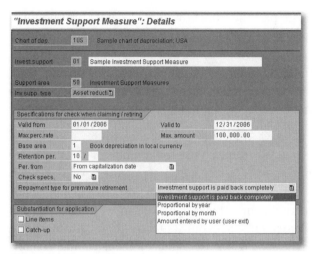

Figure 6.6 Investment Support Measure

Many subsidies (e.g., for investments made in ailing public-sector initiatives) stipulate a time period during which investment can't be sold or retired. You can also monitor investment support during the retention period and handle subsidy repayments in several ways if investments are retired during the retention period. How you configure the system determines the GL accounts posted during the different business transactions.

Before we end this chapter, let's look at the reporting capability of the investment management and asset accounting components.

Reporting

One of the unique features of investment management is that it allows you to use the *summarization database* for reporting. You can still run reports based on your database that stores transactional details, but the summarization database offers distinct benefits. For instance, reports created on the summarization database run faster, you can combine investment data from multiple SAP or non-SAP systems into it (a big advantage for decentralized corporations using multiple systems), and you can create multiple data versions to serve as snapshots of investment data at different points in time. Using multiple versions not only lets you see changes in investment data over time, but it

Summarization database

also lets you recreate past investment reports, even if corresponding appropriation requests and other objects have been deleted from the system. For example, you can create one summarization version per month or per quarter to obtain a snapshot of investment data. Note that a report from the investment management system can be based on either an online database or a summarization database—but never both.

Apart from these, reports to trace the capitalization of costs from investment measures to fixed assets are also provided. These reports show individual entries posted to fixed assets from investment measures and let you drill down to the original documents, such as goods receipt or order settlement, that contributed to the asset acquisition costs. These reports can be really useful during an audit. Additionally, many standard investment management reports are available so that you can:

> Analyze the overall and annual plan number for appropriation requests, regardless of whether they are associated with investment programs

> Compare the overall and annual plan and budget values for investment programs, program positions, appropriation requests, and investment measures

> Compare the plan and budget values of an investment program position with associated appropriation requests and investment measures

> Compare the overall, distributed, and remaining budget for the current year, previous years, and future years for an investment program position with associated investment measures

> Analyze available budget and commitments by program positions, investment measures, plants, companies, and other organizational units

> Analyze budget comparisons and distribution by budget categories, approved versus remaining budget, reasons for investment, etc.

Multiple currencies in Investment Management

At this point, it's important to discuss how to handle multiple currencies in investment management reports. In a global company, it's very likely that appropriation requests, investment measures, and even program positions in an investment hierarchy will monitor, report, plan, and budget values in different currencies. You can run investment management reports in any currency, as long as corresponding currency exchange rates are maintained. If the available data is in a different currency, it's translated into the reporting currency when the report is run. So, a steel-processing company based in North America can prepare investment management reports in U.S. dollars, even if its subsidiaries have submitted appropriation requests in Mexican Pesos, or their investment measures are in Brazilian Reais.

If depreciation methods for forecast simulation are maintained on investment measures, you can create reports to forecast future depreciation that will give you consolidated future depreciation numbers from both planned investments and capitalized assets. Planned investment values for the future that are not yet directly assigned to individual cost centers can be allocated using percentage distribution rules. For example, a mining company in the United States may have planned a three-year investment for OSHA compliance. For the depreciation forecast, the company can maintain percentage rules that distribute this amount by cost centers, by asset classes, or by years (e.g., 45 % in the first year, 35 % in the second year, and 20 % in the third year). The depreciation simulation program is sophisticated enough to avoid double counting, by eliminating current year capitalization values from the planned values.

Depreciation forecast

 Tip

In addition to reports available in the investment management component of SAP, you can also use numerous reports available in internal orders and the project system component.

For capitalized assets, asset accounting provides many standard reports to report asset balances by different criteria, such as companies, cost centers, plants, asset types, and so on. Similarly, transaction activity reports provide asset acquisitions, retirements, transfers, manual depreciation entries, and other details. Using asset worklists, you can easily and efficiently process mass changes, mass retirements, or mass transfers for hundreds of assets. Additional reports are also available to meet country-specific requirements, such as the Mid-Quarter rule report for the United States, property tax and transport tax reports for Russia, and many others.

Asset history sheet Lastly, an extremely powerful, customizable asset report called the asset history sheet is provided. This report shows the fixed asset history for a year, in a structured layout, from its opening balance to the closing balance by means of acquisitions, retirements, transfers, and depreciation. You can create as many versions of an asset history sheet as required. Each version consists of a grid like structure (see Figure 6.7) in which, for each cell, you can allocate one or more transaction type groups (discussed earlier). This design gives you the complete flexibility of creating asset reports for statutory, management, or audit purposes.

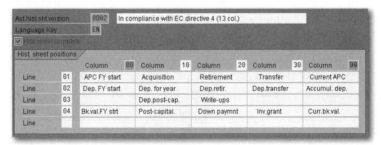

Ast.hist.sht.version	0002	In compliance with EC directive 4 (13 col.)		
Language Key	EN			
☑ Hist.sheet complete				

Hist. sheet positions

		Column 00	Column 10	Column 20	Column 30	Column 99
Line	01	APC FY start	Acquisition	Retirement	Transfer	Current APC
Line	02	Dep. FY start	Dep. for year	Dep.retir.	Dep.transfer	Accumul. dep.
Line	03		Dep.post-cap.	Write-ups		
Line	04	Bk.val.FY strt	Post-capital.	Down paymnt	Inv.grant	Curr.bk.val.
Line						

Figure 6.7 Asset History Sheet

Let's now look at an example of how a water utility company used investment management to streamline its capital investment processes.

Case Study

In this case study, we'll look at the second largest privately held water utility company in the United States. The client was located in a northern state and engaged in the purchase, production, and distribution of water. It had contracts with local city governments to distribute water primarily to more than 250,000 homes and businesses located in 223 communities and the surrounding environment. The company owned several large wells that provided more than 65,000 gallons of water per day. A large maintenance department within the company was responsible for the 173 miles of pipelines and other essential infrastructure. The company also provided services to neighboring states and municipalities for exploration of untapped groundwater, water marketing, and other supporting services.

Business Challenge

For the majority of the past decade, the company survived on very low capital investments. However, the aging infrastructure made it difficult to retain a customer base in an increasingly competitive market. It was difficult for the maintenance department to ensure that pipelines and the water infrastructure were always operating in optimum conditions. Not surprisingly, these factors began to have negative effects on company financials.

The company had started spending money on setting up a new infrastructure and maintaining the existing infrastructure. Past experience with similar projects indicated that these types of projects were invariably met with schedule delays, quality control issues, and huge cost overruns. Because external vendors carried out many activities of these projects, it was becoming difficult to manage costs. Even though the company used SAP software for its financials and procurement activities, processes for managing investments were completely offline and consisted of a large number of Excel spreadsheets. Due to these manual, resource-intensive processes, it was extremely difficult to get a timely and accurate financial status of a project. Usually, project costs were compiled and analyzed only after a project was finished, which meant that cost overruns were noticed after most of the contractors had already been paid for their services.

Additionally, top management did not have much visibility into projects initiated in response to service contracts for water exploration, marketing, and other services. Many of these contracts were performed as a partnership, and, as a result, any cost overrun directly impacted the contract profitability. The company was losing money on several contracts and, even worse, was realizing the cost overrun when it was too late-after the work had been completed.

Fortunately, management of the company decided that it was necessary to put better investment planning and budget monitoring processes in place, even if that meant postponing other initiatives and transferring money to the IT department for implementing investment management.

Solution Deployment

The organizational structure of the company was fairly simple, with only one company and two water-processing plants. Management decided to set up an investment program hierarchy based on investment objectives. Investment projects were structured based on whether the investment was for maintenance, expansion (new pipelines or infrastructure), exploration, or other services. After that decision was made, program positions were created to reflect the capital expense planning structure of the company, which consisted of division heads, area managers, and cost center managers.

The company organized a project team consisting of three full-time resources from the IT department and two people from each division representing the business side of the project. Even though Investment Management was a relatively new area for the IT team, they decided to use their existing system knowledge and augment it with additional training to complete the project in four months. This aggressive timeline created another challenge for company management: it meant that the project would go live in the middle of their January to December fiscal year. However, they decided to continue with the proposed timeline, realizing that although investment-planning processes could not be used until the next fiscal year, the benefits of budget monitoring would be realized immediately.

This decision also affected operational support and user training because many components of the system, such as fixed assets, internal orders (used for service contracts), and plant maintenance orders (used by the maintenance department) were already active, so business users were already familiar with the functionality.

The new functionality involved linking all these pieces together in a cohesive investment management planning structure and activating commitment management and budget approval functionality for budget monitoring. At the time of project go-live, approximately 437 initiatives of different sizes were in process. These initiatives were not very large volume in terms of data conversion, but they were still large enough to pose some challenges in terms of assigning those initiatives to the correct investment program positions in the hierarchy. The approved budget for the current year was entered in the system, and commitment management functionality was activated for all active projects.

Policies and procedures were put in place for the upcoming capital planning cycle so that every single investment initiative and planned service requests would be entered as appropriation requests at the appropriate organizational level. Business users would be trained over the next two months to create appropriation requests in the system and enter required details—particularly information about expected costs and revenue over the life of the initiative.

Value Achieved

The company saw immediate benefits. After doing data conversion, when the budget availability check was activated, they learned that 8 out of the 437 initiatives were already over the budget, and that another 23 initiatives were dangerously close to using up their approved budgets. Even before the project team had time to celebrate a successful go-live, company management was following up with project managers of those 31 projects by requesting status updates.

By activating the commitment management functionality, the process of budget monitoring now started at the time of placing purchase orders. Under the old process, it was possible for managers responsible for investment initiatives to place multiple purchase orders if there were delivery problems by their suppliers. This sometimes resulted in multiple deliveries of the same components and an excess of components that were never used. Under the new process, if the first purchase order uses up the approved budget, the managers are prevented from creating any additional purchase orders, thereby reducing surplus and sometimes unusable inventory.

Most important, management is able to receive accurate budget monitoring reports and to compare requested funding (plan), with approved budget and actual budget use. SAP reports are able to provide this information in real time to project managers by cost centers, divisions, and other criteria, thereby empowering project managers to take proactive actions for controlling project costs. This comparison information also gives upper-management visibility and insight and helps them identify managers and areas in the company that require additional support for project completion.

Looking Ahead

The immediate goal of the company is to use and stabilize investment-planning processes for the next capital planning cycle. After this, company management wants to focus on two areas related to capital investment projects: to improve efficiency and achieve better budgetary control.

During this project it became clear that many funding requests that made their way up in the organizational approval hierarchy would have been rejected at lower levels in the company; the company needed efficient and more formal processes in place for reviewing and approving funding requests. To address this need, the company would focus on SAP workflow to automate approvals of appropriation requests.

The company realized that purchasing processes were another area that needed improvement. The company did not use any formal, consistent process across all divisions for purchase order approvals, which in turn sometimes contributed to cost overruns of the projects. Therefore, another initiative in the project pipeline is implementation of the purchase requisitions component along with workflow in the SAP purchasing application. This initiative will ensure that purchase orders can't be created without approved purchase requisitions, thus improving budgetary controls.

Summary

In this chapter, we discussed end-to-end capitalization of the investments process from managing investment programs to final fixed assets. Following is a summary of investment management and asset accounting components discussed in this chapter.

> Create a hierarchical structure of investment programs that reflects the capital expenditure planning process of your corporate hierarchy.

> Evaluate investment alternatives using planning versions and appropriation request variants, and use a multilevel approval process for appropriation requests using workflow and status management.

> Easily obtain an overview of the planning and budgeting processes for all investment and large projects of the group while maintaining strict control over the approved budget.

> Distribute the approved budget to investment measures and monitor the available budget in real time using commitment management and budget availability checks.

> Use the highly customizable design to simultaneously calculate several types of depreciation for multiple purposes that meet local statutory requirements and consolidation requirements.

> Use the comprehensive functionality to carry out different types of business transactions during the life of an asset from acquisitions to retirements.

> Meet the business requirements of investment subsidies, leasing, insurance, and property taxes from single asset database.

In the next chapter, we'll discuss the travel management and travel accounting functionality in SAP ERP Financials.

7

Travel Management

Business travel is a large part of almost every company's budget. Employees have to travel for meetings, conferences, training, trade shows, retreats, customer visits, internal sales meeting, and a variety of other reasons. These trips are expensive and require timely reimbursement of the employee's costs and accurate accounting to the appropriate cost centers. Many companies also have to make travel arrangements and pay for the travel expenses of nonemployees such as contractors and consultants.

Even though you can process expense reimbursements through Accounts Payable (AP), it isn't always efficient, especially for large companies. For example, excessive expenses are identified only after the employee has already incurred those expenses. The AP personnel may not be able to determine the reasonableness of the expenses or may not be properly staffed to handle the detailed validation required for a large number of receipts.

To help employees comply with the company travel policy and to effectively manage travel costs, most companies have a formal travel policy that highlights acceptable reasons and expenses for business travel, along with a dedicated personnel or travel department which is responsible for making travel arrangements and validating expense

reimbursements. For companies seeking a complete travel management solution, the SAP Travel Management component can be the
answer. As you'll see, this component can be configured to meet any
combination of requirements your company may have.

Overview

The travel management component supports end-to-end business
processes for travel planning, travel booking, travel expense accounting, and expense reimbursement. Figure 7.1 provides an overview of
the functionality available for various business processes.

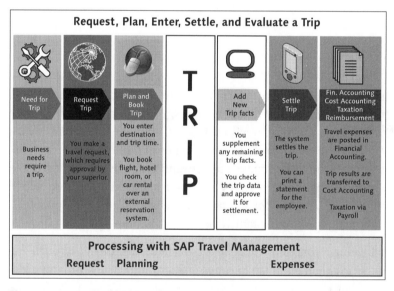

Figure 7.1 Overview of SAP Travel Management

Travel management
implementation
options

From a technical point of view, there are four different combinations
in which you can implement travel management.

> **Travel Expenses**
> You use this to record, reimburse, and report travel expenses.

> **Travel Planning and Travel Expenses**
> You use this for travel expenses and to carry out travel booking and
> reservations by integrating with the reservation systems.

> **Travel Requests and Travel Expenses**
> You use this for travel expenses and to record, track, and approve travel requests from your employees.

> **Travel Requests, Travel Planning, and Travel Expenses**
> You use all three components of travel management.

The travel request option allows your employees to make trip requests. These requests can be routed through an approval process for consideration. Enough information is captured in the travel request form to enable the approver to make a decision on the request, and information entered in the travel request can be forwarded for travel booking as well as creating the corresponding expense report.

With travel planning, you can also search through available fares and prices to make travel arrangements. And, you get functionality to improve internal compliance by setting up your own travel policy. For example, hotels with specially negotiated contracts can be given preference while still trying to accommodate travel preferences of the employee, right up to the preference of a nonsmoking room or an aisle seat. You can also use this policy to ensure travel expense compliance.

Travel expenses is the main component of the travel management component, and as discussed earlier, it can be implemented independently or in integration with other components. You can design travel expense forms to capture as much or as little information as required. In addition, expense details entered into a travel expense report can be validated for compliance, and exception reports can be created to highlight any noncompliance or exceptions. Of course, just like travel requests, you can choose to route expense reports through an approval process as well.

After an expense report is approved, it can automatically create accounting entries, ensuring that costs are posted to the proper GL accounts and cost centers. You can then choose to reimburse expenses directly to the traveler through AP (by check or direct deposit), through payroll, or by direct payment to a credit card company, if your employees use company-issued credit cards for travel expenses.

Postings and payments

Note

Implementing any travel management component requires maintaining some basic employee data in the employee mini master to differentiate it from the comprehensive employee master data required for HR or for processing payroll. Even for the employee mini master, information such as name, travel privileges, and so on is required, whereas information such as employee travel preferences is optional.

Let's move on to discuss the employee mini master and other key travel management functions.

Functions in Detail

In this section, we'll describe some of the major features of travel management using an employee mini master, travel requests and approvals, travel booking, travel expenses, expense accounting, and reimbursement, and compliance and reporting.

Employee Mini Master

Integration with SAP HCM

If you are using the SAP ERP Human Capital Management (HCM) and Payroll solutions, then your employees are already set up. In that case, you can easily extend the employee information for travel management. However, if you are not using SAP HCM, you have to create some basic information for each of your employees before you can start using travel management.

Infotypes

Different pieces of information about an employee are stored in an *infotype*. So, for example, an employee's personal data is stored in one infotype and travel preferences are stored in another. In addition, the employee's bank information is stored in another infotype for direct deposit of their pay and possibly expense reimbursements. For every employee, you have to maintain at least the following information:

> **Personal Data**
> This includes personal details such as name, gender, date of birth, nationality, marital status, and so on.

> **Organizational Assignment**
> This tells the software the different associations for the employee,

such as the company that the employee works for, the cost center the employee expenses are usually posted to, the job position that can be used to determine who the approver should be, and so on. This information is used by default when accounting entries for travel expenses are posted.

> **Travel Privileges**
This information specifies control parameters for the travel expense eligibility and reimbursement levels for the employee. These parameters provide important and necessary integration between HR and accounting.

> **Addresses**
This is where you can maintain different types of addresses for the employee, including home address, temporary address, mailing address, emergency address, and so on.

Some other pieces of information that you may want to maintain for each employee include the following:

> **Travel Profile**
Travel profiles improve the compliance with enterprise-specific travel policies, which we'll explain later. Although every employee should have a travel profile assigned, it doesn't have to be part of the employee master data. You can just let the software automatically determine travel profiles for employees based on specific criteria.

> **Communication**
Here you can maintain different communication details for the employee, such as the user login, phone numbers, email addresses, and other contact information.

> **Bank Details**
You can choose to maintain one or more bank accounts for different purposes: paycheck, deposit, expense reimbursement, and so on.

> **Cost Distribution**
If travel expenses of an employee are to be distributed across more than one cost center or more than one company, then that information is maintained along with other employee information. How-

Distribution of travel costs

ever, if this cost distribution is just for a one-off business trip or a specific expense, you can specify that information while creating the expense report without keeping it in the personnel data.

> **Flight/Hotel/Car Preferences**
This is optional information that you can maintain about the preferences of an employee, including preferred airline, preferred car rental company, automatic or manual auto transmission, smoking/nonsmoking room, window/aisle seat, and so on.

> **Customer Program**
This information pertains to travel reward programs offered by airlines, hotels, and car rental companies to which the traveler belongs. This information can be useful if the company travel policy requires travelers to transfer points/miles rewarded for business trips back to the company, so that you can use those points/miles toward other business trips in the future.

Because employee information can change at different times, and the data is valid for different timeframes, you are given a very versatile way of managing employee information. Figure 7.2 shows the different options available to maintain employee information.

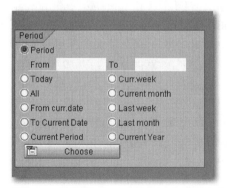

Figure 7.2 Date Options for Maintaining Employee Information

Vendor accounts for employees

If you are planning to carry out expense reimbursements using the AP component, then you'll also need to create a vendor account for every employee. This information is interlinked, that is, a vendor account maintains a link to the employee account and vice versa. And, you are given a sample program that you can use to synchronize information between vendor accounts and employee accounts automatically.

Travel Requests and Approvals

Travelers can submit all relevant and required trip data to obtain travel approval and travel booking by using travel requests. A travel request consists of the general trip data and transportation/accommodation requests.

Figure 7.3 shows a sample travel request entry screen. This screen may look complicated or crowded because it's been expanded to show as many sections as possible to give you an overview of all available features.

At the top, you'll see the General Trip Data section where you enter trip-specific details, such as the date and time of the requested trip, destination, and reason for the trip. If the trip requires traveling to more than one destination, you can enter those details under the Addnl Destinations section.

Multisegment trips

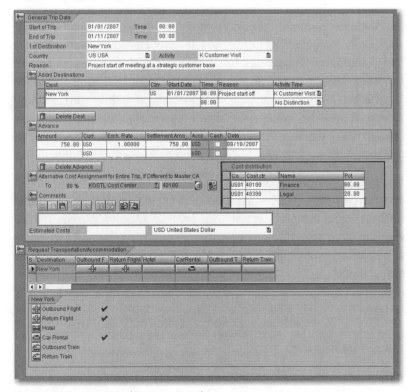

Figure 7.3 Entering Travel Request Details

By expanding the Advance subsection, you can enter details for any advance amount extended to the employee for the trip. This advance can be paid by the cash office or by AP, and of course, the advance can be in any currency.

If the trip costs have to be distributed across cost centers or even across companies, you can easily do so by specifying Alternative Cost Assignments for Entire Trip in which you specify the percentage of the distribution across cost centers and companies.

 Tip

You can specify cost distributions across cost centers or companies at three different levels: individual trips, individual expense receipts, or individual employees in the HR master data. This gives you the flexibility to distribute travel expenses at whichever level is more accurate for accounting and more efficient for data entry.

In addition, you have an option to maintain detailed Comments (possibly explaining the reason for the trip) as well as Estimated Costs at the level of the travel request. As far as transportation and accommodation requests are concerned, the individual creating the travel request has to enter only basic information, including start and end date, and destination city, and so on. For example, Figure 7.3 indicates that the traveler has requested a booking of an Inbound Flight, Outbound Flight, and Rental Car, but no hotel accommodations.

Approval of travel requests If the company policy requires such travel requests to be approved, that can be handled in several ways. You can set up the system so that no approval is required or only one level of approval is required, or you can setup an elaborate approval process using the SAP Workflow to require multiple approvals (e.g., if the trip cost is high or if the traveler is reporting to multiple managers). In any case, after the travel request is entered and approved, you are ready to carry out the travel booking.

Travel Booking

To book the travel easily, you can use the online booking functions in the travel planning component. These functions are integrated with connection to the global distribution system (GDS) that provide access to airline, hotel, and rental car providers for trip reservations. To use this functionality, you should have contractual agreements with the vendors and be able to connect with the reservation system. In addition, you have to set up the login details given by the reservation system.

The travel planning component can also be integrated with several major reservation systems. As of SAP ERP 6.0, integration with the following reservation systems is provided:

Integration with reservation systems

> AMADEUS

> SABRE

> Galileo

> HRS/Hotel Reservation System

> BIBE/Deutsche Bahn

 Warning

Synchronizing travel preferences for individual personnel isn't available with every reservation system. If this functionality is important to your company, you may want to refer to the documentation of the external system interface.

And, if necessary, you can develop your own interface programs using the SAP NetWeaver Exchange Infrastructure (SAP NetWeaver XI) technology to communicate with the reservation systems of other travel service providers, such as the reservation systems of lower cost carriers. You can synchronize with these reservation systems online for each travel plan, or you can schedule a background job offline.

So how can you use this functionality? Well, you can use it to enable travel planners to check whether travel services are available, get pricing information, and make travel reservations for airlines, rental car providers, and hotels.

Before you check on available flights and rooms and carry out reservations, you must create a *travel plan*. Each travel plan is given a unique trip number under which all travel bookings are done. If you have already created a travel request, you can create a travel plan based on that travel request and simple copy and paste the relevant information. To check the pricing and availability of transportation and accommodation options, the *Planning Manager* is provided. Figure 7.4 shows a sample screen where you can pull up the trip information entered into a travel request to check availability and booking.

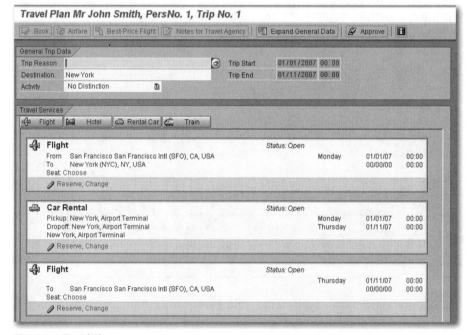

Figure 7.4 Travel Plan

Flight reservations using best-price query

Before carrying out any of the availability checks, you can modify a traveler's existing flight, hotel, or rental car travel preferences. These modifications will then be taken into account when checking the availability options.

The standard flight availability check uses a fixed price for each flight. However, if the trip includes a roundtrip, weekend stay, or any such factor that can influence flight pricing, you can use the *best-price query* available in the system. Travel planners can save their preferred query strategies (e.g., fewer connections or stopovers, roundtrip fares, etc.) for future travel planning.

Tip

> If your company has special agreements with certain hotels, or prefers particular hotels, you can create a hotel catalog specific to your company, containing all such hotels. If such a catalog is maintained and activated in the system, then any hotel availability search is done within this catalog first. If no rooms are available, the search is expanded to include other hotels.

You can set up the system so that after a travel plan has been entered, it requires approval from the manager or supervisor of the traveler. After the travel plan is approved, all necessary reservations can be made in the software, and the traveler is given the relevant information.

Travel Expenses

If you are using the travel planning component travel management, you can create an expense report based on the travel plan you already entered. If you are using only the travel expenses component, then you need to create an expense report in the system. In any case, you start preparing your travel expense report by entering the receipt details, which are then validated and subsequently reimbursed. In this section, we'll discuss how to enter travel expenses. Reimbursement and validation of expenses will be discussed later in this chapter.

As soon as you book a travel service online in the reservation system and save the travel plan, a corresponding receipt for the travel service is created in travel expenses. So if your trip details are checked for compliance with the company travel policy at the time of travel planning and travel booking, validating the expense report becomes easier. Another option is if you're using a corporate travel card or corporate credit card to pay for travel expenses, you can develop an interface to download credit card transaction details directly into the system. Some of the major credit card companies already provide such an interface to travel management.

Integration of travel planning and travel expenses

In addition, you are provided with several options for entering travel expenses, whether they are submitted for one-off business trips or company events; or they represent weekly expense reports submitted by consultants or employees who are always traveling. The option you use for entering travel expenses depends largely on your preference and convenience, as well as the program you used to create the travel plan. The level of details you can enter for each expense is the same in pretty much all the scenarios.

> **Travel Manager**
> This is the same program we discussed in the "Travel Planning" section. It can be used to create travel requests, travel plans, and expense reports. So it's more appropriate for, or at least targeted toward, the occasional user who has to enter an expense report.

> **Travel Expense Manager**
> This option gives you an overview of all trips for an employee in a tabular format. You can pick a trip from the list of trips and then enter corresponding expense details.

> **Travel Calendar**
> This option gives you an overview of all trips for an employee in calendar form. Similar to the previous option, you can pick a trip from the list and enter travel expenses.

> **Weekly Report**
> As you can see in Figure 7.5, this option gives you an overview of all weekly reports entered by an employee. This interface can be used, for example, to enter expense reports of those employees who submit their expenses every week, such as your hard working SAP consultants.

Regardless of the option you choose to enter the expense report, expenses are entered against one of the expense types that best classifies the expense. Expense types are very powerful and control several parameters, including the following:

Expense type parameters

> Whether expense reimbursement is based on individual receipts (e.g., meals reimbursement for actual expense) or per-diem (e.g., flat amount for meals reimbursement)

> What the service provider category is: airline, rental car, hotel, and so on

> Employee groups that can claim this type of expense (more about this in the "Compliance and Reporting" section)

> Whether this expense is paid by an employee and has to be reimbursed, or whether the company will need to reimburse the service provider directly

> Whether expense reimbursements are taxable for the employee

> What additional information needs to be entered for this type of expense (e.g., location, number of guests)

> Which GL accounts are posted

 Note

How these GL accounts are determined is a fairly technical subject and won't be discussed here, but you can influence the GL account posting by using the appropriate expense type.

So let's talk about the large number of standard expense types included and how you can create even more by customizing them to take advantage of the customizable screens for entering travel expenses. Figure 7.5 shows a sample screen of a weekly expense report.

Trip Data Maintain: Weekly Report

◀ Previous Week   ▶ Next Week   Simulate   Approve   Trip Status   Advances   Information   Cost Assign

Pers.No   1   Reason
Name   Mr John Smith   Destin

	Sunday	Monday	Tuesday	Wednesday	Thursday	Friday	Saturday	
Date	01/07/2007	01/08/2007	01/09/2007	01/10/2007	01/11/2007	01/12/2007	01/13/2007	
Reason								
Day Dest								
Number M's								
M/KmAllow.	0.00	0.00	0.00	0.00	0.00	0.00	0.00	0.00

Expnse Typ.	Sunday	Monday	Tuesday	Wednesday	Thursday	Friday	Saturday	Totals	
Breakfast								0.00	▲
Lunch								0.00	▼
Dinner								0.00	
Entertainment								0.00	
Hotel								0.00	
Telephone, Fax								0.00	
Flight								0.00	
Taxi, Bus								0.00	
Car Rental								0.00	▲
Gasoline								0.00	▼

Total	0.00	0.00	0.00	0.00	0.00	0.00	0.00	0.00
Advance								0.00
Payment Amount in USD								0.00

Figure 7.5 Weekly Expense Report

In this figure, you'll see that Expense Types that are paid based on individual receipts are displayed in the leftmost column (Breakfast, Lunch, Flight, Taxi, etc.), whereas per-diem expenses such as Number Mls (miles per day) are shown at the top of each column. For the per-diem expense types, per-diem numbers from the system are used (e.g., mileage rate) to calculate the equivalent expense amount.

Additional information for expense receipts In addition, for every expense, you can require that additional information be provided to support the expense. For example, you may request the customer name and business purpose for entertainment expenses. You also have the option to indicate if a portion of the receipt amount corresponds to a personal expense. This will be automatically deducted from the reimbursable expense amount. You can also scan and attach actual receipts to travel expense reports.

When entering expenses, you can choose the expense type from the available list and enter the expense amount and additional data for that expense type. After the expense details are entered, you can route the expense report through approvals before it goes to accounting for processing.

Expense Accounting and Reimbursement

After the expenses are received in accounting, the settlement run begins.

Settlement run

An approved expense report first needs to be settled. The settlement process calculates the reimbursement amounts, and it's used as the basis for posting accounting entries for receivables, payables, expenses, and so on.

The settlement process links entries in travel management (e.g., separate expense types for breakfast, lunch, and dinner) with entries in accounting (e.g., one expense account for meals reimbursement). Apart from the number of different selection criteria, such as personnel number, trip number, and so on, you also have the option to carry out this settlement run online or in the background. You can then carry out a test run to review the results before posting the results to accounting.

The settlement run also includes an option called Repeat Accounted Trips, which lets you reprocess trips that have already been transferred to accounting. This is especially important if an expense report has changed after it is posted to accounting, or if a per-diem amount has changed retroactively.

Reprocessing of expenses

Posting run

After you've reviewed the settlement results, you're ready to post these entries to accounting. You create a posting run that creates a *trip transfer document* based on the results of the settlement run.

A trip transfer document summarizes the accounting results from the settlement run that have the same GL account, tax code, cost center, and so on. You can summarize these documents by individual trips, by employee, by cost center, by company, and so on. Figure 7.6 shows the available options for summarizing while posting accounting entries.

Trip transfer document

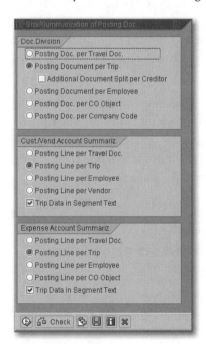

Figure 7.6 Summarization of an Accounting Posting

Tip

You may want to consider that the level of summarization you select can have an impact on how easy it is to reconcile accounting postings. So if you don't want to spend a lot of extra time reconciling, you may want to select fewer summarization options.

Validate before posting

Of course, several options are available to help reduce errors encountered while posting to accounting. For example, you have the option to Check Posting Run. When you select this option, the software validates all GL accounts in the trip transfer documents. Remember, these accounts are determined based on your system setup, and it's possible that—especially in new or distributed installations—all accounts may not exist or may not be open for posting. Depending on the results of the check, the posting run gets a status of "All Docs Checked" or "Document Errors." If there are any errors, you have a chance to resolve these errors before carrying out actual postings. Another option is the Automatic Replacement of Incorrect Account Assignment Objects. This option lets the software analyze the posting run and, if there are any cost centers that can't be posted (e.g., they are old cost centers and should no longer be used), they can be replaced by cost center from the employee master, or by using a user-defined substitution rule.

You can also carry out a posting run simulation during which the system simulates posting to accounting, so that you can identify any other errors. In case of errors, you have the option of reprocessing the posting run or rejecting it completely; although rejection of a posting run is possible only if *all* documents in the posting run have errors.

A single posting run can post all different types of accounting entries:

> Payable to employee accounts created as vendors or customers

> Payable to credit card companies

> Payable directly to service providers, such as airline/rental car companies or travel agencies

> Receivables from employees, for example, if an advance amount was more than expenses

> Posting to expense accounts determined based on expense types

> Any additional accounts based on system setup

Reimbursement

You can carry out expense reimbursement through the AP, travel management, or payroll components, depending on your organization's policy and how the expenses are incurred. The most common option is to carry out the reimbursement from AP. In this scenario, when a posting run for travel expenses is processed, payables are created in the employee accounts. You can settle these payables by check or by electronic fund transfer the same way you would make check payments or electronic fund transfers to outside vendors.

Another possible scenario is to create an electronic fund transfer directly from the travel management group. In this scenario, you send a file containing the fund transfer information to the bank. No accounting entries are generated for this reimbursement, which means the employee payables in accounting are "cleared" only as part of a bank reconciliation process.

The payroll payment option is possible, if you are using the payroll component. In this scenario, the expense reimbursement details are transferred and paid through payroll, and the accounting entries are posted along with other payroll entries.

Expense reimbursement with payroll

Finally, if expenses are charged to a corporate credit card, you can make payments directly to the credit card company. This method of reimbursement is possible whether every employee is given their own corporate credit card or whether a centralized travel department uses one or two credit cards for this purpose.

Regardless of the size of your company though, you'll want to make sure that expense reimbursement complies with statutory requirements and company guidelines.

Compliance and Reporting

To meet your compliance and reporting needs, there is functionality to support statutory compliance (e.g., taxability of expense reimbursements), as well as ensuring compliance with corporate travel policy (e.g., eligibility of different employees). So let's talk about the functions available to help you control and improve this compliance.

Employee grouping for validation

We'll start with trip expenses. Trip expense reimbursement rules and their taxability rules typically vary from country to country. Even within a country, these rules may be different based on the type of company (e.g., public sector, private sector, nonprofit, etc.). This complexity is handled by grouping relevant rules into different trip provision variants. On the other hand, you can group your employees into different groups and subgroups and assign them to different areas called personnel areas that are linked to companies. You can assign travel provision variants to any of these levels: employee group, employee subgroup, personnel area, company, and so on. By making these assignments, you have enormous flexibility when validating travel rules for each employee.

To determine which employees are eligible for which types of expenses for statutory compliance, you can use the *statutory M/A reimbursement group*. These single-character codes are assigned to the employee master part of travel privileges to determine the eligibility of an employee for specific expense types. In addition to the statutory M/A reimbursement group, you can also assign each employee to the *enterprise M/A reimbursement group*, which controls employee eligibility as it relates to your enterprise travel policy.

You can also control expense reimbursement rates at a very minute level. Figure 7.7 shows how you can use almost 10 different parameters to control expenses that are reimbursed at a flat amount, regardless of actual expenses. For an expense type that is reimbursed at a flat rate, you can specify different flat rate reimbursement amounts such as the amount billed to a customer, amount reimbursed to an employee, and the reimbursement amount that is taxable for an employee.

218

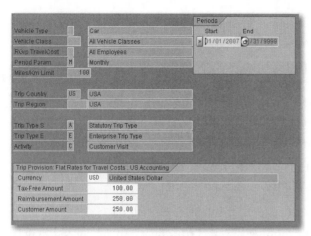

Figure 7.7 Set Flat Rate Travel Costs

You can improve compliance with the corporate travel policy in some other ways as well:

> Establish specially negotiated contracts with airlines, hotels, rental car companies, or travel agencies, and work to ensure that this contract information along with other details are used while carrying out travel booking.

> Automatically prioritize travel booking for trips based on different criteria such as the purpose of the visit, employee group (e.g., executive travel requests have higher priority), and so on.

> Establish preferred airlines based on domestic or international trips and destination cities.

> Create a preferred hotels catalog for your company.

> Require employees to provide reasons if they choose to carry out travel that does not confirm to travel policy guidelines, and also require that those trips need special approvals.

Improved compliance with travel policy

A number of standard reports that let you analyze travel trips and travel expenses before, during, and after trips have been taken are also provided. For example, you can use various information collected from trips to negotiate volume or discount contracts with travel agencies or other service providers. You can analyze travel expenses by employee, employee groups, company, cost center, geography, type and purpose of the trip, or by many other criteria.

You can also prepare exception reports to highlight trips that do not conform to your travel policy or prepare analytics to calculate per-trip, per-employee travel costs by cost center. Based on the taxability information for the different types of travel expenses, you can then create reports to help you with tax reporting and auditing.

Here are some of the standard reports delivered in SAP NetWeaver BI for travel management:

> Overview of travel expenses by different criteria

> Analytics on the number of travel trips by company, by cost center, and so on

> Analysis of expense receipt details by type of travel expenses

> Analysis of flights by airline, by cabin class, by destination, and so on

> Analysis of hotel bookings by hotel chain, by geography, and so on

> Analysis of car rental bookings by rental car companies, by geography, and so on

So now that you know about the travel management function, let's look at a case study and see how it works in the real world.

Case Study

This global conglomerate has offices in 25+ countries worldwide and spends more than $200 million dollars on travel expenses each year. Its employees travel extensively domestically and internationally, and all together they file more than 50,000 expense reports annually. Each office location has its own travel department that caters to local travel requirements.

Business Challenge

The corporate travel policy was outdated and didn't take into account local nuances for each office location, so it was difficult to enforce. This resulted in trips between the same pair of cities being reimbursed at widely different rates depending on where the booking was done.

Because travel was handled by local departments using disparate systems, it was difficult to obtain a consolidated view of the overall travel needs for the company. Without this consolidated information, it was difficult to negotiate with travel providers for preferred and discounted rates.

The expense reimbursement process was done manually through a system that required expense reports to be prepared in Excel and then manually submitted for physical signature. Then the expense report was sent to the accounting department with the accompanying receipts, and it took anywhere from four weeks to two months for some individuals to receive payments. This resulted in additional charges and write-offs, not to mention dissatisfied employees who traveled frequently.

Solution Deployment

The solution deployment involved implementing the travel expenses, expense accounting, and expense reimbursement applications with the primary goal of the project rollout being to make business processes in each of these areas more efficient and to cut travel processing costs by 13 % over the next two years.

Before embarking on the implementation of the Travel Expenses application, the organization carried out two major changes. First it created three regional travel departments to serve the Americas, Europe, and the Asia regions. This decision not only consolidated operations but also helped in head count reduction. The second change was to review and revise the travel policy to take into account the nuances and realities of traveling in each of its disparate geographical areas. This change also helped finalize the different business processes in the travel management area.

Under the new travel policy, corporate credit cards were issued to management and to employees who traveled frequently. All other employees were to use their personal credit cards for travel expenses. A worldwide contract was negotiated with a single credit card company for issuing the corporate credit cards, and an interface was developed to download the data from the credit card company and upload that data into the system.

The old, manual process for approving expense reports was replaced with an approval process using an SAP workflow. The workflow sent expense reports to the appropriate approver, who could then electronically approve or request more information on the expense report entered.

It was also decided that all expense reimbursements would be made by direct deposit to the employee bank accounts. At most of the office locations, the AP department was already using direct deposit to pay to some of the big vendors, so it was easy to extend the same technical setup and same business processes to cover the employee expense reimbursements across all office locations in all countries.

Value Achieved

Even though corporate credit cards were not issued to all employees, the change covered employees that accounted for almost 70 % of the business trips. So, the interface to download expense receipt data from the credit card company dramatically reduced the time required to get expense reports in the system. In addition, by ensuring timely payment on the corporate credit card accounts, the company was able to save on late fees and charges.

The decision to get expense receipt data electronically into the system, combined with the decision to use an SAP workflow for expense report approvals considerably reduced paperwork. This also fell in line with company's global initiative of "going green."

In addition, statutory compliance was improved by using the many ready-to-use country templates provided by SAP for travel policy compliance. SAP was set up with parameters corresponding to the corporate travel policy, thereby improving compliance with the travel policy. It was also set up to generate reports based on dollar amounts, abnormal travel volumes, and so on. This allowed the company to monitor compliance by exception, instead of having to validate every single expense report.

The use of direct deposit for expense reimbursements reduced the reimbursement time to five to seven days, and the tight integration of travel management with financial accounting allowed individual financial controllers to do better cash flow planning. And, of course, a major intangible benefit was increased employee satisfaction.

Using and accepting these new processes has ensured that the project is on target with its goal to cut travel-processing costs by 13 % annually over the next two years.

Looking Ahead

There are no plans in the foreseeable future to implement the travel booking and reservation options in SAP; however, after this project rollout is stabilized, the next phase will implement the travel request and approvals processing in SAP. This will cut out most of the process inefficiencies in the end-to-end travel-related business processes.

The major office locations worldwide are improving their infrastructure so that employees who submit expense reports manually can scan their expense receipts and attach them directly to the expense report in SAP. This will make the expense report approval process more efficient.

Finally, the SAP implementation of NetWeaver BI is another independent initiative that is being implemented. After BI is implemented, data received from the credit card company will be uploaded for advanced reporting and analytics. Information about trips mined from these reports will be used to negotiate special rates with different hotel chains and car rental companies.

Summary

In this chapter, we talked about the primary benefits of using the various functions of SAP travel management. These benefits revolve around reducing operating costs, increasing efficiency, and increasing compliance with your travel policy. As you've seen, this is a robust part of SAP that can really make your company travel policy easy to implement and enforce. Some of the key things to remember about SAP travel management include the following:

> Travel management is completely integrated with other areas of SAP, which allows you to transfer and synchronize accounting entries and personnel data with financials, HR, and payroll.

> You can improve the efficiency of your expense reimbursement accounting by streamlining the entry, settlement, posting, and reimbursement of travel expenses.

> Travel management supports more than 30 different settlement versions to meet the diverse requirements of different countries.

> By using SAP workflow, you can automate the approval processes for travel requests, travel plans, travel bookings, and expense reports to make end-to-end processes more efficient.

> You can improve compliance with your company travel policy while easily identifying and analyzing exceptions.

> Using travel management analytics and reporting, you can gather the information about your company's travel expenses and trends to help you negotiate better prices and rates with travel providers.

> By consolidating travel bookings, you can analyze trip information better.

> You can implement many of these functions (e.g., travel requests, expense entries, etc.) on an enterprise portal as part of employee self-service.

In the next chapter, we'll explore how to maintain employee information in SAP for payroll processing.

8

Payroll Accounting

In today's complex and global work environment, payroll processing doesn't just involve calculating employee payments, it also requires supporting, managing, and processing many different types of calculations that impact an employee's net earnings. Taxes, for example, have a major impact on net earnings. All employee earnings are subject to tax by federal, state, and local tax authorities, so these taxes need to be withheld from payroll, and employers are required to periodically file tax returns to all relevant tax authorities.

In addition, contribution laws dictate the various contributions that employees can make to retirement and pension plans, and these also need to be deducted during payroll processing. And of course, there are company benefits, including medical insurance, stock option plans, allowances, employee loans, etc., so the employee contributions for receiving these benefits need to be factored during payroll calculation.

Additionally, some employees may require past due taxes, alimony, child support, or other garnishments to their wages. Add to this the ever-increasing reporting requirements, either mandated by governments or required by management for operational or strategic reasons, and you need a robust payroll system.

Complex tax, benefit, and reporting requirements require a robust payroll solution

225

The SAP Payroll component not only meets these requirements, but it has the unique advantage of being completely integrated with the SAP ERP Human Capital Management (HCM) and the SAP ERP Financials solutions. Additionally, because employment, tax, labor, contribution, benefits, and information laws are different for different countries, SAP provides partially configured payroll solutions for more than 35 countries ranging from the United States, United Kingdom, and Germany to India, Argentina, and Indonesia. Because it's not practical to discuss all variations and nuances of payroll solutions for every country in a single chapter, we'll focus on SAP Payroll for the United States.

Overview

Figure 8.1 shows how the payroll solution covers a wide range of calculations needed in today's complex business environment. You can use payroll in a wide variety of processing combinations, including integration with third-party products (e.g., for time tracking or tax calculations) and third-party service providers (for payroll processing or tax processing). Because the payroll solution is integrated with other components of the SAP ERP HCM application, such as personnel administration and benefits administration, you can leverage employee and benefits information entered in those components for payroll processing. Payroll is also integrated with the GL, AR, and AP components of SAP ERP Financials, which makes it easy for you to process and reconcile different types of accounting entries.

401(k), COBRA, and FSA support

In addition, payroll supports comprehensive functionality that caters to the business processes required to run payroll in different job functions, companies, industries, and countries. You can use base earnings calculations to support several salary and wage models, or use different calculation models to structure incentive programs that are appropriate and effective for your company. Payroll is also capable of processing basic payroll remuneration, as well as any special payments (e.g., loan payments), overtime, or bonus payments. And, you can use the benefits administration component to offer different types of benefit plans to your employees, for which employee contributions and deductions are automatically calculated and deducted from the employee payroll. This includes dedicated SAP programs to support several country-specific benefits and deductions such as 401(k), CO-BRA, and Flexible Spending Accounts (FSA) for the United States.

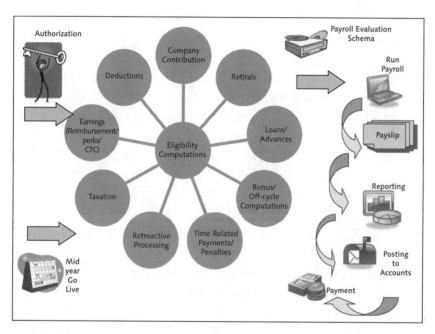

Figure 8.1 SAP Payroll: A Comprehensive Solution

You can use the powerful functionality of the Payroll Deductions component to prioritize payroll deductions and to handle arrears if all required deductions can't be made from a payroll period. The Tax component carries out tax computations by taking into consideration an employee's exemptions, prerequisites, deductions, and voluntary tax payments. You'll benefit from using the Tax Reporter provided with SAP U.S. Payroll when it comes time to prepare quarterly and annual tax forms, tax reports, and tax returns. Standard reports are available to meet other statutory, management, and analytical requirements. And, an interface tool allows you to import and export employee HR and payroll information, so that you can easily exchange employee and payroll data with third-party products or service providers. This

Comprehensive solution

227

data exchange tool is also useful if you choose to outsource payroll processing. Let's discuss this functionality in more detail.

Functions in Detail

We'll start with an overview of the payroll processes and terms specific to payroll, and then review how earnings, benefits, deductions, and taxes are calculated in a typical payroll processing sequence. Next, we'll explore how payroll entries are posted to accounting and the different ways payroll payments can be processed, and then we'll wrap it up with a look at payroll reporting and how the outsourcing of payroll processing is supported.

Process Overview

The central component of payroll is the International Payroll Driver, a program that is modified for each country to create country-specific payroll drivers that can be further customized to meet your company's requirements. A payroll driver uses a payroll schema to carry out payroll calculations. A payroll schema represents a specific sequence of completely customizable calculation rules that are used to calculate base salary, deductions, and taxes, etc. Many country-specific schemas are provided that include calculation rules relevant for each country. The payroll calculation process is also modularly designed into processing gross payroll (earnings, incentives, other payments and deductions) and net payroll (taxes, deductions, benefits, garnishments, etc.).

This modular design of the payroll calculation allows you to process complex payroll requirements of different jobs in different industries in different countries while keeping a single and consistent method and interface for business users. For example, a semiconductor company using the payroll solution can use a similar system interface whether it's calculating salary, bonus, perks, U.S. taxes, and 401(k) contributions for employees in the United States, or calculating hourly wages, medical benefits, Indian taxes, and superannuation benefits for employees in India.

Obviously, calculating payroll involves many variables that are influenced by not only country-specific laws (e.g., payroll taxes, retirement benefits) but also company-specific rules (e.g., industry, type of job, organization structure, eligibility rules) and personal status (e.g., number of dependents, location, elected benefits and deductions, membership dues). The software handles this complexity by maintaining each piece of employee information in an infotype as discussed in Chapter 7. Hundreds of generic and country-specific infotypes are provided for each payroll schema to manage employee information such as contact and address information, organizational assignment, garnishment, basic pay, insurance plans, family allowance, previous employer information, and more.

Infotypes represent a group of relevant data for an employee

Similarly, calculating your payroll requires processing many different values such as amounts, hours, percentages, and so on. With the payroll solution, such values are stored in wage types. A *wage type* differentiates between values for various business purposes and also determines how this value is posted to accounting. There are hundreds of wage types used in payroll calculation. For example, different wage types are used for different types of salary calculations (e.g., base, bonus, premium, hourly, commission), insurance payments (e.g., medical, dental, vision, AD&D), voluntary and mandated deductions (e.g., charity contributions, membership fees, garnishments), etc. In short, any uniquely calculated or reportable payroll amount is typically identified by separate wage types. This design provides you with significant flexibility in customizing, evaluating, calculating and reporting your myriad payroll processes. Throughout this chapter, we'll frequently make reference to wage types and infotypes.

Wage types

A program is available to convert and upload employee data from non-SAP systems to a format that is compatible with SAP ERP Financials payroll. This can be useful to manage employee transfers for example, if all departments or locations of your company aren't (yet) using SAP ERP Financials for payroll processing. You can transfer year-to-date data from non-SAP systems to make sure that taxes and benefits are calculated accurately.

Earnings Calculation

Indirect valuation

The payroll process starts with calculating payments that an employee is entitled to based on an employment contract, which forms the basis for calculating basic earnings (gross remuneration). In the payroll solution, the basic pay represents the salary paid every month. Note that you can include up to 40 elements in the definition of basic pay, so that it includes the salary negotiated in the original contract, other adjustments, subsequent revisions, and so on. Figure 8.2 shows the definition of basic pay. Indirect valuation of wage types is also provided. For example, by linking employees with a pay scale and by defining their pay with wage types that are indirectly valuated, you only have to maintain and revise pay scale values to influence their basic pay calculation.

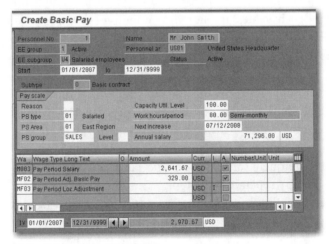

Figure 8.2 Basic Pay Calculation

Additionally, you can process recurring payments/deductions and additional payments for earnings calculation. Recurring payments/deductions are the payments or deductions made to the payroll at a specific period. The additional payments function can be used for one-off adjustments to the payroll. For example, an automotive dealer can use recurring payments for monthly payroll deductions, and use additional payments for holiday bonuses to its sales employees. Two additional functionalities also influence earnings calculation: partial period factoring and time management.

Tip

You can also maintain guaranteed wage or salary payments for an employee. For example, these guaranteed payments can be a result of union agreements (such as pay scale downgrades, provision for old age, etc.).

Partial Period Factoring

Factoring is the process used in payroll to calculate remuneration for one or more parts of a payroll period. Factoring can be necessary, for example, if an employee joins or leaves the company, if an employee is absent from the company during a period, or if parameters that influence the payroll calculation have changed during a period (basic pay of an employee is changed or an employee transfers from one cost center/company to another cost center/company).

A number of variations for calculating of partial period remuneration are provided to cater for a wide range of possible scenarios. These calculations can be based on:

> Working hours, working days or calendar day, thus enabling you to properly account for absenteeism of hourly employees as well as salaried employees

> Whether actual length and general length of a payroll period are the same or different, for example, weekly payroll is always seven days; whereas number of days are variable for monthly payroll

> Whether remuneration should be calculated by the deduction method (deducting an amount for the period of absence) or by payment method (calculating payment for the period of non-absence)

> Whether calculation should be prorated, or it's all or nothing; for example, if an employee worked for 18+ hours, full weekly allowance is paid, or no allowance is paid

 Warning

Calculation results for partial period remuneration can vary considerably from month-to-month based on the method you choose, especially if the payroll period is monthly. So, choose the method only after carefully considering your corporate policy.

We'll cover paid absences later when we talk about benefits, so for now let's discuss the interface and integration of time-management data for payroll calculation.

Time Management

If a time-management system is used along with payroll to get data from employee time tickets (time cards, punch cards, etc.), then different wage types are updated with numbers (usually hours) that are combined with rates maintained in the system to calculate payroll results. These types of calculations are especially important for facilities where most employees are paid hourly (e.g., production plants, warehouses, retail stores, etc.).

Payroll with time management involves additional complexity, but the payroll solution is capable of meeting these challenges. For example, you can do the following using time management wage types in Payroll:

> Use non-SAP, external time-management systems for recording time activity and upload corresponding information directly for payroll.

> Automatically account for duration and time of an activity based on holidays, weekends, and so on.

> Support payroll calculation for multiple shifts with shift-specific calculations, for example, overtime for weekend shifts or bonus for night shifts.

> Support higher payment for specific activities (e.g., handling of hazardous materials), or make payments using different pay scale or different job position (e.g., an associate performing supervisory activity).

> Calculate remuneration so that an employee isn't disadvantaged, when his planned working time is changed across shifts or across days.

Incentive/bonus calculation

Additionally, several calculation models to calculate bonus or incentive payments are provided. These calculations can be made based on monthly earnings, hourly wages, and also time-dependent or performance-dependent variables. The incentive calculation models for hourly wages provide considerable flexibility to provide incentives that are best suited for the working environment. For example, you can use calculation models to design incentive plans that offer a bonus if a plant worker works for 60 hours instead of the regular 40 hours in a week, as well as incentive plans that offer a bonus if a plant worker makes a widget in 3 hours instead 4 hours. Based on the incentive plans configured in the system, accurate incentive amounts are automatically calculated and included in the payroll process.

Let's move on to look at how to calculate other benefits and deductions.

Benefits and Deductions

SAP provides a benefits administration component as part of the SAP ERP HCM solution. Payroll calculations are subject to numerous deductions such as participation in benefits programs and various other items, so dedicated programs to meet the benefits and deductions requirements for specific countries are provided. A fairly common benefit provided by many companies is paid leave.

Paid Leave

Earlier, we talked about the impact of unpaid absences on the payroll calculation. However, depending on legal requirements, company policies, and union agreements, employees may be entitled to different types of leave, including sick leave, personal time off, vacation days, and disability leave. Payroll calculations need to take into account the payment eligibility of different types of leave based on the differences in compensation (e.g., for jury duty), absence quotas (only five days of paid sick leave per year), eligibility criteria (two additional weeks of paid vacation for management), etc. In addition, different types of quota calculations and leave valuations to meet such requirements are provided including:

Calculation of leave quota

> How to valuate paid leave over weekends, public holidays, other holidays, and so on

> Whether leave days are paid at a fixed rate or fixed amount, for example, fixed vacation allowance

> Whether leave days are paid as if the employee was working based on the "as-if" principle (e.g., fully paid vacation days)

> Whether leave days are paid based on parameters specified in an absence quota, for example, the first two weeks of short-term disability leave are fully paid, the next two weeks are paid at 75 %, and three weeks after that are paid only at 50 %

STD/LTD and FMLA leave

The U.S. Payroll solution also provides dedicated programs to manage leave requests received under short-term or long-term disability plans and the FMLA (Family and Medical Leave Act). Figure 8.3 shows the FMLA rule that entitles an employee to 12 weeks of leave in a calendar year if the employee meets seniority criteria and has worked for at least 1,250 hours in the past 12 months. You can also process valuation of absence quotas and modified workdays. For example, if an employee is on 5 days of paid vacation but works for 2 hours every day during that period; you can process the remuneration so that the vacation quota is reduced to 4 days, and the employee is paid for the time worked. An employee may also elect to use other benefits offered by the company.

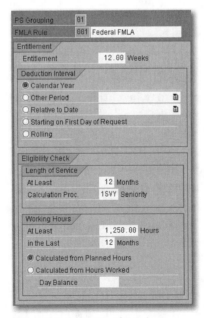

Figure 8.3 FMLA Benefits Rule

Other Benefits

If you also use the benefits administration component, then you can easily integrate benefits-based deductions and contributions entered in that component with payroll processing. The benefits administration component provides country-specific or region-specific functionality to meet legal and functional requirements. Let's first discuss some U.S.-specific benefit plans and functionalities.

Flexible spending accounts (FSAs) enable employees to set aside pre-tax income for medical care expenses. When an employee submits a medical claim, the amount can be approved for reimbursement or rejected if it doesn't qualify as a valid FSA expense. Using the integrated functionality, approved claims are automatically included for employee reimbursement during the next payroll run. The Benefits Administration component also supports management of continued health coverage of employees under the COBRA plan, although employee payments for continuing coverage can't be deducted from payroll, even for those beneficiaries who continue to be employed. You can run the ADP/ACP (Actual Deferral Percentage/Actual Contribution Percentage) nondiscrimination tests to compare 401(k) contributions of your highly compensated employees (HCE) and non-highly compensated employees (NHCE) using the earnings limit specified by IRS. If the test fails, you can use Payroll to return excess contributions to HCE.

FSA and COBRA plans

SAP also supports generic types of benefit plans that may be applicable worldwide, including:

> Health plans for medical and hospitalization coverage, where the payroll deduction is calculated based on employee eligibility and the number of dependents enrolled in the plan

> Insurance plans, such as life insurance, AD&D insurance, and so on for which the payroll deduction is calculated based on policy preferences and insurance premiums

> Stock purchase plans, for which employee contributions are deducted from payroll to buy company stock

> Automatic saving plans, so that payroll deductions are directly deposited to saving accounts.

US savings bonds

With reference to the last bullet point, SAP ERP Financials even provides programs that can interface with the National Bond and Trust Company (NBT), which provides the U.S. bond administration services. By using this interface, you can provide your employees an option to purchase US savings bonds directly through periodic payroll deductions. You can also prepare and transmit an electronic data file containing employee deductions in the format recognized by NBT. If the employer provides partial contribution for these plans, the software can separately calculate and account for employer's contributions and employee deductions. Let's discuss employee deductions in a little more detail.

Employee Deductions

The number of voluntary or mandated deductions in payroll processing can vary based on the country, the company, and even the employee. These deductions can be for insurance payments, retirement contributions, professional memberships, charitable contributions, loan payments, and so on. Figure 8.4 shows some of the benefit plans and deductions supported in payroll. Even though we won't cover every type of deduction calculation supported, we'll talk about some common functions available for these deductions.

Figure 8.4 Benefits and Deductions

An important factor influencing deduction calculations is the deduction limit. An employee may have selected multiple payroll deductions that are subject to limits due to company policy or statutory reasons. For example, the annual deduction for a 401(k) plan contribution shouldn't be more than $14,500, or the monthly deduction for medical insurance should be less than 10 % of monthly gross pay. With payroll, you can create complex rules for deduction limits, which can check different parameters and set the limits for groups of deductions. The rules can be set for groups of employees or, if required, even for individual employees. Similarly, you can specify what to do if actual deductions during the payroll process exceed these limits. For example, deductions can be made based on priorities assigned by you until the limit is reached, or deductions can be reduced by a specified percentage or amount to see if the lower values fall within the limit.

Deduction limits and arrears calculation

Priorities assigned to deductions specify the sequence in which they are processed during payroll calculation. For example, garnishment deductions (discussed later) may have a higher priority than a contribution to church. Every deduction is also qualified with parameters that determine how to manage deductions that can't be processed in the current payroll run. Continuing with the previous example, garnishment deductions have to be carried forward to future periods until they can be made by the employee; however, if an employee is unable to make the church contribution for one month, he may not want that deduction to be carried forward to future payroll.

SAP ERP Financials also supports prepayment of deductions by employees, for example, before going on a leave. This can be useful because deduction payments may accumulate if employee earnings during the leave period aren't sufficient. By making a prepayment, the employee can reduce the amount of deductions in the future when the employee returns to work.

Deduction prepayments

Now let's discuss a common payroll deduction: a loan or advance repayment.

Loans/Advances

One of the benefits provided by many companies is employee loans at a reduced interest rate, which are typically repaid through payroll deductions. With the payroll solution, you can manage multiple loans for an employee, so if an employee has three active loans, say a house loan and two auto loans, they are managed and processed independent of each other. The approved loan amount can be paid to an employee in a single payment or several partial payments, or it can be paid to a third party on behalf of an employee. For example, a financial services company that offers housing loans to its senior management can directly make loan payments to homebuilders.

Repayment method/annuity method

Typically, loan repayment installments (loan amount and interest amount) are deducted from a payroll. These installment amounts can be calculated using the repayment method or annuity method. In the annuity method, the total interest amount is calculated at the beginning and is included in the installment amount. In the repayment method, interest is calculated each period for the remaining loan balance and added to the installment amount. Employee loans typically use the annuity method because it keeps the installment amount (and thus payroll deduction) constant in each payroll period.

A special type of loan called a recurring advance is also provided. This type of loan represents an advance toward frequently occurring expenses, for example, by meeting coordinators or by sales reps, thereby eliminating the need for an employee to spend his own money until he receives reimbursement. These types of loans do not accrue any interest, and they are usually repaid only if the underlying business requirement changes or if the employee leaves that job position.

 Tip

> In some countries, the employee interest rate advantage (savings due to the difference between market interest rate and loan interest rate) is taxable. There is also support for calculating the imputed income incurred by an employee from a loan.

Apart from regular payroll deductions toward loan repayment, you can also process full, partial, unplanned, or unscheduled loan repayments. Loan deductions from subsequent payroll runs automatically adjust to reflect the new loan balance. Apart from such voluntary deductions, payroll calculation also takes into account legally mandated deductions such as garnishments.

Garnishments

Garnishment represents a legally authorized deduction from an employee's salary to satisfy an outstanding debt payment such as federal or state taxes, child support or alimony payment, loan repayment to a creditor, and so on. The Garnishment component of the payroll solution is completely customizable to meet your requirements of calculating, deducting, remitting, and communicating garnishment requests. This is especially important because garnishment rules and calculations vary depending on the creditor and type of garnishment. The garnishment calculation is based on disposable net earnings, which is the amount left from earnings after making legally required deductions. The maximum amount that can be deducted from payroll is determined by several factors, such as federal regulations, number of garnishment orders, and the net earning amount for the pay period.

For every wage type, you can specify whether and what percent of its value is included in the calculation of net disposable income (NDI). For example, almost all wage types for federal and state taxes are excluded from the calculation of disposable income. You can further customize the rules by individual states so that NDI is calculated only after deducting the earning for pension scheme contributions and group insurance payments. Similarly, you can use simple percentages, amounts, or highly complex rules to determine the nonexempt, maximum garnishment amount that can be deducted from payroll. For example, you can set up a rule so that for an hourly worker on a weekly payroll, the maximum garnishment deduction is the lower of 20 % of net earnings, or the amount left after ensuring minimum payment of $500 or minimum wage for 25 hours.

Calculation of NDI

After determining the nonexempt amount from payroll, it's compared against garnishment orders for the employee. If the available deduction amount isn't sufficient to make all garnishment payments, payments are made based on customizable priorities assigned to garnishment orders. For example, tax repayments take higher priority than student loan repayments. Secondly, you can customize the system so that if the sufficient amount isn't available for garnishment, the system will know whether to deduct the whole amount anyway and treat the negative difference as an employee advance to be adjusted in subsequent payroll, to deduct only what is possible and treat the balance as arrears, to deduct all or nothing, etc. The method you choose depends largely on the garnishment request and relevant rules and regulations.

You can also process garnishment returns, levy government-required or company-specific service charges, and make garnishment payments to creditors (discussed in the "Third-Party Remittance" section) using customizable frequency and payment methods.

Let's move on and discuss another equally important topic in payroll calculations, employment taxes.

Tax Calculations

All SAP ERP Financials customers implementing the U.S. net payroll component require a third-party product called TaxFactory© from Business Software, Inc. for employee tax calculations. Even though licensed, delivered, and supported independently, this product is an absolute requirement for U.S. tax calculations and is the only product certified to work with the U.S. payroll component. Note that even though TaxFactory carries out tax calculations, it's the SAP software configuration that determines the taxes applied for each payment or deductions of an employee, based on tax areas stored in the employee master data.

Tax Areas and Tax Models

Multiple work locations

In addition to federal taxes, U.S. payroll is subject to taxes levied by states, counties, cities, and even school districts. A *tax area* helps uniquely identify federal, state, county, city, and school district tax authorities to which the employee payroll is taxed. For example, Bradford city, Ohio and Bradford School District, Ohio are identified as two separate tax areas in the U.S. payroll component. An employee is always associated with a resident tax area based on his address. However, if an employee works in more than one tax locality, you can assign multiple work tax areas to an employee using percentages or time allocations. For example, a staffing company with an employee based in Benton, IN who spends 100 days locally, 30 days in Benton, KY, and 70 days in Benton, PA can create additional work tax areas for Benton, KY and Benton, PA, and either assign 15 % and 35 % to each tax area or specifically record tax areas and the days when the employee worked there.

While processing payroll for an employee, the system determines applicable tax authorities and uses tax models associated with each tax authority. The tax models determines applicable tax types such as Social Security, Medicare, Unemployment, Workforce Development, Worker Compensation, and so on. Wage types used in payroll calculation are indirectly linked to these tax models and provide required information for tax calculations. Another factor influencing payroll tax calculations is the withholding allowance for an employee.

W-4 Withholding Information

An employee receiving payroll in the United States is subject to Federal Employee Withholding Allowance (Form W-4) based on his tax filing status. Additionally, based on individual family, income and tax situation, an employee may choose to elect more payroll allowance or additional withholding. This withholding allowance at the federal level may or may not be applicable at the state level, or some states may allow or disallow additional withholding of taxes. The U.S. payroll component supports all these possible combinations.

As Figure 8.5 shows, you can maintain detailed employee information for the number of exemption allowances, additional withholding amounts, withholding information for additional tax authorities, Earned Income Credit status for eligible employees, and so on. You can also maintain withholding tax overrides for different purposes such as exemption from tax withholding, alternative method for tax calculation or withholding tax calculation for supplemental income. Built-in controls that ensure users don't enter withholding data that isn't allowed are also provided. For example, the system issues an error if a user attempts to enter additional W-4 withholding amounts for states that do not allow such withholding, for example, Arizona, Mississippi, and Pennsylvania.

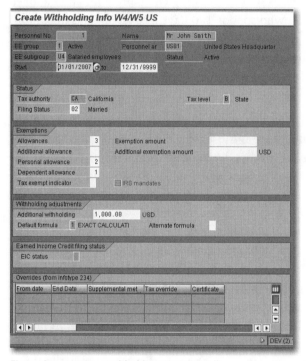

Figure 8.5 W-4 Tax Withholding (U.S. Payroll)

Partially configured tax information

Considering the myriad tax laws and their variations for tax authorities across the United States, the task of creating tax information for different tax authorities can be difficult, especially for medium to large companies. The U.S. payroll component provides templates for more than 4,000 tax authorities with corresponding information for types of taxes, rules for W-4 exemptions and allowances, and tax models, which can be customized to meet your requirements. We'll discuss tax reporting along with other payroll reporting functions soon, but in the next section, let's discuss the process of running payroll.

Payroll Processing

Payroll in SAP is always run for one or more payroll areas. A payroll area in SAP represents a group of employees for which payroll is run together, at the same time. For example, a manufacturing company can use different payroll areas to process weekly payroll (for plant workers) and monthly payroll (for office workers), or for salaried employees (to be paid on last day of the month) and hourly employees (to be paid on second day of the next month). All payroll control parameters and status information for a payroll area are maintained in the payroll control record. The payroll control record is an extremely important object that carries information such as the status of the current payroll run, the next period for the regular payroll run, the date up to which retroactive calculations have been carried out, etc. This information and status are automatically updated during the payroll process. Here is the payroll process in the payroll solution:

Payroll control record

1. Simulate payroll for one or more employees and review the log information.

2. Release the payroll run to begin the payroll process.

3. Carry out the payroll run and review the payroll results.

4. If necessary, resolve any errors and carry out payroll correction run(s).

5. Simulate the posting run for payroll accounting entries.

6. Exit the payroll run to indicate that processing is complete.

Payroll simulation runs can be useful especially when you're implementing the payroll solution for the first time or if you've made complex changes to the payroll system configuration or employee master data. A simulation payroll run doesn't update any payroll data or payroll status in the system, but it enables you to review the payroll log for any errors before the actual payroll process begins. You indicate the beginning of the payroll process by releasing the payroll run for one or more payroll areas. Due to the large quantities of data involved, a typical payroll process is carried out as a background process, during which the program goes through the payroll calculation. You can repeat the steps to review, correct, simulate, and process the payroll run until all the errors are resolved. When you carry out payroll correction runs, only those employees are processed for which the program encountered errors during a previous run. Finally, you can review payroll results and run a program to exit the payroll run, indicating that the payroll process is complete.

Off-Cycle Payroll Runs

Several variations are possible for the typical payroll process described in the earlier list. For example, if you haven't yet marked a payroll run as complete and arranged for the payments (we'll discuss this later), you can delete results of the current payroll run and start the process again, or you can carry out multiple off-cycle payroll runs for the same payroll period to pay basic remuneration, to make bonus payments, etc. This lets you process payroll per your operational and business requirements. You can associate different benefits and deductions to payroll reasons to control calculations carried out during an off-cycle payroll run. For large numbers of employees, you can configure the system to split the payroll into multiple, parallel background jobs, with each job processing certain numbers of employees. Another commonly used variation of the payroll process is retroactive processing.

Retroactive Processing

Automatic retroactive calculation

When an employee's wage data is changed retroactively, it impacts the employee's past earnings as well as tax calculations. The U.S. payroll component supports retroactive changes to employee master data and automatically calculates the effect of those changes in the next payroll run. Remember that employee information is stored in different infotypes, and for every infotype, you can control whether its information can be changed retroactively and whether that change automatically triggers retroactive payroll calculation. For example, information such as name, marital status, educational qualifications, and so on can be changed retroactively without any impact on payroll. Any retroactive changes to information such as basic pay, pension benefits, loan payments, garnishments, and so on, however, automatically trigger retroactive payroll calculation. However, changes to the system configuration (e.g., tax models) do not automatically trigger retroactive payroll calculation. As shown in Figure 8.6, for these instances, you can force the payroll program to carry out a retroactive calculation from a specific date.

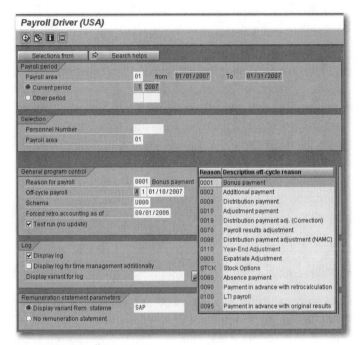

Figure 8.6 Payroll Processing

 Tip

The payroll solution stores all payroll results with two period indicators: the period *in* which the results are calculated (in-period), and the period *for* which the results are calculated (for-period). For example, it's possible to separate payroll results *for* May, calculated by a payroll run *in* May; and by retroactive payroll runs initiated *in* June, July, and November.

Typically, any overpayments or underpayments in earnings due to retroactive calculation are forwarded to the current period and taxed with the current tax authority and current tax rate. Only in exceptional scenarios (e.g., retroactive changes are made to tax models or tax authorities), will the software use tax rates and tax authorities' information from the previous time periods. This can be useful, for example, if incorrect tax configuration in tax model is corrected retro-actively. Any prior period changes to wage deductions, such as plan contributions and benefit deductions; are forwarded and processed as part of the next payroll run.

Time limits on retroactive calculation

For statutory, corporate, and operational reasons, you may have to put a limit on how far back the retroactive payroll calculation should be made. Obviously, the absolute earliest date for any retroactive cal-culation for an employee is the hire date. However, you can also set different dates as the earliest possible dates for retroactive calcula-tions for a payroll area or for an employee. The system uses the most recent of these three dates and the effective date of the retroactive change for carrying out retroactive payroll calculations. These types of controls help you keep internal checks and balances for internal and external audits. Regardless of the type of payroll run, after payroll results are finalized, the next step is posting and payments.

Posting and Payments

Payroll results contain information relevant for accounting, such as employee payables (salary, bonus, etc.), vendor payables (to tax au-thorities, plan administrators, etc.), expense entries, and so on. Let's discuss how these entries are posted to accounting.

Postings to Accounting

Symbolic accounts

We already talked about how different wage types are used to calcu-late and store these values. These results are then transferred from payroll to accounting using symbolic accounts, which map wage types to financial accounts such as GL accounts or customer or vendor accounts. This design provides you with complete flexibility to main-tain as many wage types in payroll without having to create as many financial accounts. For example, wage types for 401(k) or 403(b) con-tribution plans require only one symbolic account to post to the GL account for pensions contributions payables. Payments by employer to various health plans, on the other hand, require mapping to two symbolic accounts: the expenses GL account and to the plan adminis-trator payable account.

After payroll results are finalized, you create a posting run to carry out this evaluation and mapping of wage types to financial accounts and to create accounting entries in the form of posting documents. The posting documents contain accounting entries for payables, expenses, and other accounts, along with entries for cost centers and other objects that we'll discuss in later chapters. You should simulate a posting run before payroll run is finalized to identify and correct any problems. After the posting run has been created, you can edit it before releasing for posting to accounting. An important feature of the payroll-posting run is the ability to carry out summarization. For example, if employee health insurance expenses post to different cost centers, instead of posting multiple entries, the posting run can post one summarized entry to the GL account with cost center details in costing documents.

 Tip

> If during one payroll period, an employee has worked for more than one company; the payroll solution can automatically create accounting entries for intercompany receivables and payables between the two companies.

With the help of the document-splitting function in the new GL (refer to Chapter 2 for more details), you can also distribute payroll liabilities at a more detailed level. For example, if payroll entries are posted for two profit centers; you can choose to post the liability of employee payment only to the profit center that the employee belongs to, or you can distribute the liability across both profit centers to obtain a more accurate and complete financial picture. Many objects, such as cost center, profit center, business area, segment, and so on are supported, based on which payroll liabilities can be distributed. Activating this feature in payroll is only useful, however, if document splitting is also active for entries originating in other SAP components. Obviously, after liabilities have been created, they need to be paid.

Integration with the new GL

Payments

More often than not, payment liabilities are posted from payroll to accounting, and AP processes a payment run to settle those liabilities. You can also use bank information for employees and create an electronic payment file directly from the U.S. payroll component. This file can be sent to the bank for making payments, and you can carry out a second posting run to post payments for the liabilities generated during the first payroll run. Subsequently, you can verify accounting entries while carrying out bank statement reconciliation. (You can read more about these processes in Chapter 3 "Receivables and Payables" and Chapter 5 "Bank Accounting.") You can also make advance, one-off payments to an employee without carrying out a payroll run. Subsequently, when a regular payroll run is carried out, such advance payments are evaluated and the necessary tax and benefit deductions are carried out.

Third-party remittance

Apart from such employee payments, payroll processing can also involve payments to a large number of third parties, including government authorities, plan administrators, garnishment beneficiaries, membership organizations, and so on. These payments may have to be made at a different frequency (e.g., quarterly or annually) than the frequency of your payroll runs (e.g., weekly and monthly); or these payments may have to follow dependency rules. For example, many states require remittance of state taxes immediately after remittance is made for federal taxes.

Managing and reconciling these liabilities and payment entries between HR, payroll, and accounting can quickly become a challenging process. For this purpose, the U.S. payroll component provides a Third-Party Remittance program to control *when* and *how* such payments are made and to automatically process and reconcile these accounting entries. Figure 8.7 shows an example of a Third-Party Remittance Run.

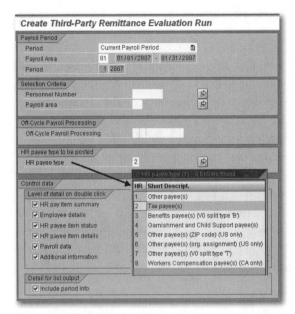

Figure 8.7 Third-Party Remittance

The sophistication of this functionality will become evident when you consider that you can specify not only simple dependency rules between payees such as the state and federal taxes discussed before but also complex dependency rules based on employee ZIP codes or organizational assignment. For example, if an employee union at an automotive company has many local chapters across the states, you can designate the regional union office as the payee based on the ZIP code of an employee. This process follows the familiar sequence of evaluation run, posting run, processing of posting run, and reconciliation of entries. Several reports are available to get the necessary information for these and other processes.

Payroll Reporting

The payroll component provides many standard and country-specific reports for operational, management, and statutory purposes to meet internal and external reporting requirements. For example, the Tax Reporter program is provided so that you can produce quarterly and annual wage and tax reports for local, state, and federal tax authorities.

Tax Reporter As you can see in Figure 8.8, the Tax Reporter can be used to create a number of employee forms as well as forms for the employer's federal tax returns. The forms are delivered per the design and requirements specified in the corresponding IRS publications. Regular updates from SAP ensure that these forms are updated with the latest changes from the IRS. You can easily transmit these tax forms electronically to local and state tax authorities. If required or accepted by relevant government authorities, you also have an option to combine data for multiple locations, multiple worksites, and even multiple tax authorities into a single electronic file. Additionally, you have access to a W-4 withholding allowances report and exemption expiration report to ensure process compliance.

Figure 8.8 Tax Reporter (U.S. Payroll)

The following are some of the other reports available in the U.S. Payroll component:

> New hire report to submit new hire data to federal and state governments

> NC-9901 report to electronically submit payroll data to the Census Bureau

> Letters outlining medical coverage for employees if applicable, as per HIPPA compliance

> Workers' Compensation report to calculate Workers' Compensation wages and premiums

Additionally, technical documentation is available so that you can create custom queries and custom reports to meet your requirements.

So far, you've seen how to use the payroll solution to maintain employee data, earnings, benefits, deductions, and tax calculations; carry out payroll processing; and generate necessary reports. In recent years, many organizations, large and small, have chosen to outsource all or some part of payroll processing, so let's see how SAP assists you in managing the difficult but sometimes necessary decision of outsourcing this key area.

Outsourcing

Considering the many government authorities with compliance and reporting requirements, as well as the inherent complexity of payroll processing, it's understandable why some companies choose to outsource payroll processing. Fortunately, with the payroll solution, you can outsource the complete payroll processing or only the processing of net payroll calculation.

Outsourcing your payroll

If you outsource complete payroll processing, you use the U.S. payroll component only to maintain employee data. So in this case, for payroll processing, you send updated employee information to the service provider, who processes the data; calculates earnings, tax, benefits, deductions, and other payments; makes payments; and sends back payroll information. With U.S. payroll, you can import this information into accounting to generate the necessary financial entries.

Another possibility is to calculate gross payroll and only outsource the net payroll processing. Under this scenario, you initiate payroll processing. And after gross payroll results are verified, this information is sent to the service provider. The service provider calculates the tax, deductions, and other components of net payroll; processes the payments; and sends back payroll information to you. You can upload this information in the Payroll component so that you can reconcile the results from the service provider to your gross payroll calculation; or you can import this information directly into accounting to generate the necessary financial entries.

> **➕ Tip**
>
> SAP supports the maintenance of outsourcing specific information for individual employees, for example, reference numbers in the outsourcing system. However, including such information in the data exchange with the service provider can increase processing time for the data export and import.

For companies with a large number of employees who are paid based on timecards (e.g., at plants, warehouses, etc.), you can export time evaluation data as an electronic file, which can be used by the service provider for payroll calculation. Another possible business scenario for U.S. companies is to outsource the processing of their payroll taxes. Programs are also provided that can export periodic or quarterly reporting data for external service providers. These programs are seamlessly integrated with the U.S. Payroll component, so the export data includes any changes due to retroactive payroll calculations. This data integrity enables the service providers to prepare accurate W-2 forms and tax reports.

Interface Toolbox for HR
Additionally, to exchange data between SAP and other third-party systems, the Interface Toolbox for HR can be used. This tool can access most of the employee and payroll information and export it in a format required by other systems. It can also be used to import data from other systems into SAP for comparison, evaluation, and reporting.

Case Study

This mining company headquartered in Canada has mining projects and properties in 11 countries in North America, South and Central

America, Australia, and Finland. The company has a global workforce of 3,500 full-time workers, excluding large numbers of temporary and hourly workers at different project sites around the world. The company develops, produces, and markets mineral resources, with future plans for engaging in discovery and acquisition projects. The company carried out a global implementation of SAP ERP components such as sales, procurement, GL, AR, and AP that went live in December, 2005. After the first wave of projects were stabilized, the company decided to concentrate on HR and payroll business processes.

Business Challenge

Because most of the regional offices ran different systems (many of the "systems" consisted of several Excel spreadsheets) for HR and payroll processes, management was painfully aware of the business risks and operational challenges. For example, at many offices, the applications for personnel management and payroll processing were separate, which required entry of common personnel data at least twice, which increased the workload and the need for staff. Disparate systems meant that the employee data wasn't always accurate or complete, which reduced the service quality of the payroll department. Adding to the complexity and administration of payroll processing; many locations, including several locations in the United States and Canada, required mid-month, end-of-the-month, and weekly payroll processing for different groups of employees and workers.

Employee transfers between locations were difficult to process due to disparate payroll systems and invariably required end-of-the-year adjustments for statutory compliance. The processing of payroll required gathering data from multiple systems and working through multiple interfaces, which meant multiple points of possible failure. Due to incorrect or incomplete employee or payroll data, approximately 15 % of the payroll checks or bank transfers (globally) generated by existing systems were incorrect and required manual processing. Another major problem area for top management was the lack of information to control labor costs in a timely fashion. Most of the time, additional costs due to overtime and double-time (as negotiated with labor unions) worked by mine workers were visible only when posted to financials, which was too late to take any corrective measures. For these reasons, gathering payroll information for analytics was a nightmarishly resource-intensive process, which is why it wasn't attempted unless required for statutory compliance.

Solution Deployment

Considering the industry reputation, Peoplesoft was a strong candidate for consideration for HR and payroll projects. However, the decision was made to go with SAP ERP HCM because of its extremely strong integration with existing systems used by the company and the availability of partially preconfigured country-specific HR and payroll components, which considerably shortened the project rollout time. It was decided to roll out the SAP ERP HCM personnel management and personnel time Management components worldwide, and implement the payroll component for the United States and Canada.

One of the main objectives of the project was to get all relevant business processes on the same system, so not much organizational change was made. The payroll frequency and operational responsibility for payroll processing of various locations and project sites remained the same. Interfaces were developed to import time data captured at mining sites for hourly and temporary workers.

The project to implement payroll was completed in 11 months, in time to go live during the open enrollment window for most of the employee benefit plans in the United States and Canada. A conscious decision was made to carry out complete payroll processing within the company, instead of outsourcing components of tax processing or net payroll. This decision was made to develop internal expertise that can be used for a future rollout of the payroll component to other countries. During the business analysis phase, more than 90 business processes were documented, including 49 payroll processes. These processes were used to develop more than 350 test scenarios that added to the timeline of the project but ensured comprehensive testing and rollout of a well-tested system.

Value Achieved

The company started realizing benefits almost immediately after the payroll system went live in the United States and Canada. The most important improvement at the operational level was a single view of employee and payroll data. This eliminated requirements of multiple data entry, reduced the chances of inaccurate or incomplete data, and helped the HR and payroll departments identify common areas of improvement. Managing different payroll runs (weekly, mid-month, and end-of-the-month) no longer required repeating the same set of complex, manual processes to consolidate data received from multiple systems. The reduction in administrative effort enabled the staff to improve the quality of their service and concentrate on more value-added activities.

In the first month after the payroll system went live, which included a number of weekly, mid-month, and end-of-the-month payroll runs at several locations, the average percentage of manual checks dropped to an astonishingly low 2 %! These checks had to be processed manually due to incorrect employee information, and the company expects this number to go down even more. The company has not yet processed any employee transfers between the United States and Canada, but the payroll staff is confident that they will be able to process any such transfer without compromising the accuracy and compliance aspects of payroll processing.

For the management, this project provided improved access and timely visibility to payroll data. Management was able to obtain payroll data for each period as soon as it was processed, which enabled them to focus on special, unplanned payroll costs such as overtime, double time, and so on and respond to staffing requirements of different mining sites. Management was also able to announce a range of incentives localized for individual mining sites because it no longer meant additional work for the payroll department. Because incentive plan details were maintained in the system, the payroll solution was able to automatically recognize and process applicable incentive bonuses based on the time and wage information and location of the employees.

The timeliness and accuracy of payments made to plan administrators was also improved due to the automatic calculation and processing of payments. Considering the detailed information available in the system for payroll calculations, the tax department is confident they will meet the upcoming deadline for tax reporting. Even though implementation of the payroll component from SAP required a moderate but permanent increase in technical support staff, the company was able to reduce the headcount of their functional staff in the payroll departments by 10 %. As the system becomes more stable and integrated, the company expects to further trim down this headcount.

Looking Ahead

Apart from the payroll rollout to other countries in Central and South America, Australia, and Finland, the company has identified two areas for the next wave of SAP projects. The first of this initiative is to process employee expense reimbursement through payroll processing. Currently, the expense reimbursement process is completely manual, except for the reimbursement payment made out of the payroll solution. The company will be able to leverage the SAP configuration done for the personnel management and payroll processing, and by enabling a few other functionalities in travel expense accounting, the company can streamline the expense reimbursement processes.

Another initiative will require implementation of the Employee Self Service component in SAP ERP HCM that enables employees to manage their own data and submit requests for routine processes via the Internet or company intranet. By extending this function, the company can allow employees to download HR and payroll forms, enroll in benefit plans during open enrollment periods, manage and request changes to personal information, and so on.

Summary

Payroll processes and operational challenges vary by country, by company, and by industry. Following are some of the functions provided by the payroll component that enable you to meet those challenges:

> Improve accuracy, efficiency, and compliance by using consolidated and consistent business processes for worldwide company locations.

> Cut down on development and deployment time of payroll solutions by using a partially configured system that can meet business requirements and localized statutory requirements.

> Provide automatic and seamless calculation of payroll deductions by integrating the payroll component with the benefits administration component.

> Calculate earnings and incentives using a variety of calculation models, as well as integrate with third-party systems to import or export time-management data for wage calculation.

> Obtain invaluable auditing and reconciliation capability by enabling authorized users to trace summarized accounting entries back to the payroll results for individual personnel numbers.

> Outsource complete or partial payroll processing or tax processing, and easily integrate calculation results back into SAP for financial accounting.

> Use many standard reports to meet the diverse information needs of federal, state, and local tax authorities, other government authorities, management, and employees.

In the next chapter, you'll see how SAP can support you in carrying out financial consolidation.

9

Consolidation

Globalization affects even the smallest businesses today. Many businesses have their own companies throughout the world, or are represented through other companies. So, when it comes time to report revenue and profits for all operations, businesses need to consolidate their data into a uniform structure. SAP ERP Financials supports this type of consolidation for both external, statutory purposes and internal, management purposes. Whether the functionality described in this chapter is relevant for your business depends not only on the size and type of your business but also on your corporate structure and statutory requirements.

Small corporations commonly consist of multiple companies created for tax benefits, which require consolidation. But, if your consolidation process doesn't involve complex currency translation or elimination requirements, you may be able to use customized reports from the SAP GL to meet your requirements.

Overview

With SAP ERP Financials, the bases for consolidation and the actual process of consolidation are separated from each other. This approach lets you consolidate companies for statutory reporting and consolidate profit centers for management reporting, while using the same consolidation processes such as currency translation, processing elimination entries, and others. This is because the consolidation design uses the same logic for a consolidation process regardless of whether consolidation is carried out for companies or for profit centers.

Companies (or profit centers, or any other consolidation unit) can be grouped into one or more consolidation groups in multilevel hierarchies for consolidation. This hierarchy can be created so that it reflects your corporate structure from a statutory or reporting point of view. You can also create parallel hierarchies, so that you can prepare consolidated reports for the same data using multiple criteria such as companies and business segments. And using the same set of programs, you can carry out consolidation based on different accounting principles as well as for different types of data such as actual, budget, and forecast.

In addition, typical consolidation tasks, such as currency translation, elimination of payables/receivables, revenue/expense, profit/loss due to inventory transfer, and investment consolidation are all supported. Data for consolidation can be collected using several different methods. For consolidation based on companies or profit centers, transactional data can be seamlessly collected from other SAP components or from other systems. You can also define rules to validate data at any stage in the consolidation process, which lets you identify and resolve data errors as they occur instead of discovering them after the final consolidated statements are prepared.

For reporting, you can create one or more consolidated financial statements to meet your reporting, audit, and analysis requirements. Additional reports are available to display control parameters and master data that influence the consolidation process, and there are additional tools for creating a variety of other types of reports.

Functions in Detail

We'll begin by describing how you can set up SAP ERP Financials to reflect your corporate structure for consolidation, and then we'll move on to talk about how to set up the software for more typical consolidation activities, including currency translation, eliminations, and investment consolidation.

Consolidation Setup

Before you can actually carry out consolidation, you have to set up the consolidation structure and specify the parameters that influence and control the consolidation process. So let's discuss the different setups required to map your corporate structure and the corresponding consolidation requirements.

Corporate Structure

To set up your corporate structure in consolidation, you need to be familiar with the differences among dimension, consolidation unit, and consolidation group. *Dimensions* are created to differentiate between different types of consolidation. For example, if you want to carry out consolidation by companies and by profit centers, you'll have to set up two different dimensions—one for each type of consolidation.

Dimension

 Tip

Even though technically it's also possible to create a single dimension that carries out consolidation based on companies and profit centers, it's recommended to use separate dimensions.

Note that how you set up dimensions doesn't have an impact on what consolidation steps you carry out. Consolidation steps follow the same logic whether consolidation is carried out by companies, profit centers, or other criteria you set up. The process steps and functionality discussed in this chapter are valid and applicable equally to any type of consolidation.

Consolidation units in the software represent individual companies, profit centers, or business areas that provide data and act as a basis for the consolidation process. Attributes of a consolidation unit specify its functional currency, whether it's included in the consolidation process, how the data for that unit is collected, and other information such as language, country, and industrial sector. *Consolidation groups* represent the level at which consolidation is carried out. A consolidation group also consists of more than one consolidation unit, although the same consolidation unit can be part of more than one consolidation group (e.g., in the case of proportional consolidation). Consolidation groups influence consolidation frequency and the currency used in the consolidation. And consolidation groups can be organized in a multilevel hierarchy to represent your consolidation structure. Figure 9.1 shows an example of consolidation hierarchies for business areas.

After you've set up the consolidation structure, you have to set up the consolidated chart of accounts.

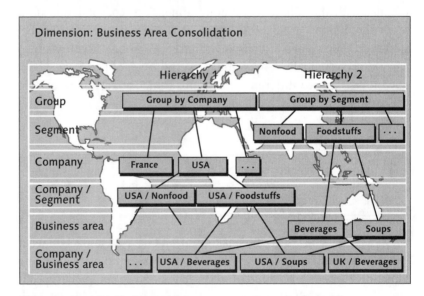

Figure 9.1 Consolidation Hierarchy

Consolidation Chart of Accounts

The consolidation chart of accounts consists of financial statement items (FS items). Information from individual companies or profit centers is aggregated into FS items and is used to prepare consolidated financial statements.

Fortunately, templates for preparing consolidated financial statements per U.S. GAAP, Japanese GAAP, or EU directives are provided. These can be used as a base while preparing your own consolidated financial statements. The financial statement definition can be created manually, or it can be copied from the chart of accounts used in the operational GL system. And the individual FS items can refer to amounts, quantities, or even statistical information. For example, you can create a statistical FS item to represent the number of employees, which can be used to report sales per employee or overhead expenses per employee.

FS items and FS subitems

Another unique feature of FS items is the ability to capture lower level details into FS subitems and report the details as supporting information for consolidated numbers. Many consolidated numbers require lower level details for statutory or management purposes. Examples of such requirements are receivables by company for intercompany receivables and payables, or gain/loss by currencies for foreign exchange gain/loss reported in consolidated statements.

In the consolidated financial statement definition, you can determine which types of lower level details are required for each FS item. With SAP ERP Financials some commonly used criteria for capturing and reporting lower level details are provided, such as currencies, partner unit (company code or profit center) from which the entry was posted, asset acquisition year and month, and a few others. In addition, you can define your own criteria for capturing lower level details for FS items by product groups, geographical regions, cost centers, customer's country, or any such criteria.

Now let's look at another important design decision consolidation: versions.

Versions

At the most basic level, *versions* let you separate the consolidation of actual numbers from the consolidation of plan or budget numbers. These versions also control dimensions and consolidation charts of accounts and other parameters. However, versions in SAP ERP provide much more flexibility and control than simply referring to different types of numbers.

You'll notice in Figure 9.2 that the definition of a version brings together different consolidation activities and parameters, each linked with its own unique version. In the example shown, while carrying out the consolidation process for Plan version, SAP ERP uses different currency exchange rates, tax rates, and corporate structure. For all other consolidation activities and parameters—such as how currency translation should be carried out, how interunit eliminations should be processed, or how investments should be consolidated—the same methods as used for consolidating actual numbers are used.

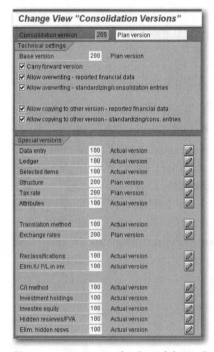

Figure 9.2 Versions in the Consolidation Process

By carefully using different versions, you can keep repetitive data entry and data maintenance to a bare minimum while meeting all of your requirements. In addition, you can create different versions for simulating what-if business scenarios, for example, the effect of a planned merger or divestiture.

Simulation scenarios

 Example

> Consider the need to restate a prior year's results due to a change in the corporate structure. By using a new version for corporate structure while keeping versions for all other consolidation tasks the same, you can restate the results of previous years per the new corporate structure.

Finally, you have to set up ledgers to store the consolidation data.

Ledgers

You can set up one or more consolidation ledgers that contain transactions and numbers to process consolidation data and prepare consolidation reports. For each ledger, SAP stores transaction currency, currency of the company (or whatever is being consolidated), and the currency in which consolidation is carried out.

For example, you may have three separate ledgers to carry out regional consolidation for the Americas, Europe, and Asia regions, and a fourth ledger that consolidates worldwide data for headquarters based in the United States. Another possible use of multiple ledgers is if you want to consolidate the same group of companies but in different currencies, for example, in EUR for statutory reasons and in USD for institutional investors. You can meet this requirement by using two separate ledgers—each one with a different ledger currency for consolidation—and then using different versions to carry out consolidation in different currencies.

This section discussed the different design decisions you must make while setting up consolidation.

Let's move on to talk about how to collect data from the different consolidation units.

Data Collection and Postings

In this section, we'll discuss how to gather data for consolidation and further processing for different consolidation units. All companies in a corporate group may not be on the same SAP ERP Financials system or version, or may not even be using it. Your consolidation reports may also require additional data that isn't available or transferable from operational systems. To meet such diverse requirements, SAP ERP Financials includes several methods to collect data for consolidation, including manually entering financial data (it isn't as bad as it sounds). Let's first look at integrated data transfer.

Integrated Data Transfer

Real-time update   If you consolidate based on one of the integration types provided by SAP (i.e., companies, business areas, or profit centers), you get three different data transfer methods so that you can easily transfer relevant data from operational systems. These three methods are real-time update, periodic extract, and data rollup.

As the name implies, the real-time method posts data to the consolidation ledger at the same time as transactional data is posted to GL in operating systems. This data transfer method can be used for consolidation based on companies and business areas but not for profit center consolidation. Companies for which you want to use this data transfer method should be on the same SAP system that you use for consolidation.

Periodic-extract   In the periodic-extract method, entries for consolidation system are
method   prepared based on the mapping between operational data and consolidated financial statements. These entries are created in parallel to the transactional data entry and are accumulated in a separate ledger—aptly called the *preparation for consolidation* ledger. As part of the consolidation preparation, you download a data extract from this ledger and upload it to the consolidation system. This data transfer

method is useful when companies aren't on the same SAP ERP Financials system, although this method is also only available for company consolidation and business area consolidation, not profit center consolidation.

The third method of integrated data transfer is to use data rollup. This is the only method available for transfer data in profit center consolidation, although it can be used for company and business area consolidations as well. Under this method, you run a process that rolls up data from transactional ledgers to the consolidation ledger (if companies are on the same SAP system) or to a data file (if companies are on different systems). If data is rolled up into a data file, then the data file is subsequently uploaded in the consolidation system.

Integrated data transfer

When you first start using consolidation, you can transfer data from operational ledgers such as GL, profit center ledger, and other ledgers; or you can create required entries manually.

In a nutshell, that is how to collect data from subsidiaries that use SAP ERP Financials. Now let's look at how to collect data manually from subsidiaries that aren't using it.

Manual Data Entry

You can design and use data entry forms for manual entry that not only capture required information but also control and influence the type of information that can be entered. Some of the factors you can decide on while designing these forms are the currency or currencies in which financial information can be entered, whether information entered should be for the period or year-to-date, and whether information is entered before or after adjusting it per guidelines for group consolidation. You can even design the form so that the breakdown details by specific criteria (by currency, by product group, for example) are also required to be entered for selected FS items.

These data entry forms can capture data for a particular year, fiscal period, chart of accounts, company, profit center, or other criteria that you've built into the form. These forms can be used to enter financial information directly in the consolidation ledger online, or you can use Microsoft Excel or Microsoft Access to gather and enter this data offline. You can transfer data from SAP ERP Financials to Access or Excel and also import data back from Access. Among other factors, the choice of method depends on your organization's policy as well as operational convenience.

Offline data collection

Especially for corporations where operations are decentralized, this offline method of data collection can be very effective (see Figure 9.3). Using Access, you can export control parameters to a database, enter required financial information and other additional information, validate and report on the entered information, and transfer the information back into SAP or Excel. As part of the control parameters, exchange rate information is also transferred from SAP to an Access database, so you can even carry out currency translation in the offline database for local reporting.

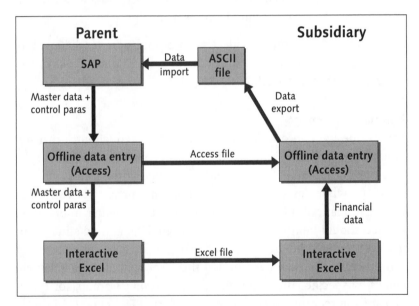

Figure 9.3 Data entry in Decentralized Corporate Structure

After the required information has been collected, you can carry out postings in the consolidation system.

Postings and Posting Levels

Changes are made to data received from companies during various steps of the consolidation process before the final consolidated statements are prepared. The software stores these changes as documents in the system, so that you can reconstruct an audit trail for your consolidated financial statements. These documents can either be a result of manual postings, or they may be created automatically when you carry out different consolidation functions such as elimination entries, and consolidation of investments. You may come across the term "standardizing entries" in the consolidation documentation. Standardizing entries are the entries posted to make data reported by individual companies compliant per the group consolidation policy.

All documents—whether they are posted manually, posted automatically, or transferred from another system—are posted in the consolidation system with a document type. Document types in the consolidation system control factors such as types of currencies in which amounts can be posted, level of details that can be entered, etc. Even though you can create and use as many different document types as required, every document type has to be associated with a posting level in SAP ERP Financials. Posting levels are used in consolidation to separate different types of entries throughout the consolidation process. So, for example, the posting level for an adjustment entry made after currency translation is different from the posting level for entries made while consolidating investments.

Posting levels

Posting levels influence multiple aspects of the consolidation process. For example, financial statement item balances are stored by posting level so that you can differentiate between the original amount loaded from the transactional system and other adjustments made at different stages in the consolidation process. Posting levels also control whether any consolidation adjustments you make are applicable for one company (e.g., adjustment entry), between two companies belonging to the same consolidation group (elimination between two companies in Europe for regional consolidation), or between companies belonging to different consolidation groups (e.g., elimination entry made at world headquarters for final consolidation).

Table 9.1 shows a sample list of posting levels used in consolidation.

Posting Level	Usage
00 or Space	Reported data loaded to consolidation system
01	Adjustment entries to reported data
02	Adjustment entries to reported data at consolidation group level
10	Standardizing/reclassification entries
12	Standardizing/reclassification entries at consolidation group level
20	Elimination entries
22	Elimination entries at consolidation group level
30	Postings for consolidation of investments

Table 9.1 Posting Levels in SAP Consolidation

Now let's look at the different consolidation functions available to automate different steps of the consolidation processes.

Currency Translation

You can post to the GL of any company in any currency as long as relevant exchange rates and control parameters are maintained in the system. Additionally, the consolidation group may consist of companies with different functional currencies. In these situations, you have to translate the financial data of individual companies from their functional currency to consolidation currency. Based on corporate structure and reporting requirements, data collected from a company may have to be translated into multiple currencies and even translated multiple times for different levels of consolidation.

The first step in this process is to group FS items that should be translated using the same method. In a very simplistic scenario, there may be just two groups of FS items: balance sheet items and income statement items. Typically, however, you'll have multiple FS item groups such as investments, stockholders equity, fixed assets, current assets, and income statement accounts—each of which needs to be translated using a different method.

The second step is to actually decide the exchange rate and translation method for each FS items group. Many currency translation methods are supported, including:

> Translate so that the net, year-to-date balance in the group currency is zero.

> Translate balances of prior months using the exchange rate from corresponding months.

> Translate balances of prior months using the exchange rate from the current month.

> Translate based on asset acquisition years.

Typically, currency translation is carried out from the functional currency of a company to the consolidation currency. If required, however, SAP ERP Financials also includes two translation methods that let you carry out currency translations directly from the currency in which the transactions are posted.

Lastly, you have to set up *consolidation translation methods* (see Figure 9.4) that consist of sequential steps with each step referring to an FS item group to be translated. This translation method is associated with one or more consolidation units. This design ensures that for all companies that use the same translation method, and all sections of a balance sheet and income statement are translated in the same way. When the currency translation process is carried out, the software translates each group of FS items based on control parameters in the translation method and then posts the results to the specified FS items.

The two types of currency translation runs are provisional and final. *Provisional currency translation* can be run any time, even if financial data contains errors or previous consolidation steps aren't completed. But, the *final translation run* is carried out only after all previous consolidation steps are completed, and all errors have been resolved. Of course, either of these translation runs can be repeated if underlying data has changed. For a repeat run, the software simply overwrites the previous results of the currency translation. New values calculated by the currency translation process are the result of different changes. Let's look at how to calculate these differences.

"Method Entries": Overview

Dimension	01	Cons chart/acct	01	Version	100	Period	1	/	2007

| Translation method | 01-10 | Mod. c-rate (TFA+ANI key date) |

No.	R	Item set 1	Description	ER ind.	Transl.
010	☐	CS01-1800	Property, Plant and Equipment	4	1
020	☐	CS01-1800	Property, Plant and Equipment	4	1
030	☐	CS01-1800	Property, Plant and Equipment	1	1
040	☐	CS01-1700	Investments		3
050	☐	CS01-2500	Equity (Without Net Income)		4
060	☐	CS01-2901	Retained Earnings - Prior Years		6
070	☐	CS01-2999	Remaining Balance Sheet (w/Net Income)	1	1
080	☐	CS01-3000	Income Statement	2	1
010	☑	CS01-1000	Balance Sheet		
020	☑	CS01-2939	Net Income - Balance Sheet/Income Stmt		
030	☑	CS01-3000	Income Statement		

Figure 9.4 Currency Translation Method

Translation Differences

Different sections of a balance sheet are usually translated using different translation methods and thus possibly using different exchange rates. This approach has the potential to create financial statements that don't have a net balance of zero. To ensure that financial statements always balance to zero, the software calculates these translation differences as follows.

SAP ERP Financials uses one of the exchange rates as the reference exchange rate. All items in a financial statement are then translated to the consolidation currency using this reference exchange rate to determine the reference value for each item. Subsequently, the translation differences are calculated as the difference between reference values and actual values (calculated based on the translation method specified for the FS item groups). Typically, the current exchange rate is used as the reference exchange rate, but you can choose any other rate as the reference.

Such translation differences can occur in the balance sheet as well as in the income statement. If you report translation differences due to balance sheet items in the balance sheet and due to income statement items in the income statement; both financial statements remain balanced, and no further processing is required. The software also allows you to report translation differences due to balance sheet items reported in the income statement and vice versa. In such cases, you have to make correcting entries to ensure that the financial statements are balanced to zero.

Transaction Differences and Temporal Differences
When an amount is translated from the functional currency of a company to the consolidation currency, the resulting change in the consolidation currency can be attributed to two factors: changes due to exchange rate and changes due to change in the underlying functional currency amount. Temporal differences represent changes in value exclusively due to a change in the exchange rate, whereas transaction differences represent a change in the value due to a change in the underlying amount.

Typically, these differences are recorded as a combined change in the group currency value. However, if you need to separately report on exchange gain/loss due to exchange rate fluctuations, you can indicate FS item groups for which temporal differences should be separately recorded. Note that temporal differences aren't carried forward across fiscal years. Instead, when the balance is carried forward to the next fiscal year, the temporal differences are merged with transaction differences.

Rounding Differences
Sometimes during currency translation calculations, small rounding differences can occur. To make sure that rounding differences are handled properly, you define one or more rounding steps in a currency translation method (e.g., the last three steps in Figure 9.4) and specify an FS item to post these differences to.

You can check for rounding differences for an FS item group. This method checks whether the net balance of the group is zero, for example, checking that the sum of all balance sheet items is zero. Another option is to check for rounding differences by comparing the net balances of two groups of FS items. This method can be used, for example, to validate that retained earnings reported in the balance sheet matches the sum of the corresponding items in the income statement. In any case, rounding differences are posted to ensure that the net balance of a group is zero or that the net difference between two groups being compared is zero.

 Tip

While validating financial data, rounding differences are calculated only in the consolidation currency. Differences in functional currency indicate that the financial data didn't balance even before currency translation was carried out. Such differences aren't allowed and are reported as errors.

After currency translation is completed, the next step involves carrying out elimination entries for business transactions between individual companies or profit centers.

Elimination Entries

In a large, multinational corporation, it's fairly common for companies in a corporate group to make loans to each other, make payments or collect money on behalf of each other, and also to sell to or purchase from each other. To avoid double counting while preparing accurate consolidated financial statements, these entries should be eliminated, that is, cancelled against each other. Even though these elimination entries can be posted using manual postings as discussed in earlier, the software can also automatically carry out these elimination entries.

One-sided versus two-sided eliminations

After you have identified groups of FS items for the elimination process, you create the elimination methods that consist of multiple steps with each step corresponding to an elimination process between a pair of FS item groups. So, for example, an elimination method may have one or more steps to process the elimination of receivables and payables, followed by one or more steps to process the elimination of revenues and expenses, and so on. While carrying out the elimination process for a consolidation group, the system processes one pair of companies at a time, and for that pair of companies, it processes one step at a time. Each step can carry out either one-sided elimination or two-sided elimination.

One-sided elimination is a simplified form of the elimination process, in which you specify only one group of FS items. The elimination process calculates the net balance of the group of FS items (e.g., revenues) in one company and posts an equal and opposite value to the offsetting FS item (e.g., expense) in the partner company. You can even choose to post the offsetting entry in the original company instead of the partner company.

However, a more typical elimination process is the two-sided elimination process that involves two groups of FS items. To carry out the elimination postings, the system compares the value of the first group of FS items (e.g., receivables) in one company, to the value of the second group of FS items (e.g., payables) in the partner company and then carries out posting of elimination entries. Any difference in values between the two FS item groups is calculated and posted as the elimination difference.

Elimination Differences

There are several possible reasons for elimination differences between two companies. These differences can be due to posting errors, differences in timing, or differences in accounting policies. Another reason for these differences can be that each company has different functional currency, and hence they report two sides of the same transaction (which could have occurred only in one currency) translated into two different currencies. These and similar types of differences that are exclusively due to changes in exchange rates are called *currency related differences*, and they can be recorded separately from other types of elimination differences.

You can decide to post elimination differences in one of the four ways. You can post them to the first group of FS items, to the second group of FS items, to the company that reported the lower of the two values, or to the company that reported the higher of the two values. With this flexibility, you can choose the appropriate course of action if, for example, a difference exists between receivable and payable numbers reported by a pair of companies in a consolidation group.

However, if the elimination difference is too large, you don't necessarily want it to be posted automatically. For this reason, you can specify a threshold value for each pair of FS items in the elimination method. Only elimination differences up to the threshold value are automatically posted by the system. Now, let's look at how to process and reconcile these elimination entries.

Processing and Reconciliation

Reconciliation lists   Typically, before the final elimination entries are posted to the consolidation system, individual companies like to review elimination entries involving their unit to analyze and correct any unexpected or unacceptable entries. For this purpose, you can run the elimination process in test mode to prepare reconciliation lists. These lists report on proposed elimination entries, including the ones where elimination differences may be higher than the threshold specified. After proposed entries in reconciliation lists are reviewed and confirmed, you can run the elimination process in update mode. In update mode, all elimination entries are made to the consolidation system, as long as the elimination difference is at or below the specified threshold value.

Other functionality includes the ability to recreate the "before" situation even after final elimination entries are posted or to reconcile elimination lists prepared in the consolidation system with the operational GL system in individual companies as long as they are on the same system. The process discussed in this section can be used to handle different types of eliminations, but additional functionality process the elimination of profit and loss incurred due to inventory transfer between companies is available.

Elimination of IPI

You can automatically eliminate profit and loss entries resulting from inventory transfer between two companies in a corporate group, that is, elimination of interunit profit and loss in inventory (IPI). An important prerequisite for using this functionality is that all required details are available and maintained. If enough accurate and detailed information isn't available, you may want to consider using manual postings to handle these types of elimination entries.

One of the decisions you have to make is whether to carry out elimination of IPI for FS items representing inventory (e.g., finished goods, raw materials, etc.) or at a more detailed level by product groups. Product groups can be defined per your corporate requirements, and they enable you to carry out elimination of IPI at a more detailed level than FS items.

During this process, inventory accounts are adjusted based on the IPI calculation. Depending on whether there is gain or loss on an intercompany transfer, the inventory value is reduced or increased by a corresponding amount. Entries that offset inventory account adjustments are made to FS items based on control parameters you specify. If you use product groups, you can specify offsetting FS items and other control parameters at the level of product groups; otherwise, this specification is made at the level of inventory FS items.

You need to know a few additional factors while processing the elimination of IPI. Adjustments made to inventory accounts include changes due to exchange rate fluctuations. Temporal differences (differences exclusively due to a change in the exchange rate) aren't recorded separately. Secondly, you can select whether the offsetting entry is posted to the company (or profit center) that supplies the inventory or to the company (or profit center) that receives and manages inventory. Lastly, you decide whether inventory adjustments should have an effect on earnings by choosing to post offsetting entries to either the income statement (earnings are affected) or to the balance sheet (earnings aren't affected).

After the system has been set up to process the elimination of IPI, you need to maintain additional financial data that provides the required information for processing. This data should be maintained for every combination of product groups and every pair of companies (or profit centers) that participate in the inventory transfer. For each of these combinations, you maintain the following information so that the system can calculate the cost of goods, which in turn can be used to calculate profit/loss on inventory transfer:

> Closing book value and quantity of goods.

> Any incidental costs (as percentage or fixed amount); from a consolidation point of view, this cost is considered as a further increase to cost of goods.

> Cost of goods manufactured; this can be either a fixed amount or can be calculated based on the percentage of sales. The percentage in this case can be the gross margin or the markup percentage.

Figure 9.5 shows in detail how all of this information is used to process the elimination of IPI.

Schema for the Calcualtion of IPI Profit/Loss		
Variable	**Formula**	**Represents**
A		(Net) book value in reporting period
B		Valuation allowance (loss allowed)
C		Valuation allowance (no loss allowed), in other words, a valuation allowance that must not change an interunit profit into a loss
D	A + B + C	Value of goods supplied / inventory value from the goods transaction
E		Incidental acquisition costs (absolute or as a percentage); need to be capitalized from the point of view of the group
F	D - E	Sales revenue
G		Profit percentage; either a markup or a gross margin
H	100 - G	Cost of goods manufactured (%)
I	(F * H) + E Or: F * (H + E)	Group cost of goods manufactured ...if incidental acquisition costs are entered as a percentage
J	A - I	Interunit profit/loss for elimination

Figure 9.5 Elimination of IPI (Interunit Profit & Loss on Inventory)

After the elimination of IPI is carried out, the next step in a typical consolidation process is to consolidate investments.

Consolidation of Investments

Consolidating investments eliminates the parent's investment with the stockholders equity of the subsidiary. SAP ERP Financials includes comprehensive functions to consolidate investments based on purchase method, proportional consolidation method, equity method, mutual stock method, and cost method. For a multilevel corporate group, the software supports the consolidation of investments using step consolidation (separate consolidation is carried out in multiple steps for each level of the corporate structure, starting at the bottom level) as well as simultaneous consolidation (consolidation occurs in a single step for the entire reporting entity). Figure 9.6 shows an example of both types of consolidation.

Investment consolidation methods

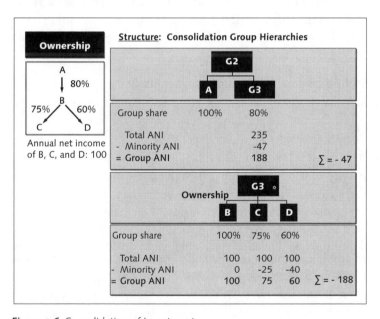

Figure 9.6 Consolidation of Investments

The consolidation of investments process goes through a specific sequence of steps to account for changes in investment and equity information for each company as well as any changes in the corporate group structure. It's difficult to discuss all of the possible functions of all of the different methods in a single chapter of a book, let alone in a single section, so we'll only focus on some of the main functions such as acquisition, capitalization, divestiture, and treatment of goodwill.

Acquisition and Capitalization

When new subsidiaries are included in a consolidation group for the first time, you carry out the first consolidation process, which eliminates the entire reported investment from the parent company against the corresponding equity reported by the subsidiary. Before carrying out any other activities in the consolidation of investments, you have to carry out the first consolidation of all new subsidiaries included in the consolidation group during that period. It's also important to specify whether the first consolidation is carried out at the beginning of the month (or any other consolidation period) or at the end of the month. This decision determines whether investment and equity changes that occurred during the month are included in the first consolidation.

Step acquisition

All consolidations of the subsidiary after its first consolidation are called *subsequent consolidations*. During subsequent consolidations, all activities for the consolidation period trigger adjustments in equity values or investment values depending on the method used for investment consolidation. If the group share of a subsidiary increases, you can carry out *step acquisition*. In step acquisition, the increase in the group shares adjusts postings in the subsidiary, and these adjustments are subsequently compared against the changes in the investment book values of the parent company.

Another possible scenario is when the book value of investments is changed in the parent company, with or without any change in its group share in the subsidiary. If the value of investment has changed along with the increase in the group share percentage, you can use step acquisition to account for proportional change. Any increase in capital without a corresponding change in the group share triggers the creation of goodwill entries.

Treatment of Goodwill

In the purchase method, any difference between the acquisition cost recorded by the parent company and the proportionate value of the subsidiary assets is recorded as *goodwill* in the consolidated balance sheet. Depending on whether the acquisition cost is greater or less than the value of assets, the difference is recorded as positive or negative goodwill. And whether goodwill is disclosed separately or is reported as part of the investment book value is determined based on the stipulated treatment in the method used for the investment consolidation.

Goodwill reported in a consolidated balance sheet is changed based on any subsequent changes to the group share or increase or decrease in capitalization. SAP ERP Financials supports several different options for handling the goodwill amount because the treatment of goodwill depends on statutory regulations, the consolidation method being used, and whether it's positive goodwill or negative goodwill.

Goodwill reporting

The three main options of handling goodwill are:

1. to offset goodwill against appropriated retained earnings
2. to reduce goodwill by amortization
3. to reduce goodwill by impairment

Under the first option, the goodwill amount is offset against appropriated retained earnings (either during the first consolidation or gradually over multiple years) so that it does not affect consolidated income. Under the second option, the goodwill is amortized over a fixed number of years or by using a fixed percentage. However, in this case, goodwill does affect the consolidated income. Under the third option, the goodwill remains as an asset on the balance sheet and is reduced only as required, after periodic impairment reviews. This option allows companies to carry out acquisitions without being forced to take periodic large write-downs of their assets.

On the other hand, negative goodwill is either reported separately as an asset or a liability, or it's offset against other noncurrent assets with any remaining difference directly impacting consolidated income.

Next, let's move on to handling the divestiture and transfer of companies.

Divestitures and Transfers

With the SAP software, total divestiture (a subsidiary completely leaves a consolidation group), partial divestiture (representing a reduction in group share of a subsidiary), and reduction in indirect investment (change in higher level company due to the divestiture of a subsidiary at least two levels below it) are supported. Keep in mind that for any of these activities to occur, the subsidiary must have undergone a first consolidation in SAP.

For the total divestiture (similar to first consolidation), you must specify whether the divestiture occurs at the beginning or end of the period. In general, total divestiture reverses all relevant entries for the company leaving the consolidation group. On the other hand, the partial divestiture process reduces the prior consolidation of investments entries. It also affects the original and accumulated amortized value of goodwill, the percentage of group shares and minority shares, and the book value of investments reported in the parent company.

Corporate transfers

If ownership of a subsidiary company isn't changed to the external entity but instead is transferred to another consolidation group within the corporate structure, you can use total transfer or partial transfer instead of the divestiture process. Similar to a reduction in indirect investment, indirect transfers that are triggered in a multilevel corporate hierarchy by total or partial transfers at lower levels are supported.

In addition to these typical consolidation processes, negative stockholders equity, distribution of dividends, calculation of minority interest, validations, reclassifications, are also supported, as we'll discuss next.

Validations and Reclassifications

You define validations to check the consistency and accuracy of data through the consolidation process. Properly designed validations can identify errors early in the consolidation process, which makes the process more accurate and efficient. You can use validation rules to validate data across consolidation groups, and the rules can be reused as required. So, for example, you can create a validation rule to check that assets are equal to liabilities and equity, and to check that the profit calculated in the balance sheet is the same as the one reported in the income statement. Then, you can run this validation rule after every consolidation activity to make sure that validations still hold true. Depending on the severity of a failed validation, you can trigger information either as a warning or as an error message.

You define reclassifications in the consolidation system to automatically reclassify values of FS items. Reclassifications can be used to make adjustments to information collected from consolidation units as well as to already-consolidated data. The power of reclassifications is shown in the following list:

> You can use the value or percentage of item A (triggering item) and reclassify it from item B (source item) to item C (destination item). For example, the percentage of repair expenses can be reclassified from sales revenue to maintenance revenue.

> You can post reclassification entries to the original consolidation unit, a partner consolidation unit, or a totally different consolidation unit.

> You can restrict the calculation of value based on several criteria such as document type, posting levels, currencies, acquisition year, partner consolidation unit, and many others.

> You can define reclassifications as periodic reclassifications, so that the system only considers periodic changes instead of the total amount for reclassification.

> You can trigger reclassification only if the value of an item is a debit or credit.

Similar to other consolidation activities, you create a reclassification method that consists of one or more steps with each step carrying out the required reclassification.

Now that we've looked at the most typical consolidation activities, let's see how to set up and execute the consolidation process.

Execution of Consolidation

SAP ERP Financials includes two programs that group all activities required for the consolidation process: data monitor and consolidation monitor. The data monitor consists of activities that collect and prepare data for consolidation, and the consolidation monitor consists of all activities required to actually carry out consolidation. These programs display individual companies in the consolidation hierarchy as rows and different data collection and consolidation activities as columns. An intersection of a row and a column displays the color-coded status (not started, errors, warnings, successful, or not relevant) of a consolidation activity for a consolidation unit. Figure 9.7 shows the typical activities in the data monitor and consolidation monitor programs.

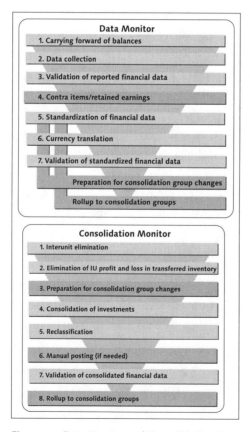

Figure 9.7 Data Monitor and Consolidation Monitor

As we discussed earlier, you can create multiple consolidation hierarchies to represent your corporate structure. Similarly, you can create as many tasks as required to carry out different data collection and consolidation activities. This ability to create your own consolidation hierarchies and consolidation activities, combined with the highly intuitive matrix layout used by the data monitor and consolidation monitor programs, provides you with highly flexible tools to perform and monitor your consolidation process.

Any activity shown in Figure 9.7 can correspond to multiple steps in the consolidation process. So, for example, in the data monitor, you may have multiple steps to carry out different types of data validations, or in the consolidation monitor, you may have multiple steps to carry out different types of elimination entries or reclassification entries.

Case Study

The client is a large consumer products company with more than 7,000 products in 16 product categories. The company, together with its subsidiaries, manufactures and sells some of the flagship products that are household names in countries around the world. The client has operations in 20+ countries in the Americas and Europe, with more than $23 billion in annual worldwide revenue.

Currently, its principal markets include North America, Latin America, and Central and Eastern Europe. The corporate structure of the company requires it to conform to statutory requirements of 21 countries and collect data from several hundred collection points scattered across approximately 34 countries. Over the past decade, the client acquired several other smaller local and multinational companies to boost its product portfolio. In addition, the client also underwent two major organizational restructurings.

Business Challenge
Rapid growth, multiple acquisitions, and organizational restructuring contributed to many challenges in the consolidation process. Even though the head office and many subsidiaries in Central Europe were

already using SAP as their primary ERP system for transactional processing, the SAP rollout to recent acquisitions was not yet complete.

Regional offices were using different systems for their daily operations and to carry out consolidations as required for statutory purposes. Management reporting from the consolidation point of view (e.g., by profit centers) was mostly not possible for many regional offices due to operational constraints. Data collection from subsidiaries mostly required manual intervention at several levels. And many locations submitted required data by using Excel spreadsheets or by faxing hard copies of reports from their individual systems.

The company was in the process of changing the management structure from a regional management model to a management model by business lines. This change necessitated a better understanding of intercompany sales, inventory exchanges, and other business transactions. It was difficult, if not impossible to get this type of information from legacy systems in a timely fashion.

Solution Deployment

Because the overall business strategy and IT strategy of the company was to eventually use SAP as the main ERP system at all worldwide locations; the choice of the SAP ERP Financials consolidation system was obvious.

This decision presented two choices for the rollout of the consolidation system. One option was to roll out the consolidation only to those regions where most of the subsidiaries were already using SAP ERP Financials and wait to roll out the consolidation to other regional offices until after their subsidiaries had started using SAP as their operational system. The second option was to roll out the consolidation to all regions regardless of whether their subsidiaries used SAP as their operational system. After considering both the options, it was decided to roll out SAP ERP Financials consolidation to all regional offices. However, to ensure the efficient collection of data from subsidiaries that didn't use it, the scope of the project also included rolling out a portal on the company intranet.

From the time requirement analysis started, it took 14 months to complete the design, development, and final rollout of SAP ERP Financials consolidation to all regional offices worldwide. Most of the project work was handled by internal resources at the SAP competency center of the company, with external consulting resources providing assistance to regional offices as required.

The monthly consolidation process started with collecting financial data from 168 locations in 34 countries. Data collection from subsidiaries that use SAP was automatic and was scheduled to run on a daily basis. Processes and policies were also instituted so that companies that do not use SAP can submit required financial information through the company intranet. Data collected from all subsidiaries was loaded into the central SAP software in which all regional and global consolidation cycles are set up.

After data from all subsidiaries of a regional office was received, the preliminary consolidation process was carried out. The preliminary consolidation process went through all of the steps of consolidation, including adjustments and reclassifications, currency translation, eliminations, and consolidation of investments. Subsequent to this process, reports were prepared and distributed to regional offices and subsidiaries for their review and confirmation. Adjustments suggested by subsidiaries were incorporated into the consolidation data, and the process was repeated again. After regional consolidations were finalized, the data was rolled up to prepare for the global and final consolidation.

Considering the number of companies, regions, and countries involved in the consolidation process, it was important to keep track of any changes in the corporate structure such as acquisitions, divestitures, transfers, and so on. The monthly consolidation cycle also included time for updating consolidation master data in SAP to reflect changes to the corporate structure.

Value Achieved

The consolidation project has considerably automated many activities of the consolidation process. Valuable analytical time of talented resources that was wasted on spreadsheet maintenance, data entry, and manual validation is now better used for much-needed analysis and compliance-related activities.

Because all regional and global consolidation cycles are now maintained in SAP ERP Financials consolidation, progress (or delay) of the consolidation process is easy to monitor. The data monitor and consolidation monitor provide visibility into subsidiaries that have or have not submitted financial data for consolidation and into consolidation processes that are at various stages of completion. The corporate consolidation group uses this information to provide necessary support to regional offices or to take corrective actions. In addition, this type of monitoring highlights business processes that contribute to delays in different consolidation processes.

Because consolidation activities are carried out in a single system, the accounting processes for consolidation were standardized and somewhat simplified. The system is able to provide a detailed audit trail for all changes made at each step of the consolidation process. This information can be used to trace numbers in the final consolidated statements to the original financial data reported by companies.

Having a single system for all consolidation activities has made huge improvements in the area of management and statutory reporting. Reporting packages can now be created so that it not only includes consolidated statements but also all supporting information. The system also supports ad hoc generation and analysis of any financial information relevant for consolidation. Regional offices can now consistently receive consolidation reports, review them, and make any corrections in a timely fashion before numbers are finalized for global consolidation.

Looking Ahead

The current scope of the consolidation process in SAP ERP Finanicals only carries out consolidation as required by legal entities. However, considering the company's goal to have management structured by business lines, it's important to obtain the same level of visibility into the financial operations of the profit centers. So one of the next initiatives is to consolidate profit centers at regional levels.

Another area under consideration is the elimination of IPI. Under the current process, this elimination is carried out for each type of inventory such as finished goods, raw materials, and other types of inventories that represent FS items in consolidated statements. This information isn't detailed enough for regional offices, so another initiative being considered is to be able to eliminate IPI by product groups, with product groups corresponding to each of the 16 product categories.

Summary

In this chapter, we learned how SAP ERP Financials gives you a highly flexible structure to help you meet your consolidation requirements. The following are some of the key features of this functionality:

> Simultaneously carry out multiple types of consolidation (by companies, by profit centers, etc.) to meet statutory and management requirements.

> Create parallel, multiple consolidation hierarchies to accurately represent your corporate structure for the consolidation process.

> Create a consolidated balance sheet, a consolidated income statement, and other financial statements to meet your reporting requirements.

> Choose from more than 10 different online and offline processes to support the collection of financial and nonfinancial data from subsidiaries.

> Automatically process different types of elimination entries for transactions between companies in a consolidation group.

> Process the elimination of IPI transfers for product groups, which can be created as per your reporting requirements.

> Consolidate investments based on the purchase method, proportional consolidation method, equity method, mutual stock method, and cost method.

> Use validation rules to validate data at each step of the consolidation process so that you can identify errors early in the process.

In the next chapter, we'll discuss the very important topic of calculation, monitoring, analysis and allocation of overhead costs.

Overhead Cost Controlling

So far in this book we've discussed how you can use SAP ERP Financials to realize the benefits of an integrated, enterprise-wide system in the areas of core accounting, such as GL, receivables, and payables. However, to make informed, strategic, and operational decisions, you need more detailed insight into the business activities of your company. To evaluate the cost efficiency of your functional areas, business initiatives, and operational activities; you need a comprehensive cost accounting system that enables you to easily and efficiently record, manage, and analyze your costs and revenues. This analysis must be at a considerably more detailed level than what is available in your financial statements without losing traceability and integration with the numbers reported there. In this and the next few chapters, we'll explore how the different components of SAP ERP Financials Controlling provide you with just that.

Considering that overhead costs represent more than 50 % of the total cost of products and services for many companies, it's an area that deserves and receives close and continued management scrutiny. This sharp increase in overhead costs is observed not only in service companies, where most of their costs are treated as overhead anyway, but also in manufacturing. Even though causes of indirect costs are

Sharp increase in overhead costs

often unclear, such indirect costs often have a bigger impact on product costs and profitability. Overhead costs such as those from planning, management, procurement, research and development, and so on are becoming increasingly important in the total cost of products or services. In this chapter, you'll learn about different functionalities and techniques that SAP has to offer to help you manage your overhead costs.

Overview

As anyone even slightly familiar with cost management will agree, *overhead costs* represent those costs that can't be directly assigned to products or services. However, this simple definition doesn't do justice to the operational hurdles involved in recording, analyzing, allocating, and reporting overhead costs with sufficient accuracy and necessary details. To overcome these operational hurdles; there are several powerful, integrated components that are part of SAP ERP Financials controlling. As mentioned in Chapter 1, these components cater to management and cost accounting requirements. In this chapter, we'll focus on Cost Center Accounting (CO-OM-CCA), internal orders (CO-OM-IOA), and activity-based costing (CO-OM-ABC). Subsequent chapters will explore other components of SAP ERP Financials controlling. Figure 10.1 shows how overhead cost controlling fits into the overall schema of operative controlling business processes.

User-defined cost structures   Cost center accounting in SAP helps you accurately plan, assign, and aggregate costs along user-defined cost structures. These cost structures can represent multiple, parallel viewpoints for cost analysis. And an easy-to-use, scalable framework is provided to simplify the cost allocation process in your company regardless of the scope or size of the cost allocation. In addition, you'll find easy-to-use functionality for tracing a cost from its allocated values to its cost origin. This helps you ensure transparency in operational processes and audit trails. You can also use cost center activities for more detailed cost management for manufacturing as well as non-manufacturing cost centers. And with the comprehensive reports available in the standard system, you can carry out detailed variance analysis by comparing actual costs with the planned, target, or forecast costs.

Value Flow for Operative Controlling

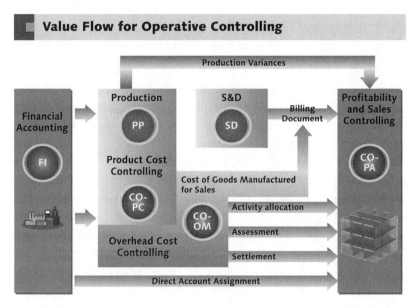

Figure 10.1 Operative Controlling

Internal orders, on the other hand, provide you with a mechanism to understand the true cost of an internal initiative, job, or relatively simple project. You can monitor internal orders through the entire lifecycle of a job by continuously assessing its costs, and even revenues, against its planned costs. Costs collected on internal orders can be allocated to other internal orders, cost centers, and so on to gain better understanding of the actual cost origins. Similar to cost centers, you can compare the actual costs of an internal order to its planned, target, or forecast costs. However, unlike cost centers, you can obtain more detailed visibility with internal orders because you can analyze costs on individual jobs instead of collective costs on a cost center.

Several techniques and methods in Activity-Based Costing (ABC) will help you gain insight into the cost-effectiveness of your business processes. With the help of ABC, you can make the real costs of business processes, products, and services more transparent. With the complete integration of ABC with other logistics components of SAP,

Gain insight into business processes

you can calculate more accurate operational costs. Such integration offers you the ability to calculate and allocate process costs based on operational parameters, such as number of invoices, purchase orders, or customer complaints processed. Template allocations allow you to develop highly complex and customizable frameworks to allocate the costs of business processes.

With the complete and seamless integration with other SAP components, you can trace allocated costs in cost management to the original postings made in SAP ERP Financials. Let's look at these functionalities in more detail.

Functions in Detail

In this section, you'll first get an overview of cost accounting in SAP, which consists of components that target the business requirements of internal, management accounting. The next several sections explore the different functionalities of recording and collecting overhead costs. After that, you'll learn about different month-end processes used for allocating these costs. Before we end this section, we'll explore reporting capabilities.

 Note

This chapter discusses collecting, recording, allocating, and settling costs. To learn more about planning costs and revenues, read Chapter 14.

Let's start with an overview of controlling—the collective cost management components of SAP ERP Financials.

Overview of Controlling

In previous chapters, we discussed different SAP components for receivables, payables, and assets, which are considered part of financial accounting in SAP. The components discussed in this chapter such as cost center accounting, activity-based costing, and so on are considered part of the cost accounting components in SAP. However, it can't be emphasized enough that all of the components of financial accounting and cost accounting are completely integrated with each other from a technical and business viewpoint. Nevertheless, cost accounting components introduce their own set of features and concepts. In this section, you'll get familiar with some of the important features and concepts of the cost accounting components starting with the controlling area.

The controlling area in SAP helps you structure your company for cost accounting. You may remember from Chapter 2 that company codes are set up from an external accounting viewpoint. So, it's possible that for statutory, tax, or business reasons; even a small company may need to set up multiple company codes even if from a cost management point of view, all of these companies are managed collectively. So you can associate multiple company codes (from financial accounting) to one controlling area (in cost accounting) regardless of whether they are in the same or different currencies. Consider the tremendous flexibility this design provides you in terms of structuring your company for cost accounting. For example, if your company has a relatively simple organizational structure, you can use one company code in financial accounting and link it to one controlling area in cost accounting. Whereas, if you are a global company, you can create one or more company codes for each of your subsidiaries in different countries, and still link all of them to a single controlling area for cost accounting.

Controlling area

 Tip

> In especially large global companies, cost management is often decentralized to regional levels such as North America, Europe, and Asia. For such an organizational structure, you can use multiple SAP controlling areas in cost management, one for each region.

Understandably, this brings up a question of managing multiple currencies in cost accounting. You can update your cost accounting business transactions in up to three currencies: the controlling area currency, the company code currency, and the currency of individual cost objects such as cost centers. This design helps provide effective cost

Multiple currencies in Controlling

management and reporting regardless of the size, scope, and structure of your organization. Table 10.1 shows different organizational structures of a company and possible currencies in cost accounting.

Example Structure of a Company and Possible Currencies	Controlling Area Currency	Currency of Company Codes	Currency of Cost Centers
A legal services company based out of and operating in the United States	USD	USD	USD
A legal services company with a head office in the United States, a subsidiary in Canada, and a sales office in Mexico managed by the U.S. company	USD	USD, CAD	USD, CAD, MXP
A legal services company with a head office in the United States and subsidiaries in Canada and Mexico	USD	USD, CAD, MXP	USD, CAD, MXP

Table 10.1 Multiple Currencies in SAP Cost Accounting

Also, it's important that all companies associated with a controlling area use the same chart of accounts and the same fiscal year. You should pay careful attention to these decisions because they have far-reaching consequences and can't be easily changed after you start using them in your live SAP system. In the next section, you'll see how SAP ERP Financials can help you record costs.

Cost Elements in SAP

Primary cost elements

All postings for management accounting are recorded and processed in the controlling area using cost elements or revenue elements. Conceptually, you can consider cost elements as accounts used in the Controlling component. For example, if you post an AP invoice for $100 travel expenses to GL account 474240 in the new GL, an *automatic and parallel* posting for $100 is also made to cost element 474240 in cost accounting. Even though this may seem somewhat redundant, this design provides you with significant advantages. This design helps you separate any further cost processing for the purpose of management or cost accounting, from the original posting carried out in the new GL for statutory, external accounting. In SAP parlance, these cost elements are called *primary cost elements*. For primary cost elements, the corresponding GL account must also exist in your chart of accounts.

Another type of cost element supported is the *secondary cost element*, which is used only for processing costs within the controlling components. As you'll see later, secondary cost elements are used in accruals, allocations, and other processes carried out strictly within the confines of CO. These processes don't have any impact on financial accounting, so for secondary cost elements, corresponding GL accounts *should not* exist in the chart of accounts. And, several types of primary and secondary cost elements are supported for different business processes. Table 10.2 provides you with a list of these different types. Even though we haven't discussed some of the business processes mentioned, the table will provide you with an overview of the powerful role played by cost elements.

Secondary cost elements

Primary Cost Elements	
Primary cost elements	These are typically debited with all primary cost postings from financial accounting and materials management (MM).
Accrual cost elements	Used with cost centers to calculate accruals based on percentage method or target=actual method. Both these methods are discussed later.
Revenue elements and Sales deduction	These cost elements are used to post revenues and sales deductions (e.g., revenues, rebates) to cost centers. These postings are only for statistical and reporting purposes.

Table 10.2 Different Cost Elements in SAP

Balance sheet accounts	These cost elements represent balance sheet accounts in financial accounting. These are also updated only for statistical and reporting purposes.
External settlement	These cost elements are useful for cost allocations (discussed later) outside of cost accounting. For example, when you want to allocate costs to fixed assets, materials, GL accounts, and so on.
Secondary Cost Elements	
Internal settlement	Unlike the cost elements used for external settlement, these cost elements are used for cost allocations within the cost accounting components.
Results analysis	These cost elements are used to record results analysis (discussed in Chapter 12) data.
Overhead rates	These cost elements are used to allocate overhead costs from cost centers to other cost accounting objects.
Assessment	These cost elements are used to allocate costs using the assessment method (discussed later).
Allocation	These cost elements are used to allocate costs during activity allocations in activity-based costing (discussed later).
Incoming orders	These cost elements are used to record sales revenues, other revenues, and costs from sales orders related to projects in SAP Project System (Chapter 11).
Earned values	These cost elements are used for earned value analysis in the SAP Project System (PS) (Chapter 11).

Table 10.2 Different Cost Elements in SAP (cont.)

You can group multiple cost elements into cost element groups and use them for your reporting, analysis, and allocation purposes. For example, you can use different cost element groups for cost elements representing your sales, marketing, R&D, and other expenses. One of the most widely used approaches for cost management is to use cost centers, so let's look at that in more detail.

Cost Center Accounting

The term cost center is so commonly used in business and accounting, that its definition may be redundant. However, for those unfamiliar with this concept, cost centers help you with recording, monitoring, and analyzing costs in your company. Cost centers are used to delineate your organization based on geography, business activities, cost responsibilities, or similar criteria. Most frequently, cost centers are created to correspond to your functional areas such as sales, marketing, HR, IT, and finance. Except in very small companies, functional areas themselves consist of multiple cost centers to enable transparent recording and reporting of costs. For example, the functional area for Info Tech may further be divided into cost centers for hardware, software, application services, consulting, and so on. Cost center managers are responsible to ensure the accurate recording and reporting of costs in their cost centers. They are also responsible for ensuring that actual costs on their cost centers remain within planned or budgeted costs. In this section, you'll see how using cost centers can help you better manage your overhead costs.

Structuring your cost centers

 Tip

Even though the focus of this chapter is on overhead costs, cost centers are also used to collect direct and allocated costs involved in the creation of products and services; which can further be used in the calculation of product costs (Chapter 12) and contribution margins (Chapter 13).

Cost Centers in SAP

Typically cost centers reflect the structure of your organization in terms of plants, offices, locations, departments, and so on. Cost centers (see Figure 10.2) contain several pieces of information that are relevant for managing, recording, and reporting costs:

> Name, department, address, and contact details of the cost center manager

> Whether you can post actual costs or carry out planning on cost centers, providing you additional control for individual cost centers

> Templates for allocating overhead costs and activity costs (discussed later)

> Area in the standard hierarchy to which the cost center is assigned

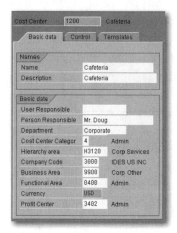

Figure 10.2 Cost Centers in SAP

Standard hierarchy The last bullet point refers to the cost center standard hierarchy, which is a special cost center group that contains *all of* the cost centers in a controlling area as a multilevel tree structure. But you have to link each cost center in a controlling area to one of the nodes in the standard hierarchy. This requirement ensures that at least one cost center group in your SAP system captures all the costs and therefore represents your whole enterprise. You can also create as many additional cost center groups as required for grouping cost centers that best meet your business requirements. As you'll see later, cost center groups are especially useful for reporting and cost allocation purposes.

Time-dependent master data Cost centers also offer you the ability to maintain time-dependent master data. Even if your company doesn't undergo frequent "reorganization," you'll still need to make changes to cost centers without affecting historical data. For example, a software company based in the United States may decide to centralize its hardware procurement for its North American companies in the United States, Mexico, and Canada. Even though going forward all IT cost centers should be managed in USD, the historical data for individual IT cost centers should be preserved in the respective currencies such as Mexican Pesos and Canadian Dollars. By providing time-dependent maintenance of master data, SAP helps you carry out such changes without losing the historical relevance and significance of data already posted. Without this capability, you may have to create a completely new set of cost centers for such changes.

 Tip

To ensure that cost center postings are consistent from statutory and accounting viewpoints, SAP automatically controls the available periods for such time-dependent changes. For example, you can't change cost center currency during a fiscal year, but fields such as the Cost Center Manager can be changed anytime.

Cost centers are cohesively integrated with other SAP components and business processes by means of the company code, functional area, profit center, business area, and so on. Not only that, but by using highly sophisticated and configurable determination strategies, SAP can automatically determine cost centers for most financial transactions resulting from business activities in procurement, sales, manufacturing, payroll, asset accounting, and other areas. This feature provides you with considerably improved accuracy in your cost center postings and reduces the time required during month-end close for analysis and adjustments.

If you want to manage your overhead costs in more detail than what Cost Center Accounting can provide, you can use cost center activities that represent activities performed in a cost center. It's relatively easy to recognize activities on production cost centers, for example, the number of units finished or number of hours worked. However, you can also classify different activities for overhead cost centers or in nonmanufacturing environments. For example, a legal services firm can use SAP activities to classify its work into pro-bono work, representation, preparing brief, reviewing documents, etc. However, there aren't any technical restrictions on what you can define as an activity, which means that a legal services firm can also use SAP activities to classify work done by different responsibility levels such as trainee,

Cost center activities

junior, partner, senior partner, etc. It entirely depends on how you want to collect and allocate the costs. Activities are available to you for cost planning, collecting, processing, and allocating. Similar to cost elements and cost centers, you can create activity groups that can be used for cost allocation and reporting. So, SAP activities provide you with a mechanism to carry out more detailed, quantity-based planning and cost allocation.

In the next section, let's take a look at internal orders that provide you with a different mechanism for collecting and managing costs.

Internal Order Accounting

Using internal orders

In Chapter 6, you were introduced to internal orders as investment measures. In this chapter, we'll only focus on using internal orders for overhead costs, although the underlying concepts are similar for both types of orders. In general, you use internal orders to plan, collect, and settle costs of any internal jobs, tasks, events, and initiatives. As compared to cost centers, internal orders help you manage and monitor costs at a more detailed level. For example, by creating separate internal orders for each customer event organized by your sales team, you can gain more insight into the true costs of different events than you would simply from a sales cost center. Similarly, by using separate internal orders for each recruiting seminar organized by your HR department, you can gain more insight into the costs than you would from costs reported on a recruitment cost center. So how you use internal orders depends on your business requirements.

Budget monitoring

Figure 10.3 shows some of the screens for an internal order entry. As you can see, an internal Order is also associated with a Company Code, cost center (Responsible CCtr), and other organizational units, so that any postings made to an internal order is also automatically posted to the corresponding SAP component. Similar to cost centers, you can use internal orders to collect, manage, and monitor costs. Also similar to cost centers, you would typically allocate a fixed budget to an internal order and monitor its performance against it. Marketing events, trade shows, and recruiting events, all have fixed budgets against which their cost efficiency is measured. In Chapter 6, we dis-

cussed the commitment management functionality for capital investment initiatives. You can use the same functionality for commitment
management and reporting on internal orders created for managing
overhead costs.

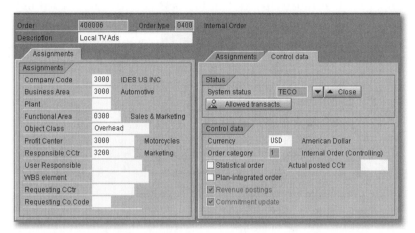

Figure 10.3 Internal Orders in SAP

However, a few factors from business as well as technical viewpoints
differentiate internal orders from cost centers. One of the differences
is that internal orders are transient in nature and have definite time
restrictions such as start and end dates. For example, when you create an internal order for a marketing event, its start date is the date
when the event was approved and internal preparation for the event
was started. Its end date is when the event is completed and all of
the accounting entries related to the event have been processed. On
the other hand, the marketing cost center that initiates this event is
more permanent in nature and doesn't have similar time restrictions.
Even though you can maintain start and end dates on internal orders
for your reporting purposes, SAP treats them only as planned dates.
There is no technical restriction in terms of what business activities
you can process on an internal order before or after these dates. To
control the processing of business activities, you are provided with
the status management function.

Differences between
cost centers and
internal orders

Status management is an extremely powerful functionality that you'll
come across in many SAP components. For example, Chapter 6 dis-

Status management

cussed using status management for appropriation requests. The premise of status management is fairly simple. Based on the current status of an internal order, status management prohibits or allows business activities that you can carry out, and it changes the status of an internal order after certain business activities are carried out. The following example shows some of the ways in which you can use the SAP status management functionality to control different business activities.

Ex   Example

You use internal orders for managing costs on trade shows and marketing events. These orders are assigned a status management profile that consists of four stages: Created, Released, Technically Completed, and Closed. You can institute the following controls for such internal orders:

> For status Created, only cost planning is allowed.

> For status Released, any costs can be posted, including costs from purchase orders and service orders for organizing the event.

> For status Technically Complete, only selected users can post financial entries, e.g., for settlement of costs after the event has been completed.

> For status Closed, no business transactions are allowed.

Similar to cost elements and cost centers, you can also create groups of internal orders for reporting and cost allocation purposes.

Now let's move on to the more detailed and complex area of managing costs using activity-based costing methodology.

Activity-Based Costing

Cross-functional view of costs

So far, what we've discussed is useful for cost management, if overhead costs can be identified or allocated with relative ease. The activity–based costing component provides an alternative form of overhead control that is particularly useful when indirect activities account for a large share of the value added to products, services or the end results. Activity-based costing provides you with a process oriented, cross-functional view of overhead costs. Unlike cost centers and internal orders, activity-based costing is considerably more complex to implement and use. However, benefits of properly instituted activity-based costing usually outweigh these efforts and challenges. With activity-based costing, you can obtain increased process efficiency, fair calculation of costs, and more transparent overhead cost calculation, as well as information made available for strategic decision making. The advantages of activity-based costing are significantly pronounced for manufacturing companies, but it can provide meaningful insights for non-manufacturing companies as well.

Business processes typically consume different resources from different cost centers. For example, a customer service call may involve cost centers for call center, engineering support, and possibly even product development and sales. Also, some business processes may carry out multiple activities from the same cost center. For example, the beginning of a procurement process may require requesting a quotation and creating a purchase order—both activities belonging to the same cost center. SAP provides you with an object called a *business process* to represent the diverse and complex world of business processes in companies. You can assign the usual organizational units such as company code, plant, cost center, and so on to a business process. Additionally, to really harness the power of activity-based costing, you have the ability to assign up to five attributes to a business process (see Figure 10.4).

Business processes and their attributes

Figure 10.4 Business Process Attributes

> Using Category, you can categorize your business processes into different categories based on functional processes such as sales,

production, accounting, and so on or in terms of complexities such as high, medium, and low.

> Using Cost Behavior, you can specify factors that influence business process costs, for example, cost of producing a widget depends on the number of widgets produced, cost of responding to a customer inquiry depends on the customer, and so on.

> Using the ranking for External value added, you can indicate the value addition of a business process from an external perspective; for example, responding to a customer complaint has a higher value addition than attending a meeting.

> Using the ranking for Internal value added, you can indicate the value addition of a business process from an internal management perspective; for example, attending a meeting provides higher value addition than responding to a customer complaint.

> The fifth attribute (Add. attributes) is freely definable, so you can decide how to use it to best analyze and report your business processes.

Calculating costs of business processes   When you carry out different business transactions, you can record activities on such business processes in appropriate units, for example, number of widgets produced, time spent in resolving a customer complaint, and so on. The total cost of a business process is calculated by using costs assigned per unit of activity. This design provides you with complete flexibility in the business processes you want to analyze and the mechanism by which you want to calculate their costs. Depending on how you choose to allocate costs collected on business processes to products, customers, and other objects, you can use two different approaches.

ABC Approaches

Push approach   The two approaches available to you in SAP for implementing activity-based costing are pure cost distribution (*Push* approach) and quantity tracing (*Pull* approach). The Push approach is an easy and straightforward method to use. In this approach, total costs are allocated based on criteria determined by you. For example, you can allocate total costs on a cost center to different business processes based on fixed percentages. Total costs of business processes are then allocated to different market segments proportional to the revenue from each market segment or based on fixed allocation percentages. You can use the distribution or assessment method (discussed later) to allocate these costs. Obviously, the disadvantage of using this approach is that even though cost calculation is carried out at a more detailed level than a cost center, the calculation isn't necessarily in proportion to the actual resource use. For example, if marketing costs are allocated to business processes such as market research and promotional events based on fixed percentages that allocation doesn't take into account the actual number of events organized.

 Note

The activity-based costing technique you choose to implement in your company has far-reaching consequences in terms of the operational demands, visibility of cost flows, and availability of information.

For more accurate or fair costing of business processes, SAP supports the *pull* approach. Under this approach, the total cost of a business process is calculated based on the actual use of resources. For example, the total cost of a purchasing cycle is calculated based on the actual hours recorded for requesting a vendor quote, creating a purchase order, receiving goods, verifying the vendor invoice, and paying for the invoice. Clearly, an accurate recording of costs at such a detailed level requires very thorough knowledge of business activities, their cost behaviors, and their cost influences. SAP provides you with several different methods to implement the Pull approach; however, due to space constraints, we won't go into the details here. The important point is that you can carry out highly complex cost allocations using fully customizable and configurable templates and formulae calculations. Figure 10.5 highlights the fundamental differences between these approaches.

Pull approach

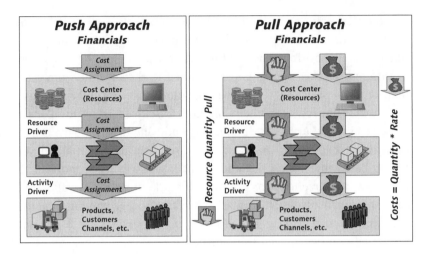

Figure 10.5 Activity-Based Costing Approaches

Activity-based costing is an extremely detailed and involved methodology and SAP matches the most demanding expectations of its implementation. In this section, we've explored only a few of the overall functionalities of this component. However, before we move on to the next topic, it's important to consider the following features of this SAP component:

What-if activity-based costing scenarios

> You can use multiple, parallel versions for calculating and analyzing the costs of business processes for all or part of your business. This helps you evaluate what-if scenarios and gain strategic insight into process costs.

> You can use activity-based costing either for statistical, reporting purposes, or as fully integrated with value flows in your cost accounting. If you use integrated ABC, it can be fully integrated with product costing (Chapter 12) and profitability analysis (Chapter 13).

> As we'll discuss in Chapter 14, you can carry out sophisticated, detailed, and integrated planning on business processes to fully integrate activity-based costing into your business from a strategic as well as an operational point of view.

So far in this chapter, we've discussed different approaches for recording and collecting costs. Now we're ready to look at different methods and techniques that you can use as part of period-end closing for allocating and settling these costs.

Period-End Closing

Period-end closing in management accounting typically involves a number of different activities for analyzing, processing, adjusting, allocating, and settling overhead costs to finally determine the product costs. In this chapter, we'll focus on overhead costs, and Chapter 12 will provide you with more details on product costing. Even though it's possible to collect overhead costs using several different methods, the techniques for cost analysis, allocation, and settlement are fairly similar. We'll review them all together to appreciate the common and consistent approach provided for managing your overhead costs. Clearly, period-end closing also involves comparing actual costs with planned costs. However, as mentioned before, the planning and budgeting functionality is discussed in Chapter 14. Let's discuss a few common concepts and functionalities shared by all of these techniques.

Common Functionalities

A particularly important concept in cost accounting is that of real costs and statistical costs. Consider an example where a group of employees spends $1,500 for attending a customer appreciation event organized by your company. Typically, this cost will get recorded on a cost center. However, as we already discussed, it's also possible to track this cost on an internal order that collects the total cost of organizing this event. This internal order in turn can be part of a bigger product launch initiative created as a project (discussed in Chapter 11). In addition to the cost center, it's also possible to post this cost automatically and simultaneously to these additional cost collectors. *Cost collectors* or *cost objects* is a generic term used to describe cost centers, internal orders, projects, and similar objects on which you can post or collect costs.

Real postings versus statistical postings

However, it will be inaccurate if this cost was counted and reported multiple times (e.g., $3,000 or $4,500) because of these parallel postings. To avoid counting the same cost multiple times, SAP treats one posting (e.g., on cost center) as the real posting and all other postings as statistical postings. The difference isn't just terminology. You can only use real costs for cost allocation to other cost centers, internal orders, and so on, whereas statistical cost postings are only for reporting purposes. So in the preceding example, costs collected on the cost center can be used in cost allocations, but costs collected on an internal order or project can't. You should keep this in mind when envisioning and designing cost flows in your company and choosing which cost collectors should collect real costs and statistical costs.

SKF for allocations   Another useful functionality in cost allocation is that of statistical key figures (SKF) which are used as a basis for cost allocation. For example, if you want to allocate cafeteria costs based on the number of employees and telephone expenses based on the number of telephone units, then you can create number of employees and number of telephone units as SKF. As you'll see later, you can use these SKF later for cost allocation. As shown in Figure 10.6, you are provided with a completely flexible definition of what these numbers represent. So, for example, you can also use information from sales, procurement, manufacturing, and other areas of your business as the basis for cost allocation. Obviously, if you use activity-based costing, using SKF based on such a wide range of criteria is a necessary part of your implementation. However, SKF can be useful even for relatively simple overhead management using cost centers and internal orders. Similar to all other components in overhead costing, you can use SKF groups for reporting and cost allocation purposes.

Sender objects and receiver objects   As discussed before, the techniques for cost allocation are fairly similar regardless of any combination of cost centers, internal orders, and activity based costing you use. Throughout the month, you post costs to different cost collectors by means of different business transactions. At the end of the month, you analyze and make any adjustment postings as necessary, for example, if an incorrect cost center was used in the original posting. Lastly, you allocate or settle the costs from sender objects (where the costs were collected) to receiver objects (where the costs will be settled to). Having considered these aspects, let's look at the available cost allocation methods.

Statistical Key Figures

8001	ABC:	Number of customer orders
8003	ABC:	Number of delivery notes
8004	ABC:	Number of new materials
8005	ABC:	Number of working hours
8006	ABC:	Number of order line items
8010	ABC:	Number of units sold/repaired
8011	ABC:	Number of customer inquiries
8013	ABC:	Number of setup transactions
8014	ABC:	Hours of production time
8015	ABC:	Repair hours I
8016	ABC:	Machine hours I
8017	ABC:	Burn-in time
8018	ABC:	Labor hours I
8100	ABC:	Number of customer complaints
8101	ABC:	Number of vendor inquiries
8102	ABC:	Number of vendor quotations
8103	ABC:	Number of customer invoices
8104	ABC:	Number of delivery contracts
8105	ABC:	Number of shipping orders
8106	ABC:	Number of stock transfers
8107	ABC:	Number of material issue slips
8108	ABC:	Number of inspection lots

Figure 10.6 Statistical Key Figures

Cost Allocation Methods

Due to the variety of transactions posted to cost centers, direct cost allocation is typically not possible. Most companies use indirect cost allocation methods such as assessment and distribution in which costs are allocated based on user-specific criteria such as percentage rates, actual amounts, planned amounts, SKF, and so on. In SAP, these allocation criteria are called *tracing factors*. The process of cost allocation is completely customizable and consistent across SAP components. You create different segments for allocating different types of costs and group them together in allocation cycles. So you can create different cost allocation cycles based on the type of costs (operational, non-operational), responsibility area (e.g., cost center managers), or any other criteria or combination of criteria. This flexibility in design provides you with an extremely versatile framework in which you can carry out cost allocations that best meet your business requirements. Allocation cycles are extremely powerful and help you control the following:

> Whether the allocation process is for actual costs or planned costs

> What percentage of costs should be allocated out, for example, allocate only 95 % of the utilities costs collected on a facilities cost center

Allocation cycles and allocation segments

311

> Whether tracing factors for cost allocation are fixed percentages, fixed amounts, fixed portions, or variable portions

> If tracing factors are variable portions, and whether they represent actual costs, planned costs, statistical costs, consumption, activities, and so on

> Cost centers, activities, business processes, cost elements, and so on that can be used as sender objects (from which costs are allocated) and receiver objects (to which costs are allocated)

Cost distribution and cost assessment

As you can see, this design is completely scalable so it remains the same regardless of the size, scope, and nature of cost allocations in your company. So you can use consistent cost allocation processes even if your organization requires hundreds of cost allocation cycles for different types of costs in multiple companies around the world. The two most commonly used indirect cost allocation methods used are cost distribution and cost assessment. One of the main differences between these two methods is that the cost distribution method retains the original GL accounts, whereas the cost assessment method doesn't retain the original GL accounts so it's used when the cost breakdown is relatively unimportant. As the example shows, both cost allocation methods are useful depending on the type of costs being allocated.

Ex **Example**

You use the distribution method to allocate utility expenses so that cost center managers can analyze the breakdown of allocated costs by water, electricity, and so on. You can use the assessment method to allocate cafeteria costs because its cost breakdown may not be important for cost center managers.

Indirect activity allocation

Another useful allocation method for overhead costs is the indirect activity allocation method for allocating activities. As we discussed before, activities provide you with more detailed recording, managing, and allocating capabilities for your overhead costs. Let's consider a scenario in a manufacturing company where a quality assurance person works on testing two types of products. Depending on the definition of this activity, you can valuate and allocate costs in several ways.

You can allocate costs based on the number of items tested for each product type, or you can do an inverse calculation and cost allocation based on the number of widgets actually tested. The latter approach can be useful if, for example, it isn't possible or practical to record and quantify the testing of the activity itself. For an iterative determination of multilevel activity allocation, you can use even more sophisticated allocation and valuation techniques such as Target=Actual Activity Allocation.

In addition to the methods just discussed, the following list shows several other methods of calculating, analyzing, and allocating costs that are discussed in other chapters:

> Overhead calculation and allocation using costing sheets (Chapter 12) with reference to calculation of product costs. The same technique is available for nonmanufacturing cost calculation and allocation as well.

> Variance calculation and analysis (Chapter 12) with reference to manufacturing cost centers. If you plan and record overhead costs by cost center activities, you can use that technique for overhead costs as well.

> Calculation framework using templates and formulae (Chapter 14) with reference to planning. The framework is available and equally applicable for calculating and allocating actual overhead costs.

> Allocation and settlement of costs collected on internal orders (Chapter 6) with reference to settlement of capital costs. The settlement process remains the same for overhead costs as long as they aren't statistical postings.

Depending on the components and functionality that you use, you may use several of these processes to analyze, calculate, and allocate your overhead costs. More than anything else, the distribution of this topic across several chapters demonstrates the highly integrated nature of the SAP software. It also demonstrates the sharing of core, common, robust functionalities across different SAP components.

Now let's discuss some of the reports available in the components discussed in this chapter.

Reporting

Master data groups

Similar to all other financial components in SAP, cost accounting components also provide an extensive list of ready-to-use reports. These reports serve a variety of purposes from management reporting operational reporting to audit trail, transaction history, strategic information gathering, detailed process logs, and, of course, analytics. When we discussed different cost allocation methods in the previous section, you may have grasped the use of different groups such as groups of cost centers, cost elements, SKF, and so on. For example, it's much easier and manageable to carry out cost allocation from a cost center group than from each cost center individually. Such groups are all the more important and relevant for reporting and analysis purposes. They not only help you keep report maintenance to a manageable level, but they also make it easier for other business users who run the reports.

 Tip

> In the cost center accounting component, you can summarize cost center transaction data into representative cost centers and use those cost centers in reports to significantly improve report performance. This can be especially useful in large companies that may use hundreds of cost centers and even larger number of reports across the company.

Reporting requirements

To make informed management decisions and corrective operational decisions, you need a significantly more detailed analysis capability in cost management reports than in financial reports. You want reports that can analyze different types of values (actual, target, statistical, commitment, etc.), over different time frames (day, month, quarter, year, cumulative, etc.), for different cost collectors (cost centers, internal orders, activities, business processes, etc.). SAP provides a large selection of standard reports to meet such requirements in all of the cost management components. Additionally, you also have access to a variety of comparison and analysis reports such as quarterly comparison (see Figure 10.7), annual comparison, actual and target cost comparison, and so on.

Cost centers: quarterly comparison

Cost elements		1st qtr	2nd qtr	3rd qtr	4th qtr	Total year
465100	Payroll tax expens	619,899.42	589,109.79	613,741.43	617,846.71	2,440,597.35
466000	Insurance	372,982.29	180,745.46	384,590.69	186,757.08	1,125,075.52
470000	Occupancy costs	1,086,699.91	864,874.78	1,100,752.24	860,182.57	3,912,509.50
471000	Machine rental	404,650.43	424,785.32	411,836.70	409,395.35	1,650,667.80
472000	Postal costs	485.54	501.78	480.67	495.29	1,963.28
473000	Postage	48,629.60	47,663.43	48,146.51	49,917.79	194,357.33
473110	Telephone Basic Fe	16,049.51	15,996.70	15,838.34	16,155.09	64,039.64
473120	Telephone Usage	408,477.18	404,035.17	391,357.69	408,977.17	1,612,847.21
474100	Travel expenses -	890,621.01	965,857.87	931,697.01	934,753.83	3,722,929.72
474210	Travel Exp. Mileag	128,183.25	132,413.72	125,644.96	129,875.43	516,117.36
474211	T&E - Meals/Ent	727.20	1,615.92	712.80	736.80	3,792.72
474220	T&E - Lodging	4,901.05	4,838.01	4,711.94	4,711.95	19,162.95
474221	T&E - Taxable	67.78			10.00	77.78
474231	T&E - Advances		864.72			864.72

Figure 10.7 Cost Center Quarterly Comparison

In addition to all of these standard reports, you have at your disposal highly flexible and comprehensive reporting tools such as Report Painter and drilldown reporting. You can use these tools to design reports that conform to your standards and meet the additional requirements of your user community. These reporting tools can be used with cost centers, internal orders, and business processes used in activity-based costing.

Let's now discuss how a software development company used activity-based costing to get a better handle on business processes and activities.

Case Study

This $950-million software company develops and supports a range of software products for hotels, resorts, and similar companies that are in the hospitality industry. Their software products help reservation, housekeeping, maintenance, food and beverages (F&B) management, and other important business areas contribute to the smooth functioning of hotels and resorts. These products work well in standalone installations as well as together as an integrated system. This enables hotel properties to choose a combination that best met their requirements. Recent additions to their products enable hotels to provide online room reservations and check-in kiosks for guests. The company is organized into separate divisions for software development, software support, hardware support, consulting services, and training services. These divisions use shared services for their finance, IT, HR, and other supporting functions. Their software products are used at hundreds of small, medium, and large properties of renowned hotel chains across the country.

Business Challenges

The biggest challenge for the company was in ascertaining the true cost of servicing a property or of maintaining one of their software products. One of the main reasons was that most of the hotel properties used multiple software products from the company. This meant that most of their consulting services and training sessions, which were typically negotiated at a fixed rate with the hotel chains, dealt with multiple products. Spot consulting and remote support services such as those via telephone, emails, and instant chat were difficult to record, track, quantify, and allocate. To add to this complexity, their creative sales representatives always managed to negotiate different product combinations and discount deals to get in new customers and sell more to their existing customers. Add to this multiple versions and several operating systems of their software products, and you have a difficult and somewhat fluid environment to ascertain costs of business activities across the divisions.

The company used a fairly stable SAP system to support its own core business functions, including the areas of financial and cost management. However, cost centers and internal orders were not enough to obtain the visibility that the management required for internal cost allocation. For example, two hotel properties may have purchased the same products at the same price; but it was difficult to establish if one of the properties used considerably more hardware and software support, and thus required another look at the pricing of their contracts. This was especially the case if most of their support requests were ad-hoc in nature and were handled via phone or email. The cost center for "remote customer support" did not capture enough details to allocate the costs in a meaningful way to provide the required visibility. So, one of the project initiatives undertaken by the IT department was to implement activity–based costing in SAP.

Solution Deployment

The most involved process during the project implementation was to determine the costing models and templates for the hundreds of business processes across all of the departments and divisions of the company. Significant efforts were devoted to preparing costing templates for calculating costs of customer facing business processes in the areas of sales, consulting, training, and, most importantly, hardware and software support. The primary goal of this analysis phase was to ensure that different divisions and departments across the company could use costing models and templates most appropriate for their business functions. At the same time, the project had to balance that goal against the consistency and standardization of business processes across the company. The project team was keenly aware of the adverse effect on data quality if the same business process in different departments or divisions used different costing templates to capture and calculate the costs.

Value Achieved

One of the major benefits obtained after activity–based costing was rolled out across the company was the extraordinary visibility into cost components of different business processes. The finance department was able to measure and analyze fixed, variable, direct, indirect, allocated, and unallocated costs of different business activities. These costs were associated with individual hotel properties (and thereby hotel chains) and software products. Subsequently, by combining these costs with revenues from customers and products in SAP profitability analysis, the company was able to carry out significantly more accurate determination of profitability by software products, hotel chains, hotel properties, and so on.

Also, activity-based costing highlighted several business processes that were not cost efficient, especially in the software support and hardware support divisions. This prompted divisional managers and senior managers of the company to start evaluating other options such as introducing more pricing tiers for different levels and types of customer support, developing a shared knowledge base to help

317

answer customer questions, and even outsourcing first-level support for some of their leading, higher margin products.

Another benefit gained from this implementation was the detailed view of so-called subprocesses or steps within a business process. Careful analysis of business processes highlighted activities that consumed a very large portion of the total cost of the process. This information was used to further analyze (sometimes offline) the costs of those activities in detail, thus creating a processing framework that helped highlight the most cost-inefficient business activities.

At the end, the successful rollout of this project caused even staunch skeptics within the company to reconsider their opinions about activity-based costing and SAP software.

Looking Ahead

The senior management believed that during the initial rollout, the true potential of activity-based costing was not used in the software development division. So the immediate focus is on reevaluating requirements of that division for the optimum use of activity-based costing. However, the company is also an avid user of SAP Business Intelligence (BI) for its financial and management reporting, so the next SAP project under consideration is to take the huge volume of detailed data generated by SAP activity-based costing into SAP BI. This will provide the users with enhanced capability for analyzing extensive cost information for their respective areas of business.

Summary

In this chapter, you discovered different methods and techniques available to you for managing overhead costs in SAP. The following quickly recaps the three major components discussed in this chapter:

Cost Center Accounting

> Using Cost Center Accounting, you can structure your organization using flexible hierarchies for reporting and cost allocation purposes, and automatically record costs originating from payroll,

fixed assets, travel management, procurement, and other areas of your business.

> Cost Center Accounting provides detailed variance analysis, which can help you compare actual costs with the planned, forecast, or target costs for deeper insights into your business activities and for taking necessary corrective or proactive actions.

Internal Order Accounting

> Using internal order accounting, you can understand the true cost of internal jobs and projects by using several planning alternatives to accurately plan for the costs, different processing methods to collect the costs through direct postings or indirect allocations, and robust settlement mechanisms to accurately settle the costs to their origins.

> Internal order accounting provides you with a comprehensive suite of features such as status management, commitments management, detailed reports, and analysis that helps you monitor your jobs through their entire lifecycles.

Activity-Based Costing

> By using activity based costing and its full integration with logistics and operational systems, you can increase the transparency of the real costs of business processes, products, and services. Template allocations in particular allow you to easily carry out complex cost allocations using business processes.

> Activity-based costing supports cost allocations at a more detailed level than is possible with overhead rates, thereby helping you lower the costs of individual departments as well as optimize the entire business process chain. Additionally, you can use activity-based costing to complement and enhance product costing by assigning costs to the business processes where they originated.

Along with other topics, this chapter also discussed how you can use internal orders in SAP for your relatively simple internal jobs and projects. In the next chapter, we'll discuss an extremely powerful SAP component called Project Systems (PS), which you can use for accounting and managing of considerably more complex projects and business initiatives.

Project Accounting

In the previous chapter, we looked at how you can use internal orders for tracking overhead costs and even capital expenditures. However, the simplicity of internal orders makes it difficult to use them for complex initiatives or projects, such as building an airport or a hospital, organizing large events such as the annual auto show or SAPPHIRE, or running R&D projects at a drug company. These projects use enormous amounts of resources and involve planning and execution of hundreds, if not thousands, of coordinated tasks and activities, so you need solutions that provide the project management functionality to plan detailed activities, manage project resources and funds, and monitor progress from a technical and commercial point of view.

Overview

This type of project management solution needs to meet complex business needs through functions (Figure 11.1) that are flexible enough to structure and design project initiatives best suited for the task. A project may involve different types of costs, such as materials, personnel, and overhead costs, so a project solution needs to be able to capture and record these costs from various sources.

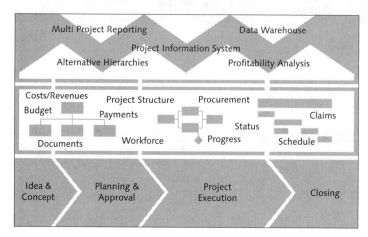

Figure 11.1 Project Management Solutions

Some projects, especially those initiated based on customer requirements, may also involve revenue-bearing elements, so a project solution needs to capture revenues on a project. This in turn requires the solution to analyze and monitor profitability of a project in almost real time and to analyze the impact of an actual or anticipated event on project profitability. Most projects also require capital planning and fund monitoring capabilities to make sure that corporate funds aren't wasted, and at the same time, that the project can meet its payment obligations.

Expected functionality

Such project management solutions seldom work in isolation because they require information exchange and coordination with a variety of sources and applications to help you successfully plan, manage, and monitor a project. For purchasing materials or external services for the project, you need integration with your procurement system. For the project resources that can be manufactured at your plants, integration with the production system can be useful. If a project requires tracking the time spent by personnel (e.g., SAP consultants or support engineers), integration with the time management system is nice too. Unless the project has an unlimited budget, effective budget monitoring and integration with the accounting and costing application is also important.

Of course, you can use an excellent project management solution that doesn't offer such integration, by building and maintaining a large number of custom interfaces; but it makes it easier for IT and the business, if all required functionality is available in a single system. As you'll see next, the SAP Project System (PS) component provides you with not only comprehensive project management functionality, but also robust integration with other SAP components.

Functions in Detail

All projects, regardless of whether they are overhead projects, capital expenditure projects, R&D projects, or manufacturing projects, incur costs and require making payments. Some projects also generate revenues and require more advanced project cash management. In this chapter, we'll mainly focus on project accounting, although occasionally we may venture into areas that are only relevant for project management.

 Tip

SAP also provides a web-based cProjects suite of products based on the SAP NetWeaver platform. Even though we won't discuss it in this chapter, cProjects integrates project management methods, management of project resources, and management of project relevant knowledge, information, and documentation.

We'll first discuss how you can use the SAP Project System (PS) component to set up your projects, followed by how to process project costs, project revenues, and cash management on projects. Later, we'll discuss some integration and other functionalities in the PS, but let's start with project structures in SAP.

Project Structures in SAP

PS in SAP doesn't have any organizational structures of its own. Depending on the project type, you can assign it different areas of your

Work Breakdown
Structure (WBS)

organization such as company code, purchase organization, plant, profit center, cost center, investment program, and so on. So, you have complete flexibility in the type, design, and structure of a project definition in SAP. Any project, large or small, can be broken down into a series of tasks, activities, and the sequence in which such activities are performed. This project structure in SAP is represented by Work Breakdown Structures (WBS), networks, and activities.

Project Networks WBSs represent project tasks in a multilevel hierarchical form based on the most suitable or relevant criteria. For example, tasks for an IT project can be structured in a hierarchy based on phases, such as requirement analysis, implementation, testing, etc.; whereas, tasks for organizing a large trade show can be structured based on functions, such as marketing, facilities, technology, catering, and so on. The individual, lowest level tasks in a project hierarchy are represented by WBS elements. On the other hand, networks help you plan, analyze, control, and monitor project schedules, dates, costs, materials, and production resources for carrying out project tasks. You create different activities such as internal activities (e.g., review, design), external activities (e.g., subcontracting), external services (e.g., consulting), or general costs, and assign them to corresponding WBS elements.

PS also provides other functionalities useful for project management to represent complex project structures in SAP:

> Milestones allow you to designate specific dates or goals in a project plan to carry out different reporting, analysis, and calculations.

> Project planning board simplifies the integrated processing of projects by presenting relevant information in a graphical view.

> Project Builder (Figure 11.2) provides you with a split-screen arrangement of project information combined with worklists, context-sensitive menus, and other features to help with daily work in PS.

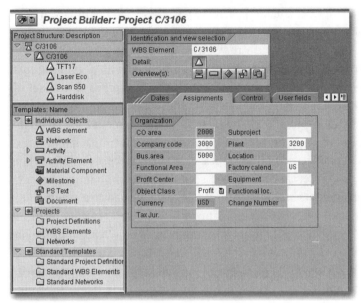

Figure 11.2 Project Definition

> Standard structures are used to prepare templates for networks, milestones and WBSs to standardize the project management process in your company.

However, because the focus of this book is on financials, let's focus on elements of PS from the project accounting and costing viewpoint.

WBS Elements

The lowest level of a WBS hierarchy consists of WBS elements that represent individual tasks of a project. Company code, business area, profit center, plant, tax jurisdiction code, and several other SAP organizational units are associated with a WBS element for analysis, reporting, and for use in accounting entries. You can control at an individual WBS element level whether it can be used in planning; whether it can be posted with actual costs, revenues or commitments; and whether it can be associated with a billing plan. These flags can be extremely useful, especially in large projects, to put system checks and controls in place against business transactions that are incorrect or not permitted.

Characteristics of WBS elements

You can plan, calculate, and evaluate costs associated with a WBS element by appropriate use of the costing sheet, overhead key, or results analysis key; and then use the settlement rule to post and transfer these costs to other objects. If you're unfamiliar with these concepts, you may want to refer back to Chapter 10. It's also possible to set up a WBS element as relevant only for statistical posting. This can be useful, for example, if you're using this WBS element (or maybe the whole project) only for reporting purposes, and capturing and settlement of actual costs is carried out using different cost objects such as cost centers, internal orders, and so on. To ensure data consistency and improve data maintenance efficiency, you can use project profiles to default these costing parameters. From the revenue planning perspective, you can associate a billing plan with a WBS element. For example, an IT project plan may include a billing plan associated with project milestones. As you'll see, the billing plans associated with WBS elements can also provide the time frame for possible incoming payments and revenues.

 Tip

> The status profile associated with WBS elements is based on standard SAP status management functionality. It determines the available statuses and corresponding business transactions that can be processed for WBS elements.

Integration with capital investments

You may recall from Chapter 6 that you can create WBS elements as investment measures. You can assign an investment profile to a WBS element and also assign one or more investment programs and the corresponding investment position and approval year to it. If you haven't yet implemented the Investment Management component but only want to use capitalization of assets, then you can associate an Asset under Construction (AuC) and depreciation parameters to a WBS element. Because these components are fully integrated with each other, SAP generates a depreciation forecast based on asset information and planned costs maintained on WBS elements. Similarly, networks and activities in PS also contain attributes that are relevant for Financials and Project Accounting.

Project Networks and Activities

You can create project networks associated with organizational units such as controlling area, company code, profit center, and so on. Also, you can use costing sheets and overhead keys to calculate cost overheads and use costing variants for evaluating actual costs. We'll cover costing variants in more detail while discussing product costing in Chapter 12; for now, just know that it's one of the most powerful tools available in SAP, and it's capable of calculating and valuating highly complex costing situations. Activities receive their default organizational assignments from corresponding project networks, but you can change the organizational assignment in individual activities; for example, R&D costs can be charged to one unit, and travel costs can be charged to a different unit.

Organizational assignments

As you can see, the design and definition of a project is completely flexible, and you can use it for projects that cross departments, functions, profit centers, divisions, plants, and even companies, regardless of whether it's a small IT project with less than a hundred tasks and activities or a highly complex construction project consisting of thousands of tasks and activities. In the next section, we'll discuss how to plan and evaluate costs in a project.

Project Costs

Detailed and accurate cost accounting of any large project is extremely important to ensure that it provides required deliverables within budget. Depending on the type and scope of a project, it may incur costs from procurement, production, subcontracting, external services, and many other business applications. The posting of actual costs simply involves assigning the appropriate WBS element, for example, while posting a financial entry or creating a purchase order. So in this section, we'll only focus on the before and after, that is, planning, budgeting, and forecasting of costs before they are posted, and settlement of costs after they are posted.

Posting of actual costs

Project Cost Planning

For relatively simple projects, such as overhead cost projects or capital investment projects, you can use manual cost planning for the WBS; whereas for complex projects involving the planning of costs, dates, resources, and so on, you should use cost planning based on project networks. For planning using project networks, costs are automatically calculated by the system based on pricing, quantity, and other information maintained on network activities.

Using manual planning, you can carry out planning for lower-level WBS elements of a project, and the system will automatically roll it up for higher levels, or you can plan at a higher level and then distribute the plan values to lower levels. Another option is to use Easy Cost Planning to quickly calculate planned values. Manual planning as well as Easy Cost Planning are generic planning methods available in SAP and are discussed in Chapter 14 in detail. However, calculating planned values based on project networks is specific to the SAP PS component.

As noted before, by using project networks, you can plan resources, in-house and external activities, and other services. Figure 11.3 shows how this planning process first evaluates individual resources, activities, and services using the corresponding rates and prices you have maintained; and subsequently uses that information along with dates to calculate planned costs for project networks. Using different costing variants, you can valuate manufactured products allocated to your projects depending on the type of manufacturing technique that is used. Chapter 12 "Product Costing" discusses valuating products using different techniques. Using this single, comprehensive cost planning process, you can take into account any procurement, manufacturing, services, and other generic activities associated with your project. This cost planning process is advanced enough to use dates specified in project networks, activities, milestones, and other project components to determine the cost distribution over the project timeline.

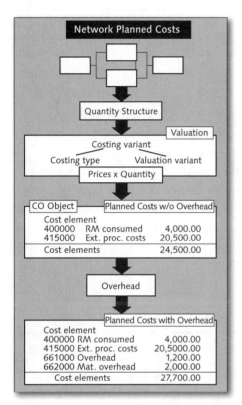

Figure 11.3 Project Network Costing

Planned costs on orders and projects

An interesting business scenario arises in SAP implementations that use both projects and orders in SAP. Depending on whether your project is an overhead project, capital project, manufacturing project, or any other type, it may be linked with different types of orders such as sales orders, internal orders, production orders, plant maintenance orders, and so on. How do you manage planned values on orders (e.g., an internal order for preparing marketing brochure) that are also assigned to a project (e.g., project for a new product launch)? SAP handles this type of business requirement by providing you with configurable options to control whether planned values on orders are added to the planned values on project or whether orders and projects are planned independently. Obviously, costs planned at the be-

Using costing variants

ginning of a project needs to be adapted, revised, and forecasted as the project progresses, and actual costs are posted.

Project Cost Forecasts

You can use the project cost forecasting functionality in SAP PS to adjust your cost planning, based on actual costs incurred so far on the project. In this process, the system helps you determine estimated costs and costs-to-complete for a project by valuating project resources and activities and then saving it in different forecast versions. This functionality can be especially useful for large projects if there are multiple alternatives to completion, or if a slight variation in costs for a key resource can have significant impact on project costs. By periodically taking into account the reality of project costs, you can choose the most cost-effective alternative and take necessary corrective actions.

 Warning

Calculating costs-to-complete for valuated project stock isn't yet supported in SAP ECC 6 Financials.

Calculation of revised costs

The actual calculation and allocation of the revised costs of a project depends on several factors such as the type of activity or resources being revalued; the extent to which activities are completed or resources have been consumed; whether the tasks are in the past, in-progress currently, or are scheduled for the future; and so on. For example, if prices have been revised for a procurement activity for which purchase orders have already been created, then the estimated cost of that activity is already reflected in the corresponding actual or commitment costs, so the cost-to-complete that activity is zero. Whereas, for an activity that is still in progress, the revised cost-to-complete is distributed between the revaluation date and the activity finish date; or if the activity is associated with an invoicing plan, these costs are distributed based on the dates in the invoicing plan.

Project Cost Budget Monitoring

Releasing budget

Using the budget monitoring functionality, you can monitor that actual costs remain within the approved budget. Budget monitoring helps you compare actual postings to projects with approved budget in real time and trigger warning or error messages if actual costs exceed budgeted costs. You can assign different tolerance limits to different types of business transactions such as purchasing activities, financial transactions, goods receipt, and so on. We covered this in Chapter 6 while discussing budget monitoring of investment measures (remember, a WBS element can also be an investment measure!). However, what is unique about budget monitoring in PS is that you can control the distribution of budgets from higher level WBS elements to lower level WBS elements. As shown in Figure 11.4, from a total budget of $15,000 at level 1, only $10,000 is distributed to lower level WBS elements; and from a total budget of $3,000 for level 2 only $1,500 is distributed to level 3, from which only $800 is distributed to level 4. This enables you to release the budget to different segments of your projects only as required.

Original Budget: WBS Element Overview

Annual Overview | Primary Costs | Activity Input

Proj. Def. C/1014
Period 2007

Annual Values

E	Lev	WBS element	Budget	Tra	Distributed	Distributable
	1	C/1014	15,000.00	USD	10,000.00	5,000.00
	2	C/1014-CON	1,000.00	USD		1,000.00
	2	C/1014-PRE	2,000.00	USD		2,000.00
	2	C/1014-EXE	3,000.00	USD	1,500.00	1,500.00
	3	C/1014-EXE-001	1,500.00	USD	800.00	700.00
	4	C/1014-EXE-002	800.00	USD		800.00
	2	C/1014-ANA	4,000.00	USD		4,000.00

Figure 11.4 Budget Monitoring

Similar to other SAP components, commitment management helps you recognize future liabilities (e.g., purchase orders) that are allocated to WBS elements. For orders that are linked to a project, you can control whether the actual cost assignment to individual orders is also deemed as the cost assignment to the project. As you can imagine, this option should be selected after you decide whether you want to carry out budget monitoring for orders and projects together or independent of each other. At period-end, you have several options to process costs accumulated on WBS elements.

Project Costs Settlement

Most period-end processing options in SAP PS are similar to the ones we discussed in Chapter 10 such as periodic reposting, overhead calculation, and so on. However, the period-end settlement process in PS has some interesting and unique features. First of all, you can settle costs from individual WBS elements directly to external cost receivers (e.g., cost center), or you can carry out multilevel settlement in which costs at lower level WBS elements are first settled to higher level WBS elements, and then settled to cost centers. Secondly, a rather unique and nifty functionality enables you to automatically generate settlement rules. This process uses customizable strategies associated with project networks and WBS elements to automatically generate settlement rules. This type of automatic generation can be especially useful for large projects with complex hierarchies because manually maintaining settlement rules can be extremely time-consuming.

Also, you have to determine the settlement process for costs collected on orders that are linked to a project. SAP supports settling these costs to the same WBS elements the orders are linked to, to different WBS elements, or to other cost receivers such as cost centers. In the next section, we'll discuss processing and calculating project revenues.

Project Revenues

Typical overhead projects or capitalization projects don't require planning, processing, and calculating revenues and profitability of a project. However, projects initiated based on customer requirements (e.g., make-to-order or assemble-to-order production scenarios) do need to be evaluated on the basis of planned revenues and its comparison with project costs to get an idea of the likely profit or loss on the project. SAP PS offers comprehensive functionality for revenue management, including revenue planning.

Revenue Planning

You can plan anticipated revenues on a project using manual planning, or you can update planned revenues based on billing plans. As discussed in Chapter 2, billing plans allow you to specify the dates and amounts for invoices sent to customers. If you've already assigned sales orders to a project, then revenue planning can be done based on billing plans from sales orders, but you can also maintain billing plans for WBS elements. This can be useful, for example, during the initial stage of a project when you haven't yet received confirmed sales orders.

 Tip

The system updates revenue planning with values combined from the billing plan maintained for WBS elements and the billing plan maintained for sales orders. This enables you to influence revenue planning in PS in addition to the values coming from the SAP Sales and Distribution component.

While distributing revenues over the project timeline for planning purposes, the system uses dates generated by the billing plan. However, if necessary, SAP PS also supports copying dates from project milestones. This can be useful, for example, if project billing is contingent upon reaching project milestones. You can use contractually agreed upon prices for billing, or you can use resource-related billing in SAP to determine billing values.

Resource-Related Billing

If pricing for project resources isn't fixed or can't be predetermined, you need to calculate customer billing based on actual resources consumed. Resource-related billing gives you this ability; for example, you can bill for actual hours on a consulting project or for actual costs in make-to-order production. The process is relatively simple and starts with a sales order item linked with a WBS element designated as relevant for resource-related billing. After resource consumption and work performed is confirmed in the sales order, you process a billing request that determines the actual amount to be billed. Calculating billing revenue consists of two steps. First, the system determines actual costs associated with consumed resources and presents it to you so that you can review and determine costs that should be billed in full, billed partially, billed later, or not billed at all. Subsequently, the process allocates the billable amount to sales order items for invoicing and records it on the project as revenues.

Billing requests

Ex Example

> During the final phase of a project, the customer requests support for an issue expected to take 8 hours. However, the engineer ends up using $150 worth of spares and spends 14 hours, for which the customer agrees to pay for 10 hours. In a billing request, you bill in full for spares, bill partially for engineer's time, and bill for travel costs later if all relevant information isn't available.

Intercompany billing

Resource-related billing can also be used for intercompany scenarios such as employees from a shared-services company working on customer projects undertaken by other companies of the same corporate group. For such business scenarios, SAP supports recording and reporting expenditures across companies so that you can use it as the basis for distributing project revenues. However, if a project uses resources managed by different profit centers (most projects do), and your company carries out parallel valuation by profit centers, you can use the transfer pricing functionality.

Transfer Pricing for Projects

The concept of transfer pricing is the same across SAP ERP Financials whether used in PS, Profit Center Accounting (PCA) (Chapter 13), consolidation (Chapter 9), or any other components. It's used by different companies for different purposes such as to determine profit margins by profit centers, for tax reporting, for management reporting, and so on. Using transfer pricing, your company can decide a particular price between profit centers for a particular service (Figure 11.5).

Transfer pricing agreements

If transfer prices are specified, then regardless of whether it's planned or actual valuation, the system writes costs and commitments to the ordering WBS element and revenue to the delivering WBS element in profit center evaluation. In PS, you use transfer price agreements to maintain transfer pricing information between two WBS elements, which should be assigned to different profit centers or different subprojects. Subprojects allow you to divide a project into smaller, different responsibility areas.

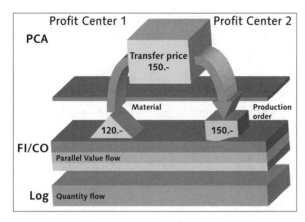

Figure 11.5 Transfer Pricing

So far, we've talked about the different ways of calculating costs and revenues on a project. This functionality in PS combined with its strong integration with SAP Sales and Distribution, provides you with a unique ability to create sales quotations for customer inquiries. This can be extremely useful when you're unable to use a standard pricing list. For example, this functionality can be useful for creating sales quotations for make-to-order products, customer projects, and so on. To help you manage payment flows arising out of these transactions, SAP PS provides you with integrated functionality for payments and cash management.

Creating sales quotations

Payments and Cash Management

For proper cash and liquidity management, especially large projects need to manage their cash flows just like a small company, with as much control and visibility as possible over incoming and outgoing payment commitments. Even for smaller projects, this information is useful in trying to understand how much cash buffer the company will need during the project duration. To carry out such analysis, monitoring, and reporting of payment flows for individual projects, you can use the Project Cash Management functionality, which automatically records relevant data from other SAP components. This functionality is used to monitor payment flows from a project point of view compared to the Cash Management component of SAP FSCM (discussed in Chapter 16), which is used to monitor payment flows for the whole business. This functionality helps you evaluate planned as well as actual payment flows.

Planned Payment Flows

Project Cash Management

Payment flows for different business transactions are calculated and evaluated differently. The Project Cash Management functionality automatically records planned payment flows from purchasing and sales transactions, while taking into account any billing plans and invoicing plans (these plans are discussed in Chapter 3). Business transactions such as purchase requisitions, purchase orders, vendor invoices, and customer invoices are recorded as commitments in project cash management. Planned payment outflows are calculated based on network costing so that outgoing payments for external activities are planned on the latest finish date, whereas outgoing payments for other resources are planned on the same date as the requirements date. Obviously, if you're using invoicing plans with any of the previously mentioned documents, the system uses dates specified in invoicing plans for planned payment flows taking into account applicable payment terms.

 Example

> A supplier invoice with payment terms of Net14 posted on March 1st shows an anticipated payment outflow in Project Cash Management on March 14th.

Automatic update of planned payment flows

Similarly, from sales transactions, you can automatically record planned incoming payments based on billing documents associated with WBS elements. Because one sales order or contract may be split into multiple billing documents, you also can record planned but unbilled payment inflows based on information from sales documents. You can ensure data integrity of the payment plan numbers in project cash management by creating subsequent documents with reference to the original document. For example, when a sales order is created based on a sales quotation, the corresponding planned payment flows are updated in project cash management. Similar to the invoicing plans on the purchasing side, if sales documents and billing documents include billing plans, then the planned incoming payments are recorded based on dates specified in billing plans.

However, if sales and purchase transactions associated with a project aren't available or aren't sufficient to provide all relevant payment flows, then you can also carry out manual payment planning for projects. This can be especially useful in the early stages of the project when the whole project structure may or may not have been finalized.

Actual Payments and Commitments

In project cash management, the payment obligations (e.g., invoice) and payments (e.g., actual payment) are recorded separately based on the dates and the payment terms from corresponding documents posted in the new GL. Apart from recording actual payment flows of incoming and outgoing payments, SAP automatically records project commitments based on purchase requisitions, purchase orders, invoice receipts, invoice issues, and down payments. Project cash management isn't automatically updated when actual payments are processed in Financials. Instead, payment-processing information is updated using a periodic transfer program into project cash management. This controlled update to project cash management data is useful from a project manager's viewpoint because it helps to ensure data consistency of their project reporting as actual processing of incoming and outgoing payments may be outside the control of individual project managers.

Controlled update of actual payments

The payment transfer program marks corresponding invoices as cleared, and thus moves it from commitment (invoice category) to actual payment. If the invoice is only partially paid, then the transfer program creates self-balancing entries so that the commitment amount and payment amounts are updated accurately. Additionally, you can also use the profit and loss adjustment program to update project cash management with details such as cash discounts, rebates, exchange rate differences, and so on. You also have the flexibility of processing payment transfers directly in project cash management without impacting the original financial posting, which is useful, for making adjustments or corrections.

Down payments in Project Cash Management

As we discussed, project cash management takes into account payment terms to actually reflect the dates when payment flows are anticipated. It's also versatile enough to handle down payments received from customers and down payments made to vendors. As shown in the example, when invoices are received, the transfer program automatically adjusts the invoice amount proportionately and reports it in project cash management.

 Example

> A 20 % down payment of $2,000 is made for a $10,000 purchase order, which gets transferred to project cash management as an actual outgoing payment. Subsequently, when a $4,000 invoice is received from the vendor; the payment transfer program clears $800 (40 % of $2,000) of the down payment against it, and it only transfers a commitment of $3,200 to project cash management.

However, in project accounting, payment transactions aren't always the result of originally planned sales and purchase transactions. Discrepancies in project deliverables either with customers or from suppliers may require processing of claims and corresponding payments.

Claims Management

Most projects have established procedures to process discrepancies in customer deliverables, identify responsibilities, and process claims and payments. To ensure protection against discrepancies in deliverables, most projects also have similar established procedures with suppliers. Even if a project does not have an established process or contractual agreement, any major discrepancy or delay in deliverables invariably results in some type of monetary or in-kind payment. Claims Management functionality of SAP PS helps you process claims with customers and vendors. Claims in SAP PS are based on a more generic, powerful concept of notifications. Notifications enable you to process different project events such as report of loss, project change orders, customer complaints, customer errors, and so on.

The PS component provides comprehensive, partially configured processes for creating and evaluating notifications and claims. Any member of your project team with proper authorization and access can create claims with a detailed description of the incident and associate it with the appropriate WBS element. For every claim (Figure 11.6), you can manage associated business partners, tasks to be performed by business partners, activities to be carried out internally, and so on. Using the standard status management and the Business Workflow functionality, you can make processing claims status dependent so that, for example, a claim isn't settled until all associated tasks and activities are completed. Additionally, you can maintain three different costs associated with a claim: estimated claim amount, required/requested claim amount, and accepted/agreed upon claim amount. These costs can be entered manually or using integrated costing scenarios.

Processing of a claim case

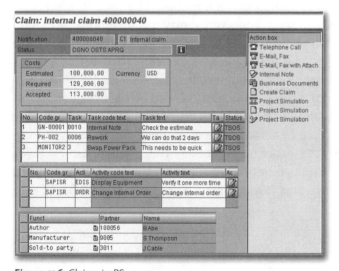

Figure 11.6 Claims in PS

For each type of notification or claim, the system can be set up to assign the appropriate costing scenario. Costing scenarios associated with a claim enable you to use powerful costing features in SAP such as costing sheets, overhead keys, results analysis keys, and settlement profiles to evaluate and process claim-related costs. The system

Costing scenarios

automatically creates an internal order to collect costs associated with the claim, and to facilitate easy reconciliation, an internal order carries all necessary references to the corresponding WBS element, profit center, business area, and so on. Estimated costs entered on a claim are automatically transferred as planned costs on the corresponding internal order, whereas settlement of the actual costs collected on internal order follows the same process as described in Chapter 10.

You may have noticed that so far in this chapter we haven't discussed procurement and production of materials, which are especially important for manufacturing projects. So in the next section, let's discuss the integration of PS with other SAP components relevant for this functionality.

Integration with Procurement and Production

Depending on the complexity and purpose of a project, it may use simple widgets, finished products that may require processing of multilevel BOM (bill of materials), intricately designed assemblies, etc. In the context of this section, we'll loosely refer to all of them as materials. A project manager may request to use these materials from existing inventory (if available), request them to be manufactured or assembled internally, or procure these materials directly. Some of these requirements may be initiated based on sales orders received from customers. SAP PS easily manages these complicated business flows and is fully integrated with SAP components such as Procurement, Production, Inventory Management, Sales and Distribution, and so on.

Typically, this stock is managed with other inventory in plants and is issued to the project as required. However, for especially complex projects, you may decide to separate inventory management and materials planning for project stock and other inventory stock. You specify relevant WBS elements in inventory movements of project stock to account for them properly in PS. Typically, from a project accounting and costing point of view, you can choose to maintain project stock on a valuated basis. This has the advantage that all goods movements of stock are valuated on both quantity basis and value basis, and corresponding postings in Financial Accounting are triggered automatically and immediately.

 Tip

> You can manage project stock on a non-valuated basis, that is, only on a quantity basis. For non-valuated project stock, individual goods movements aren't valuated and corresponding FI entries are also not posted. For such projects, stock is valuated at period-end using results analysis, and resulting entries are posted to FI. Unless there are strong and specific reasons to use non-valuated stock, SAP recommends using valuated project stock.

The advantage of using such valuated project stock is that you can easily view these stocks along with corresponding WBS elements in a project hierarchy, and because accounting entries are posted for individual goods movements, they are easier to reconcile. Following are examples of business scenarios involving valuated project stock and accounting entries in PS and FI.

Advantages of valuated project stock

> For in-house manufacturing and production, you can issue/receive project stock to/from production orders (e.g., issue semi-finished goods and receive finished products). Production orders are debited or credited as appropriate.

> Similar accounting entries are posted if the final product requires product assembly. Corresponding activities in project networks are debited or credited as appropriate.

> Delivery for a customer creates a credit posting for project stock and creates appropriate cost postings to activities in the project network.

> During cost planning, material costs are distributed over the project timeline based on invoicing plans, invoice dates, and requirement dates from project.

> Commitments from purchase orders are recorded on WBS elements, and debits arising at the time of goods receipts are automatically recorded to stock accounts in FI.

> Adjustments at the time of processing an invoice are charged to inventory accounts or price difference accounts depending on material price control.

> Of course, these are only some examples to illustrate the strong integration of SAP PS with other SAP components. These SAP processes as well as business processes are considerably more complex and involved. The focus of this chapter is on project accounting and costing, but you can refer to other fine SAP Press resources to explore Production, Procurement, Inventory Management, and other functionalities relevant for SAP PS.

In the next section, we'll look at some other features and integration functionality.

Other Functionality

Confirmations

PS is one of the most integrated components in SAP. Apart from the obvious integration with the new GL, AR, and AP, in the previous section, we discussed how PS is fully integrated with various procurement and production processes. Confirmations represent one of the important features of this integration because you can use confirmations to document and update actual work, capacity use, costs, duration, and status of different project activities, including manufacturing. Several different options are available for recording confirmations that meet diverse requirements of different types of projects and different structures of projects. You can use the standard SAP component Cross-Application Time Sheet (CATS) for recording time sheets and confirmations, you can use Microsoft Access for decentralized data entry of confirmations, or you can confirm project data over your company intranet using the corresponding functionality in PS.

 Tip

SAP also provides you with functionality called plant data collection (PDC) that you can use to confirm project activities in external, third-party systems and then transfer the data into PS.

We also discussed how you can use projects as investment measures and thus integrate PS with Asset Accounting (Chapter 6). Additionally, you can settle project results to Profitability Analysis (Chapter 13) to analyze the profitability of a project or even individual WBS elements. Project-related travel expenses can be processed using the Travel Management (Chapter 7) component. We'll discuss results analysis functionality in detail while discussing product costing (Chapter 12), but it enables you to use complicated costs and revenues calculation methods such as revenue-based, cost-based, or quantity-based analysis; percentage of completion method; several methods for inventory valuation; as well as methods based on resource-related billing.

PS also uses integrated SAP document management so that you can attach all relevant documents to projects, including project scope and charter documents, requirements documents, contracts, and even CAD drawings. PS also uses the powerful functionality of Business Workflow and provides several templates that you can use for your projects. For example, you can trigger a workflow if dates or quantities in a project are changed and a purchase order has already been created, which can help you in coordinating with your suppliers as necessary.

SAP document management

The PS itself provides a lot of other functionality that is useful for project management, resource management, and other project-related activities. For example, using capacity leveling, you can attempt to achieve optimum use of project resources, and using dates management, you can carry out comprehensive dates scheduling for different project phases. Interfaces such as OpenPS help you communicate and integrate project-related data with external products such as Microsoft Project, whereas tools such as ProMan help you obtain a structured and consolidated overview of procurement information from a variety of applications. As discussed in the next section, using project versions, you can take project snapshots to meet your requirements.

Project System interfaces

Versions

PS also provides project versioning functionality that can be especially useful for complex projects. This functionality lets you take a snapshot of a project or its subset for further evaluations, reporting, comparison, or simply for backup. Obviously, you can create the versions manually at any time, but SAP PS also provides you with the functionality to automatically trigger the creation of project versions when the project status changes to released, approved, technically completed, and so on.

 Tip

Project versions are used to create a snapshot of a project at a certain point in time, primarily for project management. Plan versions are primarily used for project accounting to evaluate different costs and revenues scenarios.

Because a large company may have several projects going on in parallel, you can group project versions into different version groups by types of project and by usage (project accountants, project managers, and so on.). These versions can be used in most project reports provided in a standard SAP system. However, if you simply want to simulate what-if scenarios, then you can use the functionality of simulation versions in SAP.

Simulation versions

You can use simulation versions for checking a hypothesis, evaluating possible risks (e.g., delay in receiving key raw material due to a shipping workers strike), and other similar scenarios that require simulating changes without impacting actual, operative project data. SAP PS provides you with complete functionality to plan costs, revenues, payments, and resources on simulation versions. Also, simulation versions can be extremely powerful because not only can you create a simulation version based on the operative project, but you can also create an operative project based on a simulation version. This can be important if a simulated scenario becomes a reality or the chosen course of action for a project. To analyze actual, planned, budgeted, and simulated project data, you can create custom reports in SAP using the Report Painter tool or use any of the standard reports provided in Project Information System.

Project Information System
SAP PS provides tools and reports for effective project monitoring, control, and execution from technical, commercial, and management points of view. Of special interest for Project Accounting are the hierarchical reports for evaluating project costs, revenues, and payments.

Using these reports, you can analyze actual values, commitments, planned values, budgeted values, sales orders, and procurement values for one project, across several projects, or for part of a project. The project analysis can be carried out for WBSs, project networks, project activities, and also for individual project components. Figure 11.7 shows an example of such a report.

Finances: Overview Report

Object	Overall--CR	Overall-- PO	Overall--pa	Overall--fin	Overall--DR	Overall- p
PRJ L-0-002	0	0	249,704-	0	0	0
PRJ T-20301	274,611-	303,093-	0	834,200	176,778	172,000
▽ WBS T-20301	274,611-	303,093-	0	834,200	176,778	172,000
▷ WBS T-20301.1	29,610-	45,000-	0	0	0	0
▷ WBS T-20301.3	245,001-	0	0	0	0	0
Result	274,611-	303,093-	249,704-	834,200	176,778	172,000
November 2006	49,595-	51,129-	249,704-	68,800	172,000-	172,000
February 2007	75,385-	78,535-	0	264,880	348,778	0
April 2007	29,610-	45,000-	0	103,200	0	0
October 2007	120,021-	128,429-	0	397,320	0	0
Result	274,611-	303,093-	249,704-	834,200	176,778	172,000
Down payments, debit	0	0	0	0	0	0
Internal Materials /	0	0	155,826-	0	0	0
External Services	29,610-	45,000-	93,878-	0	0	0
Revenues	245,001-	258,093-	0	834,200	176,778	172,000
Result	274,611-	303,093-	249,704-	834,200	176,778	172,000

Figure 11.7 Finance Overview Report

Similarly, you can use standard SAP reports that provide details of individual GL account entries to evaluate summarized totals or to carry out reconciliation with other SAP functionalities and components. For example, you can reconcile the approved budget for a project with a budget line-item report, reconcile procurement activities using a commitment line -item report, and reconcile cost accounting entries using a settlement line-item report.

For consolidated, big-picture types of reports, SAP PS provides you with a project summarization. Using this functionality, you can combine a number of different projects, internal orders, and production orders, even if those orders aren't assigned to those projects in SAP. This provides you with a highly versatile analysis tool that can be customized to summarize project data that meets your business requirements. Additional functionalities are listed here:

Project summarization

> Presentation and analysis of project data based on project structure, profit center and cost center hierarchy, capital investment program, sales order, or any custom designed hierarchy that is suitable for your project structure.

> Progress analysis process is used to determine planned and actual project progress values and to compare two sets of data. This enables you to identify cost and schedule variances early and take appropriate actions.

> Milestone Trend Analysis (MTA) is a simple method for analyzing actual and planned dates of project milestones. Project managers can use this report to analyze the impact of any delays on project milestones.

> Progress tracking enables you to closely monitor the progress of network components in projects and purchase orders in procurement. This helps you analyze the impact on projects for any actual or possible delays in procurement.

Case Study

This $230-million homebuilding company engages in the development of residential properties in the southern United States. The company primarily focuses on apartment communities and single-family homes targeted at middle-income families. The company is engaged in approximately 15 construction projects annually either as a primary contractor or subcontractors and deals with 25+ managers, 60+ suppliers and contractors, and hundreds of construction workers. Obviously, there are some similarities, but typically each construction project has its unique quirks in terms of financial, contractual, or technical requirements and obligations.

Business Challenges

Before implementing SAP PS, different areas of construction projects were primarily managed by different off-the-shelf software and a large number of Excel spreadsheets, not to mention intensely manual paper-based processes. Projects routinely experienced cost overruns and scheduling delays, resulting in disputes, soured business relationships, and sometimes even litigations. Getting all-embracing, timely status of even one project was difficult due to the overwhelming amount of information residing in mutually incompatible systems.

By their nature, construction projects involve large quantities and complex compositions of materials, numerous interdependent project activities, and careful capital management. However, because procurement, accounting, and project management were using different systems at the company, a considerable communication gap existed between these departments and personnel, which led to many decisions that were detrimental to project profitability. Lack of proper resource planning meant that many projects made urgent purchases at higher-than-market prices or had to hire temporary workers at inflated rates to meet project commitments. Payments were made to suppliers who had not met their obligations, and receivables languished due to the lack of follow-up. Most problems were noticed after the fact, when it was too late to take any corrective action.

With each new problem on a construction project, the company was becoming increasingly aware of the need to have better, accurate, and largely automatic systems in place to manage its construction projects.

Solution Deployment

The company decided to implement SAP not only because of its robust, well-integrated PS component but also because it provided comprehensive functionality to support any future business expansion such as more complex construction projects or public works projects. The project involved implementing SAP PS along with most other financial and cost controlling components such as GL, receivables, payables, fixed assets, cost center, internal order accounting, and so on. In addition to these components, the company also decided to use document management and Business Workflow functionality to enhance the efficiency of its project activities as well as back office operations.

To ensure smooth implementation, the project was awarded to an SAP consulting firm with past experience in such implementations. The project took 9.5 months to implement with the help of 16 full-time SAP consultants and a large number of dedicated users from business. Project plan templates were developed with detailed WBSs, project networks, and more than 4,300 individual activities planned in meticulous detail.

These templates provided a solid foundation that could be used for any new construction projects. Document management functionality was set up so that different project documents, such as construction plans, approvals, permits, authorizations, contracts, and other standard business documents can be easily stored and accessed from a single interface. Business workflow was configured to ensure that any new information or changes were automatically sent out to all relevant project managers, contractors, subcontractors, workers, supervisors, and back office employees.

Carefully planned change control management and claims management business requirements were configured so that even for slight discrepancies, the appropriate personnel were immediately notified so they could take necessary actions. Exhaustive training sessions were provided to all staff members in the company, and designated super users were given the responsibility of ensuring that the considerable investment made by the company in implementing SAP was followed-through by its proper use.

Value Achieved

One of the biggest benefits of implementing SAP PS was the free flow of information to all necessary people, as and when appropriate or required. Collaborative efforts between different parties involved in construction projects were not only easier to coordinate but were well received and well appreciated by all affected. The management "dream" of achieving almost real-time cost control and budget monitoring was turned into reality with the help of a budget availability check, purchase authorizations, and variance monitoring. Resource planning—for materials as well as workers—highlighted several areas of improvements in procurement, project management, and accounting functions.

Project managers were especially delighted to be able to view anticipated costs and revenues for the whole project at any given time, to carry out what-if scenarios to decide on corrective actions for possible risks, and to view the impact of any change or discrepancy on the whole project. With the help of Project Cash Management, the managers were able to view the anticipated distribution of incoming and outgoing payments over the project timeline and thus plan their capital and cash flow requirements diligently.

The management was now able to get a much-needed holistic view of the company across all projects at any time, thus providing them with a strategic, tactical, and financial advantage. Management was already observing the benefits of the powerful analytics and reporting functionality, and timely information on the progress of all projects and the use of resources. Management anticipates that the investment in SAP will be paid off in two years, which is better than some of their own construction projects.

Looking Ahead

Because with the help of SAP PS the company is able to view project schedules, resource requirements, and material requirements across all construction projects, the procurement department wants to put a preferred vendor list in place and negotiate volume discounts on standard construction materials. Another area project managers are interested in is the normalization and efficient use of resources across projects. Because the whole company now has a single view of relevant information, it will make it easier for project managers to identify any temporary surplus of resources and offer them to/request them from other construction projects in the company.

Summary

SAP PS can be used for any type of overhead, capitalization, or manufacturing projects. Following are some of the salient features of this SAP component:

> Flexible project design and integration with SAP Accounting and Logistics components provide you with complete control over the type and purpose of projects in SAP PS.

> Integration with other SAP components enables you to initiate, manage, and carry out end-to-end business processes from cus-

tomer quotation to final delivery on customer projects (e.g., make-to-order production).

> Precise planning and monitoring of costs with respect to budget creates transparency throughout the project process and enables you to tackle any problems early on.

> Availability of billing functionality such as billing plans and re-source-related billing, and complete integration with Sales and Dis-tribution helps you plan for project revenues early on to get an idea of likely profit or loss.

> Project Cash Management offers you the capability to evaluate and monitor the formation of capital on projects so that you can take proactive actions to manage your project cash flow.

> You can monitor, analyze, and evaluate technical as well as com-mercial progress of projects using a large number of standard re-ports or create custom reports per your requirements.

In this chapter, you learned how to use SAP for managing costs on your complex projects and initiatives. In the next chapter on product costing, you'll discover how SAP can help you improve the manage-ment of your manufacturing costs.

Product Costing

No matter what kind of business you're in, you're delivering some type of product or service to your customers. And regardless of whether your business is large or small, keeping your product costs under control is critical to your overall profitability. Unexpected or uncontrolled increases in manufacturing or procurement costs can have immediate and long-term effects on your company's profitability. To address this issue, SAP offers Product Costing, which provides you with an accurate, detailed, transparent, and flexible product costing framework that can help you estimate and capture the costs of your company's products and services.

The product costing tool has robust functionality to support your business needs, whether you need to reduce direct or indirect manufacturing costs, estimate costs for a proposed new product line, or anticipate costs of making changes to existing products.

Overview

Figure 12.1 illustrates how important it is to estimate the costs of products and services as accurately as possible, because they will influence decisions and cost overruns that directly impact the profitability of a product. So whether your products are manufactured for the mass market or are custom-built for a customer, you'll always risk not having timely, accurate information, if you don't have an accurate estimating framework in place.

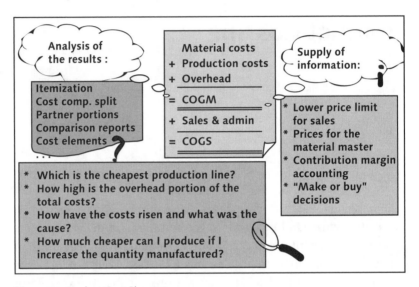

Figure 12.1 Product Cost Planning

The same is true when you're making decisions about introducing new products or when you're evaluating making changes to existing products. In either case, you need flexible tools and functionalities to help you collect, modify, and extrapolate existing information. Then you can use that information to model your assumptions about anticipated costs to make informed decisions. For custom-built products based on customer requests, it's important to have ongoing visibility of estimated, actual, and anticipated costs and revenues at each step of the process, especially if you're building a product that takes months or years.

One manufacturing environment?   Of course, you can't rely on a system that rigidly supports only one (hopefully your current) manufacturing environment. In today's market, the chances of your company being acquired or having to introduce new products with different manufacturing requirements to stay competitive are pretty great. So you need an agile system than can support your production process regardless of the industry and manufacturing environment.

It's probably unlikely that a company in the processed food industry will decide to build airplanes, but for many multinational conglomerates, the ability to use the same system for their production and manufacturing processes in different countries, industries, and manufacturing environments can be invaluable. In the next section, we'll explore the product costing functionality in detail, so that you can learn how you can use it to meet your business requirements.

Functions in Detail

With product costing, you get complete functionality for planning, calculating, controlling, managing, reporting, and analyzing costs involved in manufacturing or providing goods and services, regardless of your industry or manufacturing environment. Using the product cost planning component, you can analyze individual tasks, activities, and parts of your production processes in your own manufacturing environment. You can also identify and allocate cost breakdowns and analyze the added value of all of the activities and parts of your production processes as they relate to the total cost of the final product. For relatively simple cost planning processes, you can use the easy cost planning functionality, which can also be used in other components.

For product costing in different manufacturing environments, you are provided with different approaches to collect, report, analyze, and settle costs. You can carry out costing activities on manufacturing orders, sales orders, and orders in cost controlling. Product costing is one of the most integrated components in SAP because it can be integrated with other SAP components, such as production, procurement, inventory management, sales, materials management, project systems, overhead cost controlling, and, of course, financial accounting. With the support of a comprehensive set of processes for period-end closing, you can carry out overhead calculations, WIP (Work in

Integration with other components

Process) calculations, variance calculations, and settlement of costs to financial accounting. For those more complex orders, you can carry out complex results analysis processes for calculating cost reserves, capitalized costs, revenue surpluses, and other relevant values.

 Tip

> Even though we won't discuss any industry-specific functionality in this chapter, all of the SAP Industry Solutions provide the necessary product costing functionality relevant to that industry.

If your business demands inventory valuations in multiple currencies or based on actual prices, you can use the material ledger to calculate the actual prices of externally procured materials as well as materials manufactured in-house. This gives you the ability to value your inventory using actual prices while avoiding problems associated with using the moving average price. It also lets you estimate and control material prices, which is better than the cost management that typically comes with using only standard prices.

Unique features

Product costing in SAP also has some important differences as compared to many other major or legacy systems:

> Inventory postings do not flow through cost centers; instead, product costs are captured on production orders or sales orders and subsequently settled as appropriate.

> Product costing handles a WIP calculation, by first posting it to income statement accounts before settling it to WIP inventory accounts in the month-end balance sheet.

It's helpful to keep these differences in mind, especially during your initial system rollout, because this is when your users will be getting familiar with the system.

Let's move on to discuss some more general concepts relevant to product costing.

General Concepts

Before we delve into the details of product costing, it will be help-ful to understand the types of products and materials supported by SAP, what information you can maintain for them, and how they are processed.

Materials Management

In SAP, the material master represents the materials that a company purchases, manufactures, stores and sells. The concept of materials is more generic, and it's used to represent not just common material types, such as raw materials, semi-finished goods, and finished goods, but also trading goods, operating supplies, assemblies, packaging materials, and even services. Material types control several attributes of a material, including the information you can maintain for that type of material. So, for example, you can't maintain warehouse-relevant information for materials defined as services.

Management of special stock

Additionally, by using special stock indicators, you can separate different inventory balances for the same material. This means that the same material can have different inventory balances that are available for unrestricted use, earmarked for projects (project stock), belong to a vendor (consignment stock), and so on. This information isn't only useful for reporting, but it also influences business activities in which that inventory can be used (e.g., inventory earmarked for a project can only be processed with reference to that project).

 Tip

For a more detailed understanding of the materials management component and manufacturing processes relevant to your industry, you may want to learn more about other SAP components such as inventory management, procurement, and production.

Another concept relevant to material processing is movement types. In the same way that posting keys (Chapter 2) are used to classify different types of accounting transactions, movement types are used to classify different types of goods movements. The standard SAP soft-

Material movement types

ware provides literally *hundreds* of movement types for recording different types of inbound and outbound goods movements and goods transfers. This large number indicates the range of complex manufacturing and logistics business processes supported, and the precise control it offers in managing and influencing each process. Thankfully, for you as a business user, most of them are defaulted or used behind the scenes.

The abundance of information maintained in the material master is used in purchasing, invoicing, sales, inventory management, and in production planning and manufacturing processes. Similar to the customer and vendor information we covered in Chapter 3, material information in SAP is also stored at multiple levels.

So for sales organizations, your relevant sales information is maintained, and for manufacturing and production, the relevant plant information is maintained. This design facilitates easy maintenance of data and provides a single corporate-wide source of information. This is important because it also supports the necessary but inevitable differences that can arise in material processing between different plants, different companies, or even different countries. For product costing purposes, the relevant information, such as inventory pricing controls and inventory prices, is stored separately for each plant.

Inventory Pricing

Standard price versus moving average price

To value your inventory, you can use either the standard price or the weighted moving average price (MAP). If materials are assigned standard prices, then all of the inventory postings to it are carried out using that price. Any price differences in goods movements or material invoices are posted to price difference accounts. The SAP inventory management configuration provides a number of price difference accounts so that you can track and report different types of variances. Standard costs give you consistent values for performance measurement and can be used for estimated or budgeted values for higher level organizational planning.

You can use a number of versatile SAP tools and techniques to calculate standard cost estimates for your inventory (which we'll discuss in later chapters), but, if you use the moving average price (MAP), your material prices are *automatically* adjusted to reflect price variances in goods movements and invoices. Obviously, these are easier to maintain because the software automatically carries out the necessary calculation and because material costs tend to closely reflect actual costs. Also, because variances occur only in exceptional circumstances, there is no need to carry out formal variance analysis.

 Tip

Even though there is no technical restriction, it's recommended that you use MAP for raw materials, trading materials, and other materials when it's important and possible to capture actual procurement costs. But the standard price should be used for semi-finished, finished, and other materials manufactured in-house, when it's difficult to capture price variances in a multi-level production, or when using MAP can potentially lead to unrealistic valuations.

However, both of these pricing controls have their disadvantages.

Using standard costs requires making assumptions that may not hold true in volatile markets with price fluctuations. Standard prices of a material can't be changed during a period. And, frequent creation of cost estimates means more planning, operational, and calculation work.

But, using MAP means that any variances large or small are difficult to isolate and analyze, and there are no benchmarks to measure performance against. This may be acceptable in industries (e.g., some process industries) with highly variable manufacturing processes, but most companies like to have some visibility into variances in their processes. As we'll see later in the chapter, it's possible to have the best of both worlds in product costing by using the material ledger.

Even without the material ledger, the software will automatically calculate and maintain MAP for materials being valuated using standard costs. And, you can calculate and update standard prices for materials being valuated using MAP. This can be useful for reporting and analysis or, if necessary, to switch between inventory valuations.

So now let's take a look at some of the additional functionality in product costing.

Product Costing Overview

Obviously, product costing methodologies and requirements differ from industry to industry depending on the products being manufactured and the operational model applicable of the manufacturing environment. But this isn't a problem because it supports production processes for several types of manufacturing environments.

Manufacturing Environments

SAP supports a range of manufacturing methods and scenarios, including *make-to-stock*, *make-to-order*, *engineer-to-order*, *assemble-to-order*, *process manufacturing*, *repetitive manufacturing*, and *KANBAN*. Let's take a brief look at each of these:

> **Make-to-stock**

Make-to-stock

One of the most commonly used manufacturing environments supported in SAP. This is typically used for mass production of goods. In this environment, materials are produced independent of corresponding sales orders and sometimes even without any sales orders because the main objective is to provide customers with a finished product as soon as possible. For example, companies involved in the manufacturing of personal products, household products, office supplies, etc. Typically, in such a production environment, product costs are collected, reported, and analyzed for individual materials.

> **Make-to-order**

Make-to-order

In this next most common production environment, products are manufactured, or modified in some way, to meet specific customer orders. This environment is best for the production of small quantities of customizable products ordered in smaller quantities such as manufacturers of specialized machinery and equipment. In these situations, you typically collect, report, analyze, and settle costs based on sales orders. Figure 12.2 shows an interesting analysis of different factors involved in manufacturing processes ranging from make-to-order to engineer-to-order.

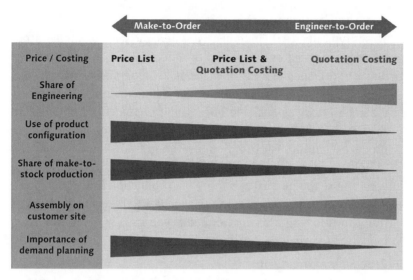

Figure 12.2 Make-to-Order to Engineer-to-Order

> **Engineer-to-order**
>
> For really complex business scenarios, such as when a product is engineered for a specific customer, you may even have the system create a project based on a customer sales order. For such environments, the production processes are managed using project networks. Of course, in such a case, product costing involves decidedly complex processes and calculations that use functionality from product costing and PS.

Engineer-to-order

> **Assemble-to-order**
>
> Another special kind of make-to-order environment supported in which a large number of finished products can be assembled from common components. In assemble-to-order environments such as those in automotive manufacturing companies, key components are planned or stocked in anticipation of the sales order, and the assembly of a customized product or service is initiated on receipt of the sales order. When you create a sales order, a customer quotation, or an inquiry with one of the assemble-to-order planning strategies, the system automatically creates an assembly order. From a product costing perspective, you collect, report, analyze, and settle costs by assembly orders.

Assemble-to-order

> **Repetitive manufacturing**

This is typically useful in industries where the same or similar products are produced over a period of time, without any defined production lots, such as consumer products, food and beverages, etc. Depending on the industry, repetitive manufacturing can be either a make-to-stock or make-to-order environment. Typically, within the framework of repetitive manufacturing, production planning of product quantities is carried out on the basis of time buckets. The in-house material flow is relatively simplified in this case because you can use the pull list to supply the production line with materials, instead of production orders specifically requesting materials from inventory. In this environment, you usually determine costs by period for analysis, reporting, and settlement.

> **Process manufacturing**

This uses a specially integrated functionality that supports manufacturing involving batch-oriented production. SAP provides process orders for the execution of process manufacturing and uses master recipes to define the process sequence necessary to manufacture products in process industries. Similar to the manufacturing environments discussed so far, you get the flexibility to decide whether to collect and analyze costs by period or by process orders. And, as you would expect from a fully integrated system such as SAP, you can even link process orders with sales orders and then collect and analyze costs based on sales orders.

> **KANBAN**

This is supported by fairly mature functionality and is largely based on the actual stock quantity in production, with required material continually provided in small quantities to the production line on an as-needed basis. If the material requirements of the production line aren't relatively constant and involve spikes and plateaus in material requirements, then that environment may not be suitable for the KANBAN method of production. For the purpose of product costing, the approach depends on how the replenishments are used to control production cycles. You can choose to collect, analyze, and settle costs by period, or you can do so based on manufacturing orders.

So now let's take a look at the different product costing alternatives available in SAP to support all of these different scenarios.

Product Costing Alternatives

Different alternatives for product costing are also provided so that you can use the best one that meets your manufacturing process.

> **Product costing by period**
>
> Lets you accumulate product costs over a period of time and then analyze debits and credits posted to it by period. This approach is particularly useful in a repetitive manufacturing environment, where the same products are manufactured using the same manufacturing processes repeatedly. However, if you really aren't interested in managing your costs for individual orders, you can also use this approach in make-to-order manufacturing environments. One of the distinguishing features of this approach is that you can use it regardless of the type of production environment you use because the cost collection and analysis can be separated from the actual production orders. This doesn't have to keep you from carrying out logistics activities, such as goods issues and goods receipts for production orders.

Product costing by period

> **Product costing by order**
>
> Lets you analyze costs at the manufacturing order level. Unlike the product costing by period approach, in the by-order approach, manufacturing orders collect costs and are used for settling those costs to financial accounting. This is particularly useful in a make-to-stock environment where you can collect costs on a production lot, and after the entire planned production quantity for the lot has been put into inventory, you can analyze any variances. Typically as part of period-end closing, you can also calculate and update WIP entries for orders that are still open and finished goods inventory for the orders that are completed.

Product costing by order

 Tip

The production campaign functionality provided, can be used for planning, analyzing, and allocating setup and clean-out costs of manufacturing a material to the actual production orders.

> ### Product costing by sales order

Lets you calculate and analyze product costs in make-to-order manufacturing environments where you want to analyze costs by customer orders that trigger corresponding manufacturing orders. However, if you carry out mass production on the basis of sales orders, you can use product costing by order in combination with this functionality. This functionality isn't just relevant for a manufacturing process because you can also use it when you are purchasing customer-specific trading goods with reference to a sales order and are reselling them to your customers. (For example, an electronics distributor can use this to valuate procurement of custom-designed electronics for one of its customer.) A distinguishing feature of this approach is that you can calculate and analyze planned costs, planned revenues, actual costs, and actual revenues for individual items in a sales order. Not only that, but this approach also offers you the ability to calculate the value of goods that have been delivered to your customers but not yet invoiced.

These approaches help you analyze costs when tangible goods are involved, but you also have support for costing that involves intangible goods and services, such as assembling a complex machine at a customer site or providing technical support services over an extended period of time. These costs can be evaluated periodically or for the entire period of undertaking. So you can evaluate setting up an engine room at a plant on a periodic basis but evaluate the whole task for construction of scaffolding. Similar to the other approaches discussed so far, the functionality to collect costs and revenues for intangible goods and services as well as carrying out complex evaluations using results analysis (discussed shortly) is also provided.

Let's move on to talk about product cost planning and the associated scenarios.

Product Cost Planning (CO-PC)

For materials valuated at the standard price, product cost planning provides you with invaluable tools and functionalities for planning and analyzing your product's costs. As before, products in this context not only refer to manufactured materials but also to services and other intangible goods provided by your company. The two main areas in product cost planning are calculating and updating planned costs.

Calculating Planned Costs

Costing variant

This functionality can be used regardless of whether you have detailed bill of materials (BOM) and routing information. And as you know, creating a cost estimate even for relatively simple finished product can be challenging. Final products can involve different materials (raw materials, semifinished products, assemblies) received from different channels (procured, subcontracted, or manufactured internally), production activities (setup, tear-down, clean-out, and actual manufacturing activities), and other cost-incurring elements, not to mention associated overhead costs. But not to worry, SAP handles these complexities easily by grouping together relevant costing parameters into what it calls a *costing variant*.

 Tip

In SAP, a costing variant is a highly versatile tool that contains all the control parameters for costing, including parameters that control how cost estimates are executed and the material prices or activity prices that are used to valuate the costing items.

So for any material cost estimate that is prepared using a costing variant, you can control the following:

> Whether costing of material movements is carried out for legal valuation, profit center valuation, or group valuation

> How the prices of materials, activities, processes, subcontracting, and other types of components are valuated

> The costing sheet used to calculate overhead, and the reference data such as BOM and routing

> Calculation of additive costs such as freight charges, insurance costs, or any other costs that have to be added manually to a cost estimate

> The timeframe for which a cost estimate and associated BOM structure and routing definitions are valid

> The purpose of creating a cost estimate, which prices are calculated, and how are they updated

Types of cost estimates

Let's discuss this last point in a little more detail because many other systems don't support as many types of cost estimates and material prices as SAP.

For example, *standard cost estimates* for materials, which are usually created at the beginning of a year and don't change during that year are supported. These cost estimates provide you with a benchmark to calculate production variances and target costs for valuating open production orders at period end. Standard costs typically remain constant throughout the year and aren't updated based on price fluctuations or changes in the product BOM.

However, unless your markets and the production processes are extremely stable, the product BOM, or at least component prices, does undergo changes during a year. So you get two additional types of cost estimates: *modified standard cost estimate*, which evaluates current BOM structures with standard prices established originally, and *current cost estimate*, which evaluates current BOM structures with current prices. With these three types of cost estimates, you can meet most of your cost planning requirements while taking into account any changes to your products.

The fourth type of cost estimate supported by SAP product costing is the *inventory cost estimate*, which is essentially used for tax and commercial valuation of your inventories.

This brings us to the different material costs and prices supported in SAP and how you update those prices.

Updating of Material Costs

We just discussed the different types of cost estimates, so take a look at Figure 12.3 to see how results of these can be updated to different price fields in the material master. In fact, this integration also works in the reverse direction because, as we discussed, you can also use different prices from the material master while preparing inventory cost estimates.

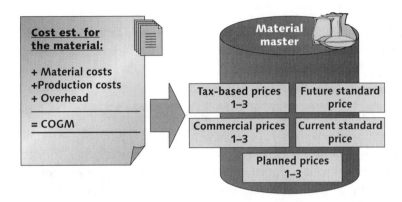

Figure 12.3 Updating Material Prices

To get a better understanding of this, let's first look at standard prices that are updated based on standard cost estimates. All goods movements for materials valuated at a standard price are valuated and posted using the current standard price in a material. SAP keeps record of this standard price separately, even if you manually modify the current standard price in a material master, so that you can reference it as required. SAP also provides you with this nifty functionality so that after evaluating and preparing a standard cost estimate, you can "mark" it to be used as a future standard price, or "release" it to be used as a current standard price.

We won't go into too much detail on inventory valuation and price updating of other prices such as commercial prices and tax-based prices because they are typically not used in the United States. However, if these valuations are relevant for you, SAP provides additional controls for preparing cost estimates, performing inventory valuation, and updating material prices.

Valuation for tax/ commercial purpose

For example, you can establish controls so that materials are updated only if the price calculated in the cost estimate is lower than the price in the material master. You also have control over whether and how much of the cost of different activities are included in valuation, so, for example, you can specify rules so that only 30 % of packaging costs and 75 % of costs of BOM items are included in a cost estimate. Of course, all of these different prices and values are available for reporting and analysis purposes as well.

So let's move on to take a look at a few of the planning aids available to you in product costing.

Planning Aids for Costing

Even though the product cost planning functionality we just discussed is extremely powerful, it may be too complex for relatively simple business scenarios. And, not all of the information required for carrying out such cost planning may always be available, for example, if you are in the process of introducing a new product. For such situations, you can use the unit costing or easy cost planning functionality provided in product costing.

Easy Cost Planning

Easy Cost PlanningCosting Models

The easy cost planning functionality provides you with a quick and easy way to calculate planned costs for a task or an activity. Using this functionality, you can design costing models to get answers to specific and relevant costing factors for a task, and then evaluate those answers to calculate the results. Consider, for example, a costing model shown in Figure 12.4 that might be used by a public works contractor for digging a ditch.

The model accepts basic information such as length, width, and depth of a ditch and the requested material (SKU #). Additionally, the costing model shown in the figure accepts information about the expected time the task will take and any additional fixed costs such as travel costs. All of thesedifferent attributes or factors provide the necessary information for calculating resource requirements or calculating estimated costs for completing a task. So you can design multiple costing models for different tasks and activities in your company, each with its corresponding set of attributes or cost factors. You can also create SAP-based or Web-based forms for each costing model so the relevant personnel can enter the required information for every costing attribute.

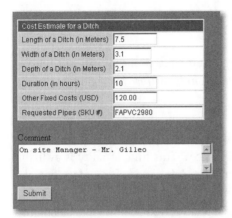

Figure 12.4 Example of Easy Cost Planning

Tip

Even if easy cost planning doesn't appear to be useful for your manufacturing environment, you may find it useful for other areas in your company that use internal orders (Chapter 10), WBS elements (Chapter 11), or appropriation requests (Chapter 6).

In the background, each costing model is associated with an ingenious functionality of cost calculation based on parameters entered on the form corresponding to the costing model, combined with a large number of criteria such as activity price in a cost center, materials, and business processes. The calculation can even make a reference to other costing models, providing you with the ability to design remarkably strong costing models.

Calculation of costs

For example, as you saw in the costing sheet shown in Figure 12.4, you can calculate material costs and labor costs for digging a ditch based on the ditch length, width, and depth. You can also calculate the material requirement for pipes based on the length of the ditch and calculate other costs and material requirements as necessary. Not only that, the potential of this functionality is further enhanced by the ubiquitous integrated nature of SAP components, so that based on results of these costing models, you can automatically trigger the creation of purchase requisitions, purchase orders, goods issues, and other business transactions.

Easy cost planning is a good option for many situations, but there is also another powerful option called *unit costing*.

Unit Costing

Spreadsheet-like framework

Unit costing provides you with a spreadsheet-like framework for planning and entering costs and prices. This functionality is available not only for materials, production orders, and sales orders but also for internal orders, WBS elements, sales order items, and so on. This functionality provides you with a relatively simple way of calculating planned costs by letting you enter individual costing items that contribute to the final cost. It also includes a mechanism for overhead calculation. Because this functionality can reference data from materials management, production, purchasing, and overhead cost controlling, it provides you with a highly adaptable tool for creating costing items that t meet your own costing requirements.

 Tip

Typically, product costing is used to plan costs in conjunction with the production planning component, whereas unit costing is used to enter cost planning information manually or to transfer it from non-SAP systems.

Some of the costing items available in unit costing functionality include the following:

> Internal activities that refer to activities performed in a cost center

> External activities that typically refer to the procurement process

> Subcontracting activities if the unit costing uses the subcontracting process

> Cost estimates and consumption of products and materials

> Costs entered manually by simply entering unit price and quantity used, regardless of what the costs may represent

For each type of costing item, an appropriate strategy is used to determine the applicable price (e.g., from material master, from purchasing, based on cost estimate, and so on), so that when you use unit costing valuation, the accurate and most current prices are used in the calculation of total costs. However, keep in mind that changes aren't automatically updated into the unit cost estimate. For example, if the unit cost estimate for a PCB assembly includes a costing item for the actual circuit board, and the price of that circuit board changes, the unit cost estimate for the PCB isn't automatically updated. You have to specifically trigger the recalculation of the unit cost estimate, so that you can control when and how any changes in component prices impact your cost estimates. Figure 12.5 gives you an example of a unit cost estimate for a CPU.

Controlled update of cost estimates

Base Planning Obj	R-1110		CPU-66								
Costing Items - Basic View											
Item	C	Resource	Plant/	Quantity	U	Value - Total	Description	Price - Total	Price Unit	Price - Fixed	Value - Fixed
1	E	4275	1420	0.033	H	2.56	Machine Hours	7,761.80	100	6,314.05	2.08
2	E	4275	1420	0.033	H	2.56	Machine Hours	7,761.80	100	6,314.05	2.08
3	M	R-1210	3200	1	PC	175.00	PROCESSOR M-375	175.00	1		0.00
4	M	R-1220	3200	1	PC	100.00	MEMORY, 8 MB	100.00	1		0.00
5	B	R-1240		1	PC	37.25	PCA	37.25	1		0.00
6	E	4275	1423	4	H	107.11	Burn-in Hours	2,677.76	100	2,384.05	95.36
7	E	4275	1420	0.017	H	1.32	Machine Hours	7,761.80	100	6,314.05	1.07
8	E	4275	1421	0.017	H	0.86	Labor Hours	5,074.97	100	3,621.89	0.62
9	M	R-1230	3200	1	PC	6.00	BIOS	6.00	1		0.00
10	G					42.15	OHS - raw material				21.08
11	S					474.81					122.29

Figure 12.5 Example of a Unit Costing

If you extrapolate this planning functionality discussion a little bit more, you can easily see how it can be useful for reference costing and simulation costing. For example, if you are planning to introduce a new product for which you haven't yet established a BOM structure, individual materials, etc, you can easily use unit costing to prepare a cost estimate for the product. And, if the new product makes use of some existing products and materials, you can include their respective cost estimates into your cost estimate as well. This functionality can also be helpful if you want to carry out what-if analysis for possible changes to your existing products and then want to analyze the impact of those changes on your cost estimates.

Now that we've looked at the different tools and functionalities available for product cost planning, let's shift our attention to cost controlling activities.

Cost-Controlling Activities

Cost-controlling activities correspond to collecting, calculating, analyzing, and settling the costs collected on products and services. Even though in an integrated system such as SAP, many costs are collected and posted on an ongoing basis, it's typically done at month end. So in this section, we'll only focus on month-end activities for product costing, which depend on several factors, such as the type of manufacturing environment you are using, the type of SAP objects you are using, whether you are costing a production order or sales order, and so on. We'll just discuss activities and functionalities that are most commonly used across different types of product costing constellations in different businesses. Typically, these activities involve calculating overhead, valuating WIP, calculating variance, and posting accounting entries.

Overhead Calculation

Costing sheets   The overhead calculation is one of the most common and most important aspects of any product costing scenario. But what is considered overhead depends on the industry, business, company, function, and statutory regulations. So to meet such diverse requirements, you get a highly flexible calculation framework of costing sheets. Using costing sheets (see Figure 12.6) you can enter a set of structured formulae for calculating overheads using three components:

> **Calculation Bases (e.g., B000–B010)**
> Let you specify cost elements based on which overhead is to be calculated.

> **Overhead Rates (e.g., C000–C003)**
> Let you specify overhead rates using customizable overhead types and overhead keys. Overhead rates can be specified as percentages (e.g., 11 % of salaries + wages) or based on quantities (e.g., $2 for every widget manufactured).

> **Credits (e.g., E01–E04)**
> Let you specify which cost center or internal order to be credited with calculated overhead.

Costing sheet rows						
Row	Base	Over rate	Description	From	To	Credit
10	B000		Material			
20		C000	Material OH	10		E01
30			Material usage			
40	B010		Production			
50		C001	Manufacturing OH	40		E02
60			Production Costs	40	50	
70			Cost of goods manufactured			
80		C002	Administration OH	70		E03
90		C003	Sales OH	70		E04
100			Cost of goods sold	70	90	

Figure 12.6 Example of a Costing Sheet

Additionally, complete flexibility as to the level at which overheads are calculated is provided, which means you can use the same overhead calculation across the whole company or use different calculations for individual cost centers, plants, internal orders, and so on. If necessary, there is even functionality to specify different overhead calculations for different groups of materials.

WIP Calculation

SAP combines diverse requirements of different types of manufacturing environments in a seemingly simple program that uses complex rules and configuration for WIP computation of unfinished products. The calculation process is decidedly more complex and more technical than the process of overhead calculation, and will most likely be configured by the team supporting your SAP implementation. However, as a business user, it will help you to be familiar with the process conceptually. Specifics of different manufacturing environments are discussed later, but conceptually, you can group similar types of costs attributable to production orders into different categories, which in turn can be grouped into cost buckets where you assign posting rules that determine accounting entries.

Warning

The WIP calculation in SAP is different from other typical systems. In SAP, material issues to production orders are immediately posted as expenses to income statement and not as balance sheet reclassifications from raw materials to WIP accounts. Subsequently, as part of the month-end processing, balance sheet entries to WIP account are posted.

Breakdown of the WIP calculation

Individual pieces of this process are completely customizable, so that you can alter the system behavior to best suit your manufacturing environment. Using an elaborate and detailed definition of cost elements, you can easily classify different types of production order costs such as settled costs, direct costs, production costs, overhead costs, and so on.

You are also provided with a highly sophisticated mechanism to map costs to these classifications based on cost elements, cost origins (which let you further subdivide costs posted to cost elements), cost centers, and several other criteria. Depending on your industry and your production environment, you may not be able to capitalize or treat all of your manufacturing costs as WIP. So, SAP also provides you with the functionality to specify costs that *must be* capitalized, *may be* capitalized, and *should not be* capitalized, for the mapping of the costs we just discussed.

The calculation process provides you with several parameters to influence the calculation of WIP, so that you can control the types of manufacturing scenarios for which the WIP calculation is carried out such as sales-order-related production, engineer-to-order production, service orders, and so on. And, as we mentioned, in especially volatile markets, cost estimates prepared at the beginning of a year may not remain valid through the year, so you can choose to valuate WIP based on standard cost estimates, current cost estimates, or alternative cost estimates.

Another equally important step in the month-end process is the calculation of variances.

Variance Calculation

There are several possible reasons actual costs of manufacturing a product vary from its planned or target costs. It can be because raw materials were received at a different price, or may be the price was the same, but different quantities of materials were used in production. Before you can take measures to reduce or at least contain your manufacturing costs, you need information that helps you trace and analyze the reasons for cost variances.

The variance calculation process helps you do that by calculating, recording, and reporting on variances due to any or all of the following possibilities:

> Variances due to differences between planned prices and actual prices of the goods consumed or the activities performed in the manufacturing process

> Variances due to differences between planned quantities and actual quantities of the goods consumed in the manufacturing process

> Variances due to the use of different components (e.g., raw materials) in the process, for example, if originally planned components were unavailable at the time of production

> Variances due to differences in scrap quantities, for example, unusually high scrap quantities than what was planned may highlight problems in manufacturing

> Variances due to differences in procurement alternatives used, for example, planned cost estimate was based on using materials from one source, whereas actual production used materials from different source(s)

> Variances due to a manufactured product being transferred to inventory at a different price than its standard price

> Variances due to difference in lot size, for example, the cost estimate was prepared for a lot of 100 widgets but the actual production lot was 150 widgets, in which case any fixed costs of the process will give rise to variances

> Variances due to the differences between planned and actual fixed costs associated with the manufacturing process

You can selectively choose the types of variances you want to track separately in your manufacturing process. All of the other variances are reported under a single intuitively obvious category of "remaining variances." Using different versions, you can calculate and compare variances based on preliminary cost estimates, current cost estimates, and alternative cost estimates. So let's talk about how to generate accounting entries using the settlement process.

Settlement process

If you recall, it's the settlement process that generates financial account postings. The process analyzes value flows generated in controlling since the previous settlement run, calculates the corresponding financial impact, and posts the appropriate entries in financial accounting. For example, an increase in costs on production orders that are still open gets posted as an increase in the WIP account, whereas completed production orders generate postings to inventory accounts and variance accounts. SAP provides you with not only the ability to control how these settlement costs are calculated but also where they can be settled. This is important because costs on production orders may be settled to inventory in make-to-stock environments but settled to sales orders in make-to-order environments.

One of the key concepts supporting this functionality is *settlement profiles* (see Figure 12.7), which control the definition of settlement rules that are used to settle costs collected on production orders. You can use these flexible settlement rules to settle costs to GL accounts, cost centers, WBS elements (recall project stock from Chapter 11), and sales orders, etc. As an example, a fairly simplistic rule may consist of 2 % and 7 % of costs collected on a production order settled to two cost centers and the remaining costs calculated as WIP. However, a settlement process may include different types of costs, although you lose that visibility by settling all costs as a single value.

Product costing provides you with the functionality of settlement structure, so that you can maintain separation of different types of costs (e.g., labor, materials, etc.) during a settlement process. These details can be important, for example, for product managers performing analysis and reporting.

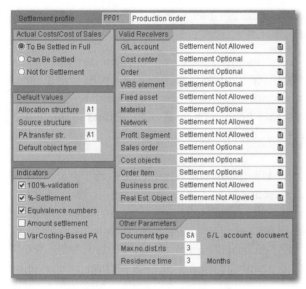

Figure 12.7 Settlement Profile

What we've discussed so far is applicable for relatively simple manufacturing processes and production orders. However, for especially complex manufacturing, you may also have to use *results analysis*.

Results Analysis

Results analysis provides you with the powerful functionality of carrying out the periodic valuation of costs and revenues on long-term projects (Chapter 11) and orders (Chapter 10). For the purpose of product costing, you can use this functionality to evaluate complex manufacturing orders typical in make-to-order and engineer-to-order manufacturing scenarios. Obviously, depending on the type of project or order being evaluated, the valuation of costs and revenues can be different. So, SAP provides you with completely customizable valuation parameters for the results analysis that control when the reserves are created or cancelled, how the profit on an order or a project is calculated, how the planned costs are evaluated to calculate the profit, how the financial postings are determined, and so on. One of the most important parameters is the results analysis method, which determines the formula used to calculate the results analysis data. The real strength of the results analysis functionality can be seen in the

Results analysis methods

number of different calculation methods it supports. The following are some examples:

> Using revenue-based methods, you can calculate interim profits based on the difference between revenues in a period and corresponding cost of sales. You can either report this difference as profit even though there may be further costs and revenues in the future, or you can report it as profit only if the profit has been realized on the market.

> Using quantity-based methods, you can calculate costs proportional to actual quantity produced and then capitalize the costs if actual costs are greater than the calculated costs, or create reserves for the costs if actual costs are less than the calculated costs. You can use a version of this method based on percentage of completion (POC) to also create corresponding postings or reserves based on revenue calculation.

> If you are using resource-related billing (discussed in Chapter 11), you can use corresponding results analysis methods to calculate cost of sales and inventory values based on the invoiced costs or the actual costs incurred. Note, however, that these methods don't calculate reserves.

Several other results analysis methods are available, and which method you actually use depends on your business requirements. Most businesses have different types of business transactions, so they end up using multiple analysis methods in parallel to evaluate their projects and orders.

In the beginning of this chapter, we discussed the functionality in product costing that helps you valuate inventory based on actual costs of the products. Now let's focus on that functionality in a bit more detail.

Actual Costing

Why actual costing?   So far, we've focused on product costing techniques that maintain inventory valuations in a single currency. However, in global companies with inventories in plants around the world, it's imperative that inventory valuations be available in different currencies, especially if inventory is carried at a plant in a country with a highly volatile currency. Valuating inventories based on standard costs, which are essentially planned costs, may not be sufficient, especially in rapidly changing market situations. At the same time, creating standard cost estimates each month after taking into account actual prices can be prohibitively time consuming, which is where material ledger helps you.

Material Ledger

The material ledger (see Figure 12.8) was introduced primarily to answer business requirements of valuating inventory in multiple currencies, tracking and analyzing price differences in inventory, and carrying out actual costing of inventories. If you activate the material ledger functionality, then valuation of all goods movements within a period is carried out using standard costs, and all price differences are recorded in material ledger. As part of period-end processing, you can valuate your inventory based on the actual price (called *periodic unit price*) calculated in the material ledger and, if appropriate, update the standard cost of materials with the periodic unit price so that goods movements in the next period are valuated using the new price.

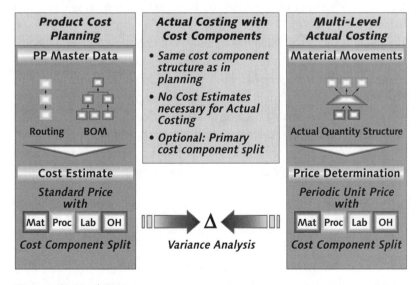

Figure 12.8 Actual Costing

Single-level and multilevel price determination

So how is price determined in the material ledger? In its simplest form, goods movements for a material are valuated at standard price, and the differences between standard price and actual price are updated in the material ledger. Using this calculation, you can take into account price differences due to a variety of reasons such as price differences in goods receipts or invoice receipts, settlement of production orders, exchange rate differences, and so on.

However, for finished and semi-finished goods or any materials that use other materials in its manufacturing process, such differences are a combination of price differences from external, direct procurement, and consumption of other materials. For such materials, you also have an option to use the material ledger to roll up differences from raw materials through semi-finished products to finished products. These approaches are called *single-level price determination* and *multilevel price determination*.

 Tip

The material ledger can also be used to valuate inventory in parallel using different accounting principles such as IAS andUS GAAP.

Of course, if neither of these approaches is relevant, then you can also calculate the moving average price (MAP) of a material as mentioned previously. Thus, you have full flexibility in choosing a price determination that is most appropriate for your business environment. The material ledger ensures that only price differences proportional to current inventory balance are reflected in the material price. Otherwise, if an invoice with a disproportionate price difference is received after all or part of the corresponding inventory has been consumed, it would distort the price. Data collected in the material ledger is processed using a costing run.

Costing Run

Typical steps in a costing run

You use a costing run at period end to calculate actual prices of the material stocks and consumption of the previous period, and to adjust balances in material stock accounts and the financial accounts. Using a sequential process, you first carry out material selection for a costing run, then let the system determine the costing sequence (e.g., costing for raw materials should be carried out before costing for semi-finished goods in which those raw materials are used), followed by single-level and multilevel price determination for materials, and finally processing of closing financial entries. Before you can proceed with material price determination and processing financial entries, you have to specifically allow or release a costing run for those processes. This helps you put in place measures of internal controls for calculating and processing costing results.

A typical costing run evaluates goods transactions in a period. But if your business requirements are to evaluate transactions over multiple periods or using different prices, you are also provided with the functionality to carry out alternative valuation runs. The advantage of an alternative valuation run versus an actual costing run is that you can create multiple alternative valuation runs that evaluate data using different aspects. This allows you to see the different valuations of your inventory balances. And, in the actual costing runs, the process differentiates among the various methods of material procurement such as subcontracting, and in-house production.

Valuation using different criteria

This helps you accurately divide material price differences to the appropriate procurement alternative. And, it's not just the procurement alternatives described earlier; the material medger is sophisticated enough to also differentiate valuation based on other criteria such as the purchasing organization (discussed in Chapter 3), supplying plant, production plant, and alternative BOM. Not only that, but if a manufacturing process produces multiple materials (e.g., joint production), the material ledger can also divide the costs accurately to individual products. At the end of the costing process, you can use the Actual Costing Information System to display your detailed costing results containing goods movements and relevant information.

The Information System contains several reports including the following:

> Material Price Analysis shows the valuated transactions and the results of material price determination with price and exchange-rate differences for a given material in a plant.

> Cost Components for Price lists the actual costs across multiple production levels so that you can analyze changes in stock, order settlements, price changes, closing accounting entries, and so on.

> Material Transaction History shows you the business transactions for a material over a period of time, so that you can review how different transactions impacted the price of a material.

For your audit trail, you have access to individual material ledger documents and price change documents so that you can verify price calculations. Additionally, standard SAP provides a large number of reports for evaluating and analyzing costing results.

Product Costing Reports

Different areas of product costing give you an extensive range of reports you can use to evaluate cost planning and cost controlling information. One particularly interesting report summarizes the analysis of costing runs because it helps you analyze the results of costing runs, compare results of one or more costing runs, or compare results of a costing run with prices in the material master. So, you can analyze variances between costing runs and the material price to evaluate the effect of updating materials with new standard prices.

 Tip

For critical materials, you can define exceptions so that materials are highlighted, if the calculated variance exceeds predefined threshold values. This helps you keep a check on inadvertently updating materials with a standard price that is abnormally different from its current price.

A cost estimate program also provides you with a comprehensive view of a material and the individual items contributing to its costs. This can be analyzed from different points of view. Figure 12.9 shows such a cost estimate for a material that shows the cost estimate of a material with individual cost items contributing to its cost of goods sold calculation. You can easily switch between different views for individual BOM components, different cost analyses, or different lot sizes. This interactive tool provides you with tremendous power for analyzing the cost of a single material. And if there is more than one procurement alternative for a material, you can display the cost estimate for each procurement alternative separately.

Costing Structure
☑ Casing
▦ Slug for spiral
▦ Flat gasket
▦ Hexagon head

Material	100-100		Casing
Plant	3000		

| Costing Data | Dates | Qty Struct. | Valuation | History | Costs |

| Costs Based On | Costing Lot Size | ☑ 10 | PC |

Cost Component View	Total Costs	Fixed Costs	Variable	Currency
Cost of goods manufactured	3,091.55	881.96	2,209.59	USD
Cost of goods sold	3,091.55	881.96	2,209.59	USD
Sales and administration cos	0.00	0.00	0.00	USD

| Cost of goods sold | ☑ ☑ ▦ ⛁ ⛁ Partner |

Itemization for material 100-100 in plant 3000

ItmNo	I	Resource			Total Value	Fixed Value	Curm	Quantity	Un
1	E	4230	1310	1422	95.48	70.37	USD	0.500	H
2	E	4230	1310	1420	0.00	0.00	USD	0	H
3	E	4230	1310	1421	0.00	0.00	USD	0	H
4	M	3000 100-110			33.00	0.00	USD	10	PC
5	M	3000 100-120			55.00	0.00	USD	10	PC

Figure 12.9 Material Cost Estimate

Additional reports provide you with the ability to analyze calculations of product costing by period, by order, and by sales order, which are the three alternatives discussed in this chapter. You can analyze actual costs, estimated costs, target costs, WIP values, and variances based on any or all criteria associated with product costing. These reports provide you with accurate, detailed, and timely information for making appropriate decisions pertaining to different aspects of your company such as procurement, manufacturing, labor management, and overhead.

An extremely useful SAP component for reporting and analysis is profitability analysis as discussed in Chapter 13. SAP product costing is fully integrated with profitability analysis and provides you with the ability to transfer costing results, production settlement results, and different variances to profitability analysis for further evaluation. The powerful analysis and reporting features of profitability analysis provide you with the additional ability to analyze results of product costing and to make more meaningful and relevant decisions.

Case Study

This automotive parts manufacturer based out of the southern United States provides different categories of electronics parts, components, and systems to automakers. The company's product offerings include climate control products, safety and security products, entertainment products, and communication products. This $3.7-billion company has more than 110,000 full-time and part-time workers at its 3 plants in the United States and its offices around the world.

Business Challenges

With the increasing challenges in the local automotive market, cost control and containment was one of the top priorities for auto manufacturers. This in turn also required their suppliers, including parts suppliers, to be increasingly efficient and effective in managing their product costs. Even though this case study focuses on challenges and benefits in terms of product costing, the decision to use SAP was made to meet overall strategic goals and enterprise-wide improvement in operational control and efficiency.

The system used to track goods consumptions and other manufacturing activities was different from the system used for inventory and stock management. The preparation of product cost estimates at the beginning of the year was done in a third system, and finance department used yet another system. Integration and data synchronization between these systems were in complete shambles. All of the information required to prepare detailed and reasonably accurate cost estimates was difficult to obtain, which translated into huge variances and unrealistic projections for revenue and cost planning. Considering the effort that went into preparing standard cost estimates even once in a year, incorporating any changes in market conditions or product specifications into standard costs was not even attempted.

Month-end product costing processes were considerably manual and required three employees more than four days to analyze material consumptions, prepare accounting entries, and carry out product cost calculations. Any trend or variance analysis of product costing data to obtain meaningful and actionable information was a time-consuming process.

Solution Deployment

The implementation of the enterprise wide rollout was awarded to a big consulting firm who used a combination of onsite and offsite large teams of subject matter experts (SME) and technical experts. Keeping in mind the prevailing sentiment at the client, the implementation partner decided not to outsource any work to its offshore centers, even though it may have helped reduce the cost of the project. Only one SME and four technical experts, assisted by a shared development team, were assigned to work on the product costing component. However, they worked closely with business users and other team members, especially in the areas of production, MRP, procurement, inventory management, and financial accounting.

The two most time-consuming and difficult areas of the project proved to be data conversion and user training. The legendary integration of SAP components made it difficult for the implementation team to prepare data from multiple, considerably nonintegrated systems. Also, even though the project team had decided to use a "train-the-trainer" approach (i.e., train key business users so that they can train other users), it did not work as well as expected. After the system rollout was technically complete, the implementation team had to carry out numerous, town hall style training sessions at several locations to increase the confidence and comfort level of business users.

However, after business users started working with the new SAP system, they were soon able to notice and appreciate—if not acknowledge—the benefits.

Value Achieved

By using SAP in all major business areas across the enterprise, several direct and indirect initiatives helped improve cost control and cost management processes. For example, by using centralized purchasing, the company was able to obtain its parts closer to its pre-negotiated prices, thereby reducing price variances. Similarly, improved production planning helped in managing temporary labor costs. The improved operational efficiencies in procurement and manufacturing translated into reduced variances. By ensuring that consistent business processes were followed at all plants, the variance analysis and other product costing activities at month end showed significant improvements.

Because procurement, production, inventory management, and financial accounting all used the same system, the process of preparing a standard cost estimate was considerably improved and streamlined. Obviously, the business processes supporting the preparation of standard cost estimates will continue to undergo improvements. However, the management had already instituted policies so that any major and relatively permanent changes to product specifications or market environment will be communicated back to cost accounting group. There, they can analyze whether the change was significant enough to be included in the standard cost of corresponding products.

The month-end product costing activities now required only two employees, and by using mostly automatic processes, they were able to finish most of the tasks in less than two days. The third employee was reassigned to enhance her capabilities. Because preparing analytical reports was almost done in real time after month-end activities were completed, managers were able to focus on analytically determining potential savings opportunities.

Looking Ahead

The company is evaluating whether its business processes and SAP rollout are ready to handle actual costing. The intent is to let the current SAP rollout stabilize, particularly in procurement and production areas, before activating actual costing in SAP.

Summary

It's impractical, if not impossible, to provide details of all of the features of SAP product costing in one chapter. However, this chapter should have given you a good overview of the robust functionality that product costing in SAP provides to meet your business requirements, regardless of your manufacturing environment.

The key things to remember about product costing include the following:

> The product costing component provides comprehensive support for multiple manufacturing environments such as make-to-stock, make-to-order, and repetitive manufacturing, etc.

> Using product cost planning, you can plan costs for materials and products to analyze their cost structure, including production costs, overhead costs, material costs, and activity costs.

> The material ledger helps you carry out actual costing to valuate inventory by taking into account inevitable price differences and also provides you with the ability to carry inventory in multiple currencies or valuations.

> You can quickly calculate planned costs using easy cost planning, and based on costing results, you can automatically trigger purchase requisitions, purchase orders, goods issues, and other relevant transactions.

> You have access to a large number of meticulously detailed reports that are part of various information systems for product costing, material ledger, mixed costing, and so on.

In this chapter, we also alluded to some functionality of the SAP ERP Financial profitability analysis component, so let's move on to the next chapter, to look at it in more detail.

Profitability Analysis

As the geographic and economic barriers come down around the world, businesses today have unprecedented access to an enormous market. This access doesn't come without challenges though. There is now intense world–wide competition, varying customer preferences, and an increasing number of factors that directly or indirectly influence your profit margins. To stay ahead of the competition and to make informed decisions, you need to see how your products and services are performing in the different market segments. And, you need up-to-date sales information by customer and product, to give your sales force much needed visibility so they can leverage all available opportunities and focus their efforts toward achieving business goals. All of this requires a system that can provide a flexible and customizable framework that gives you timely and accurate insight into the profitability of your business.

Overview

The SAP ERP Financials Profitability Analysis gives you all of the functionality required to design a customizable reporting framework that accurately meets your requirements. It gives you an integrated framework to carry out planning by various market segments, along with the functionality to capture and distribute business transaction data from other SAP components. And it provides a comprehensive reporting solution to give you advanced analytical capabilities.

There are obviously a number of factors that all companies want to use in their profitability analysis, including customers, products, customer categories, product groups, etc. However, businesses also have their own preferred, if not unique, market segments views from which they want to analyze profitability. So Profitability Analysis comes with a customizable framework you can use to define your own criteria for Profitability Analysis. And, unlike other software, SAP ERP Financials doesn't limit you into measuring profitability only based on the details available in your GL accounts. Instead, you can select from a wide variety of information from other SAP components or create custom values for your profitability analysis.

Integration with other components

This strong integration of profitability analysis with other SAP components helps ensure a smooth, real-time flow of information for reporting purposes. Sales orders and customer invoices are obviously primary sources of profitability information, but the software also enables you to gather data from parallel, supporting, and subsequent business activities such as postings in financial accounting, inventory management, overhead costing, product costing, project system, and so on. To obtain consistently structured and comparable reports, you can also distribute data from one or more profitability criteria to other undetermined profitability criteria.

Additionally, profitability analysis gives you a powerful framework for carrying out selective, multilevel, top-down or bottom-up planning by market segments. The planning aids available in the system let you easily enter, manage, forecast, and valuate planning data over a desired time frame, customer, product, or any other criteria. Not only that, the planning framework also supports sending your planning data out or receiving the planning data in from other applications.

So by using the information system, you can analyze data collected from business transactions with the planned values to carry out detailed comparisons between profitability criteria that are important to your business.

 Note

Because considering the integrated nature of profitability analysis (an appropriate reflection of activities in different areas of a company that influence or impact its profitability), we'll be referring to concepts discussed in earlier chapters, so if you need to, you can refer back to the appropriate chapters.

When considering SAP ERP Financials, one of the aspects you may want to evaluate is using Profitability Analysis with or without using Profit Center Accounting (PCA). PCA provides you with limited functionality to analyze your profitability, but it's relatively simple to implement. Also, Profitability Analysis relies considerably on other SAP components, especially the Sales and Distribution (SD) component, to provide accurate data. So you may not be able to harvest the real potential of profitability analysis, if other SAP components in your company have not yet been stabilized. With that said, let's talk about these functions in detail.

An important decision

Functions in Detail

We'll start this section by discussing profit center functionality, because it may be a stepping stone for many companies before they decide to use Profitability Analysis. Then we'll discuss building a profitability model to reflect your business requirements, followed by how information from different SAP components flows into profitability reports. This will be followed by a relatively brief section on planning, before ending the chapter with a review of the available reporting functionality.

Profit Center Accounting (PCA)

We've mentioned profit centers in passing in several chapters so far, but we haven't really talked about them in detail. So this is an appropriate chapter for that discussion because profit centers are primarily used to help you calculate the profitability of different areas within your company.

Profit center groups

With SAP ERP Financials, you can analyze costs and revenues by profit centers and assign your current assets and current liabilities to profit centers, thereby treating them as "companies within companies." Typically, profit centers in a company represent functional areas (sales, production), products (product lines, product divisions), revenue channels (retail, wholesale), or geographical areas (regions, offices). However, because only you can determine the most suitable criteria to analyze profitability of areas within your company, you have the ability to freely define profit centers as required and then group them into profit center groups for analysis, allocation, and reporting. Profit centers also support statistical key figures (as we discussed in Chapter 10), so that you can easily calculate and report commonly used analysis figures (e.g., sales per employee).

As you can see in Figure 13.1, profit centers can be assigned to most other items that carry costs or revenues, thereby eliminating the need for you to explicitly post data to profit centers. Instead, when any cost and revenue postings are made in relevant SAP components, those postings automatically flow into profit centers. If your objective is to use profit centers simply to analyze profitability, there isn't much additional work involved because you can make changes directly in the profit centers to correct or adjust your final reports. However, if you want to prepare balance sheets for profit centers, you need to consider a few additional aspects. For example, you have to decide whether to transfer balance sheet items in real time or as part of the month-end process after inventory, payable accounts, and receivable accounts are analyzed, adjusted and reconciled. If you decide to use document splitting and the zero-balancing functionality of the new GL (discussed in Chapter 2), then real-time postings and preparation of balance sheets by profit centers is far more seamless. Not only that, but because allocation processes (discussed in Chapter 10) for profit centers are supported, you can easily distribute costs, revenues, or other balance sheet items among profit centers.

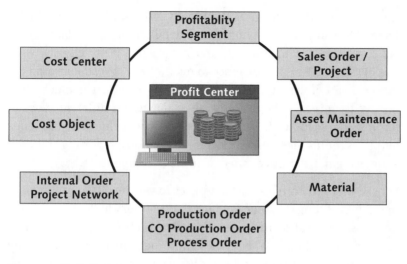

Figure 13.1 Profit Centers

 Tip

Profit centers are typically used to prepare reports based on period accounting. For the cost-of-sales approach, you have to use functional areas to classify and report business transactions.

Profit centers also support all the planning functionality and planning techniques available across different components:

> You can choose to transfer plan data online or transfer the plan information.

> You can choose to plan profit centers directly or transfer relevant planning data from cost centers, internal orders, projects, and other items.

> You can even carry out comprehensive, integrated planning in Profitability Analysis (discussed later in the chapter) and transfer those plan values back to profit centers.

> All of the allocation processes such as distribution, assessment, and overhead calculation that are supported for actual data, are also supported for processing planning data in profit centers.

Profit center

Balance sheet

Transfer pricing

Chapter 14 explores planning techniques and features available in different SAP components in much more detail, so for now let's consider another important functionality: transfer pricing. We briefly discussed this in Chapter 11 with reference to overhead or investment projects; however, profit center valuation using transfer prices is much more involved and pervasive in terms of its impact on different types of business transactions. Regardless of whether you choose to use transfer prices for managerial, statutory, or tax reasons, reporting and valuation using transfer prices affect many SAP components.

For example, you can use transfer prices to valuate different functions in product costing (Chapter 12) such as WIP (Work in Process) calculation, costing of sales orders, results analysis process, settlement process, and so on. Similarly, any sales and procurement between group companies, and inventory transfers between profit centers can also be valuated using transfer prices. Most of the allocation processes, such as distribution, assessments, accrual, overheads, settlement, and so on, also support multiple valuations; and so do the Material Ledger and the New GL. In short, you have sufficient functionality in all the components including PCA, to analyze your operational results from different points of view and in different currencies. Now that we have an overview of functionalities available PCA, let's focus our attention on Profitability Analysis.

Overview of Profitability Analysis

Even though profit centers provide you with the ability to analyze profits for areas within your company, it's not practical to create profit centers corresponding to each of your customers and products. As we shall see, Profitability Analysis provides you with the ability of calculating profitability by any criteria of your choice.

Among the first decisions you'll need to make when deciding whether to use Profitability Analysis is the consolidated level(s) at which you want to report and analyze profitability of your company, and thus create the corresponding operating concern (see Figure 13.2). The answer will be fairly simple for small- and medium-sized companies, and possibly even for many large companies. However, the answer may be different for very large, global companies and conglomerates spanning businesses in a number of countries and/ or industries. This is because the highest level for profitability analysis is an organizational unit called operating concern. Let's put this concept of operating concern in perspective. We discussed in Chapter 10 how a controlling area could encompass multiple company codes. Similarly an operating concern can encompass multiple controlling AREAS in your SAP implementation.

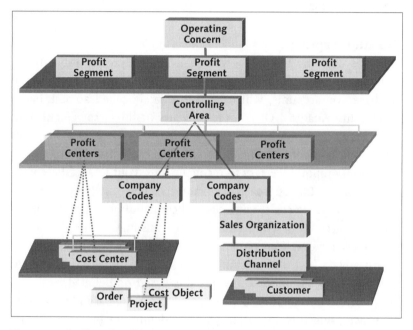

Figure 13.2 An Operating Concern

Thus an appropriately configured operating concern is capable of providing you with decidedly more global analysis across multiple divisions, geographical regions, and legal entities. This obviously brings up the question of how you manage different currencies in Profitability Analysis. The currency associated with an operating concern, which typically corresponds to the functional currency of your global headquarters, determines the primary currency for Profitability Analysis. Additionally, you also have an option to update data in the company currency, although you may want to make this decision only af-

Multiple currencies in Profitability Analysis

ter due consideration. For example, it may be useful if you choose to update the data in company currency so that you can easily reconcile Profitability Analysis reports with your financial reports. However, just like with any other application that analyzes a large volume of data, you should assess whether the corresponding increase in data volume is justified by the benefits you'll receive. After these major decisions have been made, the next decision you have to make is the approach you want to use in calculating and valuating the profitability of your business.

Valuation Approach

Account-based Profitability Analysis

As far as deciding the values you want to analyze for profitability, there are two possible approaches. One approach is to report the values based on accounts, which is appropriately called account-based Profitability Analysis. Of course, accounts in this case refer to cost elements and revenue elements as defined in the SAP ERP Financials controlling component. This approach has the advantage that your profitability reports are easy to reconcile with your financial accounting. However, this approach may not give you sufficient details in terms of analyzing costs, revenues and contribution margins. For example, an account-based Profitability Analysis may not be able to tell you that labor overhead on custom-orders built for one customer is almost always higher than similar overhead for other customers. To

Costing-based Profitability Analysis

help you carry out profitability analysis based on detailed costs and revenues, there is another approach called costing-based Profitability Analysis. Using this approach, you can define not only the criteria for which you want to analyze profitability but also the values that you want to analyze. This approach gives you a highly customizable framework for Profitability Analysis. Figure 13.3 shows a comparison between these two approaches.

 Tip

Even though individual requirements may suggest selecting one approach over another, it's also possible to use both account-based and costing-based Profitability Analysis simultaneously.

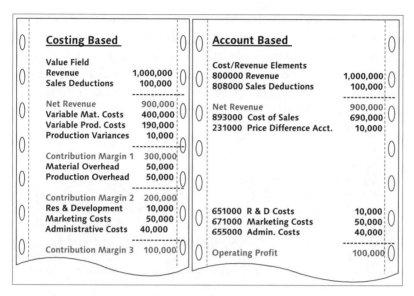

Figure 13.3 Approaches in Profitability Analysis

After you have decided on the approach or approaches you want to use, the next important decision concerns the criteria and the values that you want to analyze.

Characteristics and Value Fields

In Profitability Analysis, the criteria you want to analyze are called characteristics, and the values you want to analyze are called value fields. As we discussed before, value fields are relevant only if you plan to use costing-based Profitability Analysis because in account-based Profitability Analysis, the analysis is performed on GL accounts. So sales region, product group, plant, and customer, are examples of characteristics, whereas revenues, discounts, and cost of sales, are examples of value fields. The standard SAP ERP Financials provides many commonly used characteristics such as controlling area, company code, customer, customer group, country, and so on. You can also create as many additional characteristics as required based on values from other SAP components.

Considering the vast volume of information maintained, you can create additional characteristics, for example, that are based on the

Characteristics and value fields

customer master or the material master. If none of the existing information meets your requirements, you can even create your own characteristic definitions. Later in the chapter, you'll see how you can populate these characteristics with data values so that they can be used in analyzing profitability. Business transactions in different SAP components update the relevant characteristic values into the Profitability Analysis component.

 Warning

> You may want to carefully consider the impact on data volume and system performance while selecting characteristics to be included in profitability segments. For example, in repetitive manufacturing, customer sales order may not be an appropriate characteristic to include in profitability segments.

Similarly, if you intend to use costing-based Profitability Analysis, then you also need to specify individual value fields that are part of your profitability reports. You can select from many commonly used value fields provided or create additional value fields to analyze quantities or amounts as necessary. So, an automotive manufacturing company may analyze labor costs, healthcare costs, different types of production and procurement variances, and so on, while a rental car company may analyze number of miles driven, fuel consumption rate, fuel costs, maintenance costs, different types of insurance, etc. One of the important criteria to consider here is how the values should be aggregated over multiple periods for planning and reporting purposes. For example, to report revenue per employee in a quarterly report, monthly revenues should be added, but employee headcount should only reflect the number from last month in the quarter. We will discuss later in this chapter different strategies available for calculating and valuating these results. Business transactions in different SAP components update relevant analysis values into the Profitability Analysis component.

Profitability segments

So if business transactions from different SAP components only update relevant characteristics and values, how do you obtain consistent profitability results? You obtain your results by using profitability segments, which represent a combination of characteristic values. These segments typically correspond to market segments that are used for profitability analysis. Because components of Profitability Analysis vary by industry, by company, and possibly even within a company by divisions, you get the flexibility you need to control which characteristics are part of the profitability segment. Figure 13.4 shows you how characteristics, value fields, and profitability segments are interconnected.

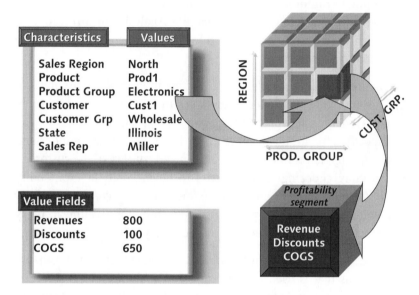

Figure 13.4 Profitability Segments

So let's discuss these two important data concepts—characteristics and value fields.

Populating and Calculating Master Data

We've already discussed how you can create your own characteristics and value fields in Profitability Analysis. So let's see how you can populate, calculate, and valuate these characteristics and value fields. For determining values for different characteristics, you can use the highly effective method of characteristics derivation.

Characteristics Derivation

Consider for example, that your profitability reports include customer number, sales region, and customer country. When an accounting entry is made to a customer, it should get updated with all three characteristic values so that you can run profitability reports at any of these three levels. However, it's highly inefficient and impractical to expect those making accounting entries to enter not only the customer number but the sales region and country of the customer as well. And, this problem can quickly reach a significant proportion based on the number of characteristics in Profitability Analysis. So SAP provides you with functionality to define rules that can automatically derive values for characteristics.

Deriving the characteristics

The concept is fairly simple. While setting up Profitability Analysis in the system, you specify derivation rules that can check one or more values to determine the resulting value for a characteristic. So you can specify derivation rules that check for the customer number and automatically determine the sales region and country of the customer. By carefully choosing characteristics to be included in Profitability Analysis, which in turn provides the foundation for creating carefully designed derivation rules, you can significantly improve the accuracy and efficiency of data collection for your analysis.

This is especially important for an SAP component such as Profitability Analysis that is used for reporting and analytics. For example, if you depend on people manually entering the sales region and country of a customer, you run the risk of not all profitability data containing the required information. In addition to these if–then type of derivation rules, you get some relatively simple rules in which all or part of one field is moved to another one (e.g., extracting the first three characters of the GL account number for structured reporting), or you can use custom development for determining values.

Characteristic hierarchies

Another useful feature of characteristics in Profitability Analysis is that you can create characteristic hierarchies for the purpose of analysis and reporting. For example, it's useful to analyze the profitability of individual customers and products; but it can provide a completely different perspective if you can also analyze the profitability of customer groups and product groups. For this reason, you can create hierarchies based on any characteristic. So, you can create customer hierarchies, product hierarchies, country hierarchies, and so on that best suit your business requirements. (We'll revisit this concept of characteristic hierarchies several times in this chapter while discussing different functionalities.)

 Tip

Using the Realignment functionality in Profitability Analysis, you can accurately reflect and incorporate changes in organizational structures to the profitability analysis data that has already been posted. This can be invaluable to handle situations such as corporate reorganization, redistribution of customers among sales areas, reassignment of sales reps, and so on.

Equally important as the derivation process for characteristics is the calculation and valuation process for value fields in Profitability Analysis.

The Valuation Process
Clearly, the valuation process is relevant only if you intend to use costing-based Profitability Analysis because in account-based Profitability Analysis, the only values posted are the ones that match with the accounts in Financial Accounting. As discussed before, you can create your own value fields in Profitability Analysis, and even if you use standard, SAP-delivered value fields, different business transactions only update selected value fields. You use the valuation process to calculate and evaluate additional information in Profitability Analysis. If you've read Chapter 12 "Product Costing," then you're already familiar with at least one of the valuation techniques in Profitability Analysis: material cost estimates.

We've already discussed product costing's strong integration with other SAP components, including Profitability Analysis. That integration especially comes into play when evaluating sales figures with material cost estimates. For example, material cost estimate in a manufacturing company may involve complex calculations that determines material costs, labor costs, and overhead costs for a finished product;

Using material cost estimates

or, in a make-to-order manufacturing environment, you may want to use costing results in Profitability Analysis after the costing run for sales orders was carried out.

If you have activated this valuation, then you can determine which cost estimates are used to valuate the cost of sales in Profitability Analysis. This can be extremely useful because you have an option to use the relevant cost estimate in your reporting, including the cost estimate based on values calculated in the material ledger. You can copy the actual cost estimate as a single value or with a detailed cost component split. You can also compare the actual cost estimate with the standard cost estimate in Profitability Analysis and analyze the variances to take the necessary action. And, you have an option to assign value fields to individual items of a cost component such as raw materials, purchased parts, production labor, production setup, and so on. The only limits to this analysis are the details available in cost components in product costing and the number of value fields you are willing to manage and analyze in Profitability Analysis.

Using costing sheets

However, what if you aren't a manufacturing company or don't really have any detailed cost estimates and variances to analyze? For this reason, SAP provides another valuation method based on costing sheets and condition techniques (see Figure 13.5). As you may remember from our discussion in Chapter 12, a costing sheet allows you to define a set of rules and conditions to calculate anticipated values. Using costing sheets, you can calculate value fields that fit the concept of using rules and conditions to determine the resulting value. So, you can use it to supplement data processed in the Sales and Distribution (SD) component of SAP, determine additional values such as sales commissions or sales rebates based on sales revenue, calculate anticipated freight charges, and so on. We won't get into the technical details of its definition, but behind each item in the third column is either a reference that can be mapped to a value calculated in sales (e.g., REVN, DISC, DISP, or COGS) or calculations that determine a value based on a percentage or some other type of calculation (e.g., PROV, OUPA, or OUTF).

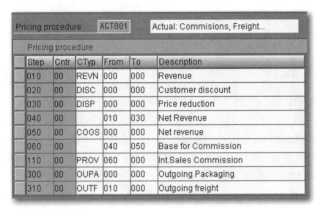

Figure 13.5 A Sample Costing Sheet

Using a valuation strategy, you determine the sequence, if and when to use a cost estimate or costing sheet, and the value field to which its results are assigned. Finally, you can choose which valuation strategy to use for the following:

> Valuation of actual data when it's posted

> Valuation of actual data during subsequent periodic processing

> Valuation of data from different sources such as financial entries, sales orders, customer billing documents, internal orders or projects, and so on

> Valuation of plan data whether it's planned manually or automatically (we'll discuss this later in the chapter)

> Planning version

So, you have access to an extremely powerful framework of valuating and calculating value fields, if you choose to use costing-based Profitability Analysis. If you use account-based Profitability Analysis, then postings are made to Financial Accounting and Profitability Analysis simultaneously, and no additional value determination needs to be carried out.

Now that we've looked at the basic concepts and master data, let's shift our focus to understanding how the actual data from business transactions posted in different SAP components flow into Profitability Analysis.

Gathering Actual Data

Profitability Analysis receives its data from other SAP components and the understanding of this data integration will not only make you an informed participant in implementing your solution but also make you appreciate the type of complex profitability analysis and reporting that you can carry out.

Flows of Actual Values

Update from billing documents

Figure 13.6 shows different actual values (planned values are discussed later) that flow into Profitability Analysis for your reports and other calculations. Let's start this discussion with the value flows from the Sales and Distribution component, in particular from customer billing documents. The update from billing documents to Profitability Analysis occurs at the same time when those values are updated to Financial Accounting (this process was discussed in Chapter 3). From billing documents, Profitability Analysis receives the revenues, sales deductions, and cost of goods sold/manufactured with or without using material cost estimates. The level of detail that you can transfer and thus evaluate in Profitability Analysis depends on the level of detail available in the billing process, although you can selectively choose not to include certain values. For example, when customers return merchandise to an online retailer, the freight costs are already incurred, so the company may choose to suppress those costs from getting transferred to Profitability Analysis.

 Tip

You may want to keep in mind that for all of the value flows discussed in this section, account-based Profitability Analysis can only receive those postings that are made to GL accounts in Financial Accounting. Any additional value flows are relevant for costing-based Profitability Analysis only.

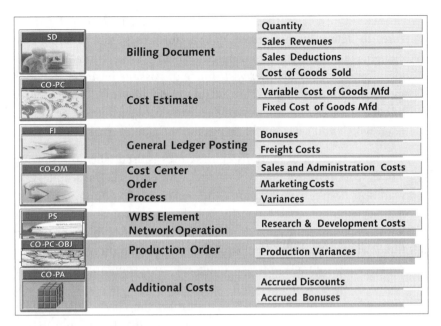

		Quantity
SD	Billing Document	Sales Revenues
		Sales Deductions
		Cost of Goods Sold
CO-PC	Cost Estimate	Variable Cost of Goods Mfd
		Fixed Cost of Goods Mfd
FI	General Ledger Posting	Bonuses
		Freight Costs
CO-OM	Cost Center / Order / Process	Sales and Administration Costs
		Marketing Costs
		Variances
PS	WBS Element / Network Operation	Research & Development Costs
CO-PC-OBJ	Production Order	Production Variances
CO-PA	Additional Costs	Accrued Discounts
		Accrued Bonuses

Figure 13.6 Actual Value Flows

However, for the market segments for which your typical sales cycles are (very) long, you may want to obtain early analysis of anticipated profitability on those deals. For such business requirements, SAP also supports statistically transferring values to Profitability Analysis from sales orders. Of course, this is only possible for costing-based Profitability Analysis, because sales orders don't create any financial postings. Though, the clever system design enables you to choose whether to transfer, and thus report, these values in the period when sales orders were created, when deliveries are planned, or when the billing is scheduled to occur. This provides you with considerable flexibility in terms of reporting your anticipated revenues. Though to ensure consistency in reporting, you should make sure that the level of information transferred from sales orders matches with the information transferred at the time of billing.

Update from sales orders

In Chapters 10 to 12, we discussed internal orders, projects and sales orders from the cost collection and cost settlement viewpoint; and how you can use them to collect costs and then settle those costs to appropriate cost receivers by using settlement profiles. As it relates to

Update from cost settlement

Profitability Analysis, these profiles in turn refer to PA transfer structures to determine how fixed and variable costs from different cost elements are transferred to different value fields in Profitability Analysis. This opens up another vast source of possible business scenarios ranging from trade shows, advertising campaigns and R&D expenses to complex make-to-order or engineer-to-order production processes, from which you can transfer values to Profitability Analysis.

Update from Financial Accounting

The same concept of PA transfer structures is used when transferring values from postings made in Financial Accounting. The seamless integration between SAP components Financial Accounting and Profitability Analysis enable you to directly enter profitability segments while making financial postings. For example, if invoices posted in financial accounting can be attributed to specific products (e.g., for expedited shipping), you can enter the corresponding profitability segment while making the financial postings. The documents are updated to Profitability Analysis based on the characteristic values found in the corresponding financial documents. If the information in original documents isn't very detailed, then values are transferred to Profitability Analysis only at an aggregated level. As you'll see later, you can subsequently distribute these values to other characteristics in Profitability Analysis. You can also post to profitability segments and cost centers (or internal orders) in parallel.

 Tip

> If you make a warehouse modification to accommodate new products, not only can you post those expenses to a (e.g., facilities) cost center but also to the corresponding product line profitability segment. The true costs are stored in a profitability segment, whereas cost center postings are for statistical purposes only.

Update from Procurement and Production

Let's continue this discussion with the procurement, production, and inventory management areas, and how you can get information from relevant transactions from each business area. For example, you can transfer values from the results of inventory revaluation to Profitability Analysis, price differences from procurement, and so on. Detailed business processes need to be taken into account when you consider integrating Profitability Analysis with your manufacturing environment. We discussed in Chapter 12 how you can use product costing to calculate and track different types of production variances, which can be used in conjunction with the PA transfer structures discussed previously. During the process of variance calculation, these production variances are determined and stored in the system. Subsequently, when production order settlement is carried out, these variances are transferred to value fields in Profitability Analysis.

Because PA transfer structures let you calculate and report details by cost elements, by combining it with different types of variances, you can carry out intricate analysis of manufacturing variances Profitability Analysis. On the other hand, calculating and transferring overhead costs to Profitability Analysis is somewhat different.

Overheads in Profitability Analysis

Unlike many other value flows discussed so far, overhead costs are typically calculated at month end as part of periodic processing, and are usually attributable and assigned to only one of the elements, such as cost centers, business processes, orders, projects, and so on, that best reflects the cause of the overhead. In Chapter 10, we discussed different methods and elements to capture, track, and calculate overhead costs. Most of those cost allocation processes are available to you in Profitability Analysis as well (see Figure 13.7).

The assessment process can be used to transfer costs to Profitability Analysis based on cost elements. If you can or must carry out cost allocation based on business processes and cost center activities, you can also use the direct or indirect activity allocation process to allocate costs to profitability segments at a more detailed level.

Allocation processes

 Example

> Costs for desktop maintenance services can be calculated and allocated based on the number of desktops repaired and serviced.

For even more detailed cost allocations, you can use a template allocation process, by creating a template to allocate IT application services costs to other functional areas, etc. Subsequently, when the costs are allocated to profitability segments, you can add further criteria such as internal orders corresponding to IT project initiatives requested by that functional area.

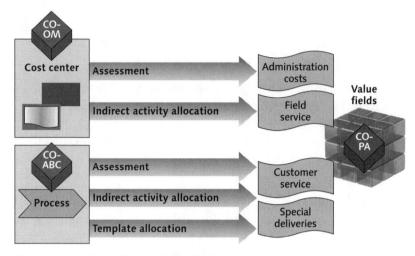

Figure 13.7 Overhead Costs in Profitability Analysis

Cross-company cost allocations

The concept of allocation cycles and a cycle consisting of multiple segments also remains the same as discussed in Chapter 10. So while allocating costs to profitability segments, you can specify senders, receivers, sending and receiving rules, and the allocation factors that best reflect the origin and cause of the overhead costs.

Considering that profitability analysis typically encompasses several companies and profit centers; an interesting constellation comes into play while carrying out cost allocations: whether to accumulate costs across companies (and profit centers) before allocating them or whether the cost allocation rules are applied separately within each company (or profit center). The right answer depends not only on the organizational structure but also on the type of costs under consideration. Luckily, both options are supported, so you can choose an option that is most appropriate.

And, of course, you have an option to manually enter or adjust postings received from other application components in to Profitability Analysis. This provides you with a mechanism to resolve incorrect allocations or classifications in Profitability Analysis without impacting the original postings. Also, as part of periodic processing, you have access to allocations and value distributions within Profitability Analysis.

Periodic Processing

You need to carry out value distribution within Profitability Analysis because not all costs and revenues can be assigned to detailed characteristics. For example, sales revenues can be assigned to individually identifiable customers and products; but it's difficult to carry out a similar assignment for common costs such as shipping and handling charges, insurance, or customs duty. The top-down distribution functionality is provided to remedy this difficulty; by using this function, you can distribute summarized values collected at one level to lower levels based on a reference you specify. Some examples of where you can use such a distribution are listed here:

Top-down distribution of costs

> Distribute values collected in a product group to individual products.

> Distribute values collected for all products in a product group to customers.

> Distribute values collected in a product group to products and customers.

> Distribute values proportional to a value field (e.g., distribution of travel expenses proportional to the number of hours billed).

> Distribute values proportional to a calculated formula based on value fields (e.g., distribution of shipping insurance costs in proportion to revenue, calculated as the difference between revenues and discounts).

> Distribute values in proportion to reference planned data (planning in Profitability Analysis is discussed later in this chapter).

> Distribute values in proportion to reference actual data (e.g., distribute freight in proportion to actual freight costs from the previous year).

You can also distribute collected values proportional to the values accumulated across multiple months (e.g., quarterly revenue) and multiple sources (e.g., accumulated freight costs posted from billing documents and financial documents). This provides you with a unique collection of techniques that can be used to distribute summarized values and prepare profitability reports that are as accurate as possible.

Periodic /multiple valuations

Another potentially significant process in Profitability Analysis helps you carry out periodic/multiple valuations. All of the data collection, distribution, and reporting discussed so far refers to sales from the point of view of a company, that is, legal valuation. However, if you use profit centers and internal prices, then managers responsible for individual profit centers will require analysis and reporting of the same data based on internal valuations, that is, transfer prices.

Fortunately, there is full functionality for carrying out parallel valuations in Profitability Analysis: processing actual data, maintaining plan data, and performing reporting and analysis. For the profit center valuation, transactions such as stock transfers between profit centers, which are typically not valuated in legal valuation, are updated and valuated using transfer prices.

 Warning

The functionality for profit center valuation is available only if you use costing-based Profitability Analysis. And, this activation almost doubles the data volume in Profitability Analysis because the system creates separate entries for legal valuation and for profit center valuation.

Data summarization

Of course, regardless of whether or not you use multiple valuations, you can reduce data volume in Profitability Analysis by summarizing the data from billing documents, financial documents, and Procurement and Inventory Management documents. Now that we've discussed the different functionality for processing actual data in Profitability Analysis, we're ready to look at the planning framework for analyzing profitability.

Planning

Even though actual business data collected in Profitability Analysis lets you analyze profitability by customers, products, market segments, and other criteria, you can really take advantage of this component by using it for the purpose of sales and profit planning. Planning in Profitability Analysis plays an important role in the integrated planning process, which is discussed at great length in Chapter 14. For now, though, our primary focus will be on aspects that are unique and specific to the Profitability Analysis component. At the core of this functionality is an environment called the planning framework.

Planning Framework

As the collage of screenshots in Figure 13.8 indicates, the planning framework provides you with a single and unified working environment from which you can model, design, execute, monitor, and carry out almost all planning functions in Profitability Analysis. It provides you with a structured outline to break down your planning process into smaller, more manageable tasks and activities. Because the planning process can vary widely between different companies, the planning framework provides you with planning levels that determine high-level planning criteria. So, planning levels in a manufacturing company may consist of product divisions, product lines, distribution channels, and so on; whereas planning levels in a professional services company may consist of practice areas, support functions, industry verticals, and so on. Almost any characteristics associated with an operating concern can be used for the purpose of planning.

Planning framework

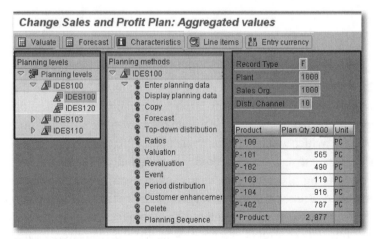

Figure 13.8 Planning Framework

Planning levels and
planning packages

However, with the exception of very small companies, planning activities are typically distributed to multiple planners based on criteria such as product lines, responsibility areas, market segments, and so on. To support this distribution of responsibilities while keeping the underlying planning processes constant and consistent, planning levels are further divided into planning packages, which typically represent a unique slice of market segment that is being planned. So, you can create multiple planning packages by product divisions, distribution channels, industry verticals, or any other criteria that best represents planning processes in your company, and then assign them to different individuals for planning. You can also parameterize relatively infrequent or global changes (e.g., change of planning year), to facilitate controlled and consistent change to planning criteria.

 Tip

Considering that there is no common source of planning data, you can plan *either* in account-based Profitability Analysis *or* in costing-based Profitability Analysis.

After you've set up and distributed relevant planning levels and planning packages, you are ready to carry out different planning activities.

Planning Activities

Planning methods

In the Profitability Analysis planning framework, you use planning methods to carry out different planning activities such as Enter planning data, Copy, Forecast, and so on (refer to Figure 13.8). Among the most important planning methods is the Enter planning data method used to enter plan data manually. You can customize the structure and the layout in which you enter planning data by using planning layouts (Chapter 14 discusses this in more detail); and you have the flexibility of entering planning data using SAP screens, a simple Microsoft Excel interface, or a simpler web interface. For example, if some part of planning information is entered by employees who don't need to have constant, continued access to the SAP software (e.g., sales representatives), you can provide a web interface so that they can enter necessary planning information on the corporate intranet. Apart from this method used to manually enter planning data, Table 13.1 provides an overview of a few other planning methods available in Profitability Analysis.

Planning Method	Use It To ...
Copy	Replace, add, or subtract planning values based on values from another year or another plan version.
Forecast	Prepare planning forecast based on customizable forecast strategies and calculation factors.
Delete	Reset or restore planning data to a previous state by deleting current planning data to zero.
Top-down distribution	Distribute plan data from a higher planning level to more detailed levels using top-down distribution techniques.
Ratios	Calculate and simulate price changes directly in Profitability Analysis without using pricing from sales.
Valuation	Calculate plan data for the value fields using available valuation techniques.
Revaluation	Revaluate plan data by applying percentage additions or deductions (increase values by 10 %).
Event	Evaluate planning data by taking into account the impact of specific events (e.g., product marketing or PR campaign).
Period distribution	Distribute planning data by using distribution keys such as equal distribution, by percentage, as before, and so on.

Table 13.1 Planning Methods

Planning sequence

You can also create a planning sequence that consists of multiple planning methods called up step-by-step for execution, thereby providing you with a consistent and controlled approach to the planning process. For most planning methods, you can choose to use actual or planned data as a reference. For planned data, you can also specify the plan version that you want to reference. Even though typically, the definition and use of different planning versions is constant across the organization, for the purpose of profitability analysis, you have to determine whether planning data is based on legal valuation or on profit center valuation for each plan version.

Before we move on to the discussion of profitability reports, let's quickly review the integrated planning functionality.

Integrated Planning

Even though Chapter 14 specifically goes into different aspects of the enterprise-wide planning process from a financial point of view, a few integration points with respect to Profitability Analysis are worth mentioning here. Previously we talked about how you can transfer different actual data flows such as order or project settlement, and overhead costs to it You can use the same techniques to transfer planned settlement data and to allocate planned overheads as well.

Integration with SOP

Profitability Analysis also provides full integration with Sales and Operations Planning (SOP), a flexible forecasting and planning tool used for sales, production and supply chain. For example, planned sales quantities from Profitability Analysis can be transferred to SOP for more detailed planning. And the best part is that since planning in Profitability Analysis can be carried out based on profitability segments; planning by different plants, product lines or product groups can seamlessly flow into SOP. In fact, this integration works in the other direction as well! If you have maintained necessarily detailed mapping between value fields and GL accounts, you can transfer planned data out of Profitability Analysis to other SAP components. Now it is time to move on to the reporting capabilities of the Profitability Analysis information system.

Information System

Instead of providing you with canned profitability reports, SAP provides you with a highly modular framework in which you can design reports that are most suitable for your company. Using this reporting tool, you can combine characteristics and value fields to design and execute drilldown reports. One of the advantages of drilldown reports is that you start out by analyzing some values (e.g., revenues, sales deductions, contribution margin, etc.) for a higher level characteristic such as all product divisions in your company. Subsequently you can drilldown to any product division to analyze same set of values for all product groups in that division, drilldown one more level to analyze all products in any product group, and so on. If you use a graphical output, you can even display multiple information windows on a screen as you drill down to analyze different criteria. For example, Figure 13.9 shows a fairly typical, albeit simple, contribution margin report that you can quickly develop in Profitability Analysis information system.

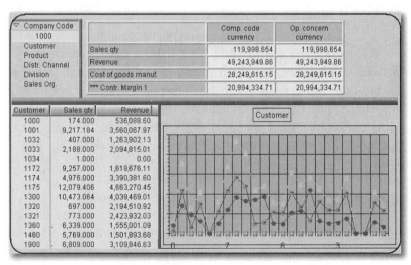

Figure 13.9 A Contribution Margin Report

Because the whole profitability structure is custom designed at the time of implementation to meet your specific requirements, it isn't even technically possible to provide any standard reports. However, to give you a jump-start in designing reports, SAP provides you with example reports for a sample operating concern. The following are some of the example reports:

> Comparison of Plan, Actual and Variance values
> Daily, Monthly, and Yearly Contribution Margin Analysis
> Monthly and Yearly Operating Profit Report
> Settlement Analysis for Internal Orders and SAP Projects
> Top-Down Distribution Analysis to Evaluate Value Distribution
> Customizable Annual Sales Plan

Report performance   Another point for consideration is the performance of profitability analysis reports, as typically these reports handle a very large volume of data. That's why SAP offers several techniques to improve the performance of reports. One of the important techniques is to create summarization levels in which you can define your requirements based on fixed characteristics and value fields, "build the levels" by populating them with data, and then use them to read data for the reporting.

Finally, particularly useful analysis tools help you check values updated in Profitability Analysis with corresponding values in Financial Accounting. You can carry out these checks for sales orders, billing documents, internal order settlements, and project settlements. These tools can be extremely useful to verify the accuracy, completeness, and validity of values reported in Profitability Analysis.

Case Study

This $3.6-billion company is headquartered in the Midwestern United States and has been operating a chain of regional supermarkets for the past two decades. Apart from temporary and seasonal help at individual locations, the company employs more than 17,000 full-time employees working at its more than 120 supermarkets in 3 neighboring states. Its supermarkets carry thousands of items organized into different product divisions and product lines ranging from produce, prepared food, seafood, and bakery items to other general products such as apparel, toys, hardware, small appliances, and school supplies.

Business Challenges

In an exceedingly competitive environment of supermarkets, the company was finding it difficult to keep tabs on its profit margins. Increased sales volume in product categories did not always translate into a corresponding increase in profit margins, and the reasons were difficult to analyze. Instead of contributing to increases in revenue, many promotional and seasonal marketing campaigns seemed to barely break even. The wastage in their perishable item products was significant, and, in some cases, it seemed to eat into otherwise profitable market segments. During the holiday season, management was noticing a huge increase in temporary labor costs without proportional impact on the bottom line. However, it was difficult to obtain data that could be used to identify any reasons or trends for this discrepancy.

Even though the company's existing back-office system did a passable job of providing profitability by location, more detailed and pertinent questions such as profitability by product categories or by product across all locations were difficult to answer without a laborious and considerably manual process. One of the reasons was that their ERP vendor did not have any solution catering to their industry-specific requirements. Another reason was that due to the lack of integration between components, it was difficult to consolidate costs and revenues originating in different areas (e.g., sales, marketing, service, procurement, overheads, etc.) to arrive at a detailed, timely, and meaningful profitability and contribution margin analysis.

However, the lack of integration among system components was not the only issue. Their system vendor was recently acquired by another ERP vendor, which gave rise to uncertainty about future support, and a somewhat inevitable push by the new vendor to thrust its own ERP system. Management decided to act proactively and change to a vendor providing a stable and fully integrated ERP system: SAP.

Solution Deployment

The switchover from the other ERP system to SAP took almost 11 months with a team of 5 full-time SAP consultants assisting the internal IT team of 12 full-time employees. Due to different acquisitions in the past, the company used 7 different POS systems; but to keep the scope of the project manageable, it was decided not to replace them as part of the current project. Modeling and implementing well thought out profitability analysis was obviously one of the top priorities for management. So from the beginning, a dedicated SAP consultant along with three key business users worked with the IT team to ensure that the processes in other SAP components were designed to provide the necessary values to Profitability Analysis.

Considering the wide range of information relevant for profitability in a complex business such as theirs, costing-based Profitability Analysis was an obvious choice. Even though the decision to use only one operating concern was an easy one, considerable time and effort was spent in determining and finalizing the profitability criteria and the profitability values. The goal was not only to get profitability by typical criteria such as stores, divisions, product groups and individual products but also to obtain visibility into the effectiveness of operational efficiency, analyze the impact of business decisions on profitability, and measure and plan profitability by product lines.

The initial focus of the team was on designing a planning framework that instituted revenue planning for all product divisions across all stores up to the level of product lines. For the product lines consisting of relatively big-ticket items, the framework was extended to a more detailed level to facilitate planning by individual products. A portal on the corporate intranet was designed to offer two-way sharing of plan data between the store managers and planners at the head office. After the design and implementation of other SAP components was stabilized, the team shifted their focus on obtaining the information from procurement and accounting systems. A generic interface was developed to collect relevant data from seven POS systems into Profitability Analysis.

Value Achieved

The company observed the trends and analyzed profitability data for four months that included one holiday season, and made many stark observations. For some stores, increased sales numbers during the holiday season were undercut by excessive spending on store decorations and other marketing ploys. Without reliable planning or historical data, many promotional campaigns grossly overestimated their effectiveness and ended up wiping out any potential increase in sales. Similarly, by comparing costs of stores in geographical proximity, the company was able to identify stores that hired a lot of extra help during the holiday season due to poor planning, excessively optimistic expectations, or both. Also, somewhat surprising were the findings where a product line as a whole seemed profitable, but individual products within the product line were not. Although these realizations shed some light on many inefficiencies and excesses, at least now the company had the actual data to take and enforce corrective actions.

Even though their previous ERP system provided a mechanism for revenue planning, it was difficult to obtain a consolidated, holistic view of the plan across product lines and across stores. With Profitability Analysis, the top management was not only able to analyze planned revenue by different criteria, but they also had the luxury of drilling down to the plan numbers entered by a store manager. All in all, after switching to SAP, the inadequacies of the previous ERP system in the integration areas became a lot more apparent; and the IT team as well as business users were glad to finally get onto a "real" integrated system.

Looking Ahead

The company is expecting its rollout of the core SAP ERP system to stabilize within the next six to eight months. The company is evaluating whether the retail industry solution offered by SAP may help with its difficulties of managing and integrating a host of smaller, isolated systems used at the company's store locations.

Summary

As you've learned in this chapter, the Profitability Analysis functionality of SAP ERP Financials provides you with profit centers as well as a customized framework of Profitability Analysis for your market segments. Some of the salient features are listed here:

> PCA provides a simplified environment to calculate profitability of areas within your company.

> Using Profitability Analysis, you can analyze profitability by product, market, customer, division, and other criteria based on financial accounts as well as flexible, custom-defined values.

> Using powerful integration, you can gather data from other SAP components such as financial accounting, sales and distribution, materials management, overhead costing, product costing, and so on.

> Using a comprehensive planning framework, you can plan sales, revenue, and profitability for different profitability segments and review the entire planning process or parts of it from multiple viewpoints.

> Using extensive reports, you can analyze contribution margin, market segment comparisons, cost estimates comparisons, and so on for individual characteristics (e.g., customers, products) or characteristic hierarchies.

> In this chapter, we explored some areas of planning in Profitability Analysis. In the next chapter, we will focus on how you can use SAP to improve your company wide planning and budgeting processes

14

Financial Planning

Business planning plays an increasingly important role in the management of any company. With the primary objective of setting financial and non-financial benchmarks across different areas of a company, this process requires participation from all divisions, locations, and departments. On the other hand, this process also enables top management to communicate and reinforce their strategy and priorities across the company through their funding decisions and budget allocations. Even though this annual, enterprise-wide planning process plans for and establishes benchmarks for sales, manufacturing, procurement, and other areas of a company; financial planning plays a central role in this process. Understandably, actual planning processes vary from company to company and are individualized based on the industry, business, and organizational structure of a company. Depending on the size of a company and the scope of the planning process, it may take from a few days to a few months; in most companies, this process is carried out toward the end of each fiscal year for the upcoming fiscal year.

Overview

As the relatively simple presentation in Figure 14.1 shows you, this enterprise-wide planning process requires close interaction and co-ordination among individual planning processes in different areas of a company. The financial planning itself consists of several other planning processes with specific financial objectives, such as profit planning, and cost planning, investment planning. SAP ERP Financials provides complete support for such intricate planning process spanning several areas in the business. You can prepare a consolidated business plan by combining several subplans from Cost Center Accounting (CO-OM-CCA), Project Systems (PS), internal orders, Profitability Analysis (CO-PA), and product costing (CO-PC).

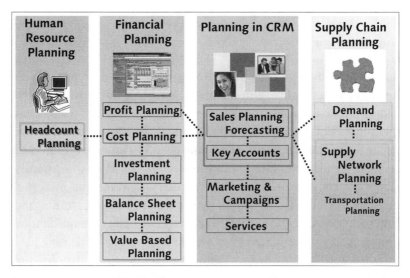

Figure 14.1 Enterprisewide Planning Process

Planning tools   SAP ERP Financials provides many planning features and functionalities that help you develop consistent planning forms regardless of whether you're planning cost centers, profit centers, projects, headcount, or any other area of your company. Integration with Microsoft Excel helps you streamline several of your planning processes by providing a familiar interface for online or offline entry of planning data. Distribution keys help you distribute the annual or quarterly plan to individual months based on different strategies. Multiple planning versions help you segregate different plans in your company based on the plan's source, periodicity, or level of details. These features help make your manual planning processes more efficient and uniform.

You never need to duplicate data entry for planned costs because costs planned on projects, maintenance orders, or other similar elements can be simply transferred to appropriate cost centers using transfer programs. On the other hand, integrated planning eliminates even such cost transfers by automatically integrating planning on cost centers, orders, projects, profit centers and so on. In fact, you can transfer detailed planning from cost centers or even Profitability Analysis back on to the GL accounts. Several planning tools are available to make your planning process as easy as possible. The efficiency improvement in the corporate planning process is evident regardless of whether you're part of a small firm with the CEO deciding on the business plan for the next year or a multinational conglomerate with hundreds of planners participating in the multilevel planning process.

Scalability

The powerful and integrated nature of corporate planning is increasingly evident in revenue planning using profit centers and Profitability Analysis. Primary and secondary costs planned in other areas of the business can be seamlessly transferred to help you in detailed profit planning. Planning methods available in Profitability Analysis help you easily prepare a profit plan with as many details as necessary for your company. Depending on the business requirements of your company, you can carry out revenue planning based on revenue numbers or sales quantities. You can easily copy, forecast, valuate, and distribute plan values across multiple versions from other plans or actual business activities, thereby considerably expediting the initial processes of your annual planning cycle. In the next section, we'll explore these functionalities in more detail.

Functions in Detail

In this section, you'll first get introduced to common planning concepts across different SAP components. Because costs and revenues originate in different areas of your company, SAP ERP Financials helps you plan for them in different components and brings everything together by means of integrated planning. So after the introduction to common concepts, you'll see how to carry out planning for costs and revenues in different SAP components. Finally, you'll learn how you can use other planning functionalities to make your financial planning processes more efficient. Let's start with common planning functionalities first.

Common Planning Functionalities

In this section, we'll look at several generic concepts, tools, and features provided to support the planning and budgeting process in your company. These powerful planning features are available and applicable across several SAP components, which helps keep your planning process consistent.

Seamless integration with Excel
One of the most useful planning functions is the seamless integration of planning screens with Microsoft Excel. By using Excel templates to collect and enter plan data, you can further distribute, delegate, and decentralize your planning tasks. This helps your team contribute to the planning process without requiring any access to SAP. Excel files with planning data can then be easily uploaded and consolidated for further analysis and modifications. Especially in a large, decentralized planning environment, the ability to gather planning data on Excel files and to upload them with minimum manual intervention can be invaluable. Even if your planning environment isn't decentralized, you can improve process efficiency by using Excel in-place for plan data entry. Excel in-place replaces the data entry part of the corresponding SAP ERP Financials screen with Microsoft Excel, thereby providing you with a familiar and easier environment for planning data entry. Figure 14.2 shows you how the familiar Excel interface is displayed in an SAP ERP Financials screen for entering cost center planning data.

Figure 14.2 Excel Integration with SAP ERP Financials Planning

Another fairly common question in your mind may be with respect to different currencies in planning. In Chapter 10, we discussed the concept of controlling area, cost centers, and other costing objects supported by the software. As we discussed, controlling objects such as cost centers may be managed in a different currency than the controlling area currency. And there is also comprehensive support for planning in multiple currencies. As the following example indicates, you can use different currencies for different aspects of your planning process.

Multiple currencies

 **Example**

> A clothing manufacturer based in the United States has a plant in Mexico that receives its materials from Brazil. The plant manager can plan the plant's material costs in Brazilian Real and all other manufacturing costs in Mexican peso. These costs are automatically and simultaneously converted into U.S. dollars, which can later be consolidated with other costs planned at the head office in U.S. dollars.

Let's now look at how you can organize this planning data.

Planning Versions

The Planning function supports multiple planning versions to help you organize your planning data, analyze what-if scenarios, and simulate different market conditions. Consider, for example, that you have created a financial plan at the beginning of a fiscal year using one plan version. In the course of a fiscal year, you can periodically reassess business conditions and market conditions and then use different

Planning versions

planning versions to maintain a changed and revised plan. This helps you compare actual business activities against what was planned originally at the beginning of a year as well as any subsequent revisions.

> ➕ **Tip**
>
> Planning versions are available and valid across different SAP components. Thus, you should ensure that different plan versions (0, 1, 2, etc.) have the same meaning across your company in cost center planning, profit center planning, business process planning, and so on.

Characteristics of planning versions

Several other factors associated with planning versions promote a disciplined planning approach. For example, for the purpose of internal controls, you can lock a planning version from further modification so that after a plan has been finalized and confirmed, its values can't be modified. You can control whether or not a plan version should be updated with actual business data. For example, if you have created several versions for the purpose of simulation only, you may not want those versions to be updated with actual data. Of course, this doesn't have any impact on your ability to analyze plan values versus actual values in reports. Moreover, there is support for these parameters separately for each fiscal year, thereby providing you with the utmost control over how these versions are used year over year. Figure 14.3 shows a sample screen of version definition.

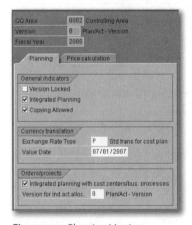

Figure 14.3 Planning Version

In the next section, we'll look at how you can enable consistent and controlled entry of plan data across your company.

Planning Layouts and Planner Profiles

Planning layouts help you organize and lay out values to be planned based on different criteria. For example, foreign subsidiaries of a globally organized religious institute may use planning layouts that accept the planned amount in local currency and simultaneously display the equivalent amount in group currency; whereas planning layouts used by plant managers of a manufacturing company will require the ability to plan based on quantities and manufacturing processes. At a group level, you may use yet another set of planning layouts for entering or displaying quarterly planning data and carrying out an annual comparison. Ultimately, the business requirements and personal preferences dictate the planned values that are entered and displayed on any planning layout. So, planning layouts help you differentiate planning activities based on what is being planned.

Planning layouts

On the other hand, *planner profiles* help you differentiate planning activities based on who is responsible for planning. Planner profiles help you carry out a controlled distribution of planning tasks and activities among planners in your company. When carefully used, planner profiles help your planning process grow with the growth in your company. For example, in a small company, where typically one or two individuals are responsible for the whole planning process, a single all-encompassing planner profile is sufficient. However, consider a large company with a decentralized planning process in which marketing departments of different subsidiaries are responsible for planning marketing expenditure. Even though they may use similar or the same planning layouts, by using properly designed planner profiles and authorizations, you can ensure that individual planners are able to carry out planning only for marketing departments of their subsidiary.

Planner profiles

 Tip

> Planner profiles also provide you with the flexibility to determine whether planned values in parallel currencies (discussed previously) are automatically calculated based on exchange rates in the system or are entered manually.

You'll gain a better understanding of planning layouts and planner profiles when we discuss manual planning later in this chapter.

In the next section, we'll look at one of the several functionalities delivered by SAP to make your planning processes more efficient.

Distribution Keys

Distribution keys planning is one of the most powerful, although somewhat underused, features. Distribution keys help you easily distribute yearly plan numbers to individual months. For example, some of the distribution keys available in the standard system are listed here:

> Equal distribution (e.g., $1,200 distributed as $100 per month)

> Distribute as before (i.e., use same distribution values as previous year)

> Distribute or copy values to following nonvalue periods (e.g., distribute or copy quarterly plan to individual months in a quarter)

> Distribute based on the number of calendar days in a period

Additionally, you can create custom distribution keys that specify the distribution of values for individual months. Such custom keys can be designed to factor in seasonal variations and similar business criteria that are specific to your industry or your business. For example, consumer electronics sales are higher during the holiday season, car dealers offer additional rebates at the end of the year, and so on. By effective use of properly designed distribution keys, you can significantly improve your planning process. Now we're ready to discuss how SAP ERP Financials can help you optimize your costs planning.

Costs Planning

In this section, we'll focus primarily on how you can use SAP ERP Financials for planning costs across different SAP components. As mentioned previously, we'll make frequent reference to the topics discussed in Chapter 10. So if you haven't already done so, you may want to read that chapter before continuing further. The process of cost planning can vary considerably in different companies in terms of how costs are planned, allocated, and analyzed. Fortunately, a number of different automatic and manual processes for your planning needs are provided. One of the most commonly used processes for planning costs on cost centers, activities, and business processes is manual planning.

Manual planning

Figure 14.4 shows an example of a screen that you can use to enter planned costs and consumption quantities for a range of accounts for a cost center in a plan version. This screen brings together several planning aspects discussed before. For example, your choice of planning layout determines that you're able to enter planned costs (Plan fixed costs) and planned consumption (Plan fixed consu) for Cost Elements; your planning profile confirms that you're authorized to enter planning data for the selected Cost Center in the selected Plan version; and distribution keys ("2") next to the amounts and the quantities indicate that the distribution in 2008 is to be carried out as it was done previously. Using Excel integration, you can display the same screen in an Excel layout or save it as an Excel file.

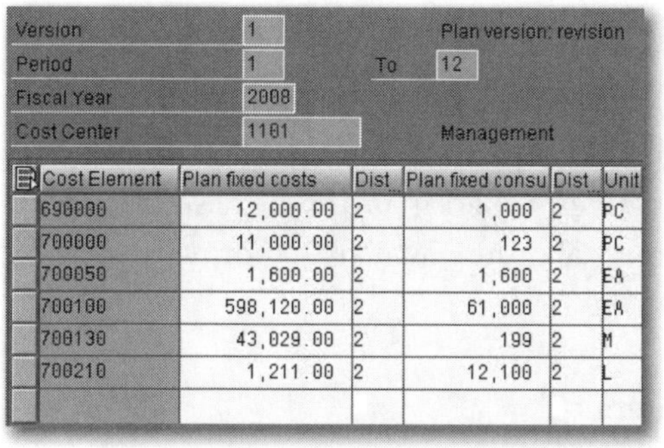

Version 1 Plan version: revision
Period 1 To 12
Fiscal Year 2008
Cost Center 1101 Management

Cost Element	Plan fixed costs	Dist	Plan fixed consu	Dist	Unit
690000	12,000.00	2	1,000	2	PC
700000	11,000.00	2	123	2	PC
700050	1,600.00	2	1,600	2	EA
700100	598,120.00	2	61,000	2	EA
700130	43,029.00	2	199	2	M
700210	1,211.00	2	12,100	2	L

Figure 14.4 Manual Planning

Planning for activities or business processes

This consistent manual planning interface allows you to easily switch among cost centers, cost elements, and other planning criteria; review and enter planned costs annually; and drill down to individual planning periods. The underlying planning framework remains the same even when you need to carry out detailed cost planning; so that you can simply switch to planning layouts that allow cost planning by activities or business processes. This SAP design of planning processes has several advantages:

> You have significant flexibility to use as many or as few planning layouts as necessary in your planning process.

> You have substantial scalability whether your planning process consists of only one or two planners or hundreds of planners around the world in a multilevel planning process.

> You can achieve easy process integration in your enterprise-wide planning because your employees have access to an identical cost planning interface in cost center planning, activities planning, business process planning, or planning of allocation factors (all discussed in Chapter 10).

These planning functionalities are useful in identifying, classifying, and analyzing specific departments or business activities in your company. However, they aren't sufficient if you want to plan costs on relatively temporary initiatives and projects undertaken by your company. Cost planning for such initiatives requires additional and somewhat different functionality. One of the reasons is that such initiatives tend to use materials and resources that need to be accounted for in cost planning.

You already read in Chapter 11 how you can plan costs and revenues on projects using SAP Project System (PS). These projects are used for considerably complex initiatives, whereas in the next section, we'll look at cost planning on internal orders, which are normally used for simpler projects and initiatives.

Planning on Internal Orders
Even though there are no technical restrictions, planning costs on internal orders is typically done only for orders that have a relatively longer time frame. And you get a range of planning functions for processing internal orders covering different levels of planning detail required at different stages of order execution. There is also support for comprehensive planning on internal orders, including multiple versions and multiple currencies so that you can carry out full variance analysis on various initiatives. Following are some of the planning functions that you can use for internal orders:

> **Overall planning**
> This is the simplest way of planning in which you maintain total planned costs on internal orders without any more details. This can be useful when more detailed planning information isn't required or available, for example, buying five computer servers.

> **Unit costing planning**
> We discussed this costing method in Chapter 12 for product costing. You can also use it for costing internal orders if you have detailed information about required activities and resources, for example, carrying out an IT upgrade project that includes installation of new hardware.

> **Easy Cost Planning**
> We also discussed this costing method in Chapter 12. Easy Cost Planning gives you not only a framework for detailed cost planning but also a way to trigger necessary purchase orders or material reservations, for example, carrying out an IT project with the help of a consulting company, which requires an approved purchase order.

> **Cost element and activity planning**
> This planning method is useful when you have detailed cost planning information available, and you can plan based on cost elements or activities, for example, setting up a new IT support center with new software, hardware, and staff.

As you can see, you have different planning alternatives to choose from based on the planning details available. These planning functions can also be used at different stages of an internal order as more details become available. This can be useful, for example, if the necessary information to carry out detailed planning isn't available at the beginning of a project. Let's look at some other planning aids available.

Planning Aids

As you can see in Figure 14.5, cost centers are posted with different types of costs from different components. We already discussed the integration of cost center planning with the costs planning on internal orders and projects. But you also have several other transfer programs to transfer plan data from other components. For example, for your fixed assets accounting, you can automatically transfer planned de-preciation to appropriate cost centers. This process helps you plan for depreciation precisely and accurately because it takes into account the exact months in which different assets will be fully depreciated. Simi-larly, if you use SAP ERP Human Capital Management (HCM) compo-nents, you can transfer planned personnel costs such as payroll, ben-efits, and so on to appropriate cost centers. Manufacturing companies that use SAP Production Planning can automatically transfer planned production activities and corresponding costs to cost centers. As any planner who has tried to accurately plan for these costs in detail can appreciate, these cost transfer programs save considerable time and effort spent in trying to gather this information from different busi-ness areas in a company.

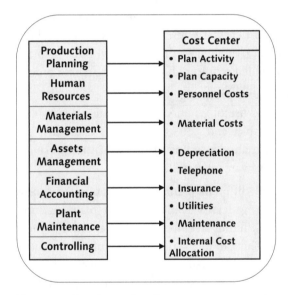

Figure 14.5 Planning on Cost Centers

Whereas the transfer programs assist in the automatic planning of costs, templates and formula planning are useful when you plan costs manually. For example, you can create templates consisting of a grid of rows and columns for the purpose of planning costs and revenues. In templates, you can use functions and formulae to calculate planned values. Following are some examples of powerful calculations that you can carry out using these features of templates and formula planning:

> Planned electricity costs = Planned employee headcount * 1350 * 12 %

> Planned maintenance services = Planned employee headcount * 3 %

> Planned travel expenses = Travel expenses of previous year * 1.20 %

> Planned telephone costs for call center = 1.5 * Number of service calls in the past year * $2.30

You use the same framework for defining these templates and formulae as you would use in Easy Cost Planning as discussed in Chapter 12. When you use SAP for planning, you not only have consistency in terms of user interfaces but also in terms of the logic and underlying functionality in different components.

However, it isn't always practical to plan costs at their origins due to time-, resource-, or information constraints. The planning process is more manageable if costs can be allocated easily. So the processes available to allocate actual costs (discussed in Chapter 10) such as distribution and assessment are also available for allocating planning costs. The advantage of these methods for you is that they are easy to use and easy to maintain. On the other hand, as we discussed, these methods only represent indirect allocation because the actual activities do not form the basis for allocation. Instead, these processes use the percentages or allocation factors you have specified for allocating planned costs. You can also use other processes for allocating planning costs such as overhead calculation, template allocation, indirect activity allocation, and so on. In the next section, we'll look at the revenue planning functionality.

Periodic allocation of planned costs

Revenue Planning

The cost planning discussed previously is only one of the pieces of overall corporate planning. You can obtain a complete view of anticipated profits (or losses) by combining planning costs with the planning of revenues. Depending on the level of detailed planning required or possible in your company; there are two primary components for carrying out revenue planning. You can carry out revenue planning on profit centers, or you can carry out more detailed revenue planning using Profitability Analysis. Also, you can transfer planning from other SAP components and add remaining or missing information as necessary for your revenue planning. In this section, we'll make frequent reference to concepts discussed in Chapter 13, so if you haven't already done so, you may want to read that chapter before continuing further. Let's start with revenue planning on profit centers.

Revenue Planning on Profit Centers

Transfer of planned costs

Most likely, you'll use profit center planning in combination with planning in other SAP components. Regardless of the scope and dimension of your corporate planning process, duplication of data entry always translates into increased time and effort, not to mention increased possibility of errors. So you get a convenient and easy-to-use data transfer process to transfer planning data from cost centers, internal orders, projects, business processes, Profitability Analysis, and manufacturing orders.

For example, you can use this transfer process (see Figure 14.6) to transfer the following:

> Planned overhead from cost centers and internal orders
> Planned overhead, manufacturing, and other costs from Project System
> Revenues from account-based or costing-based Profitability Analysis
> Planned costs from manufacturing orders

Using this data transfer process helps you considerably improve efficiency and data accuracy in your planning process, while also enabling you to segregate planning activities and tasks to appropriate areas of responsibility. However, planning data from other SAP components may not be available or sufficient to provide you with complete corporate planning. For example, planned revenues may not be available if you aren't using Profitability Analysis, and planning information for balance sheet items is typically not available in any other SAP component. But you also have the ability to enter planned data directly on profit centers.

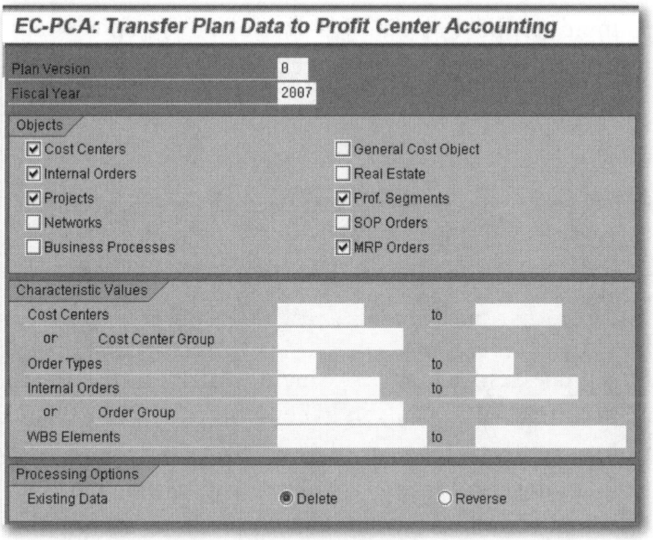

Figure 14.6 Transfer Plan Data to Profit Centers

The concepts discussed earlier such as planning layouts, distribution keys, and so on with reference to costs planning are equally relevant for direct planning on profit centers. Basically, you design your planning layouts so that it now includes profit centers, revenue accounts, balance sheet accounts, and any other criteria relevant for your revenue planning. To make your revenue planning process more efficient and distributed, you can also integrate with Excel as already discussed with any of these planning layouts. And you get a large number of ready-to-use planning layouts that help you carry out revenue planning using profit centers, profit center groups, GL accounts, functional areas, statistical key figures in multiple currencies, and different timeframes.

Manual planning for profit centers

If your planning process is modeled around planning sales quantities instead of sales revenues, you have this support with the help of representative materials. *Representative materials* represent a group

Revenue planning based on sales quantities

433

of materials with similar qualities such as manufacturing costs. You can use representative materials in your planning process so that you don't have to plan quantities by individual materials. Profit planning based on representative materials is made possible by leveraging the close integration of different SAP components. For such planning scenarios, for example, planned revenues are calculated based on transfer prices, and planned costs are calculated based on material cost estimates.

 Tip

Profit planning using representative materials uses transfer prices and cost estimates from a profit center valuation view. This also means that parallel valuation of materials needs to be active in your system.

Other common processes such as assessment, distribution, formula planning, and so on are also available when you carry out revenue planning on profit centers. However, if your business requirements and corporate planning process is capable of supporting more detailed planning, then you can carry out revenue planning using Profitability Analysis.

Revenue Planning Using Profitability Analysis

Profit planning in detail

We discussed some aspects of planning functionality in Profitability Analysis in Chapter 13. As we discussed, profitability planning provides you with a detailed look into the profitability of products, distribution channels, geographical regions, customers, or any other criteria important to your business. For example, customers who annually buy the same product in the same quantity at the same price may not be equally profitable from a business point of view because the profitability of a customer also depends on order cancellations, goods returns, shipping costs, collection costs for receivables, and similar factors. Even though it's difficult to plan individual costs, such as collection costs, by customer, you still can use the top-down distribution functionality available in Profitability Analysis to determine the estimated average cost by customer. Subsequently, you can take necessary actions by comparing actual costs (possibly approximated) and planned costs.

Revenue planning using Profitability Analysis provides you with the ability to view your entire corporate planning process in different ways depending on your business requirements. Using the planning framework, you can structure your corporate planning process and carry out all planning activities from designing and modeling to managing, monitoring, and reporting. Integration with Excel is available as well in Profitability Analysis planning, so you can enter planning data locally before loading it centrally into SAP ERP Financials. Different planning methods help you copy, forecast, valuate, transfer, and analyze planning data. As discussed previously, top-down distribution in planning helps you plan at higher levels, such as for groups of products or customers, and distribute those plan values to lower levels, such as individual products and customers.

Planning framework

As with revenue planning using profit centers, you can transfer planning data from other SAP components into Profitability Analysis for sales and profit planning (see Figure 14.7). Planned overheads from cost centers and internal orders can be settled to Profitability Analysis, planned costs and revenues from SAP projects can be transferred using sophisticated transfer structures, and similar transfer structures can be used to transfer data from product costing. An interesting constellation presents itself if you use planning on Profitability Analysis with the planning on Logistics Information System (LO-LIS). LIS consists of six, modular information systems in the areas of logistics such as sales, purchasing, plant maintenance, and so on that can be used not only to report actual business activities but also to carry out planning. From a business planning perspective, integration between Profitability Analysis and LIS provides you with extremely enhanced functionality so that you can synchronize revenue planning in Profitability Analysis with other planning processes in logistics such as procurement planning and capacity planning.

Integration with Logistics Information System (LO-LIS)

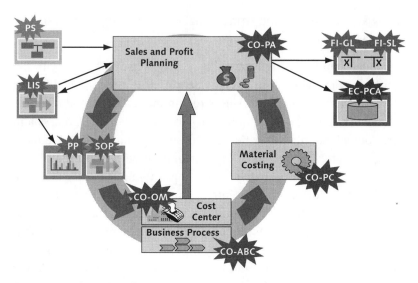

Figure 14.7 Sales and Profit Planning

This brings us to the subject of integrated planning, which is discussed in the next section along with other planning elements.

Other Planning Elements

In this section, you'll discover some of the other planning functionalities available in SAP to augment your planning process. One of the most important is integrated planning.

Integrated Planning

If you've already read Chapter 11 "Project Accounting," you got a flavor of integrated planning when we talked about cost planning on projects and on orders that are associated with those projects. As we discussed, you can either plan costs on orders and on projects independently of each other, or you can set up SAP so that costs planned on orders automatically flow into costs planned on projects. Integrated planning expands that concept to encompass all components involved in enterprise-wide planning. For example, if a cost center is linked to a profit center, or if an internal order is linked to a cost center, should the costs planned on one automatically flow to the other?

Consider an example where one cost center (e.g., customer support) requests the help of service engineers (e.g., shared services) by using an internal order. Costs for service engineers need to be planned not only on the internal order but also on the shared services cost center. If integrated planning is active, then costs planned on the internal order are also automatically planned on the shared services cost center. Whereas if integrated planning isn't active, then costs planned on internal orders aren't automatically planned on the shared services cost center.

Integrated planning

 Tip

If you activate integrated planning with Profit Center Accounting (PCA) and the new GL; planned costs from cost centers, internal orders, and other similarly planned costs are similarly transferred to PCA and the new GL automatically.

So, the integrated planning functionality can be extremely powerful in synchronizing planned values across cost centers, internal orders, business processes, activities, and profit centers. For example, such integration can be especially useful in a large company to ensure that all anticipated costs are automatically accounted for, considering that planning activities may be carried out in different areas of business by different groups of planners. In the next section, we'll look at the planning on GL accounts.

Planning on GL Accounts

In addition to the planning on cost centers and profit centers, SAP ERP Financials also offers a fairly simple framework to help you plan directly on GL accounts. For example, you can plan based on your financial statement definitions such as balance sheet. The functionality of GL planning has been considerably enhanced from previous SAP releases, so now you can also use multiple versions, integrated planning, plan allocations, and similar features for this planning. When you carry out planning on GL accounts (see Figure 14.8), you can plan total (annual) amounts and distribute it to individual (period)

Planning based on financial statements

amounts, period amounts that are automatically totaled, or a combination of individual amounts and total amounts.

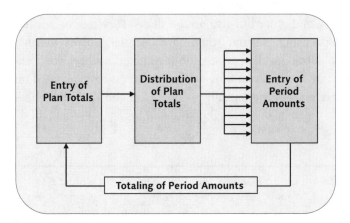

Figure 14.8 Planning on GL Account

Transferring overhead and profitability plan to GL accounts

The full range of planning functionalities such as planning layouts, planner profile, distribution keys, and Excel integration, are supported for GL planning as well. This provides you with a consistent planning interface regardless of whether you're planning overhead costs, anticipated revenues, or balance sheet items. However, one of the most beneficial features and yet another example of the robust integration offered by SAP is that you can transfer plan data from overhead costing and Profitability Analysis back into the GL planning. Such integration and data transfer capability ensures that your GL account planning is in sync with any adjustments and revisions made in the more detailed planning on cost centers and Profitability Analysis.

Lastly, let's see how you can use SAP ERP Financials planning to meet your budgeting and forecasting business requirements.

Forecasting and Budgeting

Forecasting

In addition to planning, comprehensive support for your forecasting as well as budgeting requirements across its myriad components is provided. Forecasting is typically carried out earlier in the annual planning process, and you can simply use a different plan version for your revenue and cost forecasting. For example, you can use different plan versions to maintain the primary plan as well as your quarterly plan revisions, and use yet another plan version for maintaining your forecasted values. Such separation ensures that you can compare your actual business activities with different plan numbers as well as your forecasted numbers.

On the other hand, a budget represents an approved plan and is more binding in terms of its relevancy for business planning. You may also have noticed this difference between planning and budgeting when we talked about capital investment planning in Chapter 6. We already discussed the inclusion of different plan versions to support iterative business planning process. This iterative process usually begins as a bottom-up process where department and division managers submit their planned amounts to higher management for approval. Subsequently, the approved plan (i.e., budget) is typically distributed in a top-down process in which amounts budgeted by upper management are distributed to department and division managers. Normally, version 0 is used for your approved plan/budget in Cost Center Accounting (CO-OM-CCA) and Profit Center Accounting (PCA).

Chapter 6 also introduced you to budget monitoring and availability control for capital investments, by which you can check in real time whether costs incurred on an internal order or a project are within an approved budget limit. If you want to extend that functionality to Cost Center Accounting, you can with the funds commitments function. Funds commitments enable you to reserve parts of the approved budget in advance, which may be used later in the form of purchase requisitions, purchase orders, and other expenses. However, unlike budget availability control supported for internal orders and projects, which is in real time (active), there is only support for passive budget availability control for cost centers. This means that costs and commitments posted to cost centers aren't checked in real time. Instead, several standard reports provide you with the necessary information to check for budget availability on cost centers.

Funds commitments

At this point, it's appropriate to briefly introduce the SAP component for Funds Management (PSM-FM) that provides you with a more detailed control and analysis of sources, distribution, and us-

Funds management

age of funds. This SAP component is available and developed primarily for public sector companies. Funds Management provides you with the necessary capability to budget revenues and expenditures for individual areas of responsibilities (identified as fund centers) in your company. It helps you control future funds transactions in accordance with the distributed budget and stop the budget from being exceeded. This component provides you with highly comprehensive Funds Management functionality such as the Budget Control System (BCS), budgetary ledger, and so on that you can use for detailed management of fund flows and budget management in your company. Also, similar to other SAP components, Funds Management is fully integrated with Financial Accounting (FI), Asset Accounting (FI-AA), Materials Management (MM), Sales and Distribution (SD), and other SAP components.

Now let's look at how the planning and forecasting functionality improved the corporate planning process for a manufacturer of consumer products.

Case Study

This $760-million manufacturer of consumer products is based on the U.S. west coast, with its household care and personal care products occupying prominent shelf space in most major regional supermarkets. Almost 90 % of the company sales are through supermarkets, and the company also sells its products through membership club stores and drug stores. The company is contemplating national expansion over the next five years, with the addition of several strategically located distribution centers.

Business Challenges

Even though rapid business expansion placed the company in an enviable position, its small corporate planning department was being stretched thin. Even though the company used SAP for its core financial, sales, manufacturing, and procurement, the corporate planning department was still using a hodgepodge of third-party systems and

Excel spreadsheets. This setup was just enough to carry out basic planning, but they were unable to carry out more analytical planning and forecasting based on planning strategies relevant for different business areas. The planning process involving a few hundred department managers was cumbersome and time consuming.

The planning process was carried out in several iterations with the help of numerous Excel spreadsheets, which inevitably required re-entry of data. Quality of planning data was another area of concern for managers who typically questioned it during quarterly evaluations and performance evaluations. The corporate planning department was able to conjure up revenue information for a few key customers and the top three product lines. However, strategic planning based on detailed sales and profit planning remained difficult, if not unattainable.

Even outside of the annual planning period, which extended to an excruciating three months, there were always requests for comparison reports from across the company. Preparing such comparison and analytical reports was difficult considering that the data resided in multiple, nonintegrated systems and spreadsheets. So, when the company's core operational system was scheduled to be upgraded from SAP R/3 4.6c to the latest SAP ERP 2005s and 2006, management decided to extend its benefits to the corporate planning department as well.

Solution Deployment

With full support from senior management, the planning functionality in SAP was rolled out across the company during a seven-week, rapid implementation. Involvement of business users and department managers across the company was expected, requested, and received resulting in successful completion of the project. Apart from the corporate planning department, other key stakeholders were identified as finance and sales departments who enthusiastically approved this rollout.

Profitability Analysis was used as the focal point for the company-wide planning process. Starting with the sales planning carried out for product groups and customer groups, the information was fed to Sales and Operations Planning (SOP), which, in turn, provided it as a base for Production Planning. As before, planning for overheads was carried out by cost centers; but now that information was also assessed to Profitability Analysis. Minimum user training was involved because most users affected by this project rollout were directly or indirectly familiar with SAP. Other reasons contributing to easy user acceptance included a familiar Excel interface for most planning transactions; a single, intuitive, and integrated planning framework for carrying out almost all planning activities; and user confidence in the robust system functionality based on their prior experience.

Value Achieved

With Excel integrated with SAP ERP Financials screens for most data entry and reporting transactions, most of the older planning spreadsheets were now eliminated. Even those managers who participated in the planning process but didn't have an SAP connection were able to use their familiar spreadsheets for planning purposes. Due to the integrated and consolidated planning interface available, the time taken for the annual planning process was cut down by more than 60 %. This tremendous improvement in efficiency meant that the company could continue with its ambitious and aggressive expansion plans without requiring a corresponding increase in staffing the corporate planning department for the foreseeable future.

Of course, one of the most important benefits was that now the company could carry out and include detailed customer and product segmentation at the time of planning and use it as benchmark for measuring the actual performance. There was remarkable improvement in the overall sales and forecasting process with the ability to prepare real-time reports, including any latest changes and updates from the field. The improved and integrated forecasting helped the company identify problems more quickly and take necessary corrective actions. Enterprise-wide planning processes, activities, and changes were controlled through carefully structured authorization access to help ensure data reliability. Because all changes made to planning data were automatically logged, it helped in avoiding or tracing any surprise changes in the active plan version. Overall, the project far exceeded the original expectations of its key stakeholders and business users.

Looking Ahead

The next project on the IT department's list is an enterprise-wide roll-out of SAP portals. The current plan is to provide functionality to department managers and other employees to enter plan data and obtain comparison reports through their personalized portals.

Summary

In this chapter, you saw how the integrated planning functionality in SAP ERP Financials can enhance your enterprise-wide business planning process, particularly in the area of financial planning. Some of the salient features of this functionality are listed here:

> Uniform and consistent usage of planning layouts and planner profiles help you distribute planning activities among different planners regardless of the size of your company and scope of your planning process.

> To reflect the iterative nature of corporate planning, SAP supports multiple plan versions to help you segregate your planning data based on the type of assumptions, time of creation, level of details, or other pertinent criteria.

> Detailed profit planning can be carried out using profit centers and Profitability Analysis for revenue planning, and using cost centers, internal orders, projects, business processes, and activities for costs planning.

> Powerful integration among different SAP components significantly improves the effectiveness of costs and revenue planning. Planned costs from different components can be transferred using transfer programs or can be recorded automatically with the help of integrated planning.

> Considerable efficiency improvements can be achieved in the planning process by using planning aids such as template and formula planning, transfer programs to transfer relevant costs from nonfi-

nancial SAP components, distribution keys to distribute annual and quarterly plan values, and so on.

> You can carry out planning and budgeting in multiple currencies whether you're in a global company with locations in different countries or in a company that needs to plan procurement and similar costs in different currencies.

The next three chapters explore the powerful functionality of different SAP components in the area of Financial Supply Chain Management (FSCM). The next chapter starts with credit, collections, and dispute management.

Collections, Dispute, and Credit Management

Cash flow is essential for every business. Financial managers work daily to reduce the time gap between payables and receivables to ensure efficient management of their working capital and to maximize cash availability. Everyone knows that delays in receiving payments from customers can disrupt the finely orchestrated balance of working capital, causing even the best companies to run into cash flow problems. And even if companies invest in assessing and establishing the creditworthiness of their customers, there is no guarantee of timely payments.

Regardless of the timing or reason, justified or unjustified, customer disputes do occur, and their identification, processing, and resolution involve high costs and time delays. Most of the time, disputes are identified only at the time of processing customer payments, which itself may be a late payment. This is why companies need a system that allows them to synchronize cash flows; provide better control and predictability for their working capital requirements, offer efficient payment processing and customer collections, include effective dispute handling; and implement flexible, easy-to-use and easy-to-monitor credit policies.

To give you this power, SAP ERP Financials provides the Financial Supply Chain Management (FSCM) components (Figure 15.1). These components give you the necessary visibility and control of all your cash-related processes. So let's talk about how you can use them for credit management, dispute management, and collections management.

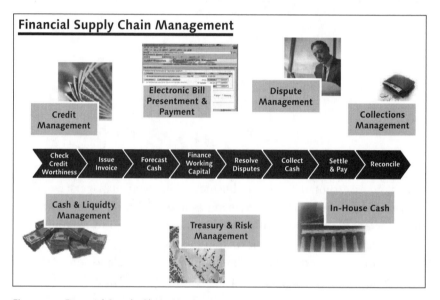

Figure 15.1 Financial Supply Chain Management

Overview

The problem with many other systems that support, or claim to support, similar requirements is that they are unable to adequately address some of the challenges faced by today's global and complex business environments. The FSCM components easily address complex issues, such as managing head office and branch office relationships of customer organizations, integrating with AR systems to automatically update corresponding disputes or collection issues, or consolidating data from multiple operational systems for credit management, dispute management, or collections management.

SAP Credit Management gives you the functionality for effective receivables and credit management by combining information from multiple Sales and Distribution (SD), Logistics Execution (LE), and Financial Accounting systems and comparing it with predefined credit limits and other customizable criteria. SAP Dispute Management controls and streamlines dispute processing by acting as a central component for handling dispute cases and enabling cross-departmental dispute resolution.

On the other hand, SAP Collections Management allows you to proactively manage your receivables by strategically determining customer follow-ups as well as recording and managing collection activities.

For relatively simple implementations with basic requirements, the limited functionality or workarounds available in the AR component may be sufficient. For example, customer disputes can be entered as sales activities, and collections can be carried out by means of the dunning functionality. You can also enter comments and descriptive texts in individual documents or in the customer master to record results of customer contacts. The functionality provided in earlier versions of SAP ERP did a fair job of meeting basic credit management requirements, and SAP ERP 6.0 continues to support that credit management functionality.

Functionality in previous versions

 Techtalk

FSCM components of SAP ERP 6.0 require SAP NetWeaver Application Server, SAP NetWeaver Exchange Infrastructure (XI), and the development of enhancements to enable its integration with SAP AR, SD, and other SAP components.

However, as you'll see in the next section, the newer functionality supported by the SAP ERP Financials FSCM components provide a more robust, open, integrated, and cross-system framework to meet more complex and advanced requirements. The main advantage for large companies is that these components can be installed on separate systems and can be integrated to collect data from other SAP applications that may be on different releases.

Functions in Detail

In this section, we'll talk about how SAP FSCM components can improve efficiency and streamline operations when you manage credit, disputes, and collections. Let's start with your organization's business requirements for managing credit.

Credit Management Requirements

Credit segments

From an organization's point of view, managing credit consists of formulating an effective credit management policy, which determines the areas of responsibility for credit management, the criteria on which credit limits of customers are determined, and the scenarios in which any further business with customers is considered at risk. In FSCM, credit segments are used by companies to differentiate credit managing, monitoring, and reporting based on criteria such as divisions, business segments, and so on. Credit limits for business partners are maintained in credit segment currency. For example, a software development company may use different credit segments for its sales, product support, and consulting business segments, or a staffing company in North America may use different segments for the United States (USD) and Canada (Canadian Dollars).

Using credit rating services

Credit-relevant information for business partners (business partners in SAP FSCM credit management correspond to customers defined in SAP SD) is managed in their credit profiles. Figure 15.2 shows an example of a credit profile for a business partner. Credit groups enable you to group your business partners for reporting purposes, such as domestic/foreign customers, small/medium/large customers, etc. Using credit ratings you can ascertain creditworthiness of a business partner.

You can also establish your own methods to determine the credit ratings of your business partners; however, most large companies choose to obtain credit ratings of their business partners from external information providers such as financial institutions or government agencies and then integrate that information in the credit management component. Because different rating agencies typically use different rating notations, FSCM provides you with the functionality to assign ranks to each of these ratings. Using ranking, you can map external ratings from different providers into a common, consistent measure to use in credit management. To use an example from Figure 15.2, you can assign the internal ranking of 002 (and interpret it as Good Credit) to credit ratings received from Moody's (Baa3), FICA (537), and D&B (2).

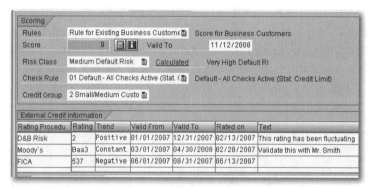

Figure 15.2 Credit Profile of a Business Partner

For internal controls, you can block a business partner in the credit management component for things such as fraud, insolvency, and bad payment history, and you can also record whether a business partner has filed for bankruptcy or if foreclosure proceedings have been initiated. Using all this information in addition to a black list and a white list (also called a negative list and a premium list, respectively) of business partners, you can influence the calculation and results of credit scores and credit limits. Let's look at these calculations in more detail.

Black list and white list of customers

Calculation of Credit Limit

Continuing to refer to Figure 15.2, credit management uses freely definable and customizable formulae in the credit rule to determine the internal credit score for a business partner. Using this credit score, it automatically determines the risk class that represents the grouping of

Credit risk determination

business partners from the perspective of credit risk, such as low risk, medium risk, high risk, and so on. Finally, using other formulae (also freely definable and customizable) associated with the credit rule, the system calculates and proposes a credit limit in each credit segment for a business partner. Of course, you can override credit scores and credit limits proposed by the system.

This completely flexible design provides what you need to define credit rules that can automatically calculate credit limits for a large number of business partners and can be as complex or as simple as required to meet the specific requirements of your industry and your company. In the credit rule formulae, you can use several different criteria from the business partner credit profile and other calculated values. For example, these formulae can be based on parameters such as industry sector, nationality, occupation, sex, street, postal code, region, foreclosure, bankruptcy, country, affidavit, risk class, credit score (to calculate credit limit), credit segment, and so on.

Ex **Example**

Here is an example of credit rule formulae:

> If Business Partner in "white list" → Score = 100
> If Foreclosure or Bankruptcy exists in customer master → Score = 35
> If Credit Segment = "IRAQ" → Limit = $100,000,000,000.00
> If Legal Form is "INC" or "LLC" → Limit = 50000 * Score
> If D&B Rating is between 0 and 10 → Limit = 21000–(Score * 8.5)

All these formulae are defined in a credit rule with a validity period (six months, year, etc.) that enables you to easily ascertain if the credit score and credit limit are still valid or whether they need to be recalculated. Using mass change functionality, you can efficiently calculate and update credit rules, credit scores, credit limits, and checking rules (discussed later) for large numbers of business partners.

Notification of changes Because you can manually override a credit score, credit limit, and other automatically calculated parameters, you can also use SAP Business Workflow to automatically trigger a notification to a credit analyst if sensitive credit-related data is changed for a business partner.

Credit Check and Monitoring

After the credit management functionality in FSCM is activated, a credit check is carried out in real time in SAP SD and AR by using checking rules.

Checking Rules

The credit profile of every business partner includes a checking rule used to calculate its credit exposure. These checking rules are freely definable and consist of a sequential execution of one or more of the following checks:

> Credit check based on credit insurance, collateral, and other information

> Credit check based on maximum document value to ensure that order or delivery values can't exceed certain value (e.g., for new customers)

> Dynamic credit check that only evaluates credit exposure within a specific time frame (credit horizon)

> Credit check based on maximum dunning level reached (refer to Chapter 2 for more details on dunning process in SAP)

> Credit check based on the maximum age of oldest open item

> Credit check based on payment behavior index calculated using DSO (Day Sales Outstanding)

If the available checking rules and credit limit calculations aren't sufficient for your credit management processes, you can create your own routines to influence credit limit check calculations.

To meet the diverse requirements of different companies in different industries, you can carry out credit checks at the time of creation (or modification) of a sales order, goods delivery, or goods issue. Determining the most appropriate option for you depends on your business and your industry. Typical time frames among order creation,

Checking against available credit limits

delivery creation, and (if applicable) goods issue also influence this decision. For example, for an airline or shipping industry, these time frames can span years; for make-to-order manufacturers, it can be months; and for e-commerce companies, it can be a few days or almost instantaneous (e.g., purchasing and electronically downloading software). Credit limits are checked in real time and are updated in credit management to calculate credit exposure.

Credit Exposure

Calculation of exposure

For every credit segment, you can choose whether credit exposure calculations should be calculated based on open sales orders, open deliveries, open invoices, or open accounts receivables. Factors discussed before that influence when to carry out the credit check and are also relevant in determining how to calculate credit exposure. Additionally, credit management provides you with the unique functionality to evaluate the credit exposure of a business partner by different categories, such as open orders, open deliveries, open billing documents, open receivables, and so on. Figure 15.3 shows an example of a credit exposure report. This type of information provides you with a more detailed view. For example, during a credit block the details help you determine whether to release the transaction for further processing, temporarily increase the credit limit, or reject the transaction.

Reports in Credit Management

In addition to credit exposure, additional reports and evaluations let you analyze credit profiles, credit segments, and credit limit use by business partners. Additional information available for business partner analysis includes criteria such as dunning level and dunning amount, date and amount of last payment, date and amount of oldest open item, highest balance and total sales volume in the past 12 months, gross total of payments with or without a cash discount, and average arrears in payments, etc. Detailed logs and extracts help you understand the system response based on the transactional information received from other components.

Credit Exposure

Partr	Cr.Seg	BP Message	Name of Cr. Exp. Cat.	Seg Exp	Curre	Cr. Expos.	Mess
CMS1	0000	CMS0000001	Open Orders	23,173.84	EUR	28,768.00	USD
		CMS0000001	Open Items from FI	5,799.90	EUR	7,200.00	USD
		CMS0000001	Delivery Value	5,373.43	EUR	6,670.58	USD
	0000			34,347.17	EUR	42,638.58	USD
	3000	CMS0000001	Open Orders	28,768.00	USD	28,768.00	USD
		CMS0000001	Open Items from FI	7,200.00	USD	7,200.00	USD
		CMS0000001	Delivery Value	6,670.58	USD	6,670.58	USD
	3000			42,638.58	USD	42,638.58	USD
CMS1				34,347.17	EUR	85,277.16	USD
				42,638.58	USD		
CMS2	0000	CMS0000002	Open Items from FI	24,971.81	EUR	31,000.00	USD
		CMS0000003	Open Items from FI	13,291.45	EUR	16,500.00	USD
		CMS0000010	Open Orders	73,370.85	EUR	73,370.85	EUR
		CMS0000010	Open Items from FI	168,358.31	EUR	209,000.00	USD
		CMS0000011	Open Items from FI	10,472.05	EUR	13,000.00	USD
		CMS0000012	Open Items from FI	233,607.22	EUR	290,000.00	USD
	0000			524,071.69	EUR	73,370.85	EUR
						559,500.00	USD
	3000	CMS0000002	Open Items from FI	31,000.00	USD	31,000.00	USD
	3000			31,000.00	USD	31,000.00	USD
CMS2				524,071.69	EUR	73,370.85	EUR
				31,000.00	USD	590,500.00	USD

Figure 15.3 Credit Exposure Report

Even though the credit management functionality is much improved and enhanced, SAP ERP 6.0 also supports the original credit management functionality that was available in SAP R/3 versions.

Comparison with SAP R/3 Credit Management

Although not as advanced and flexible as the functionality of the credit management component, the functionality of previous SAP R/3 versions is still sufficient, if your company's credit management requirements are relatively simple. Instead of credit segments, R/3 credit management uses credit control areas to subdivide credit management from an organizational point of view; the credit rules engine isn't available, so you have to maintain credit rating and credit limits individually for every customer. And instead of complex checking rules, you have to choose from limited options that meet most basic credit checking requirements. Table 15.1 compares these two functions.

	R/3 Credit Management	FSCM Credit Management
Master data	Customer account in AR	Comprehensive functionality of SAP Business Partner
Financial data	Only from AR	From AR, contracts accounting, and others
Monitoring of credit exposure	For simple one Financial and one SD system	Across multiple Financial, SD, and CRM systems
Customer scoring and rating	Not available	Credit rules engine
External credit rating information	Only through third-party, partner products	Support for any XML-based service
Rule-based definition of credit limits	Not available (you manually assign credit limits to customers)	Credit rules engine
Support for Business Workflow	Only in SD system	Workflow capability for any credit event
Analysis capability	Customer fact sheet and other R/3 reports	Credit Manager Portal, including support for NetWeaver BI
Connectivity to non-SAP systems	Not available	Connectivity possible through XI Server

Table 15.1 Comparison of Credit Management Functionality

Regardless of the credit management system being used, the credit-worthiness of a customer and a successful credit check doesn't guarantee receipt of payments. Customers may dispute and withhold payment or underpay invoices for any number of reasons. You can use the dispute management component to manage such disputes.

Dispute Management Overview

A customer dispute can arise at any stage, including order processing, order fulfillment, invoicing, or later. The dispute can be for any reason, such as late delivery, quality issues, or to force resolution to other issues. The dispute may be communicated in any form such as calling customer support, sending a complaint letter, or withholding invoice payments. In this section, we'll only focus on using dispute management to manage and monitor customer issues and disputes based on payment deductions. The dispute management component helps you manage dispute cases and provides robust integration with SAP Accounts Receivable.

At the core of the dispute management component are completely flexible and fully customizable dispute case templates that you can use to efficiently create dispute cases relevant for your business. It also offers several pieces of information that you can include, record, calculate, or reference in a dispute case (see Figure 15.4).

Roles in Dispute Management

You can enter business partner information and contact information directly in a dispute case or let the system automatically copy it from AR. To effectively manage cross-departmental coordination for dispute resolution, a dispute case differentiates among the three roles of a processor, a coordinator, and a person responsible, which all can be different from an employee who creates a dispute case. A *coordinator* is the central contact person and is responsible for resolution of the dispute case, for example, a customer support representative. A *person responsible* is typically the person that is impacted financially if the dispute hasn't been resolved, for example, a cost center manager. Whereas a *processor* is typically the person responsible for processing or carrying out an activity and can change as dispute resolution moves through different stages.

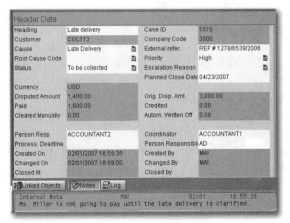

Header Data					
Heading	Late delivery		Case ID	1075	
Customer	COL112		Company Code	3000	
Cause	Late Delivery		External refer.	REF # 1278/6539/2006	
Root Cause Code			Priority	High	
Status	To be collected		Escalation Reason		
			Planned Close Date	04/23/2007	
Currency	USD				
Disputed Amount	1,400.00		Orig. Disp. Amt	3,000.00	
Paid	1,600.00		Credited	0.00	
Cleared Manually	0.00		Autom. Written Off	0.00	
Person Resp.	ACCOUNTANT2		Coordinator	ACCOUNTANT1	
Process. Deadline			Person Responsibl	AD	
Created On	02/01/2007 16:55:35		Created By	MAI	
Changed On	02/01/2007 18:09:00		Changed By	MAI	
Closed At			Closed by		

Linked Objects   Notes   Log

Internal Note   MAI   02/01   16:55:35
Ms. Miller is not going to pay until the late delivery is clarified.

Figure 15.4 Information in a Dispute Case

Example

> For a dispute about shipping charges for a delayed shipment, a coordinator may first assign shipping personnel as a processor, who confirms that the shipment was delayed; followed by account manager as a processor, who decides that credit for shipping charges should be given; and lastly someone in AR as a processor, to processes credit to the customer.

Other unique characteristics of dispute cases include the following:

> For easy auditing, reconciliation, and communication, you can track several different amounts associated with a dispute case such as original dispute amount, current disputed amount (which can be different if the dispute has been partially resolved), amount paid, amount credited back to the customer, amount adjusted (cleared) manually, and amount written off.

> You can carry out powerful root cause analysis by assigning root cause to a dispute case in addition to a reason for dispute. For example, dispute reasons can be late delivery, but the root cause of this problem may be supplier or transportation issues.

> With every dispute case, you can maintain different types of notes such as customer description, additional description, internal note, internal reply, concluding remark, customer reply, and so on.

> You can create case search profiles to make it easier for employees to search for dispute cases using information relevant to them. This is in addition to the standard personalized "My Dispute Cases" worklist for an employee where he is identified as coordinator, processor, or person responsible.

Dispute case Myworklist

> If necessary, you can restrict visibility of the information in a dispute case and attached documents based on user role and authorizations.

Another extremely useful functionality of a dispute case is its ability to store and link all relevant documents and objects for case processing. So, you can associate customer information, credit information, the original invoice from the Sales or CRM application and many other documents and links (see Figure 15.5) that help you process a dispute as accurately and quickly as possible.

In the next section, we'll discuss processing of a case.

Figure 15.5 Linked Objects in a Dispute Case

Processing a Dispute Case

Processing a dispute case is largely controlled by its processing status. SAP FSCM provides you with status management functionality that you can customize to determine the routing and processing of a dispute case in different stages. For example, a utility company may

Status Management

use a status management process that routes a customer complaint through processing stages of new, information requested, waiting for response, under investigation, closed or voided, confirmed, and so on. Status management also controls which actions you can take depending on the status of a case. So, you can decide, for example, whether a case that has been "voided" can be reopened by changing its status back to "in-process."

Business Workflow for dispute processing

You can simplify dispute case processing even further by combining it with SAP Business Workflow, which enables you to automatically and electronically notify the appropriate employee. For example when a case coordinator assigns AP personnel as a processor, he automatically receives an email indicating that his action is required on a dispute case. After the necessary action is completed (e.g., credit posted to customer account), he can update the status and return the case back to the case coordinator. Sometimes, a dispute case needs to be escalated because either a case processor isn't responding to the action request, an irate customer calls repeatedly, or case resolution is taking longer than an internally established benchmark.

Regardless of the reason, in dispute management, you can assign an escalation reason to a dispute case to inform the supervisor, manager, or other employees that a dispute case has reached a critical stage. Similarly, you can add or modify new customers, business partners, open invoices, disputed items, and information while processing a case. Depending on the dispute case template you're using, you can customize which functions are available while processing a dispute case.

So let's see how you can generate different correspondence while processing a dispute case.

Correspondence

Processing correspondence

As we discussed before, different actions taken on a dispute case generate different types of external and internal correspondence. For example, a credit card company that receives a call for a disputed charge typically sends out printed letters to the customer in the beginning and in the end to inform about the receipt of complaint and the results of the internal investigation. Or, when a case gets assigned to remote account managers, they may be informed by fax of relevant information about the case. To manage the processing of relevant correspondence activities, you can use the powerful Post Processing Framework (PPF) that works behind the scenes.

Necessary correspondence can be triggered automatically, or the processor, coordinator, or person responsible can initiate it manually. The template associated with a dispute case type controls several factors relevant for correspondence such as available types of correspondence, whether they are triggered automatically, what triggers the correspondence, and how they are processed (e.g., fax, printout, email, SAP Business Workflow). Typically, as part of day-end processing, you can collectively process all correspondence requests.

Because the dispute management functionality primarily focuses on customer issues that are translated into payment deductions, it's fully integrated with the SAP AR component.

Integration of Dispute Management

The strength of the dispute management component is evident in its integration with SAP AR—particularly, the ability to automatically create dispute cases from AR items and the ability to update and take action on open dispute cases based on activities in a customer account. In its simplest form, this integration enables you to create a dispute case directly from commonly used AR programs such as while processing an open line-item list, a customer account clearing, and incoming payments. Similarly, from a dispute case, you can access open items in a customer account and insert their reference to the dispute case.

Automatic creation of dispute cases

Additionally, a highly sophisticated program that can automatically create dispute cases in dispute management based on residual items created in AR is provided. Typically, these residual items on a customer account are created as a result of payment activity such as incoming payments, lockbox processing, bank statement processing, electronic check processing, and so on. The criteria, logic, and default values for dispute cases are determined based on a custom interface integrating

AR with dispute management and default parameters (case type, reason, priority, etc.) specified in the system configuration.

 Tip

> Refer to Chapter 2 and Chapter 5 for more details on incoming payments, lockbox processing, bank statement processing, electronic check processing, account clearing, residual items, and more.

Automatic reopening of dispute cases

Additionally, payment activities in a customer account automatically update relevant dispute cases. For example, if a dispute case is created for $500, and a customer pays $100, the corresponding dispute case is updated so that the original dispute amount remains $500, but the current dispute amount changes to $400, and the paid amount is updated with $100. Dispute cases are also updated based on manual account clearing or credit memo processing. This type of integration also enables you to take corrective actions. Consider an example of a dispute case that is marked as closed based on a customer check payment processed in accounting. Subsequently, if the bank rejects the check, and the invoice becomes unpaid again, that information can be used to automatically reopen the corresponding dispute case in dispute management!

Another helpful functionality is the automatic write-off of dispute amounts. The logic and criteria used by this write-off program can be influenced using custom development. For creating an accounting entry for write-off, the program determines the corresponding GL account based on the reason assigned to a dispute case and the corresponding cost center based on the person responsible assigned to a dispute case. Similarly, a custom development can be used to automatically close dispute cases that meet certain criteria, for example, cases that are in the status "customer reply requested" for more than 60 days.

Whereas dispute management assists you in managing your receivables after recognizing customer dispute, the collections management component helps you with proactively initiating contacts for due or overdue receivables.

Collections Management Overview

Collections management supports the evaluation and prioritization of receivables based on collections strategies to help you follow up with customers for payment reminders and record their response in the system for follow-up actions. Collections management uses freely definable and customizable collection strategies to automatically prepare daily worklists with relevant information for all collection specialists, that is, employees responsible for follow-up with customers and collections. Because collection strategies are at the core of the collection management component, let's dig deeper.

Collection Strategies

Collection strategies (see Figure 15.6) primarily consist of collection rules that are used to select, evaluate, and prioritize customer receivables and create worklists for collection specialists. Collection rules reflect the reason a customer is to be contacted. A collection rule formulates the prerequisites and conditions that a customer must fulfill to be included in the collection processing. Various collection rules are delivered based on the following:

> Total of all items overdue since "n" days

> Amount of individual items overdue since "n" days or due within "n" days

> Total amount to be collected

> Customer has paid less than minimum amount since "n" days

> Customer has items in legal dunning procedure

Overdue Periods	Due Date Periods				
Overdue Period 1	[ ] 1	To	30	Days	
Overdue Period 2	[ ] 31	To	60	Days	
Overdue Period 3	[ ] 61	To	90	Days	
Overdue Period 4	≥ 91	To		Days	

Assignment of Rules			
Collection Rule	Val	Name of Prerequisite	Name of Condition
CR0000002A	25	Risk Class A, B	Total of all items overdue since 30 days: Total amount larger than 5,000.00 USD
CR0000002A	25	Risk Class C, D, E	Total of all items overdue since 15 days: Total amount larger than 2,000.00 USD
CR00000003	20		Individual items overdue since 30 days: Amount larger than 1,000.00 USD
CR00000013	15		Broken Promises to Pay: Total amount larger than 10.00 USD
CR00000018	5		There is a resubmission due for the customer

Figure 15.6 Collection Strategies

Customer receivables are selected for further processing if they satisfy one or more of these rules. You can even use rules as prerequisites for evaluating other rules. For example, you can prepare a rule that selects an item overdue for 5 days, only if the corresponding customer is also deemed a high credit risk. The process than evaluates selected items and assigns valuation points, which represent a number assigned by you to indicate the weight associated with a collection rule. For example, you may assign 5 points for total amounts between $100 and $1,000, 15 points for total amounts between $1,000 and $5,000, 25 points for total amounts more than $5,000, and so on. Selected customers are evaluated based on these valuation points. To avoid abnormally skewing the final results, you can specify maximum valuation points that a collection strategy can assign to a customer.

 Tip

A collection strategy can be customized so that it factors in payment terms offered to customers (10 % in 10 days, 5 % in 20 days, Net 30 days) while evaluating and reporting amounts to be collected.

Finally, so you can focus on receivables that are at higher risk, the report to create the worklist prioritizes customers based on the percentage ratio of their evaluation. The priorities are also freely definable, so you can evaluate customers as A, B, C, or Very High Risk, High Risk, and Medium Risk. Final worklists for collections specialists are created using all this information.

Collection profiles From an organizational point of view, the flexible design of the collection management processes makes them easily configurable and scalable regardless of the size and structure of your organization. Your companies are grouped into collection segments (similar to the credit segments discussed before), and collection segments are grouped into one or more collection profiles. Similarly, collection specialists are grouped into collection groups, which are in turn associated with a collection profile. So, a small start-up pharmaceutical company may use only one collection segment with one employee performing the roles of collections specialist and collections manager. Whereas decentralized collection processing at a multinational financial institution with hundreds of collection specialists may require multiple collection segments worldwide, each comprised of local companies and associated with a group of collection managers and collection specialists.

While preparing worklists for collection specialists, the report determines the default collections group based on the collection profile associated with a company. All specialists in a collection group collect open receivables with the same collection strategy, which helps collections managers ensure that the performance of all specialists in a group is evaluated using the same basis. Let's discuss the collections worklist and activities in more detail.

Collections Worklists

Worklists are created based on a default collections group and collections specialists associated with a collections profile. An easy maintenance program enables you to assign a substitute collections specialist if the main collections specialist is unavailable for any reason. Additionally, you can use the distribution method enhancement to allocate unassigned receivables items to collection specialists who have fewer numbers of items in their worklist or who have a worklist with a lower evaluation score and thus possibly quicker, easier interactions with customers. From worklists, collections specialists can easily branch out to a detail screen (see Figure 15.7) that shows them all relevant customer information and supports various collection activities. The details include customer contact information, past payments, open invoices, and due as well as overdue receivables conveniently grouped into different time periods (< 5 days, 5–15 days, 15+ days, etc.).

Distributing collections workload

Collection activities and their outcome can take different forms. For example, a collections specialist may not be able to reach the customer, or a customer may request later follow-up, highlight a dispute, or promise to make payment by a specific date. The collections management component provides support for recording, managing, and reporting different types of custom-defined collection activity results such as customer contact not necessary, customer could not be reached, message left on answering machine, promised to pay, customer dispute, and so on.

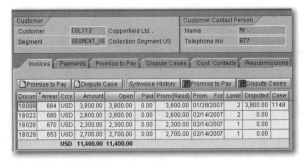

Figure 15.7 Collection Activities

Collections Activities

Promise-to-pay | If a customer responds by promising to pay one or more invoices, you can create promise-to-pay records in collections management with the promised amount and promised date of payment. Even if you enter the promise information for multiple invoices, Collections Management tracks it at the individual invoice level. The strong integration between AR and collections management ensures that when incoming payments from customers are processed, promise-to-pay records are updated with the appropriate status depending on whether the promised amount was paid in full (status = kept), in part (status = partially broken), or not at all (status = broken). You also have an option to maintain tolerance days so that if a payment is received within a certain number of days, the promise is still considered as kept. This can help you, for example, with payments that are promised on Friday but are received on Monday. By using appropriate collection rules, you can make sure that partially broken or broken promises show up on the collections worklist again. Figure 15.8 shows an example of entering a promise-to-pay record.

Figure 15.8 Promise-to-Pay Record

Another fairly common result of a collections activity is a request by the customer to follow up or call again after some time period. For this purpose, you can create resubmission requests and specify the date when the item should be included in the collections worklist again. Similarly, you can record any customer disputes by creating dispute cases and any other information in detailed notes with each collection activity. A processing screen presented to a collections specialist always shows all details, including priority, outstanding amount, amount to be collected, amount promised, amount broken, amount under dispute, amount already dunned, last dunning date, last payment date, last contact date, and so on.

Apart from these activities carried out by collections specialists, processes are also available for collections managers. Because creation of an appropriate collections worklist is completely dependent on the accurate definition of collection strategies, from time to time collections supervisors can tweak the strategies to adapt to customer payment patterns. Similarly, supervisors can analyze the performance of collection specialists in his group by using a worklist statistics report that shows daily open items, successful customer contacts, attempted customer contacts, and so on for each collections specialist.

In the next section, we'll explore integration of the collections management component with other SAP components.

Collections Management Integration

Similar to other SAP components, collections management is also fully integrated with other relevant SAP components. We already discussed how, because of this integration, incoming payments in AR automatically update promise-to-pay records created in collections management. For this integrated process to work seamlessly, you are provided with a program that can be enhanced to synchronize customer data in AR with business partners' data for collections management. Similarly, a mass change program lets you update collection profiles in business masters. Other customer master data that is available in collections management include dunning levels to exclude customers from collections processing if legal proceedings have already been initiated against them, payment authorization to exclude those customers from collections processing who have authorized direct debit of their bank accounts, and so on.

Collections management is also linked with the credit management and dispute management components. We already discussed how a collections specialist can create a dispute case while processing a collections worklist. Similarly, in dispute management, if a dispute is unjustified, and the amount should be collected from customers, you can set the status of that dispute case as "to be collected."

This integrated functionality is evident in the definition of collection strategies, which can consist of collection rules based on the following:

> AR data such as open items, dunning and payments information, customer master information, and so on

> Dispute management data such as the status of a dispute case and the disputed amount at the individual invoice level

> Credit management data such as risk class, credit limit, use of credit limits, etc.

> Collections management data such as promise-to-pay amount, contact data resubmission data, and so on

Case Study

This regional bank based out of the southeastern United States operates 37 retail banking branches in 4 neighboring states. It's primarily focused on consumer products and services, including bank accounts and consumer credit cards. The bank has recently started to offer corporate banking products to small- and medium-sized businesses in the area and expects to grow by 25 % in that segment over the next 5 years.

Business Challenges

Even though the company's consumer credit cards business was the most lucrative and had the most potential to grow, it also generated a large number of consumer inquiries, disputes, and chargebacks. After implementing SAP five years ago, the bank had seen measurable efficiency improvement in its backend operations and frontend, customer-facing systems. However, disputes and chargebacks were still processed manually for the most part, and that processing was costly, cumbersome, and time-consuming. Each month, the customer support center of the bank received approximately 400 calls for disputes and chargebacks. It took a relatively large staff on an average, 17 days to resolve each case. This delay translated into an increase in the volume of impatient consumers calling multiple times to check the status of the same case, which in turn also meant increased capacity requirements for the customer service group.

The resolution process required searching for information in disparate sources and rekeying and keeping track of the information in a complicated, convoluted, hodgepodge of internally developed systems. More time was wasted in searching for and filing information than was spent in making informed decisions to move forward in the dispute-resolution process. Decisions and supporting information was scattered across physical printouts and file folders, faxes, Excel documents, Word documents, and internal emails.

With the business strategy anticipating and demanding growth in the consumer credit cards segment, an increase in number of disputes and chargebacks was inevitable. So, the bank decided it was time to implement an automated and more sophisticated dispute-management system that could provide the required functionality to process dispute cases efficiently and quickly.

Solution Deployment

The bank decided to use a standalone server system for installing SAP dispute management because for their frontend and backend systems, they were still using SAP R/3 4.6C. The project plan and budget allocation was already made to upgrade the system to SAP ERP 6.0. However, that project was not expected to go live for another year considering the sensitive nature of financial information that they were involved in and keeping in mind all of the rules and regulations they had to comply with. On the other hand, the implementation of the dispute management component was a quick nine-week implementation requiring one full-time and one part-time internal SAP resource, and dedicated business representatives responsible for getting this project through. The payback of an efficient dispute management system was deemed higher even after factoring in system changes required after the upgrade to ERP 6.0.

Considerable time of the project was spent in deciding and designing three aspects of the system: a dispute case template that included all relevant information, identifying all different types of documents that can be/should be linked to a dispute case, and SAP Business Workflow for processing and escalating dispute cases. Benchmark time limits were established for different types of dispute cases and different stages of case processing.

Personnel at the central customer service center and those responsible for dispute management and dispute resolution were trained to ensure that all dispute cases were entered, managed, processed, and resolved using consistent business processes. Employees were requested to enter any relevant data, comments, notes, communication records, documents, or anything related to a case as soon as possible to the appropriate dispute case. The root cause reasons, although not necessarily as detailed and as many for a manufacturing company, were established to analyze the types of disputes and identify any procedural changes that could be made.

Another aspect of the project that consumed considerable time was developing interfaces to convert dispute cases from the current system to the SAP dispute management component. It was decided to convert not only currently open cases but also dispute cases of the past two years. Of course, this also meant carrying out the time-consuming but necessary activity of searching for relevant information and electronically converting it to a format that can be linked to a case in dispute management.

Value Achieved

Definite, measurable benefits were visible soon after the dispute management software was implemented and stabilized. Even though information for old cases is still being converted and loaded into the system, for the new dispute cases, the average processing time was reduced by five days, which is an improvement of almost 33 %. Even though currently there has not been any reduction in staff personnel, after the backlog is cleared, and processes are streamlined, the resource requirement is expected to reduce.

Considerable improvement in efficiency and decision making was achieved by designing and implementing SAP Business Workflow along with dispute management. The workflow process ensured that if an employee processing a dispute case was unavailable, it got assigned to another employee with a lower workload. Managers were easily able to identify cases that were stuck at any particular stage for too long and take the necessary action to move it forward. Previously, the escalation process was unstructured and unorganized, many times resulting in consumers closing their accounts before managers had a chance to review and respond to them. With the new process combined with the escalation feature in the dispute management component, everybody involved with the case was immediately made aware if the case needed more urgent attention.

And, of course, everyone involved simply loved the comprehensive access to all relevant information from a single system in a structured and consistent manner. An employee was able to add comments, add information, or attach relevant files to a dispute case at any time, which resulted in greater transparency in dispute processing. It also allowed the dispute coordinator to promptly and accurately respond to status requests from consumers. Now employees were spending more time making effective dispute resolution decisions than searching for or filing information.

Looking Ahead

The bank is evaluating the SAP collections management component to see if it can be used to improve business processes involving its new corporate banking products. Because the bank engages in business with large numbers of small- and medium-sized businesses, one of the major benefits of such an implementation will be the bank's ability to automatically prepare prioritized worklists for collections follow-up. The IT department is still in the process of building a proof-of-concept and cost-benefit analysis for such an implementation, but initial results seem encouraging.

Summary

The credit management, dispute management, and collections management components of SAP ERP Financials FSCM provide you with many features and functionalities to improve the efficiency of your cash management:

> Using the advanced credit rules engine, you can automatically evaluate, calculate, and maintain credit scores and credit limits for business partners.

> You can control credit risk via real-time credit allocation to operational transactions, ongoing monitoring, and flexible reporting to evaluate credit exposure based on different internal and external criteria.

> Optimize, streamline, and accelerate cross-departmental dispute resolution, and use root cause analysis to uncover flaws in existing business processes.

> Using the collections management functionality, you can increase the share of collected receivables, avoid or reduce write-offs, and increase on-time payments.

> Using efficient dispute management and proactive collections management, you can reduce your average DSO (Days Sales Outstanding), increase customer profitability and improve working capital forecast

In the next chapter, we'll look at the functionality available in Cash and Liquidity Management, another SAP ERP Financials FSCM component.

16

Cash and Liquidity Management

Financial planning has become increasingly important in the new global economy where reduction in working capital and the effective use of liquidity can considerably influence the future course of a company. Being aware of cash and liquidity information in a timely fashion helps a business take necessary actions to maximize returns and reduce costs. This is especially true for global companies operating in multi-currency environments, where such information can help them manage risks associated with exchange rate and interest rate fluctuations around the world.

Even though almost all companies recognize and acknowledge the need for having such information, the operational hurdles make it difficult for many to achieve their objectives. Multiple systems, inconsistent processes, different sources of information, as well as difficulty in recording and comparing actual data with planned numbers in a timely manner, impact the optimum use of funds. The cash and liquidity management component of SAP can help you streamline your cash planning and liquidity forecasting processes.

Overview

As shown in Figure 16.1, effective cash management not only involves analyzing current and short-term cash and liquidity positions but also managing banking activities by improving transactional efficiency. For example, by switching from manual payments to electronic payments, you can use your funds for a few more days, or by using SAP to (at least partially) automate bank account reconciliation, you free up valuable time and resources that can focus on more value-added cash management activities. By using lockbox processing or a similar electronic interface for processing payments from your customers, you can collect your receivables quicker and thus improve the availability of working capital.

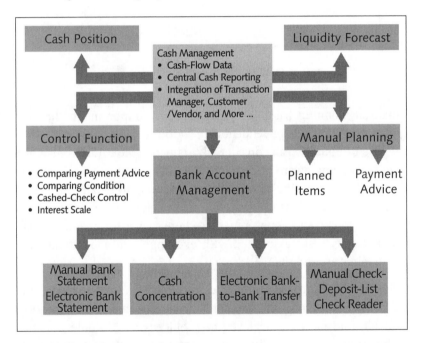

Figure 16.1 Cash Management Overview

The electronic payments, bank statement reconciliation, lockbox, and other banking transactions have been discussed in detail in Chapter 5 "Bank Accounting." Additionally, Chapter 3 "Receivables and Payables" discussed AR and AP processes such as self-billing, ERS (Evaluated Receipt Settlement), invoicing plans, and billing plans that can be used to improve working capital management.

The financial planning process starts with gathering relevant transactional data and organizing it by current and expected payment inflows and outflows. SAP provides a completely customizable framework to structure cash position and liquidity forecast statements to meet your business requirements. By using seamless integration with your banking partners, you can monitor daily bank account balances for available funds and prepare liquidity forecasts that are as accurate as possible.

After cash position and liquidity forecast statements are finalized, the advanced cash concentration functionality helps you prepare fund transfer proposals that you can review and manage payment flows that are anticipated but not yet recorded in the system. Fund transfer proposals can be easily converted into payment advices, which in turn can be used by the payment program to post relevant accounting entries and also generate electronic fund transfer requests for your banking partners.

For medium- and long-term liquidity planning and risk management, SAP helps you create customizable planning structures that best meet your financial planning requirements and compare actual payment flows to the planned liquidity, so that you can take proactive and corrective actions. Let's look at this functionality in more detail.

Functions in Detail

As we'll discuss later, the cash management component is provided for preparing short-term cash positions and liquidity forecasts, and the liquidity planner is used for medium- to long-term liquidity planning. As we've already discussed, the bank accounting component provides additional capabilities such as electronic payments and bank statement processing that can further improve your cash management and working capital management.

Levels of cash management

Even though data collection for cash management in SAP needs to be enabled for each company, the analysis and reporting is possible for lower organizational levels such as branch, location, and division of the company, as well as higher organizational levels such as groups of companies, geographical regions, and countries. In this section, we'll discuss how SAP is able to gather relevant data from transactional systems and provide near real-time access to cash management information, followed by the cash concentration process. At the end, we'll discuss available functionality for medium- and long-term liquidity planning. Let's start with the planning process first.

Planning Process

You can use the comprehensive functionality to define cash management statements that meet your business requirements. Defining multiple, customizable statements make it possible for treasury and finance managers to obtain and analyze information that only pertains to their responsibility area; whether it consists of branch offices, regional offices, or worldwide companies with a centralized treasury.

To prepare cash management statements that are relevant for analysis and are as accurate as possible, it isn't sufficient to collect information about expected fund inflows and outflows. You also need to be able to assign source, timing, and likelihood to the payment flows so that you can analyze the information for different time periods and responsibility areas, and so you can proactively take necessary action. Let's first discuss the process of gathering and classifying data for cash management.

Data Gathering and Classification

Planning types

You can post manual entries in Cash Management for anticipated payment flows or balance information. SAP uses planning types to differentiate between different types of manual planning entries such as available opening balance, and payment advice postings, etc. Figure 16.2 shows an example of a manual planning entry for 1000 Euro in a bank account managed in U.S. dollars.

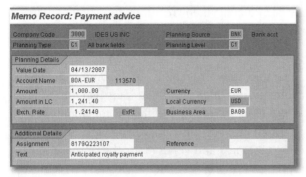

Figure 16.2 Manual Entry of Planning Data

You can use this manual planning to record exceptional or unanticipated payment flows, but most of the actual and anticipated payment
flows are usually the results of different business transactions. Full
integration with other SAP components ensures that data relevant for
cash management is automatically updated in the cash and liquidity
management component.

SAP provides planning sources to differentiate actual or anticipated
payment flows originating in different components, and planning levels to classify different types of fund inflows and outflows. Following
are some examples of the planning sources and corresponding planning levels:

Planning sources and planning levels

> **Bank accounting**
> Bank statement postings, cash concentr tion, float balances, etc.

> **Receivables and payables**
> Different types of incoming and outgoing payments, down pay-
> ments, letter of credits, and so on.

> **Treasury management**
> Loans, options, and investment postings, etc.

> **Logistics**
> Purchase requisitions, purchase orders, and sales orders, etc.

By assigning appropriate planning levels to all GL accounts relevant
for cash management, you can separate in your reports fund outflows
because of check payments (typically cleared in 5-7 days) and fund
outflows because of bank transfers (typically cleared in 1-2 days).

Planning levels for AR and AP

Depending on your cash management requirements, you can create as many planning levels as required.

Assigning planning levels for receivables and payables requires more information. For example, the probability of incoming payments from low-risk customers and high-risk customers isn't the same, and the time it takes to clear payments is different for domestic vendors and foreign vendors, etc. For this reason, you can use planning groups to group your customers and vendors for the purpose of cash management. Planning groups are freely definable and can represent customer and vendor accounts based on their business volume, industries, and types of business relationship. These planning groups in turn are associated with planning levels so that you can display them separately in cash management statements. Let's move on to discuss how you can use SAP to define these statements.

Definition of Statements

Multiple statement definitions

As discussed before, SAP provides you with the ability to create multiple, customizable cash position and liquidity forecast statements. A statement in this context can consist of groups of accounts, planning levels, and planning groups. Thus treasury department at the global headquarters of a company can use a statement that includes information from worldwide companies for all planning levels and planning groups, whereas a treasury manager at a branch office can use a statement that only refers to local bank accounts.

The standard SAP programs that prepare these reports provide extremely powerful analysis capabilities. For example, you can display fund inflows and outflows in multiple currencies (Figure 16.3 shows a modified screen) and then drill down to actual and anticipated activities in a single currency. You can also do the following:

> Easily switch between a summarized view showing group subtotals and a detailed view showing all planning groups and planning levels.

> Display the GL account number (for reconciliation with financial entries) or display corresponding mnemonic names assigned for cash management purposes.

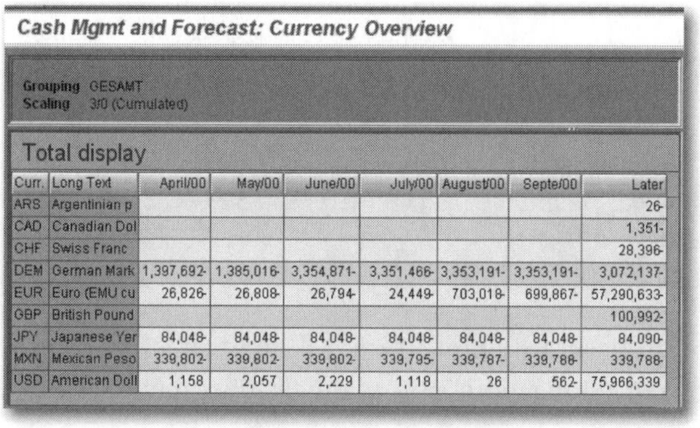

Cash Mgmt and Forecast: Currency Overview

Grouping GESAMT
Scaling 3/0 (Cumulated)

Total display

Curr.	Long Text	April/00	May/00	June/00	July/00	August/00	Septe/00	Later
ARS	Argentinian p							26-
CAD	Canadian Dol							1,351-
CHF	Swiss Franc							28,396-
DEM	German Mark	1,397,692-	1,385,016-	3,354,871-	3,351,466-	3,353,191-	3,353,191-	3,072,137-
EUR	Euro (EMU cu	26,826-	26,808-	26,794-	24,449-	703,018-	699,867-	57,290,633-
GBP	British Pound							100,992-
JPY	Japanese Yen	84,048-	84,048-	84,048-	84,048-	84,048-	84,048-	84,090-
MXN	Mexican Peso	339,802-	339,802-	339,802-	339,795-	339,787-	339,788-	339,788-
USD	American Doll	1,158	2,057	2,229	1,118	26	562-	75,966,339

Figure 16.3 Cash Management–Currency View

> Prepare daily, weekly, or monthly statements, and adjust the time interval between the displayed columns. So, you can easily create a quarterly statement by using an increment of 3 in a monthly statement.

Adjusting time intervals

> Prepare statements that can show ending balances or delta balances (i.e., changes). The ending balance reports can be useful for management reporting, whereas delta balance reports can be useful for analysis.

> Assign different planning levels to separately display blocked payments and special GL items (both discussed in Chapter 3).

Another extremely useful functionality for cash management planning is the ability to assign distribution percentages to a planning level to manage the inherent uncertainty in the liquidity forecast. For example, you may have assigned a single planning group to most of your low-risk customers who pay by the invoice due date. By default, the liquidity forecast would display all of their receivables on the planned date, even though you may receive actual payments a few days before or after that date. Considering this uncertainty, it can be difficult to obtain reliable liquidity forecasts, especially if the amounts involved are high. However, in SAP, you can assign percentages to planning levels so that the planned amount is automatically distributed over a few days before and after the planned date.

Ex Example

> If a planning level is assigned distribution percentages of 10 % (-1), 70 % (0), and 20 % (+1), then corresponding receivables of $10,000 on a planned date will be displayed in the statement as $7,000 on the planned date, $1,000 on the day before the planned date, and $2,000 on the day after the planned date.

Managing the uncertainty

After the cash position and liquidity forecast statements have been created and finalized (along with any manual adjustment entries), treasury managers can decide whether any fund transfer needs to be made to meet liquidity requirements or for cash concentration.

Cash Concentration

Most companies have multiple bank accounts for operational efficiency, business relationships, or many other reasons. For the most effective use of funds, companies need to strike a balance between having enough funds in each bank account to meet its operational needs and transferring any excess funds to bank accounts that offer the most beneficial conditions. For example, companies can choose to keep most funds in a bank account that offers the maximum interest rate and transfer funds only as required to the bank account used for payroll processing. The cash concentration functionality helps you process fund transfers among bank accounts for efficient cash management.

Using intermediate accounts

All bank accounts participating in a cash concentration process are linked together into a group. To meet different cash concentration requirements of different companies, regions, or business functions; you can create multiple groups, with each group linking together relevant bank accounts. To take advantage of say lower bank transfer charges, you can also define an intermediate bank account for cash concentration fund transfers. In such a case, funds are first transferred from the original bank account to the intermediate bank account, and subsequently from the intermediate bank account to the target bank account. As may be necessary for most large companies, the cash concentration process can link bank accounts (including intermediate bank accounts) across multiple companies.

Funds transfer decisions during the cash concentration process depend on several factors, including the business objective and activity volume associated with the bank account. As shown in Figure 16.4, for every bank account, you can maintain several specifications that influence the cash concentration process. Planned Balance represents the planned, target balance of the account at the end of the cash concentration process. However, if the actual account balance is within the Deficit Tolerance and Excess Tolerance limits (in the example shown, if the account balance is between $5,950 and $6,050), no funds transfer is requested or carried out. This enables you to process fund transfers only if account balances are outside of tolerance limits. Also, to avoid creating fund transfers for very small amounts, you can specify the Minimum Amount for payment advices. In addition, you can specify a Planning minimum balance for a bank account. The cash concentration process creates funds transfers only if the bank account balance is less than zero or more than this balance.

Cash concentration parameters

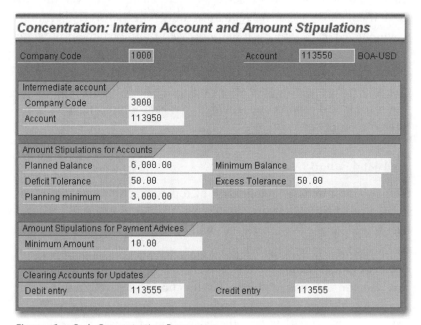

Figure 16.4 Cash Concentration Parameters

> **Tip**
>
> By specifying the planning currency, you can process cash concentration even across bank accounts maintained in different currencies. If managed in a different currency, account balances are converted into planning currency for cash concentration.

Cash concentration proposal

An automatic cash concentration program is provided that takes into account the minimum balance requirements and planning horizon (to factor in expected fund inflows and outflows) to create a cash concentration proposal for a bank account grouping. You can make several changes to this cash concentration proposal. For example, you can tweak minimum balances for bank accounts to factor in anticipated fund requirements that may not have been captured in the system yet. You can change or delete proposed fund transfers, or even create new payment advices for additional funds transfers. After the cash concentration process has created payment advices, you can directly post them into cash management accounts and convert them into payment requests, which can be processed by the payment program (refer to the payment program section in chapter 3 and chapter 5). Alternatively, you can create necessary forms or letters to communicate these fund transfer requests directly to the banks. Additionally, other tools and reports are provided that can be used for cash management purposes.

Tools and Reports

This section discusses a collection of topics that although not interrelated provide functionality and reports that are relevant to Cash and Liquidity Management. Let's start with interest calculation.

Interest Calculation

You can use the *interest calculation* function to verify interest calculated by your bank or to post relevant accounting entries for interest calculation. In either case, the calculation process is influenced by the interest indicator maintained in the GL account master data. This interest indicator controls several factors:

> Whether interest is calculated based on account balance or as arrears calculation, that is, interest is calculated for every open receivable or payable transaction separately.

> The frequency at which interest calculation is carried out, for example, monthly, quarterly, semi-annually, etc.

> The calendar used for interest calculation, such as

  – Bank Calendar (1 year = 360 days, 1 month = 30 days)

  – French Calendar (1 year = 360 days, 1 month = exact number of days)

  – Gregorian Calendar (1 year = 365 days, 1 month = exact number of days)

  – Japanese Calendar (1 year = 365 days, 1 month = 30 days)

> Minimum amount of interest (e.g., $5.00), only above which the settlement is processed. This helps you avoid interest postings of small, minor interest.

> The actual interest rate.

You can also specify an interest percentage that is relative to a reference interest rate. For example, interest on most loan accounts and bank accounts in the United States is pegged to the prime rate published by the central Federal Reserve Bank. When you update the reference interest rate in the system, subsequent interest rate calculations are automatically performed at the revised rate because corresponding interest indicators are linked to the reference interest rate.

Reference interest rates

 Tip

The interest calculation program also provides the cash pooling feature, by which you can calculate interest based on the combined balance of multiple accounts belonging to different companies, as long as the accounts are in the same currency.

When you run the interest calculation program, it uses interest indicators and associated parameters to calculate the interest amount for the accounts. Results of this program can be used to verify interest calculations done by banks or other business partners; or you can use these results to post corresponding accounting entries in the new GL. The interest calculation program is sophisticated enough to handle back-dated entries separately. Let's say after carrying out the interest calculation run, you had to post a back-dated entry that should have accrued interest for the past three months. Obviously, you can't recalculate for past three months on other items because it would create duplicate postings.

Processing back-dated entries

The interest calculation program automatically identifies back-dated entries based on their value date (calculated at the time of posting), calculates the interest separately, and reports or posts it as required.

The next section discusses another useful tool available in this component called cashed check analysis.

Cashed check analysis

To carry out a liquidity forecast that is as accurate as possible, it helps to analyze the pattern of how long it takes for issued checks to be cleared. If you issue large numbers of checks from several bank accounts, then it is neither practical nor efficient to manually carry out such analysis. To assist you in carrying out such analysis, you can use a report that analyzes the average outstanding period of checks for every bank account and every vendor. This program analyzes the average outstanding period separately for checks that have been cashed and for checks that have not yet been cashed.

Average days by grading amount

Figure 16.5 shows the report output that lists, for every vendor, the number of checks, total amount, and average number of days. Another unique functionality available is the use of grading amounts to calculate the average outstanding period. This is especially useful because, typically, the checks with large amounts are submitted for encashment sooner than the checks with small amounts. By using up to eight grading amount thresholds (less than $1,000, between $1,000 and $5,000, more than $5,000, etc.), you can obtain average outstanding days for checks in different amount ranges. Subsequently, you can use this information in cash management by instructing the programs to use the average number of outstanding days based on amount limits.

Outstanding Checks Analysis per G/L Account and Vendor

Outstanding Checks Analysis per G/L Account and Vendor
CoCde: 1000 G/L Acct: 113101

Days	Vendor	CoCd	Name 1	City	Number	Total
22	1000	1000	C.E.B. BERLIN	Berlin	9	298,621.71
4	1002	1000	Müller KG	Rosenheim	1	188,155.41
28	1003	1000	Gusswerk US	HARBOR CITY	1	580.32
8	1007	1000	Bike Retail & Co.	Hannover	6	9,454.85
0	1940	1000	Brain Associates	London TW3 LN2	1	3,719.65
7	1991	1000	Schneider AG Deutschland	Frankfurt	2	13,352.65
13	1992	1000	IDES UK	London	2	1,100.30
8	1993	1000	Snyder Inc.	NEW YORK	2	7,950.59
13	1995	1000	Schneider GmbH	Walldorf	1	991.91
10	4711	1000	Cinsa GmbH & Co. KG	Ravensburg	16	178,481.78
3	51000	1000	SAPSOTA AG	Nordenham	1	10,781.31
4	91011	1000	Lampen und Deko GmbH	Stuttgart	1	8,180.87

Figure 16.5 Outstanding Checks Analysis

The next section discusses some of the reports and interfaces available for cash management reconciliation and data analysis.

Reports and Interfaces

The primary reports of this component are obviously the cash position and liquidity forecast statements discussed earlier. Additionally, you have several other reports to manage, reconcile, and analyze cash management data with other systems. Following are some of the reports and interfaces available in the cash and liquidity management component:

> Payment advice journal that provides a record of daily planning activities that were entered, changed, archived, or reactivated for cash management

> Bank terms comparison report to compare interest rates of two bank accounts and their planned balance as of a particular date

Comparison of bank terms

> Reports to reconcile cash management data with the data in the new GL, in materials management, in sales and distribution, and so on

> Reporting tool to create customized drill-down reports based on cash management data

> An interface to create different file formats so that you can create payment advices externally (e.g., Microsoft Excel) and later load them into the system using an upload program

Market data
management

SAP also provides interfaces and programs for market data management. We'll discuss this functionality in more detail in Chapter 17, "Treasury and Risk Management," but for the purpose of cash management, you can use this functionality to interface with external systems to obtain reference interest rates and currency exchange rates. These interfaces can eliminate the need for manually maintaining relevant information, especially if you carry out business activities in multiple currencies or manage large number of deposit and credit accounts for which interest rates are tied to different reference rates.

Now, let's talk about the other interfaces and programs that support distributed cash management.

Distributed Cash Systems

Central system and
sending systems

For efficient cash management, more and more global companies are using a centralized treasury group that manages cash and liquidity requirements for all the group companies. To support these cash management requirements, tools and functionality are provided to manage distributed cash systems. Your technical team will ensure linking SAP systems used at different locations; however, you have to designate one SAP system as the central treasury system (typically at the group head offices) and other systems as the operational, sending systems (typically the regional or branch SAP systems).

To obtain a consistent, consolidated view of cash positions and liquidity requirements, you can use the mapping of company code, planning levels, and planning groups (optional) between sending systems and receiving system. The information exchange can be initiated by the sending systems or the receiving system. For example, your branch offices can send their cash positions at the end of each day, or your centralized treasury department can request weekly updates from each of the branch offices.

What we have discussed so far describes the available functionality of the cash and liquidity management component of SAP ERP Financials. The cash position and liquidity forecast reports available in this component provide you with basic functionality to assess your cash and liquidity requirements. However, to carry out medium- and long-term liquidity planning, you need the comprehensive features of the liquidity planner.

Liquidity Planner

While the case and liquidity management component provides the necessary information for short-term planning; for medium-term and long-term liquidity planning, you can use the liquidity planner component to plan and monitor the payment flows in your company. For the most effective use of the liquidity planner, you can create a planning structure consisting of liquidity items (discussed next) that represent payment flows that are planned as part of medium-term or long-term liquidity planning. As discussed later, the actual payment flows in the operative ERP Financials system are assigned to these liquidity items, which can be later transferred to BPS (Business Planning and Simulation) in the SAP NetWeaver BI component for liquidity planning and reporting.

 Tip

Up to the SAP R/3 4.70 version, SAP provided a component called cash budget management (CBM) to meet requirements of medium-term and long-term liquidity planning. Upgrades to newer versions of SAP, including ECC 6.0, require you to migrate from CBM to the Liquidity Planner.

Liquidity items determine which incoming and outgoing payments should be planned in the company, how detailed this planning should be, and which payment flows can be traced back to actual postings so that you can carry out plan and actual comparison. Liquidity items can be as detailed as required to meet your planning requirements. Typical payment inflows used in liquidity planning are receivables from trade customers, receivables from group companies, dividends, and interest income; whereas typical payment outflows used in liquidity planning are the payables to trade customers, payables to group companies, payroll expenses, and tax payments. Let's now see how these items can be used to carry out liquidity calculation.

Liquidity items

Liquidity Calculation

As discussed before, liquidity items provide the structure for preparing liquidity analysis, that is, the current liquidity situation. To prepare accurate liquidity statements, you need to analyze new receivable/payable items that should be included in liquidity statements and also analyze cleared or paid items that must be removed from the liquidity statements. In SAP, you use the assignment process to link liquidity items to accounting entries in financials.

 Warning

> If you use liquidity planner without BPS or BI, you'll only be able to assign actual payment flows to liquidity items using SAP ERP Financials. You'll require a workaround (e.g., third-party product) for carrying out liquidity planning and reporting.

Liquidity calculation area

When you activate the liquidity calculation, relevant accounting entries from FI are updated into a separate data area in the system called the liquidity calculation area. Subsequently, the assignment process attempts to automatically assign liquidity items to the accounting entries, thereby classifying payment flows as per their origin and usage. It is important to be familiar with how the software carries out this assignment to help you as a business user to work with your team in fine-tuning the system rules. This won't only ensure that most transactions are assigned to accurate liquidity items, but it will reduce the number of manual adjustments you'll have to make later. The most commonly used assignment processes assign liquidity items on the basis of bank statement entries and based on financial documents, including customer and vendor invoices. Let's discuss these assignment processes in more detail.

Assignment Based on Bank Statement

Because all fund inflows and outflows impact bank accounts, and all bank account transactions are captured in a bank statement, the best way to assign liquidity items to transactions is to start from bank statement items. In its simplest form, the assignment process checks assignment rules (queries) defined in the system to determine the corresponding liquidity item. SAP provides highly customizable functionality to enable you to create queries that are as detailed as necessary to meet your liquidity analysis requirements. For example, Figure 16.6 shows a query called UTIL_PYMNT that checks whether payment notes of a bank statement item contains *Elec* in it, and whether the payment is under 500 USD. If these conditions are met, the query proposes Liquidity Item 127000 (OC Other Expenses) to the assignment program.

 Tip

> Default system behavior is to display sales/purchase tax and withholding tax included in the liquidity items corresponding to revenue or expenses. Additional programming is required if you want to display tax amounts in separate liquidity items.

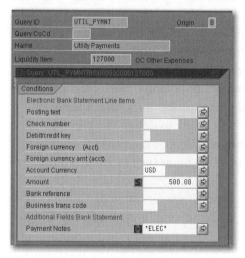

Figure 16.6 Bank Assignment Query

During the assignment process, the program goes through every bank statement item to determine the appropriate liquidity item and evaluates assignment rules (queries) in the sequence you specify. You can use this feature to your advantage by structuring the query sequence that is appropriate for each bank account. For a bank account that is used for payroll, for instance, you can assign queries so that liquidity

Assignment rules and queries

items relevant to salaries and taxes are evaluated first; whereas for a bank account used for investments, you can assign a sequence so that liquidity items relevant for interest and dividends are evaluated first. In addition, a large number of selection fields are provided for you to use to evaluate bank statement items.

However, assignment based on bank statement items may not be accurate enough or may not be relevant (e.g., if you don't use the electronic bank statement functionality discussed in Chapter 5). For those scenarios, you can attempt to assign liquidity items based on financial documents.

Assignment Based on FI Documents and Invoices

This assignment process analyzes financial documents, instead of bank statements, to evaluate information used to determine liquidity items. For example, while evaluating a payment clearing entry (Dr Outgoing payment account, Cr Bank account), the assignment program attempts to determine the corresponding information document that contains vendor information (e.g., Payment document–Dr Vendor, Cr Outgoing payment account) and evaluates the information document to derive the appropriate liquidity item. Financial documents typically contain more information than bank statements, so this option provides you with an ability to design complex queries to determine liquidity items. For example, you can create queries so that payments are classified into liquidity items such as software expenses, hardware expenses, and consulting services based on industry of the vendor Figure 16.7 shows a simple query for assigning Liquidity Item VENDOR_EXT to all items posted to vendor reconciliation account **161000**.

 Tip

There are two options to determine liquidity items for cross-company documents such as company A paying an invoice on behalf of company B. You can determine the liquidity item based on the intercompany receivable account in company A or from the original invoice document in company B.

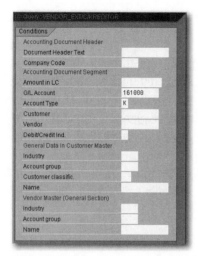

Figure 16.7 Assignment Query for Vendors

Because this logic attempts to determine documents posted to customer or vendor accounts based on entries posted to a bank account, you may run into a situation where multiple line items posted to bank account (N) are linked to multiple information items posted to customer or vendor account (M). In the Cash and Liquidity Management component, this is referred to as an *N:M Relationship*. We won't go into technical details here, but the assignment program is versatile enough to handle such a scenario by creating virtual line items and offsetting line items to automatically determine and assign liquidity items.

N:M relationships

If your liquidity planning is even more detailed and complex, then you can use the program to assign liquidity items based on invoice documents, which consists of two steps. The first step is similar to the assignment based on financial documents. If the program finds a liquidity item, then it starts the second step of processing in which it attempts to find and evaluate the original invoice document for determining a more accurate or detailed liquidity item. This provides you with the ability to create even more complex rules for determining liquidity items. For example, if the first step determines a liquidity item corresponding to AP, the second step in the process can be used to determine liquidity items based on information from vendor in-

Assignment based on invoices

voice documents. This in turn enables you to perform liquidity analysis at a very detailed level.

After the transaction data has been processed through these assignment programs, you can review liquidity statements, and, if necessary, you can manually adjust the assignment of liquidity items. As discussed before, to use the reporting and planning capabilities of liquidity planner, you are required to use BPS, NetWeaver BI, or other third-party tools. Let's now look at a case study of how a major airline transformed its cash management using the functionality available in the cash and liquidity management component.

Case Study

This corporation has more than $35 billion in annual revenue and through its subsidiaries operates a passenger airline in the United States. The passenger airline provides scheduled service to more than 135 global destinations. The company has a strong presence in 79 countries for its main passenger airline business. Group subsidiaries have presences at worldwide strategic locations to provide supporting services such as logistics, maintenance, catering, IT services, and so on. During the last quarter of the millennium, as the company expanded its global business, it also aggressively ventured into other areas such as leisure travel and financial services for aircraft leasing.

As the company built up its global business, the treasury operations became decentralized. Regional locations were using independent, incompatible processes, making the worldwide treasury operations difficult to manage. With over 125,000 full-time employees, temporary workers, partners, and suppliers worldwide; global payment management, cash planning, and liquidity forecasting were becoming crucial for the treasury. The unexpected and sudden downturn of business after 2001 combined with a soft economy prompted the business decision to take a careful look at treasury operations to reduce working capital requirements and save as much cash as possible to successfully navigate through the turbulent times ahead.

Business Challenges

Worldwide, the company had more than 250 bank accounts with a large number of local, and in many cases, smaller, banks. Lots of bank accounts meant increased account management fees, personnel requirements for operational activities, and no strong banking relationships that can be achieved by consolidated banking operations. Large numbers of bank accounts also meant that inactive accounts were under the radar screen of treasury managers, even if they contained large account balances.

The treasury department at the headquarters had difficulty collecting reliable and accurate data from subsidiaries in a timely manner. This was because cash management information at most locations was collected from individual bank websites and then manually entered into internally developed, ad-hoc systems and Excel spreadsheets. Obtaining a consolidated view of the company's global cash and liquidity position meant consolidating information from a large number of different systems.

Because treasury management was unable to obtain cross-company cash management information in a timely manner, it translated into situations where one location had to borrow money at a higher cost from an external bank, while another location in the same country had idle money in a dormant bank account at a less-than-optimum interest rate. Because the company was already using SAP ERP Financials for its accounting, receivable, payable, and banking operations; using SAP for cash and liquidity management was a no-brainer decision.

Solution Deployment

The complete rollout of the cash and liquidity management component to all worldwide locations took 18 months. As anticipated by the project management team, a large percentage of that time was spent in implementing business policies and procedures for treasury management at all locations and in carrying out administrative work with numerous banks for opening and closing bank accounts. Twenty senior level SAP resources from the internal IT department that already supported their existing SAP applications were allocated to this project. External consulting help was neither planned nor required for the project implementation. However, a considerable time commitment was expected and received from the treasury managers and finance managers at all of the company subsidiaries and locations.

After careful consideration of local requirements and centralized treasury operations, global banking relationships were streamlined and consolidated (as possible) with 3 major global banking partners. Over 250 bank accounts before the project were reduced to a more structured and manageable 119 bank accounts in 8 major currencies. The treasury operations were reorganized so that the central treasury department was based in the United States, with regional treasury centers in Hong Kong (for Asia), London (for Europe), and Canada (for the Americas). Cash management information from local subsidiaries was collected in the SAP systems at the regional centers, which in turn sent that information to the SAP system used by the treasury department at the headquarters.

For the purpose of cash concentration, processes were set up to keep cash flows from each location in its country to meet its own requirements, and to sweep any residual amount to bank accounts maintained (if possible in the same currency) at regional treasury centers. Homegrown systems and Excel spreadsheets were replaced with standard cash position and liquidity forecast statements in SAP, which were implemented at all locations so that the format and context of the information remained the same regardless of whether statements were created for a location, a branch, a company, a country, or the global operations at the headquarters.

Value Achieved
Reorganization and centralization of treasury operations in SAP made considerable improvements in the efficiency with which information was collected and analyzed, and the company was able to reduce its working capital requirements by 12 % in the first year after the project went live. SAP was able to provide treasury managers and finance managers worldwide with clear, day-to-day, more accurate visibility of cash positions with regards to their area of influence.

Cash position and liquidity forecast statements were not only able to gather information from and for individual companies but also across all business segments and business activities, such as purchasing, sales, service, and so on. And the ability to review cash positions in multiple currencies in a timely fashion enabled the treasury department to minimize currency risk, reduced borrowing costs, and provided improved management of monetary flow. By careful planning and using information available from SAP, the company was able to identify underused and underperforming funds and invest surplus liquidity with more favorable returns.

Fewer bank accounts meant lower management and administration fees and a reduction in transaction costs to the tune of almost $225,000 a year. Using the cash concentration proposals created from SAP, all locations that had banking relationships with one of the three banking partners were able to manage, initiate, and carry out electronic fund transfers, thereby enabling the locations to right-size their treasury departments.

Summary

You can do the following by using the cash and liquidity management component of SAP:

> Enhance the visibility of cash flows and liquidity flows, and improve your financial position through increased control of working capital.

> Determine and efficiently manage liquidity by departments, branch offices, regional offices, or companies.

> Increase operational efficiency by using various programs that support international or country-specific formats for electronic banking.

> Use multicurrency reporting to identify expected liquidity risks in one or more currencies.

> Use the sophisticated cash concentration program to optimize cash management by preparing and executing fund transfer requests.

> Use the Liquidity Planner for centralized, medium-term, and long-term liquidity planning.

In the next chapter, we'll discuss more complex functionality of Financial supply chain management (FSCM) application components for treasury management and risk management.

Treasury and Risk Management

For optimum financial management, companies large and small invest surplus liquidity in financial markets for improved returns as well as to finance short-term and long-term investment projects. Easy access to information and open economies around the world make it possible to identify most suitable investment opportunities anywhere in the world. Major financial institutions also provide an array of financial products in different financial markets to help their clientele grow their investments. However, along with these investment opportunities and increased returns also come risks and regulations. Different financial products such as securities, derivatives, and foreign exchange, are processed, managed, and traded in different markets and are subject to different market-specific and country-specific regulations. For treasury departments, it is challenging to ensure compliance with local rules and regulations while working toward the organizational goals and achieving maximum possible investment returns.

Additionally, investing in global financial markets in complex financial products amplifies associated risks and the need for risk management. Sudden and unanticipated fluctuations in market price, interest rates, and exchange rates can severely impact returns on invested capital. Treasury departments must be able to easily calculate and analyze different types of risks to take proactive actions that steer investment strategy in the appropriate direction. Most treasury departments also put in place continuously enforceable risk-management policies that limit their exposure to any one area of financial markets. The SAP ERP Financials Treasury and Risk Management component provides all of these, and then some.

Overview

Scales of treasury operations

Regardless of whether your treasury operations consist of a few traders sporadically investing in a single financial market or a large number of traders in subsidiaries around the world constantly trading in different financial markets, treasury and risk management provides a structured and controlled framework for trading, back-office processing and risk management of treasury investments. You can use efficiency improvements offered by advanced and integrated treasury and risk management, regardless of whether your treasury operations are exclusively for your group of companies or investing in financial markets is your primary business activity.

Functionality offered by this component is robust enough to handle complexities of different financial products, including complex derivatives and hedging contracts. The system can determine market risk and default risk on trades based on risk models and available market data and can also control exposure to different market, industry, and geographical segments in real time. Comprehensive back-office functionality enables you to carry out activities such as trade settlement, securities account management and reconciliation, printing correspondence, and carrying out adjustments as a result of corporate actions such as a stock split.

Using different analysis, evaluations, and reports available in the standard SAP system, you can calculate, anticipate, and analyze the impacts of market fluctuations on your investments. Using a powerful simulation functionality, you can carry out complex testing of such impacts on hypothetical market scenarios on your current or potential investments. The following section discusses these functionalities in more detail.

Functions in Detail

In this section, we'll first look at unique characteristics of treasury and risk management and then look at types of financial instruments that are supported by the transaction manager. We'll also look at the trading, back-office processing, and accounting of sample transactions. Subsequently, we'll discuss risk analyzers that are available for different types of risk management.

Concepts and Terminology

The treasury operations of any large, global corporations trade a variety of financial products such as securities, bonds, derivatives, foreign exchange, and so on. These products are traded in different financial markets governed by different sets of rules and regulations. Regardless of the size of the treasury operations, controls are necessary for issues related to internal and external compliance. For seamless and efficient processing, it's necessary to recognize and process diverse accounting provisions of different types of transactions. Even though your SAP team will manage the technical configuration and setup, you should be familiar with how the software manages complex requirements of different financial products, treasury transactions, and your organizational structure.

Financial Products

The complex world of financial products is represented in the treasury and risk management component by contract types, product categories, and product types. Contract types represent different financial markets such as securities, derivatives, money market, and foreign exchange. Product categories represent different financial instruments of a certain contract type such as term deposits and commercial papers (money market), stocks and bonds (securities), and so on. Product types represent more detailed classification of financial instruments. For example, stocks can be further classified into domestic stock, foreign stock, and so on.

A large number of product categories are supported and numerous, partially configured product types are provided (see Figure 17.1). If necessary, you can also create additional product types to meet your requirements. Transactions in the TRM component are processed at the level of product types.

Figure 17.1 Product Categories and Product Types

Treasury Transactions

Transaction types Depending on the financial products being processed, you use *transaction types* to represent different treasury transactions such as sales and purchase of securities, borrowing, investment, hedging, etc. Transaction types enable you to control financial product-specific parameters. For example, for money market products, you can specify the basis and discounting method used to calculate NPV (net present value), for commercial papers, cash flow relevance, and so on. For securities and derivatives, you can specify rules to determine contract, order, payment, and settlement dates; whether accrued interest calculation should be carried out for bonds; and so on. All transaction types share some common features regardless of the financial instruments being processed:

> You can use multiple memo books for financial transactions, to maintain comments and notes by traders, back office, accounting, and so on.

> For every transaction type, you can use separate document numbering for actual transactions, offers and quotations, hypothetical (what-if) transactions, and underlying transactions (e.g., currency trade for a Forex option).

> You can assign a limit group to each transaction for limit management, which we'll discuss later in this chapter.

> You can determine the processing sequence of a deal such as contract: contract–settlement, order–contract–settlement, with or without settlement, and so on.

Now let's look at the functionality available to meet your organizational control requirements.

Organizational Controls

From the organizational point of view, you can use Business Workflow and status management functionality to assign approval procedures to treasury transactions. These approval procedures can have up to three approval levels and can be independently triggered at the time of creation, changes, or reversal of transactions based on several parameters. This can be especially useful in large treasury operations to implement internal checks and balances.

 Tip

> For each company, you can independently specify whether it allows the short sale of securities.

Treasury and risk management uses the standard SAP authorization functionality to control user access to different transactions and activities. Depending on their authorizations, users can process treasury activities as trade controllers, limit managers, risk controllers, back-office processors, fund managers, staff accountants, treasury managers, and so on. Also, users have to be specifically set up as traders in individual companies before they can process trading transactions.

Authorization roles

Restrictions by
trader, business
partners
Additionally, traders can be restricted to transact only specific contract types (e.g., money market, derivatives), product categories (e.g., term deposits, commercial papers), product types (e.g., domestic stock, foreign stock), and transaction types (e.g., Purchase, Sale, Exercise). You can place similar restrictions for depository banks and issuers so that no one inadvertently places a derivative order for a business partner responsible for only managing money market transactions.

Portfolio hierarchies
You can manage one or more portfolios in each company to group your investment positions and use them along with other criteria to create multilevel portfolio hierarchies. With the availability of more than 15 criteria (e.g., company code, currency, country, trader, product type, etc.), you can create highly complex portfolio hierarchies that meet your management, analysis, and reporting requirements. Figure 17.2 shows an example of a portfolio hierarchy for global treasury operations with country, trader, securities account, and product type as its criteria.

In addition, you can use master agreements to manage money market transactions to ensure that it meets predetermined investment criteria such as who to invest with, how much to invest, in what increment, and so on.

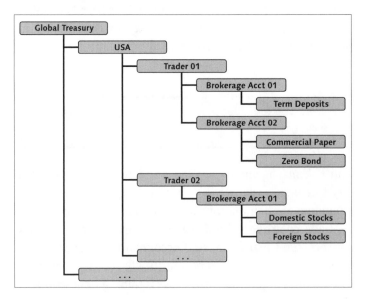

Figure 17.2 Portfolio Hierarchy

Let's now look at processing different types of treasury transactions.

Transaction Management

Transaction management collectively refers to end-to-end processes encompassing front-office activities (deal capture, exercise, valuation, limit checks, etc.), back-office activities (correspondence, settlement, process monitoring, etc.), and accounting activities (posting to accounting, parallel valuation, hedge accounting, etc.). However, you first need to create relevant master data that can be used for these transactions.

Master Data

For efficient processing and seamless integration with other components, you need different types of data such as bank accounts, securities accounts, debt management and borrowing agreements, and data for the actual financial products. In Chapter 5, we discussed how SAP supports management of house banks and bank accounts. Similarly, different types of securities accounts are supported, such as investment accounts, margin accounts, lending accounts, and futures accounts. Later you'll see how to set up different business partners such as security issuer and depository bank, and you'll learn standing instructions to carry out recurring activities.

Securities accounts

Regardless of whether it's a stock, bond, warrant, or any other financial instrument, every financial product is represented as a class (associated with a product type) in treasury and risk management and represented as a class position in a securities account. For example, the definition of Google (name, stock symbol, stock exchange, etc.) is created as a class, whereas when you purchase 10,000 units of Google at $1,000.00 each, it creates a position. For all supported financial products, SAP provides you with the functionality to enter comprehensive master data relevant for trading, reporting, and managing, including data unique to specific product types. Obviously, it isn't practical to discuss every piece of information collected for all financial products supported by treasury and risk management, but the following list will give you an idea of the wide range of data maintenance capability

Class and position

available to you. For a financial product (class in SAP), you can maintain the following:

> Search terms to easily find a financial product, for example, CUSIP number, CBOE number, Ratings (Moody's, S&P), etc.

> The exchanges at which you want to trade the class (NASDAQ, LSE, etc.)

> Dividend, distributions, and bonus information for stocks

> Dates, rates, frequency, and currency for interest calculation for bonds

> Call rights for the issuer or bond holder for callable bonds

> Redemption schedules for asset-based securities (ABS) or mortgage-based securities (MBS)

> Underlying product type for futures transactions such as reference interest rate for interest futures, or security index for index futures, and so on

After all relevant master data is maintained, you are ready to process trades.

Trading

Financial transaction

In spite of the wide range of financial instruments and different types of business transactions supported by treasury and risk management, the system provides a single, simple interface for entering most types of trades. At the core of any trading activity is a financial transaction posted in the transaction manager. Financial transactions provide you with access to all relevant information about a trade in a structured format. This includes information about counterparty; securities account; trading activity, such as quantity, unit price, market value; and so on. Total costs, including brokerage and commission, automatically create necessary payment flows that can be used in accounting settlement. Apart from standard display, change, and reversal, SAP provides you with several other processing options (see Figure 17.3):

> **Settle**
  Using this function, you can settle financial transactions and con-

vert planned payment flows proposed in the transaction entry into actual payment flows.

› Give Notice

Depending on the financial instrument underlying the trade, this function is useful to settle an OTC option, carry out outstanding interest payments of swaps and cap/floors, or terminate the contract resulting in settlement payment for FRA (forward rate agreements).

Position management and date check

› Roll Over

This function can be used to roll over current investment to a new term, with any possible changes in investment amount, interest rates, and so on.

› Expiration

Typically for options and derivatives, this function can be used to set the expiration date for a trade. Trades without any values are deleted.

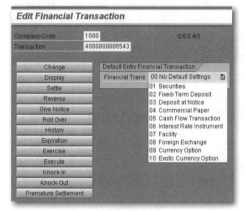

Figure 17.3 Edit Financial Transaction

› Exercise

This function is used to exercise an option, and as applicable, create a cash settlement based on the difference between strike and market price.

> **Execute**
>
> This function changes a transaction from an order to an actual contract that is released for trading and further processing.

> **Knock-In**
>
> This function activates a currency barrier option for exercise of expiration. This type of option becomes effective only if the underlying trades are at a predetermined level on or before a fixed date.

> **Knock-Out**
>
> This function activates a currency barrier option for expiration. This type of option expires if the underlying trades at a predetermined level on or before a fixed date.

> **Premature Settlement**
>
> Using premature settlement, you can break down full or part of forward exchange transactions into subsequent transactions.

Additionally, several fast-entry programs are provided for entering trade information for different money market and foreign exchange transactions. These programs enable you to enter your trades as quickly as possible while capturing all relevant and required information. Other useful features for trading include the consumption sequence that can determine whether securities are sold based on manual assignment or based on LIFO (Last-in-first-out) or FIFO (First-in-first-out) strategy; the position management functionality, which gives an overview of investment positions based on selected criteria; and the date check functionality, which checks whether an entered date falls on a nonworking day or on a holiday. This last function can be useful if you are placing a trade to be executed on a foreign stock exchange that follows a different holiday schedule.

Regardless of the type, financial instrument, and volume of trading transactions, they are seamlessly integrated with accounting and other back-office components.

Accounting and Back Office

Flow types   Using the transaction manager subledger (similar to receivables and payables subledgers discussed in Chapter 3), you can report and reconcile transactional activities posted in treasury and risk management. The seamless integration between treasury transactions and accounting entries is achieved by every transaction type automatically generating relevant flow types. Flow types are used to classify different payment flows associated with a deal, support different accounting processes, use complex posting specifications to determine accounting entries, and provide powerful integration between treasury and risk management and other components.

Ex Example

A transaction type that records a money market purchase automatically triggers a flow type that denotes an increase in investment amount. This flow type in turn, determines the accounting implications of this transaction, and using posting specifications behind-the-scenes, it prepares an account entry to debit the investment position account and credit the bank clearing account.

The proposed accounting entries are then reviewed by accounting and the back office and released for posting. A transaction type can also automatically propose one or more derived business transactions such as income tax, capital gains tax, or withholding tax. Thus, a transaction type that records nominal interest not only can trigger inflow of interest income but also outflow of tax liability. In the following section, we'll see some other accounting processes that are supported by the integration of treasury and risk management.

Other Accounting Processes

To assist in period-end accruals and deferrals typically at large treasury operations, SAP provides a program to automatically post accruals and deferrals based on flow types. After preparation of financial statements, these entries are then reversed using a reversal program. The accruals and deferrals may be necessary for flow types corresponding to interest or dividend payments, option premiums, and so on. You can choose between posting these accounting entries with or without impact to the income statement.

Investment valuation

Another period-end activity is the valuation of investment portfolios to accurately reflect investment valuation on financial statements. The robust design and functionality of treasury and risk management helps you valuate money market, securities, currencies, and derivatives using appropriate valuation methods:

> One-step or two-step price valuation for most product types

> Amortization valuation for loans and bonds

> Index valuation for index-based financial instruments

> Security valuation based on price changes

> Foreign currency valuation

> Other methods for derivative valuations

 Tip

One unique and especially useful functionality (for large, global companies) is the ability to carry out parallel valuation of investment positions per different valuation guidelines such as US GAAP and IAS .

Typically, these valuations are performed at the end of the fiscal year, but you can also run the valuation process in SAP during the year and subsequently reset the valuation. This enables you to evaluate and analyze your investment portfolios anytime during the year.

Now let's look at some of the important back-office activities.

Back-Office Activities

The back office of most treasury departments is responsible for carrying out necessary supporting activities for the deal execution and securities account management. As shown in Figure 17.4, the option of collective processing provides a summarized view of relevant information for all transactions. From the collective processing screen, you can branch to a detailed screen to carry out necessary processing. For the purpose of cash management, you can use the position monitor tool that combines cash flow information from cash and liquidity management with the financial transactions entered in treasury and risk management and presents a consolidated view of current and anticipated payment flows.

Transaction Management: Collective Processing

Contract	Product/transact.cat. (descr.)	T	Transaction structure
12/29/05	Stock-Purchase	200	5,000.00000 Units 63.500000 EUR
12/29/05	Stock-Purchase	201	2,000.00000 Units 62.000000 EUR
12/29/05	Stock-Sale	202	3,000.00000 Units 69.800000 EUR
12/29/05	Stock-Purchase	203	1,000.00000 Units 49.000000 EUR
12/29/04	Stock-Purchase	204	750.00000 Units 52.400000 EUR
12/29/04	Stock-Sale	205	450.00000 Units 58.300000 EUR
01/28/04	Bond-Purchase	212	EUR 1,000,000.00 - 100.000000%
01/03/04	Fixed-term deposit-Borrowing	500	USD 10,000,000.00 + 3.5000000 %
01/03/04	Commercial Paper-Purchase	503	EUR 9,426,551.00 - 3.0000000 % Yield
01/04/06	Interest rate instrument	504	EUR 12,000,000.00 - 4.0000000 %
01/03/06	Interest rate instrument	501	EUR 25,000,000.00 - <EUREUR01YM> - 0.4
01/03/06	Interest rate instrument	502	CHF 30,000,000.00 - 3.5000000 %
01/03/06	Foreign exchange-Forex	400	EUR 6,944,444.44 - 1.440000000
01/04/06	Foreign exchange-Forex	401	EUR 5,925,925.93 + 1.350000000
01/04/06	Foreign exchange-Forex	402	EUR 5,555,555.56 - 1.440000000
03/24/06	Foreign exchange-Forex	403	EUR 10,000,000.00 - 1.314070000
01/07/05	CAP/FLOOR-Purchase	601	5.0000000 % 40,000,000.00 EUR
01/07/05	CAP/FLOOR-Purchase	602	3.5000000 % 20,000,000.00 USD
01/03/04	SWAP-Swap	603	ReceiverSwap 100,000,000.00 EUR
01/07/04	SWAP-Swap	604	Payer Swap 20,000,000.00 EUR
01/07/04	FRA-Purchase	605	10,000,000.00 USD 4.0 % USDLIB01YM
01/07/06	OTC options-Purchase	606	100,000.00000 Units 80.000000 EUR
01/07/06	OTC options-Purchase	607	Swap for the swapInterest rate sw 100.00 EUR
01/07/06	OTC options-Purchase	608	EUR 8,333,333.33 - 1.440000000 Put
01/07/06	OTC options-Purchase	600	EUR 7,092,198.58 - 1.410000000 Put

Figure 17.4 Collective Processing

Treasury and risk management is fully integrated with other components, so any payment flows requiring outgoing payments (e.g., for purchase of securities) can automatically generate payment requests. As discussed in Chapter 5, you can use the payment program to automatically process payments based on these payment requests. Payments in the same currency to the same business partner can be combined using the powerful *netting* functionality. For example, using netting, you can offset receivables for stock sales with the payables for a new term-deposit and derivatives position, and make a net payment to settle all three transactions, thereby reducing transaction costs, charges, and other fees.

Automatic payment processing

Almost all transactions processed in treasury and risk management require some form of communication to record, inform, confirm, or

Correspondence processing

instruct some aspect of the deal. Treasury and risk management supports a wide range of physical and electronic correspondence options such as printouts, faxes, emails, and other electronic communication. Rather than having to decide correspondence requirements for every transaction, you can maintain highly customizable standing instructions with which you can automatically trigger necessary printouts or other electronic communication for treasury transactions. For example, you may automatically email confirmations for money market investments, automatically print and fax confirmations for securities purchases, and may require manual printing of derivative investments. Using a correspondence monitor, you can manage, request, execute, delete, or even repeat any printouts or electronic communications. SAP even allows you to maintain counter-confirmations for your correspondence. A correspondence status will change to "reconciled" only after you have confirmed the receipt of counter-confirmation from your business partners.

The back office component also provides transactions to process most typical corporate actions such as stock split, reverse split, stock swap (initiated by the company), stock transfer, and so on. All of these functionalities help you process treasury transactions. However, to ensure that the actual performance of your portfolios is in line with your investment strategies, you also need to calculate, evaluate, and analyze the returns of your portfolio.

Portfolio Analyzer

The portfolio analyzer allows you to measure the performance of your treasury portfolios using different calculation methods and compare the results with corresponding benchmarks. We discussed before how treasury and risk management helps you group your investments into portfolios and how you can create multiple portfolio hierarchies for reporting and evaluation for internal controllers, dealers, managers, and others. The portfolio analyzer calculates rates of returns for every node and every level in a hierarchy so that you can calculate investment performance by product types, traders, securities accounts, currency, country, and many other criteria.

The portfolio analyzer brings over capital flows from treasury trans-actions as portfolio analyzer flows (PA flows) forr yield calculation. Depending on how these capital flows impact revenue and position values, you can decide their impact on yield calculation. For example, the impact on yield calculation will be different for interest income versus reclaimable tax payments. Such performance-neutral capital flows are eloquently referred to as exogenous capital flows in portfolio analyzer settings. Considering that even a reasonable size of treasury operation involves a large number of capital flows, SAP provides a program to automatically propose these settings, which can be further modified as needed. Let's move on to discuss the yield calculation.

Performance neutral payment flows

Yield Calculation

The system supports four different methods for calculating rates of return (yield): time-weighted rate of return (TWRR), money-weighted rate of return (MWRR), Dietz method, and Modified Dietz method. These formulae and calculation methods are too detailed and complex for the scope of this chapter, but suffice it to say that SAP supports highly advanced evaluations that uses different yield curves, exchange rates, Forex volatilities, interest rate volatilities, index volatilities, security volatilities, market prices, and so on.

Typically, different portfolio values are calculated and updated for reporting and analysis as part of day-end processing. Each calculated value (called key figure) is based on one of the evaluations discussed previously and can reflect transaction values or summarized aggregated results. Invested amount, average cost, quantity, market price, realized or unrealized gain/loss, year-to-date income, and bid/ask difference are all examples of key figures. A group of key figures (called a key figure hierarchy) is linked with one or more portfolio hierarchies, which greatly improves evaluation efficiency because during the processing, all key figures can be evaluated for all nodes and levels of associated portfolio hierarchies. Evaluation results for these runs are stored in an area called the results database. Obviously, calculation of key figures is interdependent both from the business as well as the calculation point of view. For example, calculation of the current

Key figures and results database

gain/loss key figure depends on first calculating key figures for original cost, quantities, and market price.

 Tip

> The portfolio analyzer creates versions of portfolio hierarchies and its calculations of rates of returns and benchmarks. This helps in back testing and also for reproducing historical data for comparison and decision making.

Benchmarking

Apart from obtaining portfolio information from Transaction Manager and getting market data either through manual entry or automatic data feed (discussed later), Portfolio Analyzer provides you with the ability to maintain benchmarks to compare and evaluate investment performance. Benchmarks can be created with reference to market data such as index value or reference interest rates, or you can create composite benchmarks that are calculated based on percentage weights of multiple, individual benchmarks. Benchmarks are assigned to individual nodes in a portfolio hierarchy, so, for example, you can evaluate performance of portfolios managed by different traders against a consistent benchmark such as S&P 500. For the evaluation of actual results and benchmarks, SAP provides the Analyzer Information System.

Analyzer Information System

The Analyzer Information System (AIS) is a highly flexible tool that helps you analyze key figures stored in the results database as well as key figures calculated on-the-fly based on completely customizable formulae. Using multiple subscreens, AIS enables you to analyze any key figure for any node or level in a portfolio hierarchy. Figure 17.5 shows a sample output from AIS. You can also display other information using AIS:

> Individual positions that make up the number displayed in the summary (e.g., Euro Money Market positions in Figure 17.5)

> Risk hierarchy and maturity bands (we'll discuss this later in more detail)

> Daily, weekly, monthly, quarterly, semi-annual, or annual historical trend

> Calculation bases and evaluation procedures used for the calculation, which is helpful for reconciliation or audit

By careful definitions of portfolio hierarchies and key figure hierarchies, this tool can meet most of your reporting requirements. However, to protect current investments and evaluate new ones, companies also need detailed and actionable views to potential risks to their investments.

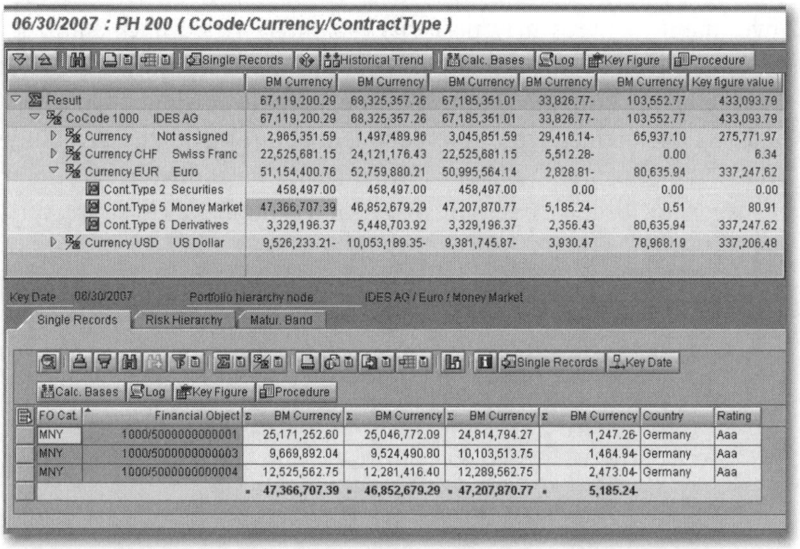

Figure 17.5 Analyzer Information System

Market Risk Analyzer

The market risk analyzer allows you to evaluate transactional activities on a global basis for potential risks due to fluctuations in exchange rates, interest rates, and security prices. The risk management functionality provides you with not only the ability to take proactive actions to protect your current investments but also the ability to evaluate investment opportunities for potential risks. Risk manage-

Integration with SAP SEM

ment is strongly integrated with the strategic enterprise management (Strategic Enterprise Management) components of SAP for reporting and analysis, although in this chapter we'll only focus on organizational aspects and risk evaluation in SAP ERP Financials.

Organizational Aspects

Risk hierarchies

From an organizational perspective, to obtain consolidated and consistent view of risk evaluations, risk management provides risk hierarchies that provide a structured grouping of different risks. During risk evaluations, all applicable risks are evaluated for all positions and all levels of portfolio hierarchies; for example, a money market investment in Euros may pose risks in interest rate fluctuations as well as exchange rate fluctuations. Figure 17.6 shows an example of a risk hierarchy. With the ability to define multiple portfolio hierarchies and risk hierarchies, you have complete control over the flexibility and visibility of risk evaluations, whether it's for individual portfolio managers or for the treasury manager of a centralized global treasury department.

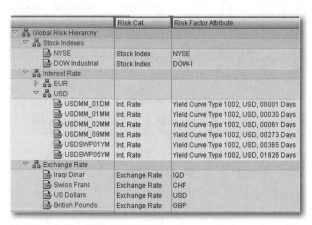

Figure 17.6 Risk Hierarchy

Profitability Analysis

In addition to characteristics available in the standard system such as portfolio, trader, product types, and so on, you can create your own characteristics for risk analysis and also evaluate them in the Profitability analysis component (Chapter 13). This enables you to calculate profitability and evaluate risks on the same set of organizational criteria. Apart from the AIS, you have access to highly sophisticated evaluations:

> Net Present Value Analysis

> Mark to Market Valuation and Position Analysis

> Sensitivity Analysis based on durations, convexities, exposures

> Currency Exposure Analysis that can be used to assist in currency hedging

> Gap Analysis, position and maturity volumes, cash flows, and liquidities analysis using advanced maturity bands (periods) definition

> Value-at-Risk Analysis using probability factors that can account for the uncertainty of future market developments

Risk management also provides comprehensive simulation functionality.

Simulation

Using the simulation functionality in risk management, you can create a long-term forecast of your company's financial development based on different scenarios. Two important aspects of simulation functionality in risk management are definitions of scenarios (a set of actual or hypothetical values) and market data shifts (anticipated changes). This seemingly simple functionality is capable of highly complex simulations. For example, in a scenario definition, you can maintain a combination of values for exchange rates, exchange rate volatilities, yield curves, interest rate volatilities, security prices, security volatilities, security indexes, and index volatilities. A fairly simple simulation consists of applying one of these scenarios to a portfolio hierarchy, although the scenarios themselves may be simple (e.g., U.S. dollar depreciates by 3 % against the Euro) or complex (including fluctuations in several exchange rates, interest rates, indexes, and volatilities).

Simulation scenarios

To carry out even more advanced simulations, risk management provides the functionality of *scenario progressions*, which involves defin-

Scenario progressions

ing a series of chronological scenarios separated by (subject to) market data shifts. A market data shift in this context represents absolute or percentage changes in exchange rates, yield curves, indexes, securities, or volatilities. Figure 17.7 shows a definition of a market data shift for yield curves in different currencies. Scenario progressions enhance your ability to carry out fairly long-term simulations based on anticipated changes in securities, currencies, and derivative markets (during different timeframes). In addition to market data shifts, you can also create "shifts" or distribution of values based on due dates, liquidation (sale), and use (of available credit lines). Even though these evaluations provide you with powerful risk analysis capabilities for fluctuations in prices and rates, to manage and limit your investment exposures to the risks of default, you should use the credit risk analyzer.

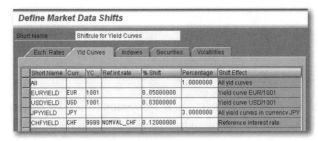

Figure 17.7 Market Data Shift Definition

Credit Risk Analyzer

Risk management offers you the ability to measure, analyze, control, and limit exposure to the risks of default or delinquency. Large treasury operations working in a global investment environment need to assess risks and creditworthiness of business partners, issuers, and counterparties; allocate results of risk assessments to treasury transactions and investment positions; and limit the exposure so that it's manageable. Using the credit risk analyzer, you can calculate default risks for every treasury transaction and assign it to all affected segments such as portfolio, and trader.

Exposure amount and attributable amount To accurately assess the amount at risk, SAP uses the total amount at risk (exposure amount) and configurable variables that indicate

514

how high the risk is, to calculate risk-adjusted amount (attributable amount). If the default is certain, then the attributable amount and exposure amount are same. The attributable amount is calculated for every expected incoming cash flow after taking into consideration the expected loss and the unexpected loss. Let's look at this calculation in detail.

Attributable Amount

To calculate the attributable amount, first the Credit Risk Analyzer needs to determine risk profiles for individual transactions. Figure 17.8 shows default risk classifications as supported by Credit Risk Analyzer. The assignment functionality in Risk management allows you to bundle risk parameters into different risk rules and assign them to different treasury transactions. For example, depending on the complexity of treasury operations, you can create one risk rule for all money market transactions or separate risk rules for term deposits, commercial papers, loans, and so on. You can either assign these risk rules as part of day-end processing or automatically at the time treasury transactions are created in Transaction Manager.

Assigning default risks to transactions

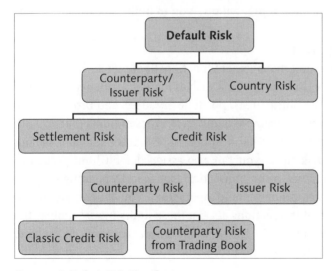

Figure 17.8 Default Risk Classification

Some of the configurable factors that influence the calculation of risk-adjusted attributable amount are listed here:

> Customizable formulae based on advance payment amount, return payment amount, nominal amount, and value-at-risk amount.

Recovery rate on
defaults

> Recovery rate percentage that represents the proportion that may still be paid in case of a partner default (e.g., as part of bankruptcy proceedings)

> Add-on factors percentage that indicates the risk premium taking into account potential positive market value changes

> Percentage probabilities of default for different credit ratings (A, AA, B, C, etc.) and different time periods

> Existence of a collateral agreements or collateralization using collateral amounts or securities

If a transaction contains more than one risk at one point in time (e.g., counterparty credit risk, issuer credit risk, and settlement risk), then the system generates several attributable amounts at the same time. Whereas risk-adjusted attributable amount provides visibility to risks of default, Limit Management allows you to limit the exposure itself.

Limit Management

You can use the limit management functionality to set and monitor exposure limits for different criteria such as market segments, countries, companies, geographical areas, portfolios, traders, and profit centers. Figure 17.9 shows an example of different types of limits that you can maintain in limit management. Similar to the automatic and default assignment of risk rules, you can also assign default limit groups to treasury transactions in the transaction manager. Depending on your organizational requirements and operational convenience, you can validate the actual transactions against these limits in real time as the transactions are entered in Transaction Manager, or you can evaluate them as part of your day-end processing.

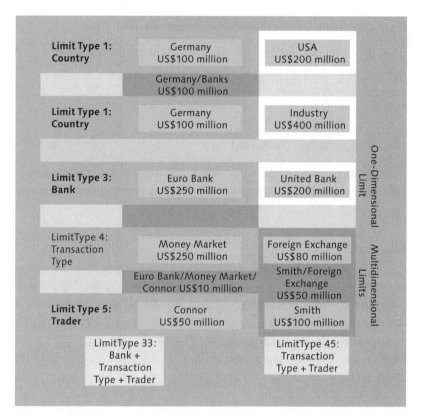

Figure 17.9 Limit Types

Additionally, you can easily lock the limits against changes, transfer unused limits between different objects, or increase one or more limits temporarily to enable traders to process financially important transactions in volatile markets. Even the process for establishing limits can be set to work in accordance with the principle of dual control, so that new limits aren't active until they are released by two employees. If a transaction is subject to multiple types of limit checks, the system calculates and evaluates each type of limit to determine if that transaction violates any established trading limits. On a daily basis, you can generate utilization reports that show you the amounts drawn up or used from available limits for any and all criteria for which the treasury group has established exposure limits. Another unique functionality available to you is to be able to reserve a free

Utilization reports

limit for a certain time period, to make sure that the anticipated deal goes through without any problems of exceeding any limits. In the next section, we'll look at other functionality available in treasury and risk management.

Data Maintenance and Reporting

This section focuses on functionalities that support or enhance the capabilities that we have discussed so far in this chapter. Let's start with the concept, roles, and influence of business partners.

Business Partner

As we mentioned, business partners play an important role in treasury and risk management. Security issuers, depository banks, counterparties, borrower entities, and guarantors, etc are all maintained using a consistent user interface of business partners. For each business partner, you can maintain a wide variety of information ranging from addresses, bank details, tax details, and regulatory reporting, to account management, payment controls, dunning, and correspondence. Even though the concept of business partners is shared by several SAP components, maintenance of recurrently used standing instructions for payments, authorization, and correspondence are of special significance for treasury management.

Standing instructions   Payment details refer to bank account, payment method, and currency for payment. This information is used while carrying out settlement payments based on treasury transactions and is linked with product types and transaction types. So, for example, you can make payments to different accounts based on whether the settlement was for money markets or securities. To expedite payment entry, you can also use repetitive codes discussed in Chapter 5. On the other hand, standing instructions for transaction authorization ensure that a business partner is authorized for processing specific contract types, product categories, and product types. For any large treasury operation with hundreds of different investment partners and an almost equal number of financial instruments, these authorizations provide internal controls to ensure, for example, that a currency exchange transaction isn't processed with a brokerage responsible only for derivatives. Lastly, standing instructions for correspondence help you send necessary confirmations and information from SAP to your business partners when the relevant transaction is processed in the transaction manager.

Now let's look at how to maintain market data in treasury management.

Market Data Management

Obviously, for transaction processing and continuing evaluations, you need the relevant and latest market prices, and rates. For a global treasury department processing a wide variety of complex financial products, a large volume of such information may be required on a daily basis or even in real time. For a small, simple, low-volume treasury department, however, relatively infrequent and manual update of market data may be sufficient. Treasury management supports both these extremes and everything in between by providing you with three options for data update: entering data manually, using the file interface, and using a real-time data feed.

 Tip

Exchange rates and interest rates that are uploaded using market data management are shared by both treasury and risk management and cash and liquidity management.

Manual data entry is possible using direct entry into SAP or using spreadsheets. If you use the file interface, SAP makes the process easier by enabling you to first export the structure in which the required data needs to be prepared. To make the data upload even easier, SAP provides you with conversion functionality to use to convert currency names, exchange rate types, security codes, interest rates, etc from the codes used by your data provider to the corresponding codes defined in the SAP system. On the other hand, if your treasury operations require a continuous update of price, rates, and so on, then

File interfaces and data feed

you first need to obtain corresponding software and hardware from third-party data providers (e.g., Dow Jones, Reuters, Telerate) or arrange to receive this data via Web Services. Using translation tables, you can map and convert current and historical incoming data to the codes used in your SAP system. The responsibility of providing data, file formats, and necessary software and hardware remains with the data provider, but the available information from the data feed can be updated or accessed in treasury and risk management with a desired frequency.

Using one of the available data update methods, you can load any of the data in the following table in treasury and risk management. Using real-time data monitors, you can monitor the frequency and changes to relevant market data. We've already discussed how this information can be used in various reports and risk analyzers to valuate their portfolio positions and evaluate their risks. Another option to manage your risks against market fluctuations is to use hedging.

Hedge Management

Hedging contracts   To insure against market fluctuations, global companies routinely hedge their exposures by making investments that specifically reduce or cancel out risks in another investment. Without hedging, an unanticipated large movement in exchange rate can easily erode the profitability of a deal or, in extreme cases, even the future viability of a company's operations. With the treasury and risk component, you can manage hedging relationships in the transaction manager. These hedging relationships can represent independent hedging contracts or derivative (currency exchange, options, etc.) transactions already in the securities accounts. SAP supports various types of hedging contracts such as cash-flow hedges, fair-value hedges, net investment in foreign subsidiary, etc. Figure 17.10 shows an example of a Forex hedging transaction.

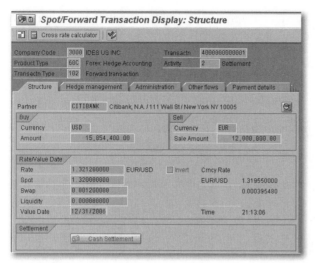

Figure 17.10 Hedging Transaction

Because of its full integration with other SAP components and functionalities, hedge management can easily calculate the market value of a derivative financial instrument using market data from market data maintenance and mark-to-market valuation from risk management. To test the effectiveness of hedging relationships for statutory and reporting purpose, you can define different hedge strategies that factor in the following criteria:

> The ratio range within which a hedging relationship is considered effective.

> Calculation parameters such as price/NPV, evaluation types, and so on used for hedge assessment calculation and hedge measurement calculation.

> The method for ineffectiveness measurement for cash flow hedges. Currently, SAP supports two methods from FAS 133:

  – Method 1 of the methods suggested in DIG issue G7 in FAS 133

  – Method laid out in FAS 133, par 30 (b)

The valuation of hedging relationships and realized gains and losses provides complete and automatic integration to accounting, and several reports in the standard system provide you with the ability to carry out prospective and retrospective assessments.

In addition to the standard reports such as AIS and limits utilization reports available for the portfolio analyzer, market risk analyzer, and credit risk analyzer, you can use tools such as drilldown reporting and SAP Query to create additional, custom reports to meet your organizational requirements.

Summary

The treasury and risk management component of SAP provides the following high-value benefits to a treasury department, large or small:

> Improved efficiency, uniform data entry, and consistent reporting for optimum global financial management

> Support for centralized, decentralized, or partially centralized treasury operations to best meet your organizational requirements

> Ability to process treasury operations involving a wide variety of financial instruments such as money market products, securities, currencies, derivatives, and commodities

> Seamless and transparent integration with financial systems to accurately and automatically post accounting entries for treasury transactions, in compliance with relevant statutory requirements

> Ability to evaluate current, proposed, and hypothetical transactions for different types of risks such as fluctuations in market price, rates, exchange rates, risks of settlement, and delinquency

> Multiple options to transfer data or integrate data from external applications, including an open interface to market data providers

> Comprehensive and flexible reporting with AIS, a large number of standard reports, integration with NetWeaver BI, and tools for creating custom reports

A   Glossary

ABAP   Advanced Business Programming Language. The SAP programming language

Account Assignment   A tool that specifies of which accounts to post to from a business transaction

Account Determination   An automatic function that determines the accounts for posting amounts in Financial Accounting

Account Reconciliation   A procedure for ensuring the reliability of accounting records by comparing the balances of the business transactions posted

Accrual   A method used to distribute expenditures, revenue, receivables and losses for the correct period, based on the origin of these amounts

Accrual Engine   Tool in General Ledger Accounting that can be used to calculate and post accruals automatically

Accrued Tax   A tax included in the cost of purchases and payables to the tax authorities at regular intervals of time

Acquisition Tax   An acquisition tax is due on cross-border movement of goods and services within the European Union

Activity Type   A unit in a controlling area that classifies the activities performed in a cost center

Additive Cost   A material based cost that you can enter manually in the form of a unit cost estimate and then add to an automatic cost estimate

Assessment   A method of internal cost allocation by which the costs of a sender cost center are allocated to receiver CO objects using an assessment cost element and on the basis of the keys defined by the user

Asset Class   The main criterion for classifying fixed assets according to legal and management requirements

Asset Subnumber   A unique number, that in combination with the main asset number, identifies an asset in the SAP system

Authentication   The process of verifying the identity of a computer user to provide access to a system or data

Authorization   The authority to execute a particular action in the SAP system

Availability Control   An internal active funds controlling system that can identify possible budget underruns or overruns when funds are being committed in respect of transactions assigned to projects

Balance Carryforward   The transfer of an account balance from the previous year

Bill of Exchange   A promise to pay in the form of an abstract payment paper detached from the original legal transaction

Bill of Lading   Documents issued by sender of goods that are shipped with goods

Bill of Material   A complete, structured list of the components called BOM items that make up a material

Bill-to Party   A person or company that receives the invoice for a delivery or service

Billing Document   A generic term for customer documents such as invoices, credit memos, debit memos, pro forma invoices, and cancellation documents

Book Depreciation   Set of laws for the valuation of fixed assets for the balance sheet

Budget   An approved cost structure for an action or project in a particular period of time

Budget Category   Classification of the budget of a capital investment program such as capital expenditure, expenses

Business Area   An organizational unit of financial accounting that represents

a separate area of operations or responsibilities within an organization

Business Partner   A natural or legal person or a group of natural or legal persons, not part of the business organization; but with whom a business interest exists

Business Process   Process in a company that uses resources and can involve the activities of different departments

Capitalization Key   A structure that enables you to capitalize debits on an investment measure using different percentage rates for each depreciation area

Characteristic   The characteristics in Profitability Analysis represent those criteria according to which you analyze your operating results and your sales and profit plan

Characteristic Derivation   A rule consisting of multiple steps that define which values of derived characteristics can be determined from the values of other characteristics

Chart of Accounts   A classification scheme consisting of a group of general ledger accounts

Clearing Procedure   A procedure by which open debit and credit items posted to an account are cleared

Commitment   A contractual or scheduled commitment that is not yet reflected in Financial Accounting but that will lead to actual expenditures in the future

Company Code   The smallest organizational unit of Financial Accounting for which a complete self-contained set of accounts can be drawn up for purposes of external reporting

Compliance   The process businesses use to comply with regulations such as Sarbanes-Oxley or health and safety regulations

Consignment   A form of business in which a vendor (external supplier) maintains a stock of materials at a customer (purchaser) site

Consolidation   An accounting procedure whereby the financial operating results of the companies within the group are combined to create overall results for the group in accordance with the entity theory

Consolidation Group   A user-defined group of multiple consolidation units and/or consolidation groups for purposes of consolidation and reporting

Consolidation Unit   The smallest element of the corporate group structure that can be used as the basis for performing a consolidation

Controlling Area   An organizational unit within a company, used to represent a closed system for cost accounting purposes

Controlling Area Currency   The currency in which cost accounting is performed

Corporate Services   One of the four main applications areas of SAP ERP that offers tools such as real estate management, enterprise asset management, and travel management

Correspondence   The printed correspondence of a company such as order confirmations, dunning notices, payment notifications

Cost Center   An organizational unit within a controlling area that represents a defined location of cost incurrence

Cost Element   Classification of the organization's valuated consumption of production factors within a controlling area

Cost of Sales Accounting   A type of profit and loss statement that matches the sales revenues to the costs or expenses involved in making the revenue

Costing Method   A method of creating a cost estimate such as product costing, unit costing, multi-level unit costing, easy cost planning

Costing Sheet   A definition consisting of base lines, calculation lines and totals line that determine how values posted in the SAP system are calculated

Costing Variant A tool that contains all control parameters for costing, including parameters that control how cost estimates are executed and the material prices or activity prices that are used to valuate the costing items

Credit Control Area An organizational unit that represents an area responsible for granting and monitoring credit

Cycle A collection of rules for cost allocation

Data Monitor A tool that manages the transfer of individual financial statement data into the consolidation system

Default Risk Risk of an unexpected loss in the value of a receivable due to a worsening of the credit standing of a business partner

Deferred Revenue The amount of revenue that has been invoiced and not recognized

Depreciation Area An area showing the valuation of a fixed asset for a particular purpose such as financial statements, taxes, management accounting

Distribution Key A tool used to distribute annual planned values over the planning periods in accordance with certain rules

Down Payment A part of the full price paid at the time of purchase or delivery with the balance to be paid later

Dunning Area An organizational unit within a company from which dunning is conducted

Earned Value Describes the costs incurred to bring a project element to its current degree of completion

Easy Cost Planning A method of costing based on costing models that enables costs to be planned quickly and easily

Engineer-to-order A manufacturing environment, in which complex production activities under essentially one-off conditions are undertaken for a specific customer

Enterprise Resource Planning (ERP) A type of application that is used to integrate all the data and processes of a business or organization with the goal of maximizing the efficiency of operations. See also SAP ERP

Fiscal Year Variant A variant that specifies the number of periods and special periods in a fiscal year and how the SAP system is to determine the assigned posting periods

Foreign Currency A currency that differs from the company code currency (country currency)

Formula Planning A tool for IT supported planning of costs using mathematical dependencies

Functional Area The areas in which costs were incurred in cost-of-sales accounting

GL Account Master Record A data record containing information that controls how data is entered into a GL account and how that account is managed

Goodwill The differential amount on the assets side and arises during the consolidation of investments

GR/IR Clearing A function that determines price variances between valuated goods receipts and invoice receipts

Grace Period The period within which an employee must provide evidence of insurability or within which an employee can submit FSA claims relating to the previous plan year

Group Currency The currency assigned to a consolidation group, and used in the consolidated financial statements

Hard Currency A country specific second currency used in countries with high rates of inflation

Impairment Test A method for treating goodwill in the consolidation of investments

Imputed Interest The interest, which represents the interest gain lost because of the capital tied up in assets

Index Series A mathematical series for representing price rate increases

Input Tax A tax that is charged by the vendor

Internal Order An instrument used to monitor costs and, in some instances, the revenues of an organization

IPI (Interunit Profit and Loss) A situation that occurs when internal trading partners buy and sell goods and services from each other

Inventory Costing A costing procedure that determines how the materials in inventory are valuated before the balance sheet is prepared

Investee A company is an investee if another company has investments in it

Invoicing Plan A listing of dates on which invoices for purchase order items covering materials or services are to be entered and subsequently paid

Journal A list of all Financial Accounting postings in a period

Jurisdiction The geographical region (country, state, city or any other level) in which a law or other types of directives is valid

Kanban A procedure for controlling production and material flow based on a chain of operations in production and procurement; also a card sent by a consumer to the supplier to signal for replenishment

Key Figure   A value calculated from other values in a report using report cells

Knock-in   An activity to effect the right to exercise an option that is linked to a rate rise above a certain level, or fall below a certain level

Knock-out   An activity to cancel the right to exercise an option that is linked to a rate rise above a certain level, or a fall below a certain level

Leasing Type   An indicator that controls whether the leased asset is handled for bookkeeping purposes as operating lease or capital lease

Ledger   A specialized framework that determines how values and quantities are entered and presented for a particular area of accounting and for reporting or evaluation purposes

Ledger Group   A combination of ledgers for the purpose of applying the functions and processes of general ledger accounting to the group as a whole

Local Currency   The currency of a company code (country currency) in which the local ledgers are managed

Main Asset Number   The unique number that identifies a fixed asset in the SAP system, in combination with

the company code and the asset sub number

Make-to-order Production   A type of production in which a product is manufactured for a particular customer

Make-to-stock Inventory   An inventory of goods that were not manufactured for specific sales orders or projects

Mark-to-market Value   A price that has to be paid, or that can be achieved, under current market conditions in order to close a position

Material Cost Estimate   A tool for planning costs and setting prices for materials

Material Ledger   A tool that collects transaction data for materials whose master data is stored in material master

Material Master   A data record containing all the basic information required to manage a material

Milestone   Events used in a project to designate significant events or the completion of a project phase

Mixed Costing   A costing method that uses multiple cost estimates to calculate a mixed price for a material

Movement Type   A classification key indicating the type of material movement such as goods receipt, goods issue, physical stock transfer

Moving Average Price A price that changes in consequence of goods movements and the entry of invoices and is used to valuate a material

mySAP Enterprise Portal A solution that unifies all types of enterprise information, including business applications, databases, stored documents, and internet information

mySAP Financials A mySAP solution that helps companies improve their processing and interpretation of financial and business data, their handling of financial transactions, and communication with their shareholders

mySAP Human Resources A mySAP. com cross-industry solution that delivers key strategic, analytic, and enabling facilities for human resource management, administration, payroll, organizational management, time management, and legal reporting

Note to Payee The fields on data media that include information on regulated line items relevant for the business partner

Off-cycle Payroll Run Payroll run that is carried out in addition to the regular payroll run for a specific day and for individual employees

Open Item Management A stipulation that the items in an account must be used to clear other line items in the same account

Operating Concern A representation of a part of an organization for which the sales market is structured in a uniform manner

Option A limited right to accept or reject a contract offer within a certain period, fixed by the business partner according to price and quantity

Output Tax A tax levied on customers at all levels of production and trade

Overhead Cost Controlling The activities related to the coordination, monitoring and optimization of overhead costs

Overhead Key A tool that enables you to calculate a percentage overhead rate for specific orders or materials

Overhead Rate The rate at which overhead is allocated to direct costs to charge cost objects with the proportion of the overhead costs attributable to them

Payee A business partner to whom payments are made

Payer A person or company that pays the bill

Payment Method A method that specifies how payment is to be made: check, bill of exchange, or bank transfer

Payroll Area A group of employees included in the same payroll run

Payroll Control Record Summary of administrative functions in payroll for payroll area

Payroll Infotypes Infotypes for the evaluation of payroll results

Periodic Allocation An allocation method by which the costs collected on a cost center during a period are allocated according to allocation bases defined by the user

Personnel Area An organizational unit representing an area in an enterprise delimited according to personnel administration, time management, and payroll accounting criteria

Personnel Subarea An organizational entity that represents part of a personnel area

Pipeline Material Something that flows directly into the production process from a pipeline, a pipe, power transmission lines, or similar means

Plan Version A tool that enables different data to be run in parallel for the same object

Posting Date Date on which a business transaction is transferred into one or more accounting ledgers on document entry.

Posting Key A two-digit numerical key that determines the way line items are posted.

Posting Level A classification of posting entries in the consolidation system

Preliminary Costing A process that determines the planned costs for objects such as orders

Prenotification Procedure for verifying bank account details for a direct deposit

Price Control An indicator determining the procedure used for material valuation

Price Difference The difference between the valuation price of a material and the price used for a movement with an external amount

Pricing Procedure A procedure that defines the conditions permitted for a document and the sequence in which the system takes these conditions into account during pricing

Primary Cost Element A cost element whose costs originate outside of CO

Primary Costs The costs incurred through the consumption of goods and services that originate from outside the company (that is, from the procurement market).

Process Driver A measure for the usage of business processes by receiver objects

Processing Class Wage type characteristic that determines how processing is conducted during the payroll run

Procurement Card A payment card issued on behalf of a company to employees for purchasing items up to a given amount

Product Costing A tool for planning material costs and prices

Product Hierarchy An alphanumeric character string for grouping materials by combining different characteristics

Profit Center An organizational unit in accounting that reflects a management-oriented structure of the organization for the purpose of internal control

Profitability Segment An object within profitability analysis to which costs and revenues are assigned

Project Version The status of a project at a particular time or in a particular action

Promise-to-pay Commitment from a customer to pay an invoice in the future

Purchase Requisition A request or instruction to purchasing to procure a quantity of a material or service so that it is available at a certain point in time

Quantity Structure The basis for calculating costs in a material cost estimate

Realtime Update A data transfer method that updates every business transaction relevant to the general ledger in the totals records of the consolidation ledger

Reconciliation Account A GL account to which transactions in the subsidiary ledgers such as in the customer, vendor or assets area, are updated automatically

Record Type A key that separates data in Profitability Analysis according to its source

Recurring Entry A periodically recurring posting made by the recurring entry program on the basis of recurring entry original documents

Reference Interest Rate A value reference in the condition structure of an interest dependent transaction

Report Painter A tool for creating reports that meet specific business and reporting requirements

Representative Material A material chosen to represent a group of materials with similar qualities

Request for Quotation A request from a purchasing organization to a vendor to submit a quotation for the supply of materials or provision of services

Resource-related Billing You use cost related billing when invoicing customers for work done in customer projects, materials used or other related costs

Results Analysis A periodic revaluation of long-term orders and projects

Results Analysis Method A method that determines how the results analysis data such as capitalized costs or the cost of sales is calculated

Revaluation (FI-AA) An adjustment to asset values to compensate for a reduction in the value of a currency because of inflation or when adopting market value principles for the valuation of fixed assets

Risk management Identifying and planning for potential risk in business, including performing risk analysis, monitoring, and developing responses for possible risk scenarios

Sales and Operations Planning A forecasting and planning tool for setting targets for sales, production, and other supply chains based on historical, current, or estimated data

Sales Organization An organizational unit in Logistics that structures the company according to its sales requirements

SAP All-in-One An integrated software system built on business SAP Best Practices for the small to midsize company

SAP Business One SAP's offering for the smaller end of the mid-market

SAP Business Suite A comprehensive business solution from SAP that includes SAP ERP, SAP Customer Resource Management, SAP Product Lifecycle Management, SAP Supply Chain Management and SAP Supplier Relationship Management

SAP NetWeaver SAP's technology platform for most of its solutions that allows for the integration of various application components, and for composing services using a model-based approach

SAP NetWeaver Business Intelligence (SAP NetWeaver BI) A component of the SAP NetWeaver platform that offers data warehousing functionality via repositories of data, and tools for information integration

SAP NetWeaver Exchange Infrastructure (SAP NetWeaver XI) A feature in SAP NetWeaver that allows you to integrate processes, thereby allowing applications to communicate with each other

SAP Tech Ed An annual SAP conference spotlighting technical knowledge and skills related to SOA and SAP NetWeaver, including hands-on workshops and technical lectures

SAP xApps Composite applications that customers of SAP can buy to enable additional business processes. See also Composite application

SAPPHIRE SAP-run annual conferences that take place in a variety of cities and countries to expose business decision-makers to SAP's latest offerings

SAP R/3 The SAP client/server architecture based software introduced in 1992, which was a predecessor of SAP ERP

Sarbanes-Oxley Act A US regulation initiated in 2002 to regulate financial reporting and accountability

Scalability The ability of a system to be grown or built on easily with increase in business requirements or user base

Secondary Cost Element A cost element used to allocate costs for internal activities

Segment Division of a company that can create its own financial statements for external reporting

Settlement (CO) Full or partial allocation of costs from one object to another

Standard Cost A cost that is based on an activity unit and that remains stable over a relatively long period of time

Statistical Posting The posting of a special GL transaction where the offsetting entry is made to a specified clearing account automatically

Summarization A method summarizing the data of account assignment objects so that costs can be analyzed at a higher level

Symbolic Account Customizing object used for posting payroll results and data from personnel cost planning and simulation to accounting

Target Costs The costs expected to be incurred when a specific quantity is produced or in the performance of a particular activity

Tolerance An accepted deviation from specified values

Transaction Currency Currency in which a particular document is posted

Transfer Price The price charged for transfer of a product from one business unit to another

Translation Difference The difference in reporting currency that occurs when an amount in local currency is valued using different exchange rates between two periods

Validation The process of checking values and combinations of values as they are entered into the SAP system

Valuation Class A classification that determines the GL accounts that are updated as a result of a valuation relevant transaction or event such as goods movement

Valuation Method A method that can be used for multiple charts of accounts

Variable Costs A portion of the total cost that varies with the operating rate and the lot size

Variance Category A classification of variances based on their cause

Wage Type Object in Payroll and Personnel Administration in which the user or the system stores amounts and time units that are used, for example, for calculating pay or for determining statistics

Wage Type Group Grouping of wage types according to specific business criteria

WBS Element A structural element in a work breakdown structure representing the hierarchical organization of a project

WIP Calculation A procedure during period-end closing that calculates that work in process for the production orders and process orders

WIP Stock Work-in-process Stock

Withholding Tax A form of taxation deducted at the beginning of the payment flow

Year-end Closing An annual balance sheet and profit and loss statement, both of which must be created in accordance with the legal requirements of the country in question

Yield Curve A summary of reference interest rates, including the determination of the interest calculation method, the quotation type and the financial center

Index